Aircraft Radio Systems

Aircraft Radio Systems

J Powell
BA, CEng, MIERE, GradIMA

Pitman

PITMAN PUBLISHING LIMITED
128 Long Acre, London WC2E 9AN

PITMAN PUBLISHING INC
1020 Plain Street, Marshfield, Massachusetts 02050

Associated Companies
Pitman Publishing Pty Ltd., Melbourne
Pitman Publishing New Zealand Ltd., Wellington
Copp Clark Pitman, Toronto

First edition 1981
Reprinted 1984

Library of Congress Cataloging in Publication Data

Powell, James, 1943–
  Aircraft radio systems.

  Bibliography: p.
  Includes index.
  1. Airplanes – Radio equipment.   I. Title.
TL695.P68   629.135   80-20454
ISBN 0-273-08444-5

Text set in 10/11 pt Press Roman
by L.M.A. Ltd. Southampton, Hants.
Printed in Great Britain at The Pitman Press, Bath

ISBN 0 273 08444 5

Contents

Preface

The cockpit and equipment racks of modern aircraft, large and small, are becoming filled with ever more sophisticated systems. This book attempts to describe a certain class of such systems, namely those which rely for their operation on electromagnetic radiation. The subject matter is complex and wide-ranging, hence not all aspects can be covered in one volume. In deciding where the treatment should be light or perhaps non-existent, I have asked myself two questions: (1) which aspects can most usefully be covered in a book; and (2) at which group of people involved in aviation should a book covering such aspects be aimed?

The answer to (1) must be 'describe the theory'. One can, and indeed must, read or be told about how to operate the systems; how to navigate using the systems; how to solder, crimp and change items; how to use test equipment, etc. but proficiency is impossible without practice. On the other hand gaining an understanding of how a particular system works is more of a mental exercise which can be guided in a book such as this. This is not to say that more practical matters are neglected, since it would not help one's understanding of the theory of operation not to see, at least in words and pictures, how a particular system is controlled, presents its information, reacts to the environment, etc.

Having decided the main line of attack the more difficult question of depth of treatment must be answered; in other words which group should be satisfied? Pilots need a superficial knowledge of how all the systems work; maintenance engineers on the ramp and in the hangar a more detailed knowledge; workshop engineers must have an understanding of the circuitry for perhaps a limited range of equipments; while designers should have the greatest depth of knowledge of all. It is virtually impossible to draw dividing lines, but it is hoped that if enough theory is given to satisfy the aircraft radio maintenance engineer then the book might be useful to all groups mentioned.

The depth of treatment varies, it being impossible to cover everything, or indeed anything, to the depth I would have liked. In particular few details of circuitry are given since I feel most readers will be more interested in the operation of the system as a whole. Nevertheless, some circuits are given purely as examples. Should the reader need circuit knowledge, the equipment maintenance manual is the best place to find it, assuming he knows the system and he has a basic knowledge of electronics.

The state of the art of the equipment described is also varied. I did not see the point of describing only equipment containing microprocessors, since the vast majority of systems in service do not use them as yet. On the other hand if the life of this book is not to be too severely restricted, the latest techniques must be described. Within the pages that follow, analogue, analogue/digital, hardwired digital and programmable digital equipments all find a place.

As stated previously, the book is aimed primarily at the maintenance engineer. However, I hope several groups might be interested. This poses problems concerning the background knowledge required. For what I hope is a fairly substantial part of the book, any reasonably intelligent technically minded person with a basic knowledge of mathematics and a familiarity with aircraft will have no difficulty that two or perhaps three readings will not overcome. There are parts, however, where some knowledge of electronics, radio theory or more sophisticated mathematics is needed. In three chapters where the going gets a bit tough, I have relegated the offending material to an appendix. Some background material is covered in Chapter 1, in particular, basic radio theory and a discussion of digital systems in so far as coding and computers are concerned.

If you are one of the few people who plough all the way through the Preface to a book, you may have decided by now that this book is concerned with theory and little else. That this is not so may be clear if I outline briefly the contents of each chapter. An introduction saying a few words about the history and function of the system is followed by a fairly thorough coverage of the basic principles. In some chapters the next item is a discussion of the installation, i.e. the units, how they are interconnected, which other systems they interface with and any special considerations such as cooling, positioning, type of antennas and feeders, etc. This, together with a description of controls and operation, puts some practical meat on to the bare bones of the theory which continues with a consideration of the block diagram operation. In certain chapters the order: installation − controls and operation − block diagram, is reversed where I thought it was perhaps to the reader's disadvantage to break up the flow of the more theoretical aspects. A brief look at characteristics, in practically all cases based on ARINC publications, and testing/maintenance concludes each chapter.

Most chapters deal with one system; none of them is exclusively military. The exceptions are, in reverse order, Chapter 13 where I look at the current scene and review some systems we should see in the next few years; Chapter 12 which is a bringing-together of some of the previously covered systems; Chapter 6 covering Omega, Decca Navigator and Loran C; Chapter 2 which covers both radio and non-radio communications; and Chapter 1 where some chosen background material is given.

I should point out that this is not a textbook in the sense that everything is examinable in accordance with some syllabus. The reader will take from the book however big a chunk he desires, depending on his background knowledge, his profession, the examinations he hopes to take and, of course, his inclination. Some will have, or end up with, an understanding of all that is included herein, in which case I hope the book may be seen as a source of reference.

Acknowledgements

A number of manufacturers have given valuable assistance including the supplying of material and granting permission to reproduce data and illustrations. Without the generosity of the following, this book would have been of very limited use.

Bendix Avionics Division
Boeing Commercial Aeroplane Company
British Aerospace
Communications Components Corporation
The Decca Navigator Company Limited
Field Tech Limited
Hazeltine Corporation
IFR Electronics Inc
King Radio Corporation
Litton Systems International Inc., Aero Products Division
Marconi Avionics Limited
MEL Equipment Company Limited
RCA Limited
Rockwell-Collins (UK) Limited
Ryan Stormscope
Tel-Instrument Electronics Corporation (TIC)

Although I am grateful to all the above, I must reserve a special word of thanks to Mr Wayne Brown of Bendix, Mr A. E. Crawford of King and Mr T. C. Wood of RCA, who arranged for the dispatch of several expensive and heavy maintenance manuals in reply to my request for information. These manuals, and indeed all other information received, were used in the preparation of this book and continue to be used in the training of students at Brunel Technical College, Bristol, England.

I also wish to thank all my colleagues at Brunel who have helped, often unwittingly, in conversation. In particular my thanks go to John Stokes, Clive Stratton and Peter Kemp for proof-reading some of the chapters and also Leighton Fletcher for helping with the illustrations. May I add that, although I received technical assistance from the above, any mistakes which remain are obviously mine. I would be grateful to any reader who might take the trouble to point out any errors.

Finally, my thanks to Pauline Rickards, whose fingers must be sore from typing; to the publishers who displayed great patience as the deadline for the submission of the typescript came and went; and, most of all, to my wife Pat and son Adam who showed even more patience and understanding than Pitmans.

Bristol,
England   J.P.

1 Historical, technical and legal context

Introduction

This book deals with airborne systems that depend for their operation on the generation and detection of that intangible discovery the radio wave. Such systems split naturally into two parts: communications and navigation. The former provide two-way radio contact between air and ground, while the latter enables an aircraft to be flown safely from A to B along a prescribed route with a landing safely executed at B.

An understanding of such systems requires a working knowledge of basic electronics, radio, computer systems and other topics. A book of this length cannot provide all that is necessary but it was thought that some readers might appreciate a review of selected background material. This is the objective of Chapter 1. It may be that on consulting the list of contents, the reader will decide to omit all or part of this chapter. On the other hand, some readers may decide that more basic information is needed, in which case, the list of recommended books will help point the way to sources of such material.

Historical Background

In 1864 James Clerk Maxwell, Professor of Experimental Physics at Cambridge, proved mathematically that any electrical disturbance could produce an effect at a considerable distance from the point at which it occurred. He predicted that electromagnetic (e.m.) energy would travel outward from a source as waves moving at the speed of light. In 1888 Hertz, a German physicist, demonstrated that Maxwell's theory was correct, at least over distances within the confines of a laboratory. It was left to the Italian physicist Marconi to generate e.m. waves and detect them at a remote receiver, as he did by bridging the Atlantic in 1901. Other notable landmarks in the development of radio include:

1897   First commercial company incorporated for the manufacture of radio apparatus: the Wireless Telegraph and Signal Company Limited (England), later the Marconi Wireless Telegraph Company Limited.

1904   Fleming's (British) discovery of the thermionic valve – the diode.

1904   First patent for a radar-like system to a German engineer, Hülsmeyer. Workable but not accepted.

1906   De Forest's (American) invention of an amplifying thermionic valve (triode).

1911   Direction-finding properties of radio waves investigated.

1912   Discovery of the oscillating properties of De Forest's valve.

1936   The first workable pulse radar.

1939   Invention of the magnetron in Britain.

1948   Invention of the transistor by Bardeen, Brattain and Shockley (Bell Telephone Laboratories, USA).

1958   First active communications satellite launched (project SCORE).

To bring us up to date, in the early 1970s the first microprocessor appeared from Intel (USA) leading directly to present-day microcomputers.

Paralleling the progress of radio was the second of the three great developments of the twentieth century, i.e. powered flight in heavier-than-air machines. (The other two developments referred to are electronics and applications of nuclear physics; the reader is concerned with two out of three.) There can be few people who have not heard of Wilbur and Orville Wright; who designed and built the first successful powered aircraft which Orville flew for the first time at 10.35 on 17 December 1903, making a landing without damage after 12 seconds airborne. Since then landmarks in aviation, with particular reference to civil aviation, include:

1907   First fatality: Lieut. T. E. Selfridge, a passenger in a Wright Flyer.

1909   Bleriot (French) flies the English Channel.

1912   Sikorsky (Russian) builds first multi-engined (four), passenger (sixteen) aircraft.

1914   World War I. The years 1914-18 saw

advances in performance and a vast increase in number of aircraft, engines and pilots.

1919   Sustained daily scheduled flights begin in Europe.

1928   Whittle (British) publishes thesis on jet engine.

1929   First blind landing by Doolittle (American) using only aircraft instruments.

1937   Flying-boat service inaugurated from Britain to the Far East. Britain to Australia took 8 days in 1938, either by KLM or Imperial Airways.

1939   Inaugural air-mail service between Britain and North America using flying-boats and in-flight refuelling.

1939   First jet-powered flight by He 178 (German).

1939   World War II. The years 1939-45 saw the growth of world-wide military air transport services, and the USA established as the postwar leader in civil aviation.

1944   International Civil Aviation Organisation formed at Chicago conference.

1945   American Overseas Airlines operate scheduled flights over North Atlantic with landplane (DC 4).

1952   First civil jet aircraft, the Comet 1, goes into service with BOAC.

1953   First civil turboprop aircraft, the Viscount, goes into service with BEA.

1954   Previously unknown problem of metal fatigue discovered in Comet 1. Withdrawn.

1956   Tu 104 first jet aircraft to commence sustained commercial service.

1958   First transatlantic jet service by BOAC with the Comet 4. (PAA's Boeing 707-120 follows three weeks later.)

1965   First short-haul jet to enter service, the BAC 1-11.

1970   Boeing 747 introduced; the first of the Jumbo Jets.

1970   First civil aircraft supersonic flights, Concorde and the Tu 144.

From the time of the Wright brothers to the present day, the non-commercial side of civil aviation, known as general aviation (business and private) has grown with less spectacular firsts than its big brother, so that now by far the largest number of civil aircraft are in this category.

It was inevitable that the new toys of radio and aircraft should be married early on in their history. Later the vast increase in air traffic made it essential that radio aids, in both communication and navigation, should be made full use of, to cope safely with the crowded skies. In 1910 the first transmission of e.m. waves from air to ground occurred. Speech was conveyed to an aircraft flying near Brooklands Airfield (England) by means of an e.m. wave in 1916. By the 1920s, radio was being used for aircraft navigation by employing rudimentary direction-finding techniques (Chapter 3). The introduction of four-course low-frequency range equipment in 1929 provided the pilot with directional guidance without the need for a direction-finder on the aircraft.

Steady progress was made up to 1939, but it was World War II which gave the impetus to airborne radio innovations. Apart from very high frequency (v.h.f.) communications, introduced during the war, a number of radio navigation aids saw the first light of day in the period since 1939. These systems are described in the following chapters.

Basic Principles of Radio

Radiation of Electromagnetic (e.m.) Waves and Antennas

If a wire is fed with an alternating current, some of the power will be radiated into space. A similar wire parallel to and remote from the first will intercept some of the radiated power and as a consequence an alternating current will be induced, so that using an appropriate detector, the characteristics of the original current may be measured. This is the basis of all radio systems.

The above involves a transfer of energy from one point to another by means of an e.m. wave. The wave consists of two oscillating fields mutually perpendicular to each other and to the direction of propagation. The electric field (E) will be parallel to the wire from which the wave was transmitted, while the magnetic field (H) will be at right angles. A 'snapshot' of such a wave is shown in Fig. 1.1 where the distance shown between successive peaks is known as the wavelength.

The velocity and wavelength of an e.m. wave are

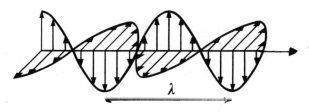

Fig. 1.1 An electromagnetic wave

directly related through the frequency of the alternating current generating the wave. The law is:

$$c = \lambda f$$

where:
c is the speed of light (3×10^8 m/s).
λ is the wavelength in metres.
f is the frequency in Hertz (cycles/s).

A radiating wire is most efficient when its length is equal to half a wavelength. Thus for a frequency of 100 MHz the wire should be $(3 \times 10^8)/(2 \times 100 \times 10^6) = 1\cdot5$ m long, in which case it is known as a dipole. In practice many airborne radio systems do not make use of dipole antennas since their size is prohibitively large, except at very high frequencies, and the radiation pattern is not suited to applications where energy needs to be transmitted in or received from a certain direction.

A close relative of the dipole is the unipole antenna which is a $\lambda/4$ length conductor mounted vertically on the metal fuselage which acts as a ground plane in which a reflection of the unipole is 'seen' to form a dipole. Thus a v.h.f. communication (comm.) unipole would be less than 60 cm long (centre frequency of the band is 127 MHz). Two unipoles are sometimes mounted back to back on the vertical stabilizer to function as a dipole antenna for use with VOR (Chapter 4) or ILS (Chapter 5).

At frequencies in the region of 2-30 MHz (h.f.) a dipole would be between 5 and 75 m. Since the dimensions of aircraft fall, roughly speaking, within this range of lengths it is possible to use the aircraft as the radiating or receiving element. A notch or slot cut in a suitable part of the airframe (e.g. base of vertical stabilizer) has a large oscillating voltage applied across it, so driving current through the fuselage which in turn radiates. The notch/airframe load must be 'tuned' to the correct frequency for efficient transmission. Without tuning, little energy would be radiated and a large standing wave would be set up on the connector feeding the notch. This is due to the interaction of incident and reflected energy to and from the antenna. An alternative type of antenna for this band of frequencies is a long length of wire similarly tuned, i.e. with variable reactive components.

For frequencies within the range 10-100 kHz the maximum dimension of even large aircraft is only a small fraction of a wavelength. At these frequencies capacitive type antennas may be used. One plate of the capacitor is the airframe; the other a horizontal tube, vertical blade or a mesh (sometimes a solid plate). The aircraft causes the field to become intensified over a limited region near its surface. The resulting comparatively strong oscillating E field between the capacitor's plates causes a current to flow in twin feeder or coaxial cable connected across the antenna. The airborne systems operating in the relevant frequency band are the receive-only systems covered in Chapter 6 (Omega, Decca and Loran C). Although ADF (Chapter 3) receives signals in the band of frequencies immediately above those considered in this paragraph, one of its two antennas (sense) utilizes the principles discussed.

An alternative to the capacitance antenna is the loop antenna which is basically a loop of wire which cuts the H field component of the e.m. wave. The field is intensified by use of a ferrite core on which several turns are wound. Use of two loops mounted at right angles provides a means of ascertaining the direction of arrival (ambiguous) of an e.m. wave. Such antennas are used for ADF (loop) and may also be used for Omega.

At frequencies above, say, 3000 MHz the properties of waveguides may be used. A waveguide is a hollow metal tube, usually of rectangular cross-section, along which an e.m. wave can propagate. If the end of a waveguide is left open some energy will be radiated. To improve the efficiency, the walls of the waveguide are flared out, so providing matching to free space and hence little or no reflected energy back down the guide. Such an antenna is called a horn and may be used for radio altimeters (Chapter 11).

Associated with the wave propagated along a waveguide are wall currents which flow in specific directions. A slot, about 1 cm in length, cut in the waveguide so as to interrupt the current flow will act as a radiator. If several slots are cut the energy from them will combine several wavelengths from the antenna to form a directional beam. The direction depends on the spacing of the slots. Such antennas may be used for Doppler radar (Chapter 10) and weather radar (Chapter 9).

The theory of some of the more esoteric antennas used on aircraft is a little sketchy and design is finalized, if not based, on empirical data. However the antenna is designed, it will only see service if it performs its function of transmitting and/or receiving e.m. waves in and/or from required directions. The directivity of an antenna, or the lack of directivity, is most clearly defined by means of a polar diagram. If we take a transmitting antenna and plot points of equal field strength (one value only) we have such a diagram. The same antenna used for receiving would, of course, have the same polar diagram. If the diagram is a circle centred on the antenna, as would be the case if the plot were in the plane perpendicular to a dipole, then the antenna is said to be omnidirectional in the plane in which the measurements were made. A practical antenna cannot be omnidirectional in all planes, i.e. in three dimensions.

The e.m. Spectrum and Propagation

As can be seen from the previous paragraph, the frequency of the radio wave is an important consideration when considering antenna design. In addition the behaviour of the wave as it propagates through the earth's atmosphere is also very much dependent on the frequency.

However, before considering propagation, we will place radio waves in the spectrum of all e.m. waves (Table 1.1). In doing so we see that the range of frequencies we are concerned with is small when

Table 1.1   The electro-magnetic spectrum

Hz	Region
10^{25}	Cosmic rays
10^{21}	Gamma rays
10^{19}	X rays
10^{17}	Ultraviolet
10^{15}	Visible
10^{14}	Infra-red
10^{11}	Radio waves
10^{4}	Electric waves

compared with the complete spectrum. By general agreement radio frequencies are categorized as in Table 1.2. There is less agreement about the letter designations used for the higher radio frequencies which are tabulated with approximate frequency ranges in Table 1.3. Finally, Table 1.4 lists the frequencies used for airborne radio systems by international agreement.

Table 1.2   Radio frequency categorization

Name	Abbreviation	Frequency	
Very low frequency	v.l.f.	3-30	kHz
Low frequency	l.f.	30-300	kHz
Medium frequency	m.f.	300-3000	kHz
High frequency	h.f.	3-30	MHz
Very high frequency	v.h.f.	30-300	MHz
Ultrahigh frequency	u.h.f.	300-3000	MHz
Superhigh frequency	s.h.f.	3-30	GHz
Extremely high frequency	e.h.f.	30-300	GHz

Table 1.3   Approximate bands for microwave frequencies

Letter designation	Frequency range (GHz)
L	1-3
S	2·5-4
C	3·5-7·5
X	6-12·5
K	12·5-40
Q	33-50

Table 1.4   Airborne radio frequency utilization (exact frequencies given in relevant chapters)

System	Frequency band
Omega	10-14 kHz
Decca	70-130 kHz
Loran C	100 kHz
ADF	200-1700 kHz
h.f. comm.	2-25 MHz
Marker	75 MHz
ILS (Localizer)	108-112 MHz
VOR	108-118 MHz
v.h.f. comm.	118-136 MHz
ILS (Glideslope)	320-340 MHz
DME	960-1215 MHz
SSR	1030 and 1090 MHz
Radio altimeter	4·2-4·4 GHz
Weather radar (C)	5·5 GHz
Doppler (X)	8·8 GHz
Weather radar (X)	9·4 GHz
Doppler (K)	13·3 GHz

In free space, all radio waves travel in straight lines at the speed of light. Such a mode of propagation is known as the space wave. In addition, two other modes of propagation are used with airborne radio equipment: the ground wave and the sky wave. A fourth mode known as tropospheric scatter is used only for fixed ground stations since elaborate and expensive equipment must be used at both ends of the link due to the poor transmission efficiency.

The ground wave follows the surface of the earth partly because of diffraction, a phenomenon associated with all wave motion which causes the wave to bend around any obstacle it passes. In addition, the wave H field cuts the earth's surface, so causing currents to flow. The required power for these currents must come from the wave, thus a flow of energy from wave to earth takes place causing bending and attenuation. The attenuation is a limiting factor on the range of frequencies which can be used. The higher the frequency the greater the rate of change of field strength, so more attenuation is experienced in maintaining the higher currents. Ground waves are used for v.l.f. and l.f. systems.

Radio waves striking the ionosphere (a set of ionized layers lying between 50 and 500 km above the earth's surface) are refracted by an amount depending on the frequency of the incident wave. Under favourable circumstances the wave will return to the earth. The distance between the transmitter and point of return (one hop) is known as the skip distance. Multiple hops may occur giving a very long range. Above about 30 MHz there is no sky wave since insufficient refraction occurs. Sky wave propagation is useful for h.f. comm. but can cause problems with l.f. and m.f. navigation aids since the sky wave and ground wave may combine at the receiver in such a way as to cause fading, false direction of arrival or false propagation time measurements. At v.l.f. the ionosphere reflects, rather than refracts, with little loss; thus v.l.f. navigation aids of extremely long range may be used.

Above 30 MHz, space waves, sometimes called line of sight waves, are utilized. From about 100 MHz to 3 GHz the transmission path is highly predictable and reliable, and little atmospheric attenuation occurs. Above 3 GHz attenuation and scattering occur, which become limiting factors above about 10 GHz. The fact that space waves travel in a straight line at a known speed and, furthermore, are reflected from certain objects (including thunderstorms and aircraft) makes the detection and determination of range and bearing of such objects possible.

Modulation

Being able to receive a remotely transmitted e.m. wave and measure its characteristics is not in itself of much use. To form a useful link, information must be superimposed on the e.m. wave carrier. There are several ways in which the wave can carry information and all of them involve varying some characteristic of the carrier (amplitude or frequency modulation) or interrupting the carrier (pulse modulation).

The simplest, and earliest, way in which a radio wave is made to carry information is by use of Morse Code. Switching the transmitter on for a short time-interval, corresponding to a dot, or a longer time-interval, corresponding to a dash, enables a message to be transmitted. Figure 1.2 illustrates the transmission of SOS, the time-intervals shown being typical.

In radar the information which must be superimposed is simply the time of transmission. This can easily be achieved by switching on the transmitter for a very short time to produce a pulse of e.m. energy.

When transmitting complex information, such as speech, we effectively have the problem of transmitting an extremely large number of sine waves. Since the effect of each modulating sine wave on the radio frequency (r.f.) carrier is similar, we need only consider a single sine wave modulating frequency. The characteristics of the modulating signal which must be transmitted are the frequency and amplitude. Figure 1.3 shows three ways in which a pulsed carrier may be modulated by a sine wave while Figs 1.4 and 1.5 show amplitude and frequency modulation of a continuous wave (c.w.) carrier.

Both amplitude modulated (a.m.) and frequency modulated (f.m.) carriers are commonly used for airborne systems. With a.m. the amplitude of the carrier represents the amplitude of the modulating signal, while the rate of change of amplitude represents the frequency. With f.m. the amplitude and frequency of the modulating signal is represented by the frequency deviation and rate of change of frequency of the carrier respectively.

Both a.m. and f.m. waves have informative parameters associated with them. With a.m. if the

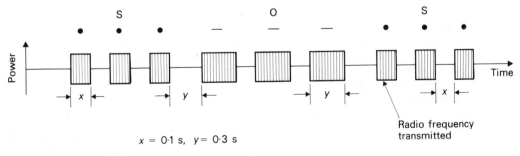

$x = 0.1$ s, $y = 0.3$ s

Fig. 1.2 Morse code: SOS

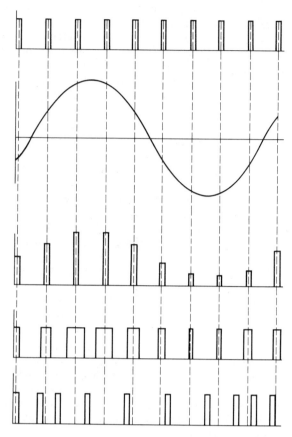

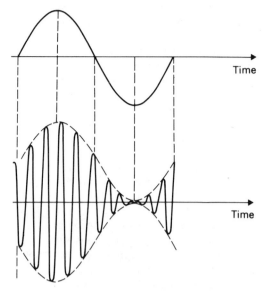

Fig. 1.4 Amplitude modulation

Fig. 1.3 Pulse modulation – from top to bottom: unmodulated carrier, modulating waveform, pulse amplitude modulation, pulse width modulation and pulse position modulation

carrier amplitude is V_c and the modulating signal amplitude is V_m then the modulation factor is V_m/V_c. This fraction can be expressed as a percentage, in which case it is known as the percentage modulation or depth of modulation (note sometimes depth of modulation is quoted as a decimal fraction). Figure 1.4 shows 100 per cent modulation. With f.m. the parameter is the deviation ratio which is given by the ratio of maximum frequency deviation (f_d max) to maximum modulating frequency (f_m max). The ratio f_d/f_m is called the modulation index and will only be constant and equal to the deviation ratio if the modulating signal is fixed in frequency and amplitude.

In Figs 1.3, 1.4 and 1.5 the modulated signal is illustrated in the time domain, i.e. with time along the horizontal axis. It is instructive to look at the frequency domain representations as shown in

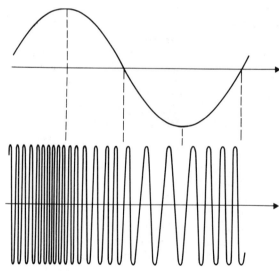

Fig. 1.5 Frequency modulation

Fig. 1.6 where a single sine wave of frequency f_m is the modulating signal. It can be seen that several frequencies are present, so giving rise to the idea of bandwidth of a radio information channel. The most significant difference between a.m. and f.m. is that the a.m. bandwidth is finite whereas, in theory, the f.m. bandwidth is infinite. In practice the f.m. bandwidth is regarded as finite, being limited by those extreme sidebands which are regarded as significant, say 10 per cent of amplitude of the largest frequency

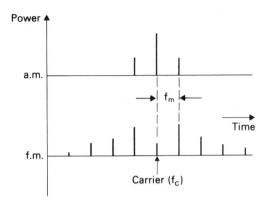

Fig. 1.6 Amplitude modulation and frequency modulation spectrums for a pure sine wave modulating signal of frequency f_m

component. The relative amplitudes of the carrier and sidebands depend on modulation factor and index for a.m. and f.m. respectively.

In any information link there is a relationship between the bandwidth and the amount of information which can be carried, hence high-fidelity stereo broadcasts occupy a wide bandwidth. It is not, however, desirable to have as wide a bandwidth as possible since (a) the number of available channels is reduced; (b) electrical noise, generated at all frequencies by electrical equipment and components, and by atmospheric effects, will be present in the receiver channel at a greater power level the wider the bandwidth. The signal power to noise power ratio is a limiting factor in the performance of receiving equipment.

The information in an a.m. wave is repeated in each of the sidebands; the carrier frequency component has no information content. As a consequence, at the expense of more complicated transmitting and receiving equipment, we need transmit only one sideband. Single sideband (s.s.b.) transmission conserves bandwidth, with attendant advantages, and is found in airborne h.f. comm. systems.

Multiplexing

In most airborne systems the required number of channels is obtained by allocating non-overlapping bands of frequencies centred on specified discrete carriers. This is known as frequency multiplexing.

Shannon's sampling theory shows that a sine wave of frequency f_m can be completely specified by a series of samples spaced at no more than $1/2 f_m$ second(s). To transmit speech where the highest

frequency component is 3000 Hz we need only transmit a sample of the instantaneous amplitude every $1/6000 = 0.000\ 166\ 7$ s (= $166.7\ \mu s$). Thus we have time-intervals during which we can transmit samples of other signals. The number of signals we can time multiplex on one carrier link depends on the duration and frequency of each sample. The shorter the sample duration the greater the bandwidth required, confirming the statement made earlier that more information requires wider bandwidths.

Basic Receivers and Transmitters
A much simplified transmitter block diagram is shown in Fig. 1.7. This could be called the all-purpose block diagram since it could easily be converted to a

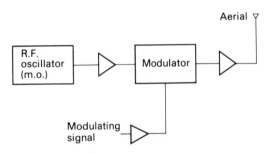

Fig. 1.7 Basic radio transmitter block diagram

low-level a.m. transmitter, (little if any amplification of the carrier before modulation), a high-level a.m. transmitter (little if any amplification of the carrier after modulation), an s.s.b. transmitter (introduce a band pass filter after the modulator) or an f.m. transmitter (introduce a frequency multiplier after the modulator). Obviously in the above examples the circuit details would vary greatly, particularly in the modulators, and if detailed block diagrams were drawn the underlying similarities in structure would be less obvious.

The most basic type of receiver is a tuned radio frequency (t.r.f.), however this is rarely used. The standard receiver configuration is the superhetrodyne (superhet) shown in Fig. 1.8. The desired r.f. is converted to a constant intermediate frequency by taking the difference frequency after mixing the received signal with the output from a local oscillator (l.o.). Since most of the amplification and selectivity is provided by constant frequency and bandwidth stages the design problem is eased.

In both the transmitter and the receiver, r.f. oscillators have to be tuned to different frequencies. In the transmitter it is the m.o. (master oscillator), while in the receiver it is the l.o. Modern practice is

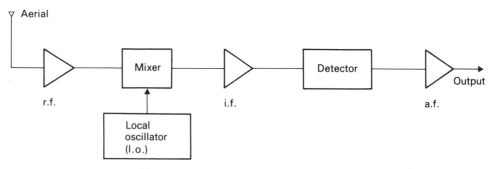

Fig. 1.8 Basic superhetrodyne receiver block diagram

to use a frequency synthesizer with a single crystal to provide stability and accuracy.

Digital Systems

Coding

Most of the airborne systems in use are basically analogue, i.e. they deal with signals which represent various quantities continuously and smoothly. For example in DME a very small increase in range results in a corresponding increase in time; we say time is an analogue of distance. With a digital system, information is represented by a number encoded in some suitable way.

Since it is difficult to detect many different voltage or current levels only two are used, and this leads naturally to expressing numbers to the base 2 (binary code) where the only digits are 0 and 1. It remains to define electronic representations of 0 and 1 in an unambiguous way. Various methods are used with (a) being by far the most common, in the non-exhaustive list which follows.

(a)	Voltage level	no voltage	= 0
		high voltage	= 1
(b)	Pulse polarity	positive	= 1
		negative	= 0
(c)	Pulse position	a time interval is split in two halves:	
		pulse in first half	= 1
		pulse in second half	= 0
(d)	Phase change	at specified read time a sine wave:	
		changes phase (180°C)	− 1
		does not change phase	= 0

In all of the above the logic may be reversed (positive and negative logic). Thus we can represent a binary digit (bit) by an electrical signal, but if the number to be represented is larger than 1, we must combine bits into some intelligible code.

Binary code has been mentioned; this is simply counting to the base 2 rather than the base 10 (decimal code) as we do normally. Unfortunately, binary numbers soon become very large, for example $91_{10} = 1\ 0\ 1\ 1\ 0\ 1\ 1_2$ (the subscripts indicating the base), so octal (base $8 = 2^3$) and hexadecimal (base $16 = 2^4$) may be used. The machine may still deal with a 1/0 situation but the numbers are more manageable when written down, for example $91_{10} = 133_8 = 5B_{16}$. Note, in the examples given, if we split the binary number into groups of three from the right (least significant bit, l.s.b.) we have 1, 011, 011$_2$ = 1, 3, 3$_8$, i.e. each group is the binary code for an octal digit. Similarly 101, 1011$_2$ = 5, B$_{16}$.

Binary and hexadecimal codes are used in digital computers, octal code is used for the ATC transponder (Chapter 8). The task of frequency selection is one which lends itself to coding, and among several which have been used, the two most common are binary coded decimal (b.c.d.) and two from five (2/5). Both of these codes retain the decimal digit 'flavour' of the number to be encoded at the expense of using extra bits. To represent 91_{10} we consider the decimal digits 9 and 1 separately to give:

$$91_{10} = 1\ 0\ 0\ 1\quad 0\ 0\ 0\ 1_{b.c.d.},$$
$$91_{10} = 1\ 0\ 0\ 0\ 1\quad 1\ 1\ 0\ 0\ 0_{2/5}$$

Equivalents for all the codes mentioned are given for decimal numbers 0 to 15 in Table 1.5.

It can be seen from the above that more bits than are absolutely necessary are used for b.c.d. and 2/5.

Table 1.5 Various code equivalents

Base				Code		
10	2	8	16	BCD		2/5
0	0000	0	0		0000	01001
1	0001	1	1		0001	11000
2	0010	2	2		0010	10100
3	0011	3	3		0011	01100
4	0100	4	4		0100	01010
5	0101	5	5		0101	00110
6	0110	6	6		0110	00101
7	0111	7	7		0111	00011
8	1000	10	8		1000	10010
9	1001	11	9		1001	10001
10	1010	12	A	0001	0000 11000	01001
11	1011	13	B	0001	0001 11000	11000
12	1100	14	C	0001	0010 11000	10100
13	1101	15	D	0001	0011 11000	01100
14	1110	16	E	0001	0100 11000	01010
15	1111	17	F	0001	0101 11000	00110

If the bits are transmitted serially, one after the other in time down a line, then more time is needed for the transmission of a number than would be needed if binary code were used. If the bits are transmitted in parallel, one bit per line, then more lines are needed. This has a certain advantage in that the redundancy may be used to detect transmission errors, for example 1 0 1 1 0 could not be a 2/5 code and 1 0 1 0 could not be b.c.d.

Error checking can also be used with binary codes. We will always be restricted to a certain maximum number of bits, one of which can be designated a parity bit used solely for error detecting. Suppose we had eight bits available, each group of eight bits would be called a word of length 8 (commonly called a *byte*). The first seven bits of the word would be used to encode the decimal digit (0 to 127) while the eighth would be the parity bit. For odd parity we set the parity bit to 0 or 1 so as to make the total number of ones in the word odd; similarly for even parity. Thus 6_{10} = 00001101 odd parity or 6_{10} = 00001100 even parity. Error correcting (as opposed to detecting) codes exist but do not find use in airborne equipment as yet.

To consider a practical application of the above — suppose a particular frequency is selected on a control unit, we may have the following sequence of events:

1. information from controller: 2/5 code;
2. conversion from 2/5 to binary;
3. microcomputer processes binary data;
4. conversion from binary to b.c.d.;
5. b.c.d. fed to frequency synthesizer;
6. conversion from b.c.d. to special code;
7. special code fed to readout device.

So far we have only discussed the coding of numerical data. The ISO (International Standards Organisation) alphabet No. 5 is a seven-bit word code which can be used to encode upper and lower case letters, punctuation marks, decimal digits and various other characters and control symbols. The full code may be found in most of the latest ARINC characteristics and will not be repeated here, however, examples are A ≡ 1 0 0 0 0 0 1, % ≡ 1 0 1 0 0 1 0, etc. A parity bit may be added to give a byte.

Where a limited number of actual words need to be encoded, e.g. 'distance', 'speed', 'heading', etc. special codes may be designated. Such codes are described in ARINC specification 429-2 digital information transfer system (DITS) which is discussed in Chapter 13.

Microcomputers

The microprocessor has brought powerful computers on to aircraft to perform a number of functions, including the solution of navigation equations, in a more sophisticated way than before. A microcomputer consists of a microprocessor and several peripheral integrated circuits (chips), to help the microprocessor perform its function.

There are four basic parts to computers, micro or otherwise: memory, arithmetic logic unit (ALU), control unit and the input/output unit (I/O). In a microcomputer the ALU and control unit are usually combined on a single chip, the microprocessor or central processing unit (CPU). Figure 1.9 illustrates a basic system.

The memory contains both instructions and data in the form of binary words. Memory is of two basic types: read only (ROM) and random access (RAM). The ROM does not remember any previous state which may have existed; it merely defines a functional relationship between its input lines and its output lines. The RAM could be termed read and write memory, since data can be both read from memory and written into memory, i.e. its state may change. Information in RAM is usually lost when power is switched off.

The ALU contains the necessary circuitry to allow it to carry out arithmetic operations, such as addition and subtraction, and logical functions such as Boolean algebra operations (combinations of NANDs and NORs etc.).

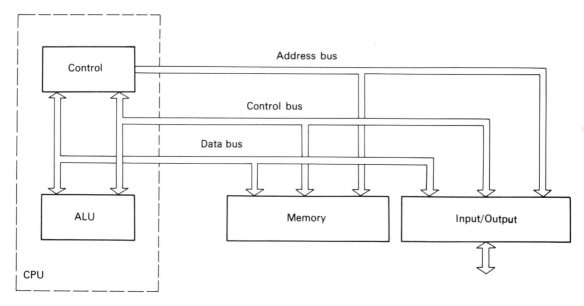

Fig. 1.9 Basic microcomputer organization

The control unit provides timing instructions and synchronization for all other units. The control signals cause the other units to move data, manipulate numbers, input and output information. All this activity depends on a set of step-by-step instructions (known as the program) which reside in memory.

The I/O unit is the computer's interface with the outside world.

From Fig. 1.9 it can be seen that the units are interconnected by three main buses. A bus is several electrical connections dedicated to a particular task. A unidirectional bus allows data flow in one direction only, unlike a bidirectional bus where flow is two-way. In a microcomputer we usually have:

1. address bus: sixteen unidirectional lines;
2. data bus: eight or sixteen bidirectional lines;
3. control bus: the number of lines varies with the system and may have both unidirectional and bidirectional lines.

To operate, each step-by-step instruction must be fetched, in order, from memory and executed by the CPU. To keep track of the next step in the program, a program counter is used which increments each time an instruction is fetched. Before an instruction can be executed, it must be decoded in the CPU to determine how it is to be accomplished.

On switch-on, the program counter is set to the first stored instruction. The address (location) of this first instruction is placed on the address bus by the program counter causing the instruction to be fetched

from memory, on the data bus, to the control unit where it is decoded. The program counter automatically increments by one count, and after the current instruction has been executed the next instruction is fetched. This basic cycle of:

fetch
decode
increment
execute

is repeated continuously. During the execution of an instruction data may have to be fetched from memory, for example to add two numbers the instruction will need to tell the CPU not only that an addition operation is necessary, but the location, in the memory, of the numbers to be added.

The rate at which instructions are executed depends on the complexity of the instruction and the frequency of the system clock. Each pulse from the clock initiates the next action of the system; several actions per instruction are needed. Often the clock circuit is on the CPU chip, the only external component being a crystal.

The I/O data flows via logical circuits called *ports*. These ports may be opened in a similar way to that in which memory is addressed. In some systems the I/O ports are treated as if they were RAM — an address opens a particular port and data flows in or out of that port depending on whether a read or write signal is present. A variety of chips are used for I/O, some of which are very basic; others (programmable ports) more flexible.

The program which is resident in ROM is subdivided into routines. Some routines will be running continuously unless stopped; others may only be called for when the need arises. For example, a navigation computer will continuously compute the aircraft position by running the main routine (or loop) which instructs the ALU as to which calculations must be carried out using data available in memory. This data must be updated periodically by accepting information from, say, a radio navigation sensor. When data is available from the external equipment, an interrupt signal is generated and fed to the microcomputer on an interrupt line. Such a signal causes the computer to abandon the main routine and commence a service routine which will supervise the transfer of the new data into memory. After transfer the main routine will recommence at the next step, remembered by a CPU register.

The topics discussed in the paragraphs above can all be classified as hardware or software. The hardware is the sum total of actual components making up the computer: chips, active and passive discrete components, and interwiring. Software comprises programs, procedures and the languages or codes used for internal and external communication. Software determines the state of the hardware at any particular time. In an airborne computer both the software and hardware are fixed by the designer. The operator does not have to program the computer in the sense that he must write a routine; however, he plays his part in how the computer will function by, for example, selecting a switch position which will cause certain data to be presented to him by the computer, inserting a card (hardware), on which coded instructions or data (software) have been written, into a card reader, etc.

Examples of the use of microcomputers are considered in some of the chapters to follow. These applications, and the above brief discussion, should give the reader a basic idea on how computers work; for details of circuitry and programming consult the readily available specialist literature.

Categorization of Airborne Radio Equipments

Frequency and Modulation
Since the techniques involved vary greatly with the r.f. and type of modulation used, it is often useful to categorize equipment as to the band of frequencies in which it operates (see Tables 1.2 and 1.3) and as being pulsed, a.m. or f.m. From both the design and maintenance point of view, the frequency at which equipment operates is perhaps more important than the modulation used, at least in so far as the choice of components and test equipment is concerned.

The higher the frequency the greater the effect of stray capacitance and inductance, signal transit time and skin effect in conductors. In the microwave region (s.h.f. and the high end of u.h.f.) waveguide replaces co-axial cable, certainly above 5 GHz, and special components whose dimensions play a critical part in their operation are introduced (klystrons, magnetrons, etc.).

Analogue-Digital
These terms have already been mentioned and certain aspects of digital systems have been discussed. In modern airborne systems the information in the radio and intermediate frequency stages, including the 'wireless' r.f. link, is usually in analogue form (the exception being secondary surveillance radar (see Chapter 8), to be joined in future by microwave landing systems, data link and the replacement for SSR (see Chapter 13)). In addition commonly used transducers such as synchros, potentiometers, microphones, telephones and speakers are all analogue devices. Not all transducers are in the analogue category, a shaft angle encoder used in encoding altimeters is basically an analogue to digital converter.

With the exception of the above almost everything else in current equipment is digital, whereas previously systems were all analogue. There is a further subdivision within digital equipment into those using a combination of hardware and software (computer-controlled) and those using only hardware (hardwired logic). The trend is towards the former.

Function
The two basic categories with regard to function are communications and navigation. If navigation is defined in its widest sense as safe, economical passage from A to B via selected points (waypoints) then communications systems could be considered as belonging to the navigation category. If, however, communications systems are regarded as those systems capable of transmitting speech over radio or wire links, and all other systems as navigation, we are obeying a sensible convention. The introduction of data links will require some amendment to the definition of communications systems, since non-navigational data will be transmitted but not as a speech pattern.

Navigation systems may be subdivided into radio

and non-radio, but only the radio systems concern us here. Another possible subdivision is position-fixing (on a map), height-finding, landing aids and environment-monitoring. For the latter we have weather avoidance systems, while radio altimeters belong to the height-finding category and instrument landing systems belong to the landing-aids category; different types of these subdivisions of the category of navigation systems will be considered in Chapters 9, 11 and 5 respectively. Position-fixing systems may be further subdivided into self-contained and ground-station-based. The former uses dead

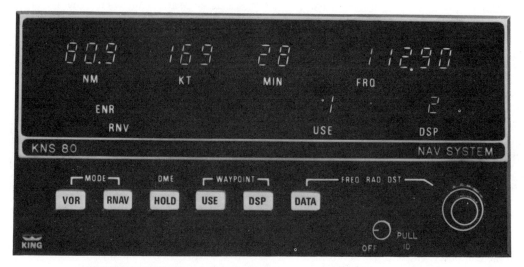

KNS 80 INTEGRATED NAVIGATION SYSTEM (VOR/DME/RNAV/ILS)

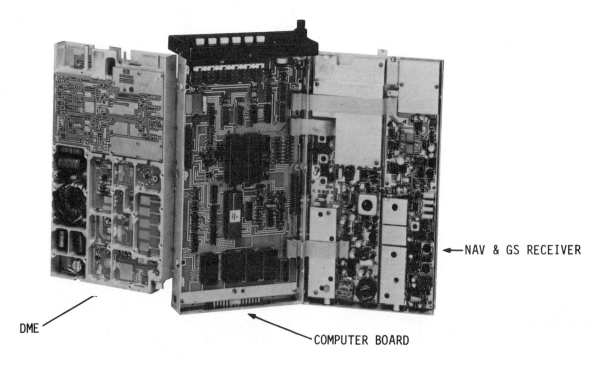

Fig. 1.10 KNS 80 integrated navigation system
(courtesy King Radio Corp.)

reckoning to compute the aircraft's position while the latter uses a variety of methods: rho-theta, rho-rho, rho-rho-rho, theta-theta and hyperbolic.

The Greek letters ρ (rho) and θ (theta) are used to represent distance (range) and angle (bearing) to a fixed point of known location. The pilot can determine (fix) his position if he knows:

(a) ρ and θ to one fixed point;
(b) ρ to three distinct fixed points;
(c) θ to two distinct fixed points.

A rho-rho system gives an ambiguous fix unless the aircraft is at the midpoint of the line joining the two stations to which the range is known. With hyperbolic systems position-fixing is achieved by measuring differences in range; ambiguity may be avoided by various techniques (Chapter 6).

One item of navigation equipment overlaps the boundaries between the different methods of position-fixing, namely Omega; this uses dead reckoning in conjunction with rho-rho, rho-rho-rho or hyperbolic methods. Two systems, VOR (Chapter 4) and DME (Chapter 7) are used together to give a rho-theta fix.

With miniaturization of circuitry, it is now possible to house several systems, which were previously physically separate, into one box. It is still possible to categorize by function, but we must bear in mind that the circuit implementation may be intimately connected. Such an example is given by the King KNS 80 integrated navigation system (Fig. 1.10) which incorporates VOR, DME and ILS (Chapters 4, 7 and 5) as well as area navigation facilities (Chapter 12). Other equipment may group together systems operating within the same band of frequencies such as v.h.f. comm. and v.h.f. nav. (VOR and ILS).

Figure 1.11 illustrates the navigation systems in use on a Boeing 747 with a typical fit; different operators may take up different options. This diagram includes non-radio (mainly in the top half) as well as radio systems, and illustrates the interrelationships between them especially with regard to display (right-hand side). A similar diagram for the communications systems is included in Chapter 2 (Fig. 2.15). The large number of radio navigation systems, some duplicated or even triplicated for safety, present the problem of where to position the antennas. The solution for the Boeing 747 is shown in Fig. 1.12.

Navigation Nomenclature

Figure 1.13 and Table 1.6 define the most commonly used terms in aircraft navigation. All of the quantities defined, with the exception of heading, can be found using radio systems, or are input by the pilot at some stage of the flight, usually prior to take off.

Interference

The e.m. environment of an aircraft radio system is such that it may suffer from interfering signals and/or noise, man-made or natural, and cause interference itself to other systems. Interference may be either radiated or conducted.

As the aircraft flies through the atmosphere, it picks up electrical charge due to frictional contact with atmospheric particles (precipitation static) and also while flying through cloud formations, within which very strong electric fields exist (electrostatic induction). An uneven distribution of charge will cause currents to flow in the aircraft skin; possibly in the form of a spark, between parts of unequal potential. Any spark results in a wide band of radiated r.f. which will be picked up by radio systems as noise and possibly mask wanted signals. To avoid this type of interference, a bonding system is used comprising numerous metal strips which present very low resistance links between all parts of the aircraft.

In addition to discharges within the aircraft, a discharge will occur to atmosphere if a sufficiently large difference in potential exists. The discharge cannot be avoided, but in an attempt to keep the activity as far from antennas as possible, static dischargers are fitted to the trailing edge of the mainplane, tailplane and vertical stabilizer in order to provide an easy path for it. By providing a number of discharge points at each discharger the voltage is kept low. The bonding system carries the large currents involved to those parts of the airframe where the static dischargers are fitted. Lightning conductors, such as on the inside surface of the non-conducting nose radome, and lightning dischargers connected to the lead-in of wire antennas and some notch antennas, help conduct any strike to the bulk of the airframe, so preventing damage to equipment. A wire antenna will also have a high resistance path between it and the airframe to allow leakage of any static build-up on the antenna.

Sparks occur in d.c. motors and generators, engine ignition systems, etc. Capacitors are used to provide a low resistance r.f. path across brushes, commutators and contacts, a form of protection known as suppression.

Another form of interference is capacitive and inductive pick-up and cross-talk between adjacent

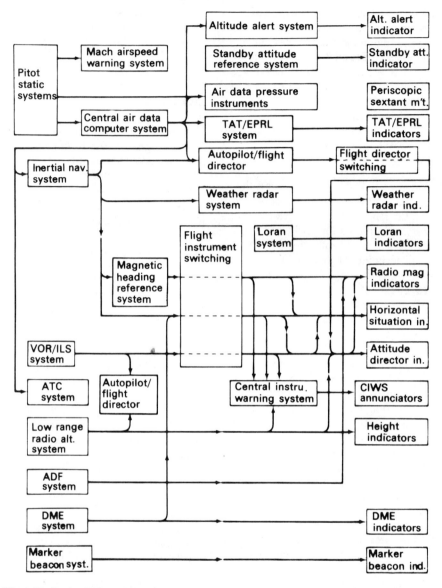

Fig. 1.11 Boeing 747: typical navigation systems fit
(courtesy Boeing Commercial Aeroplane Co.)

cables. Pick-up is the term used when the interfering source is a.c. power (400 Hz in aircraft), while cross-talk is interference from a nearby signal-carrying cable. The problem arises out of the capacitance and mutual inductance which exists between the cables. A pair of wires may be twisted together to reduce both types of interference – the pick-up or cross-talk on adjacent loops, formed by the twist, tending to cancel out. An earthed metallic screen or shield will provide an effective reduction in capacitive interference but low-frequency inductive

pick-up is not appreciably affected by the non-magnetic screen. At high frequencies skin effect confines the magnetic fields of co-axial cables to their interior. Most signal-carrying cables are both screened and twisted; some, where integrity is especially important, e.g. radio altimeter output, may have double screening.

The screen around a wire must be earthed in order to be effective. However if both ends of the screen are earthed, an earth loop may be formed since the complete circuit through the screen, remote earth

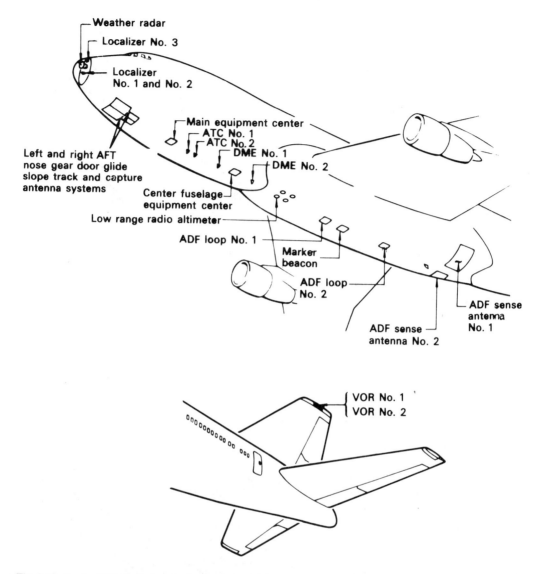

Fig. 1.12 Boeing 747: typical navigation systems aerial locations (courtesy Boeing Commercial Aeroplane Co.)

points and the airframe is of non-zero resistance. As a consequence, interfering sources may cause a potential difference to exist between the ends of the screen. The resulting current flow and its associated H field would cause interference in the inner conductor. Earth loops are a particular problem in audio systems and must be avoided.

The earth points for screened cables and a.c. power must be remote from one another. If a screen were to be connected directly to an a.c. power earth, conducted mains interference may result. Another form of conducted interference is cross-talk where a number of signal carrying wires are brought together, e.g. audio signals being fed to an interphone amplifier. Suitably designed potential divider networks keep this conducted cross-talk to a minimum (Chapter 2).

Adequate separation of antennas operating within the same frequency band is necessary to prevent mutual interference by radiation. Frequency and time domain filtering may be used in helping to avoid such interference, the former in c.w. systems, the latter in pulsed systems. Different polarization (E field direction) will assist in preventing cross-coupling between antennas.

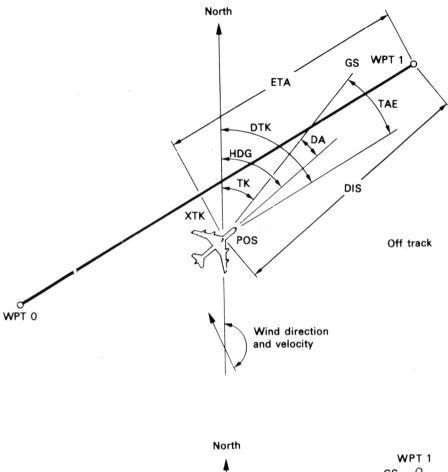

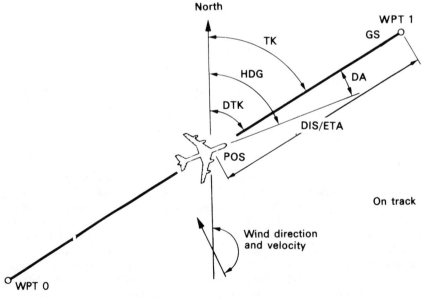

Fig. 1.13 Navigation nomenclature (courtesy Litton Systems
International Inc., Aero Products Division)

Table 1.6   Navigation nomenclature — abbreviations

Abbreviation	Meaning
HDG	Heading — angle, measured clockwise between North and the direction in which the aircraft is pointing.
TK	Track — direction in which the aircraft is moving.
DTK	Desired Track — direction in which the pilot wishes the aircraft to move.
DA	Drift Angle — angle between heading and track measured to port (left) or starboard (right).
TAE	Track Angle Error — angle between track and desired track, usually quoted as left or right.
GS	Ground Speed — speed of the aircraft in the direction of the track in the 'plane' parallel to the earth's surface (map speed). Compare with air speed which is the speed of the aircraft relative to the air mass through which it is moving.
POS	Position.
WPT	Waypoint — a significant point on the route which may be used for reporting to Air Traffic Control, turning or landing.
DIS	Distance to go from position to waypoint.
XTK	Cross Track — the perpendicular distance from the aircraft to the line joining the two waypoints between which the aircraft is flying.
ETA	Estimated time of arrival.

Adjacent channel interference occurs when a receiver's bandwidth is not sufficiently narrow to attenuate unwanted signals close to the required signal. Second or image channel interference may occur in superhet receivers when an unwanted signal is separated from the required signal by twice the intermediate frequency and lies on the opposite side of the local oscillator frequency. A high intermediate frequency will help reduce second channel interference since the image will be outside the r.f. bandwidth, the separation being greater. Unfortunately for a given Q factor, the bandwidth of the intermediate frequency amplifiers will be wide for this solution to the second channel problem. Increasing channel separation is not really acceptable since demand for more channels is forever rising. Some receivers employ two intermediate frequencies produced by two mixer stages and two local oscillators; this can give good adjacent and second channel rejection.

Magnetic fields associated with electronic and electrical equipment will interfere with the magnetic compass. Units are marked with their 'compass safe distance' as appropriate but care should also be taken with cables, particularly for d.c. power.

Maintenance

This is not the place to go into great detail on this important practical topic but some notes of a general nature are in order to supplement the notes included in most of the following chapters. In practice the maintenance engineer relies on his training and experience and also regulations, schedules and procedures laid down or approved by national bodies responsible for aviation in general and safety in particular.

The aircraft maintenance engineer, of whatever specialism, is responsible for regular inspections of equipment as laid down in the aircraft schedule. For the radio engineer an inspection will consist of a thorough examination of all equipment comprising the radio installation for cracks, dents, chafing, dirt, oil, grease, moisture, burning, arcing, brittleness, breakage, corrosion, mechanical bonding, freedom of movement, spring tension, etc. as applicable. In carrying out specific tasks the engineer should look for damage to parts of the airframe or its equipment which are not directly his or her responsibility. Vigilance is the key to flight safety.

Carrying out functional tests when called for in the schedule, or when a fault has been reported, should be done in accordance with the procedure laid down in the aircraft maintenance manual. A word of warning should be given here, since procedures are not always what they should be: often testing of certain aspects of a system's function are omitted and, rarely, there may be errors in the procedure. A thorough knowledge of the system is the best guard against mistakes or omissions which, if noticed, should be amended through the proper channels.

Modern equipment usually has sufficient built-in test equipment (BITE) and monitoring circuits to carry out a comprehensive check of the system. With radio systems, however, special portable test equipment must be used in addition to BITE in order to be in a position to certify the system as serviceable. Test sets should be capable of testing by radiation and of simulating the appropriate signals to test all functions not covered by BITE.

The r.f. circuits, including antennas and feeders, are often neglected when functional tests are carried out. In particular test set antennas should be correctly positioned if a false impression of the receiver sensitivity or power output is to be avoided.

When fault-finding a complete functional test should be carried out as far as possible in order to obtain a full list of symptoms. Naturally symptoms such as a smell of burning or no supply must call a halt to the procedure. Fault-finding charts in maintenance manuals are useful but there is no substitute for knowledge of the system.

One should not forget the possible effects of non-radio systems and equipment when investigating reported defects. Poor bonding, broken static dischargers, open circuit suppression capacitors, low or inadequately filtered d.c. supplies, low voltage or incorrect frequency a.c. supplies, etc. will all give rise to symptoms which will be reported by the pilot as radio defects.

Sometimes symptoms are only present when the aircraft is airborne and the system is subject to vibration, pressure and temperature changes, etc. A functional test during engine runs will go part way to reproducing the conditions of flight.

One should mention the obvious hazard of loose articles; so obvious that many aircraft accidents have been caused in the past by carelessness. Tools and test equipment, including leads, must all be accounted for when a job is finished. A well-run store with signing-in and signing-out of equipment is an added safeguard to personal responsibility.

Installation of equipment should be in accordance with the manufacturer's instructions which will cover the following:

1. Weight of units: centre of gravity may be affected.
2. Current drawn: loading of supplies should be carefully considered and the correct choice of circuit-breaker made.
3. Cooling: more than adequate clearance should be left and forced air-cooling employed if appropriate. Overheating is a major cause of failure.
4. Mounting: anti-vibration mounts may be necessary which, if non-metallic, give rise to a need for bonding straps.
5. Cables: length and type specified. Usually maximum length must be observed but in some cases particular lengths are necessary. Types of cable used must provide protection against interference and be able to handle current drawn or supplied. Current capabilities are reduced for cables in bunches.
6. Antenna: approved positions for particular types of antenna or particular types of aircraft are laid down by aviation authorities.

Strengthening of the structure around the antenna in the form of a doubler plate will probably be necessary. A ground plane is essential and must not be forgotten if the antenna is to be mounted on a non-conducting surface. If the antenna is movable, adequate clearance should be left. Any alignment requirements must be met.

7. Interface: compatibility with other systems/ units must be ensured. Both impedance matching (including allowing for capacitive and inductive effects) and signal characteristics should be considered. Loading of outputs should be within limits. Particular care should be taken in deciding where synchro devices obtain their reference supplies. Programming pins for choice of outputs and/or inputs must be correctly connected.
8. Compass: safe distance.
9. Radiation hazards.

The last item in the above non-exhaustive list raises the topic of safety. Electric shock is an obvious hazard when working on aircraft and it should be remembered that one is liable to receive a shock from radiating antennas, particularly h.f. antennas. A radiation hazard exists with all transmitting antennas, thus the operator should ensure no-one is working, particularly doping or painting, near an antenna when the associated transmitter is on. The particular hazards of microwave radiation are considered in Chapter 9. It is up to all personnel working on aircraft to become aware of the dangers of harmful substances, the use (and position) of fire extinguishers, the dangers of mixing oil or grease with oxygen, elementary first aid, warning symbols, etc.

Regulating and Advisory Bodies

All countries set up bodies which are responsible for matters concerned with aviation e.g. CAA (UK), FAA (USA), Bureau Veritas (France), etc. These bodies draft air law and issue regulations concerned with the licensing of engineers and aircrew, aircraft operations, aircraft and equipment manufacture, minimum equipment fits (including radio), air traffic control, etc. They are also the bodies charged with seeing, by means of examinations and inspections, that the law is obeyed.

Aviation is an international activity and co-operation between countries is essential. This co-operation is achieved mainly through the ICAO, an agency affiliated to the United Nations. All nations which are signatories to the Chicago Convention on Civil Aviation 1944 are member-states of the ICAO which was an outgrowth of that convention.

Table 1.7 Organizations, orders and conference concerned with aircraft radio systems

Abbreviation	Organization
ARINC	Aeronautical Radio Inc.
ATA	Air Transport Association
AEEC	Airlines Electronic Engineering Committee
CAA	Civil Aviation Authority
CAP	Civil Aviation Publication
FAA	Federal Aviation Agency
ICAO	International Civil Aviation Organization
IFRB	International Frequency Registration Board
CCIR	International Radio Consultative Committee
ITU	International Telecommunications Union
TSO	Technical Standard Order
WARC	World Administrative Radio Conference

The ICAO issues annexes to the convention, Annex 10 being of particular significance to aircraft radio engineers since it is concerned with aeronautical telecommunications and, among other things, lays down a minimum specification for airborne radio systems. The material published by the ICAO does not automatically become the law or regulations in all member-states; ratification is necessary and may not take place without considerable amendment, if at all. In particular, system specifications emerge in forms considerably different from Annex 10, although similar in content. In the USA specifications are issued in the form of TSOs while in the UK there is CAP 208, Volume 1 with its companion Volume 2 listing approved equipment under various classifications.

Licensing of engineers is one area in which, as yet, there is little international standardization in accordance with Annex 1. The licensed aircraft radio maintenance engineer is unknown in the USA but, of course, organizations operating with the approval of the FAA do so only if they employ suitably qualified personnel. In the UK the licensed engineer reigns supreme, except in the certification of wide-bodied jets and supersonic transports where a system of company approval of personnel exists, the company itself being approved by the CAA for the operation and maintenance of such aircraft. France has no system of state licensing, it being left to the operators to assess the competency of its maintenance personnel under the watchful eye of officials.

Of further interest to those concerned with aircraft

radio, the Chicago convention provides that aircraft registered in contracting states may carry radio transmitting apparatus only if a licence to install and operate such apparatus has been issued by the appropriate authorities of the state in which the aircraft is registered. Furthermore, radio transmitting apparatus may only be used over the territory of contracting states, other than the one in which the aircraft is registered, by suitably licensed flight crew.

Various non-regulatory bodies exist with a view to extending co-operation across national boundaries in respect to aircraft equipment and maintenance. ARINC is one such organization. It is a corporation the stockholders of which are drawn from airlines and manufacturers, mostly from the USA. As well as operating a system of aeronautical land radio stations ARINC sponsors the AEEC, which formulates standards for electronic equipment and systems designed for use in airliners as opposed to general aviation. Characteristics and specifications published by ARINC do not have the force of law but nevertheless are, in the main, adhered to by manufacturers who wish to sell their equipment to the airlines.

A specification relating to the presentation of maintenance information is the ATA 100. A standard layout for technical publications relating to aircraft has been promulgated and widely adopted. Of particular interest to readers are Chapters 23 and 34 of the maintenance manual which cover communications and navigation respectively. In addition to prescribing layout, a set of standard symbols for electrical wiring diagrams has been issued.

So far, bodies concerned with aircraft and their equipment have been considered; in addition organizations concerned with telecommunications should be mentioned. The ITU is an agency of the United Nations which exists to encourage international co-operation in the use and development of telecommunications. The CCIR is a committee set up by the ITU to deal with radio communications. Among topics of interest to the CCIR are spectrum utilization and aeronautical mobile services. The IFRB has also been set up by the ITU for the assignment and registration of radio frequencies in a master frequency list. In November 1979 an international conference (WARC '79), with representatives from 154 countries, met in Geneva to consider radio regulations and re-allocate frequencies. The results of WARC '79 will not be published while this book is being written but it is unlikely that the frequencies allocated to aeronautical mobile services will suffer significant amendment — the cost would be too great.

2 Communication systems

Introduction

There is a fundamental need for communication between aircrew and ground controllers, among the aircrew and between aircrew and passengers. External communication is achieved by means of radio-telephone (R/T) link while internal communication (intercom or audio integrating system) is by wire as opposed to wireless. Although intercom. is not a radio system, it is included in this chapter because of its intimate relationship with the aircraft radio systems. Voice recorders and in-flight entertainment systems are also considered since they are usually the responsibility of the aircraft radio technician/engineer.

The first items of radio equipment to appear on aircraft were low-frequency (l.f.) communications sets in the World War I days of spark gap transmitters. Intercom was by means of a Gosport (speaking) tube. By the 1930s the early keyed continuous wave (c.w.) (radio-telegraphy) was beginning to be replaced by R/T although 'key-bashing' had its place as long as aircraft carried radio operators. Early R/T was within the l.f. and h.f. bands, the sets operating on only one or very few frequencies. With airfields widely spaced and low-powered transmission, there was little interference and so the need for many channels did not arise.

The situation has drastically changed since World War II; air traffic and facilities have increased with the consequent demand for extra channels which cannot be provided in the l.f., m.f. or h.f. bands. Fortunately v.h.f. equipment has been successfully developed from early beginnings in World War II fighter control.

The current situation is the v.h.f. is used for short-range communication while h.f. is used for long-range. A large airliner, such as a Boeing 747, carries three v.h.f.s and dual h.f. In addition, in such aircraft, selective calling (Selcal) facilities are provided by a dual installation such that a ground station can call aircraft either singly or in groups without the need for constant monitoring by the crew. Provision for satellite communication (Satcom)

on v.h.f. frequencies is often found; unfortunately aeronautical communications satellites are not to be found (1979).

The audio integrating system (AIS) complexity depends on the type of aircraft. A light aircraft system may provide two transmit/receive channels for dual v.h.f. comms and receive only for dual v.h.f. nav., ADF, DME and marker. Each receive channel has a speaker-off-phone switch while the microphone can be switched between v.h.f. comms 1 and v.h.f. comms 2. A multi-crew large airliner has very many more facilities, as described later.

V.H.F. Communications

Basic Principles

An aircraft v.h.f. comms transceiver is comprised of either a single or double conversion superhet receiver and an a.m. transmitter. A modern set provides 720 channels at 25 kHz spacing between 118 MHz and 135·975 MHz; until recently the spacing was 50 kHz giving only 360 channels. The mode of operation is single channel simplex (s.c.s.), i.e. one frequency and one antenna for both receiver and transmitter. If provision for satellite communication is included in accordance with ARINC 566 then in addition to a.m. s.c.s. we will have f.m. double channel simplex (d.c.s.), i.e. different frequencies for transmit and receive.

Communication by v.h.f. is essentially 'line of sight' by direct (space) wave. The range available can be approximated by $1·23\,(\sqrt{h_r} + \sqrt{h_t})$nm where h_r is the height, in feet, above sea level of the receiver while h_t is the same for the transmitter. Thus, with the ground station at sea level, the approximate maximum range for aircraft at 10 000 and 1000 ft (30 000 and 3000 m) would be 123 and 40 nm respectively.

Installation

A single v.h.f. installation consists of three parts, namely control unit, transceiver and antenna. In addition crew phones are connected to the v.h.f. via

Fig. 2.1 KY 196 v.h.f. comm. transceiver (courtesy King
Radio Corp.)

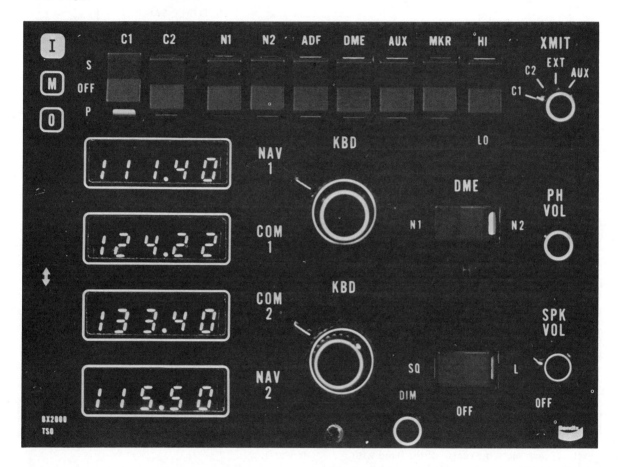

Fig. 2.2 CN-2011 v.h.f. comm./nav. equipment
(courtesy Bendix Avionics Division)

selection switches in the AIS. Light aircraft v.h.f.s
usually have a panel-mounted combined transceiver
and control unit, an example being the King KY 196
illustrated in Fig. 2.1. The current trend is for
combined COM/NAV/RNAV; Fig. 2.2 illustrates the
Bendix CN-2011, a general aviation panel-mounted
unit comprising two comms transceivers, two nav.
receivers, glidepath receiver, marker receiver,

frequency control for internal circuits and d.m.e. and
last but not least, audio selection switches. Such
equipment will be considered in Chapter 12.

Figure 2.3 shows one of a triple v.h.f. comms
installation as might be fitted to a large passenger
transport aircraft: VHF2 and VHF3 are similar to
VHF1 but are supplied from a different 28 V d.c. bus
bar and feed different selection switches in the AIS.

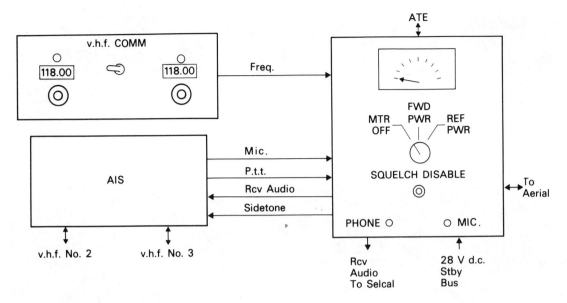

Fig. 2.3 Typical v.h.f.1 installation

Controls and Operation

The transceiver, which is rack-mounted, contains all the electronic circuitry and has provision for the maintenance technician to connect mic. and tels direct, disable the squelch, and measure VSWR. These provisions for testing are by no means universal but if the system conforms to ARINC 566 a plug is provided to which automatic test equipment (ATE) can be connected. A protective cover for the ATE plug is fitted when the unit is not in the workshop.

The antenna can take various forms: whip, blade or suppressed. In a triple v.h.f. comms installation these may be two top-mounted blade antennas and one bottom-mounted; an alternative would be two blade and one suppressed within the fincap dielectric. The whip antenna is to be found on smaller aircraft. All antennas are mounted so as to receive and transmit vertically polarized waves.

The blade antenna may be quite complex. It will be self-resonant near the centre of the band with bandwidth improvement provided by a short-circuited stub across the feed terminal or a more complicated reactive network built in which will permit height and hence drag reduction.

Controls and Operation

It is common to have in-use and standby frequencies available, the former controlling the transceiver frequency. This is the situation in Fig. 2.3 where we have two sets of frequency controls and two displays, the in-use one being selected by the transfer switch and annunciated by a lamp above the display.

Frequency control is achieved by concentric knobs, the outer one of which varies the tens and units while the inner one varies the tenths and hundredths. An alternative is shown in Fig. 2.1 where there is one frequency control and two displays. On rotating the frequency knobs clockwise or anticlockwise, the standby frequency only will increment or decrement respectively. Standby may then become in-use by operation of the transfer switch. There are many controllers in service with only in-use selection.

Some or all of the following switches/controls may be provided by manufacturers on request.

Volume Control A potentiometer, which allows variable attenuation of audio, prior to feeding the AIS may be fitted as a separate control or as a concentric knob on the frequency selector(s). Such a volume control may have sidetone coupled through it on transmit.

Squelch Control A squelch circuit disables the receiver output when no signals are being received so preventing noise being fed to the crew headsets between ground transmissions. The squelch control is a potentiometer which allows the pilot to set the level at which the squelch opens, so allowing audio output from the receiver. When the control is set to minimum squelch (fully clockwise) the Hi and Lo squelch-disable leads, brought to the control unit from the transceiver, should be shorted, so giving a definite squelch-disable.

Mode Selector Control Provides selection of normal a.m., extended range a.m. or Satcom. If the Satcom antenna has switchable lobes such switching may be included in the mode switch, or could be separate.

On-Off Switch Energizes master power relay in transceiver. The switch may be separate, incorporated in mode selector switch as an extra switch position, or ganged with the volume or squelch control.

Receiver Selectivity Switch Normal or sharp selectivity. When Satcom is selected sharp selectivity automatically applies.

Block Diagram Operation (KY 196)

Figure 2.4 is a simplified block diagram of the King KY 196 panel-mounted v.h.f. comm. transceiver. This equipment, intended for the general aviation market, is not typical of in-service transceivers since frequency and display control is achieved with the aid of a microprocessor; however within the lifetime of this book such implementation will become commonplace.

Receiver The receiver is a single conversion superhet. The r.f. stage employs varactor diode tuning, utilizing the tuning voltage from the stabilized master oscillator (s.m.o.). Both the r.f. amplifier and mixer are dual gate field-effect transistors (f.e.t.). The r.f. amplifier f.e.t. has the input signal applied to gate 1 while the a.g.c. voltage is applied to gate 2. The mixer connections are: gate 1, signal; gate 2, s.m.o. The difference frequency from the mixer, 11·4 MHz, is passed by a crystal filter, providing the desired narrow bandpass, to the i.f. amplifiers. Two stages of a.g.c.-controlled i.f. amplification are used; the first of which is a linear integrated circuit.

The detector and squelch gate utilize transistors on an integrated circuit transistor array. A further array is used for the squelch-control circuitry. Noise at 8 kHz from the detector output is sampled and used to close the squelch gate if its amplitude is as expected from the receiver operating at full gain. When a signal is received, the noise output from the detector decreases due to the a.g.c. action; as a consequence the squelch gate opens allowing the audio signal to pass. The squelch can be disabled by

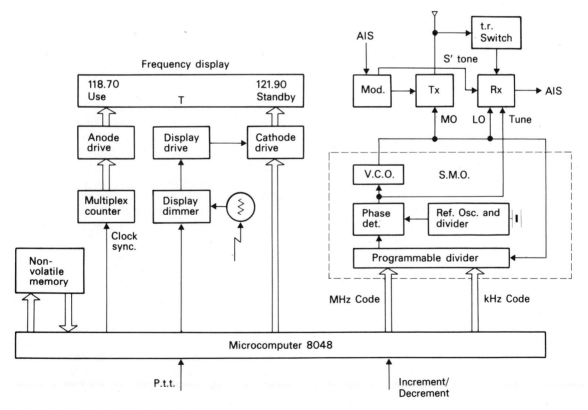

Fig. 2.4 King KY 196 simplified block diagram

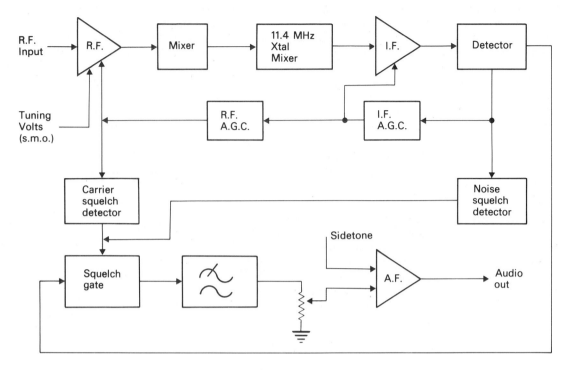

Fig. 2.5 King KY 196 simplified receiver block diagram

means of a switch incorporated in the volume control. When the received signal has excessive noise on the carrier, the noise-operated squelch would keep the squelch gate closed were it not for carrier-operated or backup squelch. As the carrier level increases, a point is reached where the squelch gate is opened regardless of the noise level.

The mean detector output voltage is used to determine the i.f. a.g.c. voltage. As the i.f. a.g.c. voltage exceeds a set reference the r.f. a.g.c. voltage decreases.

The detected audio is fed via the squelch gate, low-pass filter, volume control and audio amplifier to the rear panel connector. A minimum of 100 mW audio power into a 500 Ω load is provided.

Transmitter The transmitter (Fig. 2.6) feeds 16 W of a.m. r.f. to the antenna. Modulation is achieved by superimposing the amplified mic. audio on the transmitter chain supply. The carrier frequency corresponds to the in-use display.

Radio frequency is fed from the s.m.o. to an r.f. amplifier. This input drive is switched by the transmit receive switching circuits, the drive being effectively shorted to earth when the press to transmit (p.t.t.) button is not depressed. The transmitter chain comprises a pre-driver, driver and final stage all broad band tuned, operated in Class C and with modulated collectors. The a.m. r.f. is fed via a low-pass filter, which attenuates harmonics, to the antenna. On receive the t.r. diode is forward biased to feed the received signal from the antenna through the low-pass filter to the receive r.f. amplifier.

The modulator chain comprises microphone pre-amplifier, diode limiting, an f.e.t. switching stage, integrated circuit modulator driver and two modulator transistors connected in parallel. The pre-amp output is sufficient to subsequently give at least 85 per cent modulation, the limiter preventing the depth of modulation exceeding 100 per cent. The mic. audio line is broken by the f.e.t. switch during receive.

Stabilized Master Oscillator The s.m.o. is a conventional phase locked loop with the codes for the programmable divider being generated by a microprocessor. Discrete components are used for the voltage controlled oscillator (v.c.o.) and buffers while integrated circuits (i.c.) are used elsewhere.

The reference signal of 25 kHz is provided by an oscillator divider i.c. which utilizes a 3·2 MHz crystal to give the necessary stability. Only seven stages of a fourteen-stage ripple-carry binary counter are used to

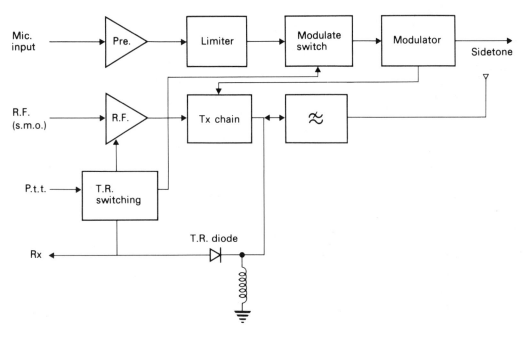

Fig. 2.6 King KY 196 simplified transmitter block diagram

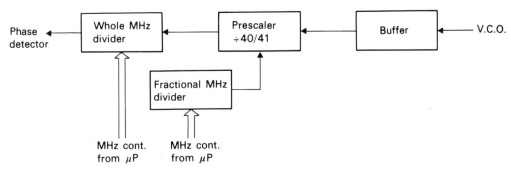

Fig. 2.7 King KY 196 simplified programmable divider block diagram

give the necessary division of $2^7 = 128$. This reference, together with the output of the programmable divider, is fed to the phase detector which is part of an i.c., the rest of which is unused. The pulsating d.c. on the output of the phase detector has a d.c. component which after filtering is used to control the frequency of the v.c.o. by varactor tuning. If there is a synthesizer malfunction, an out-of-lock signal from the phase detector is used to switch off the s.m.o. feed to the transmitter.

The programmable divider consists basically of three sets of counters as shown in Fig. 2.7. The buffered v.c.o. output is first divided by either 40 or 41, the former being so when a discrete MHz selection

is made; i.e. zeros after the displayed decimal point. The prescaler which performs this division is a u.h.f. programmable divider ($\div 10/11$) followed by a divide-by-four i.c. The whole MHz divider uses a 74LS162 b.c.d. decade counter and a 74LS163 binary counter which together can be programmed to divide by an integer between 118 and 145, hence the prescaler and whole MHz divider give a total division of 4720 (40 × 118) to 5800 (40 × 145) in steps of 40. Thus a required v.c.o. output of, say, 130·00 MHz would be achieved with a division of 5200 (40 × 130) since 130 MHz ÷ 5200 = 25 kHz = reference frequency.

The 25 kHz steps are obtained by forcing the

prescaler to divide by 41, the required number of times in the count sequence. Each time the division ratio is 41, one extra cycle of the v.c.o. frequency is needed to achieve an output of 25 kHz from the programmable divider. To see that this is so, consider the previous example where we had a division ratio of 5200 to give 130·00 MHz, i.e. 5200 cycles at 130·00 MHz occupies 40 μs = period of 25 kHz. Now a prescaler division ratio of 41 once during 40 μs means 5201 cycles of the v.c.o. output occupy 40 μs so the frequency is $5201/(40 \times 10^{-6}) = 130·025$ MHz as required. The prescaler ratio is controlled by the fractional MHz divider, again employing a 74LS162 and 74LS163. The number of divide-by-41 events in 40 μs is determined by the kHz control code from the microprocessor and can be anywhere from 0 to 39 times. Therefore each whole megacycle can have $N \times 25$ kHz added where N ranges from 0 to 39. This produces 25 kHz steps from 0 kHz to 975 kHz.

Microprocessor and Display The microprocessor used, an 8048, contains sufficient memory for the program and data required in this application to be stored on the chip. In addition to this memory and, of course, an eight-bit c.p.u., we have an eight-bit timer/counter and a clock on board. Through twenty-seven I/O lines the 8048 interfaces with the programmable divider, display drive circuits and non-volatile memory.

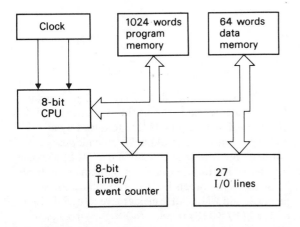

Fig. 2.8 8048 eight bit microcomputer (courtesy King Radio Corp.)

The 8048 has been programmed to generate a binary code for the 'use' and 'standby' frequencies. The code, as well as being stored in the 8048, is also stored in a 1400-bit electrically alterable read only memory (EAROM). This external memory is effectively a non-volatile RAM, the data and address being communicated in serial form via a one-pin bidirectional bus, the read/write/erase mode being controlled by a three-bit code. When power is applied the microprocessor reads the last frequencies stored in the EAROM which are then utilized as the initial 'use' and 'standby' frequencies. In the event of failure of the EAROM the microprocessor will display 120·00 MHz as its initial frequencies. The EAROM will store data for an indefinite period without power.

The 'standby' frequency is changed by clockwise or counterclockwise detent rotation of the frequency select knobs. 1 MHz, 50 kHz and 25 kHz changes can be made with two knobs, one of which incorporates a push-pull switch for 50/25 kHz step changes. The microprocessor is programmed to increment or decrement the 'standby' frequency by the appropriate step whenever it senses the operation of one of the frequency-select knobs.

The code for the frequency in use is fed to the programmable dividers from the microprocessor. 'Use' and 'standby' frequencies are exchanged on operation of the momentary transfer switch. When the transceiver is in the receive mode the microprocessor adds 11·4 MHz to the 'use' frequency code since the local oscillator signal fed to the receiver mixer should be this amount higher than the desired received carrier in order to give a difference frequency equal to the i.f.

Both 'use' and 'standby' codes are fed to the display drivers. The 'use' code represents the transmit frequency and is not increased by 11·4 MHz in the receive mode. Each digit is fed in turn to the cathode decoder/driver, an i.c. containing a seven-segment decoder, decimal point and comma drives and programmable current sinks. The decimal point and comma outputs (i and h) are used to drive the segments displaying '1', '.' and 'T' (*see* Fig. 2.10). The 'T' is illuminated when in the transmit mode.

The display is a gas discharge type with its intensity controlled by a photocell located in the display window. As the light reaching the photocell decreases the current being supplied to the programming pin of the cathode decoder/driver from the display dimmer circuit decreases, so dimming the display.

Time multiplexing of the display drives is achieved by a clock signal being fed from the microprocessor to

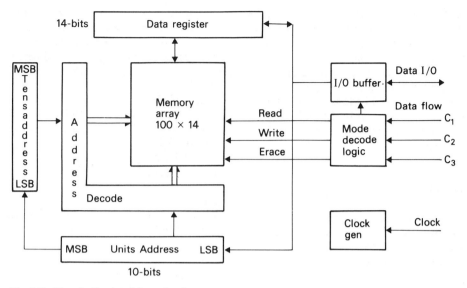

Fig. 2.9 Electrically alterable read only memory, e.a.r.o.m.
(courtesy King Radio Corp.)

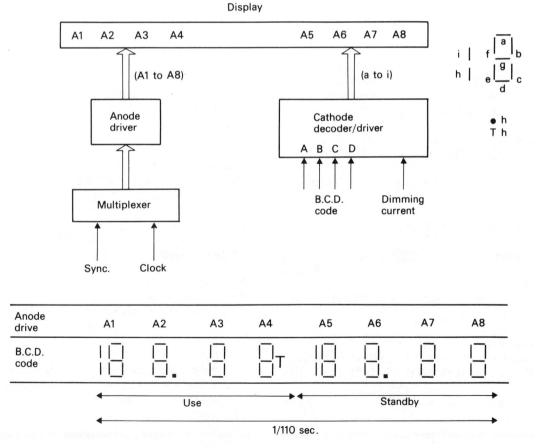

Fig. 2.10 King KY 196 simplified display drive block
diagram

a 1 of 8 counter/multiplexer so that the anode drives (A1 to A8) are switched sequentially. As the anode drives are switched the appropriate b.c.d. information from the microprocessor is being decoded by the cathode decoder/driver, the result being that the necessary segments of each digit are lighted one digit at a time at approximately 110 times per second. A synchronization pulse is sent to the multiplexer from the microprocessor every 8 cycles to maintain display synchronization.

Characteristics

The selected characteristics which follow are drawn from ARINC Characteristic 566 covering airborne v.h.f. communications and Satcom Mark 1. Details of Satcom and extended range a.m. are not included.

System Units
1. V.h.f. transceiver;
2. modulation adaptor/modem – f.m. provision for Satcom;
3. power amplifier – Satcom and extended range;
4. pre-amplifier – Satcom and extended range;
5. control panel;
6. remote frequency readout indicator – optional;
7. antennas – separate Satcom antenna.
   Note: 1 and 2 may be incorporated in one line replaceable unit (l.r.u.).

Frequency Selection
720 channels from 118 through 135·975 MHz, 25 kHz spacing.
Receiver muting and p.t.t. de-energization during channelling.
2/5 channel selection.
Channelling time: $\leqslant 60$ ms.

Receiver

Sensitivity
3 μV, 30 per cent modulation at 1000 Hz to give S + N/N $\geqslant$ 6 dB.

Selectivity
Minimum 6 dB points at ± 15 kHz (± 8 kHz sharp).
Maximum 60 dB points at ± 31·5 kHz (± 15 kHz sharp).
Maximum 100 dB points at ± 40 kHz (± 18·5 kHz sharp).

Cross Modulation
With simultaneous receiver input of 30 per cent

modulated off-resonant signal and an unmodulated desired signal, the resultant audio output shall not exceed −10 dB with reference to the output produced by a desired signal only when modulated 30 per cent (under specified signal level/off resonance conditions).

Undesired Responses
All spurious responses in band 108-135 MHz shall be down at least 100 dB otherwise, including image, at least 80 dB down.

Audio Output

Gain
A 3 μV a.m. signal with 30 per cent modulation at 1000 Hz will produce 100 mW in a 200-500 Ω load.

Frequency Response
Audio power output level shall not vary more than 6 dB over frequency range 300-2500 Hz.
Frequencies $\geqslant$ 5750 Hz must be attenuated by at least 20 dB.

Harmonic Distortion
Less than 7·5 per cent with 30 per cent modulation.
Less than 20 per cent with 90 per cent modulation.

AGC
No more than 3 dB variation with input signals from 5 μV to 100 mV.

Transmitter

Stability
Carrier frequency within ± 0·005 per cent under prescribed conditions.

Power Output
25-40 W into a 52 Ω load at the end of a 5 ft transmission line.

Sidetone
With 90 per cent a.m. at 1000 Hz the sidetone output shall be at least 100 mW into either a 200 or 500 Ω load.

Mic. Input
Mic. audio input circuit to have an impedance of 150 Ω for use with a carbon mic. or a transistor mic. operating from the (approx.) 20 V d.c. carbon mic. supply.

Antenna
Vertically polarized and omnidirectional.

To match 52 Ω with VSWR $\leqslant 1.5 : 1$.

Ramp Testing

After checking for condition and assembly and making available the appropriate power supplies the following (typical) checks should be made at each station using each v.h.f.

1. Disable squelch, check background noise and operation of volume control.
2. On an unused channel rotate squelch control until squelch just closes (no noise). Press p.t.t. button, speak into mic. and check sidetone.
3. Establish two-way communication with a remote station using both sets of frequency control knobs, in conjunction with transfer switch, if appropriate. Check strength and quality of signal.

NB. Do not transmit on 121.5 MHz (Emergency). Do not transmit if refuelling in progress. Do not interrupt ATC-aircraft communications.

H.F. Communications

Basic Principles

The use of h.f. (2-30 MHz) carriers for communication purposes greatly extends the range at which aircrew can establish contact with Aeronautical Mobile Service stations. This being so, we find that h.f. comm. systems are fitted to aircraft flying routes which are, for some part of the flight, out of range of v.h.f. service. Such aircraft obviously include public transport aircraft flying intercontinental routes, but there is also a market for general aviation aircraft.

The long range is achieved by use of sky waves which are refracted by the ionosphere to such an extent that they are bent sufficiently to return to earth. The h.f. ground wave suffers quite rapid attenuation with distance from the transmitter. Ionospheric attenuation also takes place, being greatest at the lower h.f. frequencies. A significant feature of long-range h.f. transmission is that it is subject to selective fading over narrow bandwidths (tens of cycles).

The type of modulation used, and associated details such as channel spacing and frequency channelling increments, have been the subject of many papers and orders from users, both civil and military, and regulating bodies. ARINC Characteristic No. 559A makes interesting reading, in that it reveals how conflicting proposals from various authorities (in both the legal and expert opinion sense) can exist at the same time.

The current and future norm is to use single sideband (s.s.b.) mode of operation for h.f. communications, although sets in service may have provision for compatible or normal a.m., i.e. carrier and one or two sidebands being transmitted respectively. This s.s.b. transmission and reception has been described briefly in Chapter 1 and extensively in many textbooks. A feature of aircraft h.f. systems is that coverage of a wide band of r.f. and use of a resonant antenna requires efficient antenna tuning arrangements which must operate automatically on changing channel in order to reduce the VSWR to an acceptable level.

Installation

A typical large aircraft h.f. installation consists of two systems, each of which comprises a transceiver, controller, antenna tuning unit and antenna. Each of the transceivers are connected to the AIS for mic., tel. and p.t.t. provision. In addition outputs to Selcal. decoders are provided. Such an installation is shown in Fig. 2.11.

The transceivers contain the receiver, transmitter, power amplifier and power supply circuitry. They are mounted on the radio rack and provided with a flow of cooling air, possibly augmented by a fan. A transceiver rated at 200 W p.e.p. needs to dissipate 300 W when operated on s.s.b. while on a.m. this figure rises to 500 W. Telephone and microphone jacks may be provided on the front panel, as might a meter and associated switch which will provide a means of monitoring various voltages and currents.

Coupling to the antenna is achieved via the antenna tuning unit (ATU). Some systems may employ an antenna coupler and a separate antenna coupler control unit. The ATU provides, automatically, a match from the antenna to the 50 Ω transmission line. Closed-loop control of matching elements reduces the standing wave ratio to $1.3 : 1$ or less (ARINC 559A).

Since the match must be achieved between line and antenna the ATU is invariably mounted adjacent to the antenna lead-in, in an unpressurized part of the airframe. For high-flying aircraft (most jets) the ATU is pressurized, possibly with nitrogen. Some units may contain a pressure switch which will be closed whenever the pressurization within the tuner is adequate. The pressure switch may be used for ohmmeter checks or, providing switch reliability is adequate, may be connected in series with the key line thus preventing transmission in the event of a leak. Alternatively an attenuator may be switched in to reduce power.

Light aircraft h.f. systems in service are likely, for

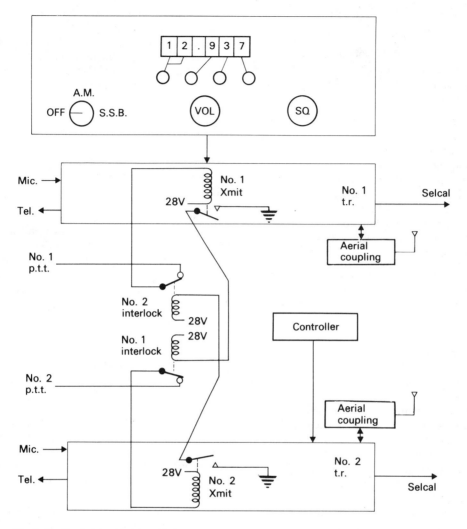

Fig. 2.11 Typical dual h.f. installation

financial reasons, to have a fixed antenna coupler. Such a system operates on a restricted number of channels (say twenty). As a particular channel is selected, appropriate switching takes place in the coupler to ensure the r.f. feed to the antenna is via previously adjusted, reactive components, which make the effective antenna length equal to a quarter of a wavelength, thus presenting an impedance of approximately 50 Ω. The required final manual adjustment must be carried out by maintenance personnel on the aircraft.

The antenna used varies greatly, depending on the type of aircraft. For low-speed aircraft a long wire antenna is popular although whip antennas may be found on some light aircraft employing low-powered h.f. systems. The aerodynamic problems of wire antennas on aircraft which fly faster than, say, 400 knots, have led to the use of notch and probe antennas which effectively excite the airframe so that it becomes a radiating element.

Modern wire antennas are constructed of copper-clad steel or phosphor bronze, giving a reduced r.f. resistance compared with earlier stainless-steel wires. A covering of polythene reduces the effects of precipitation static. Positioning is normally a single span between forward fuselage and vertical stabilizer. Larger aircraft will have twin antennas while a single installation, possibly in a 'V' configuration, is more common for smaller aircraft. The r.f. feed is usually at the forward attachment via an antenna mast. The rear tethering is by means of a tensioning unit.

The antenna mast is subject to pitting and erosion

of the leading edge; a neoprene covering will provide some protection, nevertheless regular inspections are called for. Protection against condensation within the mast may be provided by containers of silica gel which should be periodically inspected for a change in colour from blue to pink, indicating saturation. Hollow masts are usually provided with a water-drain path which should be kept free from obstruction.

The two most important features of the rear tethering point are that the wire is kept under tension and that a weak link is provided so as to ensure that any break occurs at the rear, so preventing the wire wrapping itself around the vertical stabilizer and rudder. On light aircraft a very simple arrangement of a spring, or rubber bungee, and hook may be used. The spring maintains the tension but if this becomes excessive the hook will open and the wire will be free at the rear end. On larger aircraft a spring-tensioning unit will be used to cope with the more severe conditions encountered due to higher speeds and fuselage flexing. The unit loads the wire by means of a metal spring, usually enclosed in a barrel housing. A serrated tail rod is attached to the tethering point on the aircraft and inserted into the barrel where it is secured by a spring collet, the grip of which increases with tension. The wire is attached to a chuck unit which incorporates a copper pin serving as a weak link designed to shear when the tension exceeds about 180 lbf. Some units incorporate two-stage protection against overload. Two pins of different strengths are used; should the first shear, a small extension (3/16 in.) of overall length results, thus reducing tension and exposing a yellow warning band on the unit.

Notch antennas consist of a slot cut into the aircraft structure, often at the base of the vertical stabilizer. The inductance of the notch is series-resonated by a high-voltage variable capacitor driven by a phase-sensing servo. Signal injection is via matching circuitry driven by a SWR sensing servo. Since the notch is high 'Q' the input is transformed to a voltage across the notch which is of the order of thousands of volts. This large voltage provides the driving force for current flow in the airframe which serves as the radiator.

A probe antenna, which is aerodynamically acceptable, may be fitted at either of the wing-tips or on top of the vertical stabilizer. Again series tuning provides the necessary driving force for radiation. The probe antenna, as well as the wire antenna, is liable to suffer lightning strikes, so protection in the form of a lightning arrester (spark gap) is fitted. Any voltage in excess of approximately 16 kV on the antenna will cause an arc across the electrodes of the nitrogen-filled spark gap, thus preventing discharge

through the h.f. equipment. Build-up of precipitation static on antennas, particularly probes, is dealt with by providing a high resistance static drain (about 6 MΩ) path to earth connected between the antenna feed point and the ATU.

It is important in dual installations that only one h.f. system can transmit at any one time; this is achieved by means of an interlock circuit. This basic requirement is illustrated in Fig. 2.11 where it can be seen that the No. 1 p.t.t. line is routed via a contact of the No. 2 interlock relay, similarly with No. 2 p.t.t. The interlock relays will be external to the transceivers often fitted in an h.f. accessory box. While one of the h.f. systems is transmitting the other system must be protected against induced voltages from the keyed system. In addition, with some installations, we may have a probe used as a transmitting antenna for both systems and as a receiving antenna for, say, No. 1 system. The No. 2 receiving antenna might be a notch. It follows that on keying either system we will have a sequence of events which might proceed as follows.

HF 1 keyed:
1. HF 2 keyline broken by a contact of HF 1 interlock relay;
2. HF 2 antenna grounded;
3. HF 2 ATU input and output feeds grounded and feed to receiver broken.

HF 2 keyed:
1. HF 1 keyline broken by a contact of HF 2 interlock relay;
2. HF 1 probe antenna transferred from HF 1; ATU to HF 2 ATU;
3. HF 2 notch antenna feed grounded;
4. HF 1 ATU input and output feeds grounded and feed to receiver broken.

Controls and Operation
Separate controllers are employed in dual installations, each having 'in-use' frequency selection only. Older systems and some light aircraft systems have limited channel selection where dialling a particular channel number tunes the system, including ATU, to a pre-assigned frequency, a channel/frequency chart is required in such cases. With modern sets, indication of the frequency selected is given directly on the controller.

The controls shown in Fig. 2.11 are those referred to in ARINC 559A; variations are common and will be listed below.

Mode Selector Switch. OFF-AM-SSB The 'turn off' function may be a separate switch or indeed may not be employed at all; switching on and off being achieved with the master radio switch. The 'AM' position may be designated 'AME' (AM equivalent or compatible) and is selected whenever transmission and reception is required using a.m. or s.s.b. plus full carrier (a.m.e.). The 'SSB' position provides for transmission and reception of upper sideband only.

Although use of the upper sideband is the norm for aeronautical h.f. communications some controllers have 'USB' and 'LSB' positions. In addition 'DATA' and 'CW' modes may be available. The former is for possible future use of data links by h.f. using the upper sideband — the receiver is operated at maximum gain. The latter is for c.w. transmission and reception, morse code, by 'key bashing', being the information-carrying medium.

Frequency Selectors Frequency selectors consist of, typically, four controls which allow selection of frequencies between 2·8 and 24 MHz in 1 kHz steps (ARINC 559A). Military requirements are for a frequency coverage of 2 to 30 MHz in 0·1 kHz steps, consequently one will find systems offering 280 000 'channels' meeting these requirements in full or 28 000 channels meeting the extended range but not the 0·1 kHz step requirement.

When a new frequency is selected the ATU must adjust itself since the antenna characteristics will change. For this purpose the transmitter is keyed momentarily in order that SWR and phase can be measured and used to drive the ATU servos.

Squelch Control Normal control of squelch threshold may be provided. As an alternative an r.f. sensitivity control may be used, but where Selcal is utilized it is important that the receiver operates at full sensitivity at all times with a squelch circuit being employed only for aural monitoring and not affecting the output to the Selcal decoder.

Audio Volume Control Provides for adjustment of audio level. Such a control may be located elsewhere, such as on an audio selector panel, part of the AIS.

Clarifier This control is to be found on some h.f. controllers. With s.s.b. signals while the phase of the re-inserted carrier is of little consequence its frequency should be accurate. Should the frequency be incorrect by, say, in excess of ± 20 Hz deterioration of the quality of speech will result. A clarifier allows for manual adjustment of the re-inserted carrier frequency. Use of highly accurate and stable frequency synthesizers make the provision of such a control unnecessary.

Indicator A meter mounted on the front panel of the controller may be provided in order to give an indication of radiated power.

Block Diagram Operation

Transceiver Figure 2.12 is a simplified block diagram of an a.m./s.s.b. transceiver. The operation will be described by function.

Amplitude Modulated Transmission The frequency selected on the controller determines the output from the frequency synthesizer to the r.f. translator which shifts the frequency up and provides sufficient drive for the power amplifier (p.a.). The mic. input, after amplification, feeds the modulator which produces high-level amplitude modulation of the r.f. amplified by the p.a. The r.f. signal is fed to the ATU via the antenna transfer relay contact.

The PA output signal is sampled by the sidetone detector which feeds sidetone audio via the contact of the de-energized sidetone relay and the sidetone adjust potentiometer to the audio output amplifier.

Single Sideband Transmission Low-level modulation is necessary since there is no carrier to modulate at the p.a. stage, hence the mic. input, f_m, is fed to a balanced modulator together with a fixed carrier frequency, f_c, from the frequency synthesizer. The balanced modulator output consists of both sidebands $f_c + f_m$ and $f_c - f_m$, the carrier being suppressed. The required sideband is passed by a filter to the r.f. translator after further amplification.

If we consider an audio response from 300 to 3000 Hz we see that the separation between the lowest u.s.b. frequency and the highest l.s.b. frequency is only 600 Hz. It follows that the filter used must have very steep skirts and a flat bandpass. A mechanical filter can be used in which an input transducer converts the electrical signal into mechanical vibrations, these are transmitted by mechanically resonant metal discs and coupling rods and finally converted back to an electrical signal by an output transducer.

Frequency translation is by a mixing process rather than a multiplicative process since if the u.s.b. $f_c + f_m$ were multiplied by N we would radiate a frequency of $N(f_c + f_m)$ rather than $f_t + f_c + f_m$. The amount by which the u.s.b. is translated, f_t, is determined by the frequency selected on the controller. Final amplification takes place in the p.a. prior to feeding the r.f. to the ATU.

To obtain sidetone from the p.a. stage a carrier would need to be re-inserted. A simpler method,

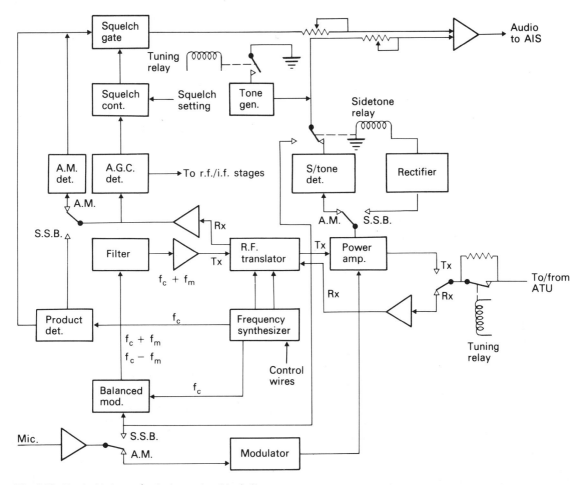

Fig. 2.12 Typical h.f. a.m./s.s.b. transceiver block diagram

which nevertheless confirms that a signal has reached the p.a., is to use the rectified r.f. to operate a sidetone relay. When energized the contact of this relay connects the amplified mic. audio to the output audio amplifier.

Amplitude Modulated Reception The received signal passes from the ATU via the de-energized antenna transfer relay contact to an r.f. amplifier and thence to the r.f. translator. After the translator normal a.m. detection takes place, the audio so obtained being fed to the output stage. A variety of a.g.c. and squelch circuits may be employed.

Single Sideband Reception The circuit action on s.s.b. is similar to that on a.m. until after the translator when the translated r.f. is fed to the product detector along with the re-inserted 'carrier' f_c. The output of the product detector is the required audio

signal, which is dealt with in the same way as before.

Antenna Tuning Unit Figure 2.13 illustrates an automatic ATU simplified block diagram. On selecting a new frequency a retune signal is sent to the ATU control circuits which then:

1. keys the transmitter;
2. inserts an attenuator in transceiver output line (Fig. 2.12);
3. switches on the tuning tone signal generator (Fig. 2.12) and drives a tune warning lamp (optional);
4. switches on reference phases for servo motors.

The r.f. signal on the input feed is monitored by a loading servo system and a phasing servo system. If the load impedance is high then the line current, I_L, is low and the line voltage V_L is high. This is detected by the loading servo discriminator which

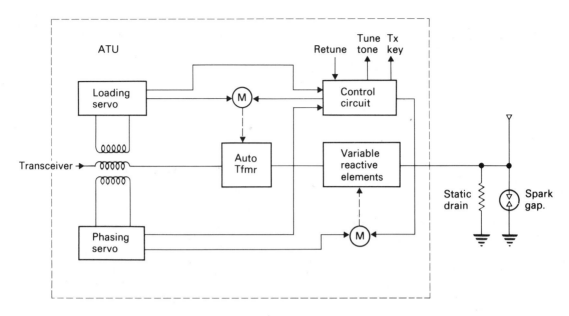

Fig. 2.13 Typical h.f. a.t.u. block diagram

applies the appropriate amplitude and polarity d.c. signal to a chopper/amplifier which in turn provides the control phase for the loading servo motor. The auto transformer tap is driven until the load impedance is 50 Ω.

Should I_L and V_L not be in phase this is detected by the phasing servo discriminator which applies the appropriate amplitude and polarity d.c. signal to a chopper/amplifier which in turn provides the control phase for the phasing servo motor. The reactive elements, inductance and capacitance, are adjusted until I_L and V_L are in phase.

As a result of the action of the two servo systems a resistive load of 50 Ω is presented to the co-axial feed from the transceiver. When both servos reach their null positions the control circuits remove the signals listed previously.

Characteristics
The following brief list of characteristics are those of a system which conforms with ARINC 559A.

Frequency Selection
An r.f. range of 2·8-24 MHz covered in 1 kHz increments.
Method: re-entrant frequency selection system.
Channelling time less than 1 s.

Mode of Operation
Single channel simplex, upper single sideband.

Transmitter
Power output: 400 W p.e.p. (200 W p.e.p. operational).
Absolute maximum power output: 650 W p.e.p.
Mic. input circuit frequency response: not more than ± 6 dB variation from 1000 Hz level through the range 350 Hz to 2500 Hz.
Spectrum control: components at or below f_c −100 Hz and at or above f_c +2900 Hz should be attenuated by at least 30 dB.
Frequency stability: ± 20 Hz. Shop adjustment no more often than yearly. Pilot control (e.g. clarifier) not acceptable.
Interlock: only one transmitter in a dual system should operate at a time on a 'first-come, first-served' basis, this includes transmitting for tuning purposes.

Receiver
Sensitivity: 4 μV max.; 30 per cent modulation a.m. (1 μV s.s.b.) for 10 dB signal and noise to noise ratio.
A.g.c.: audio output increase not more than 6 dB for input signal increase from 5 to 1 000 000 μV and no more than an additional 2 dB up to 1 V input signal level.
Selectivity:
s.s.b., 6 dB points at f_c + 300 Hz and f_c + 3100 Hz, ± 35 dB points at f_c and f_c + 3500 Hz.
A.m.: to ensure proper receiver operation (no adjacent channel interference) assuming operations on 6 kHz spaced a.m. channels.

Overall response: compatible with selectivity but in addition no more than 3 dB variation between any two frequencies in the range 300-1500 Hz (for satisfactory Selcal operation).
Audio output: two-wire circuit isolated from ground, 300 Ω (or less) output impedance supplying 100 mW (0·5 Selcal) into a 600 Ω load.

Ramp Testing and Maintenance

Whilst regular inspection of all aircraft antennas is called for, it is particularly important in the case of h.f. antennas and associated components. Any maintenance schedule should require frequent inspection of antenna tensioning units and tethering points in the case of wire antennas, while for both probe and wire antennas the spark gap should be inspected for signs of lightning strikes (cracking and/or discolouring).

A functional test is similar to that for v.h.f. in that two-way communication should be established with a remote station; all controls should be checked for satisfactory operation and meter indications, if any, should be within limits. Safety precautions are particularly important since very high voltages are present on the antenna system with the resulting danger of electric shock or arcing. No personnel should be in the vicinity of the antenna when transmitting, nor should fuelling operations be in progress. Remember with many h.f. systems a change of frequency could result in transmission to allow automatic antenna tuning.

Selcal

The selective calling (Selcal.) system allows a ground station to call an aircraft or group of aircraft using h.f. or v.h.f. comms without the flight crew having continuously to monitor the station frequency. A coded signal is transmitted from the ground and received by the v.h.f. or h.f. receiver tuned to the appropriate frequency. The output code is fed to a Selcal decoder which activates aural and visual alerts if and only if the received code corresponds to the code selected in the aircraft.

Each transmitted code is made up of two r.f. bursts (pulses) each of 1 ± 0.25 s separated by a period of 0.2 ± 0.1 s. During each pulse the transmitted carrier is 90 per cent modulated with two tones, thus there are a total of four tones per call; the frequencies of the tones determine the code.

The tones available are given by the formula

$$f_N = \text{antilog} \left(0.054(N-1) + 2.0\right),$$

where $N = 12, 13 \ldots 27$,

giving a total of sixteen tones between 312·6 and 1479·1 Hz. The tones are designated by letters A to S omitting I, N and O so a typical code might be AK-DM. There are 2970 codes available for assignment using the first twelve tones, the addition of tones P, Q, R and S (1976) bring the total to 10 920. Codes or blocks of codes are assigned on request to air carrier organizations who in turn assign codes to their aircraft either on a flight number or aircraft registration-related basis.

Figure 2.14 illustrates a single Selcal system. Large passenger transport aircraft would normally carry two identical systems. The decoder will recognize a received combination of tones on any of five channels which corresponds to that combination selected on the code select and annunciator panel. When the correct code is recognized the chime switch and appropriate lamp switch is made. The lamp switch supply is by way of an interrupter circuit so that the lamp will flash. A constant supply to the chime switch causes the chimes to sound once. Each lamp holder, designated HF1, HF11 etc. incorporates a reset switch which when depressed will release the latched lamp switch and chime switch. The tone filters in the decoder will typically be mechanically resonant devices.

Variations in the arrangement shown and described are possible. Mechanically the control and annunciator panel may be separate units. Should the operator require aircraft registration-related codes there will be no need for code select switches, the appropriate code being selected by jumper leads on the rear connector of the decoder.

Although five reset leads will be provided they may be connected individually, all in parallel to a single reset switch or to the p.t.t. circuit of the associated transmitter. In this latter case isolation diodes (within the decoder) prevent 'sneak' circuits, i.e. keying one transmitter causing one or more others to be keyed.

The lamp and chime supplies shown can be changed at the operator's option. Possibilities are to reverse the situation and have steady lights and multi-stroke chimes, or have steady lights and single-stroke chime, in which case the interrupt circuit is not used.

The Selcal systems which do not comply with ARINC 596 may not provide facilities for decoding of five channels simultaneously. A switch is provided on the control panel with which the single desired channel can be selected; in this case only Selcal codes received on the corresponding receiver will be fed to

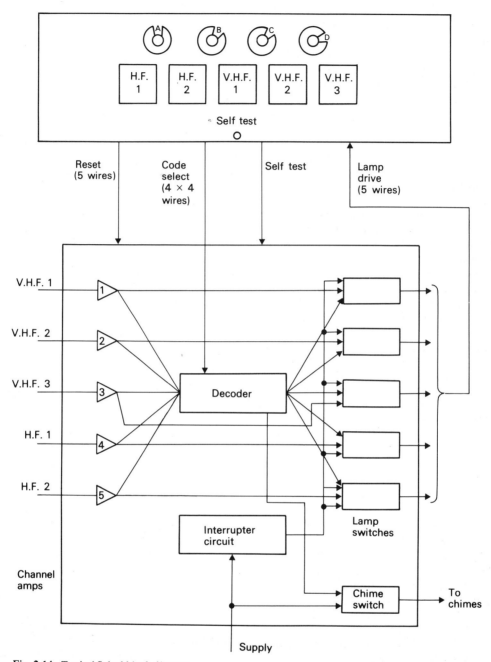

Fig. 2.14 Typical Selcal block diagram

the decoder. Only one annunciator lamp is required.

Code selection in an ARINC 596 system is achieved by means of a 'b.c.d.' format. Each of the four tone selectors has four wires associated with it; for any particular tone an appropriate combination of the wires will be open circuit, the rest grounded. If the

tones A to S are numbered 1 to 16 (0) the open wires will be as given by the corresponding binary number; e.g. tone M-12-1100, so with the wires designated 8, 4, 2 and 1 wo ooo 8 and 4 will be open. Note this is not really b.c.d. but is nevertheless termed so.

Testing of Selcal is quite straightforward. If

possible a test rig consisting of a tone generator in conjunction with a v.h.f. and h.f. transmitter should be used, otherwise permission to utilize a Selcal-equipped ground station should be sought.

Audio Integrating Systems (AIS) — Intercom

Introduction

All the systems in this book exhibit a variety of characteristics but none more so than AIS. In a light aircraft the function of the audio system is to provide an interface between the pilot's mic. and tel. and the selected receiver and transmitter; such a 'system' might be little more than a locally manufactured panel-mounted junction box with a built-in audio amplifier and appropriate switching. In contrast a large multi-crew passenger aircraft has several

sub-systems making up the total audio system. The remainder of this chapter will be concerned with the AIS on a Boeing 747.

It is unusual to consider all the systems and sub-systems which follow as part of AIS, a term which should perhaps be restricted to the system which provides for the selection of radio system audio outputs and inputs and crew intercommunications. However a brief description of all systems which generate, process or record audio signals will be given. The following services comprise the complete audio system:

1. flight interphone: allows flight deck crew to communicate with each other or with ground stations;
2. cabin interphone: allows flight deck and cabin crew to communicate;

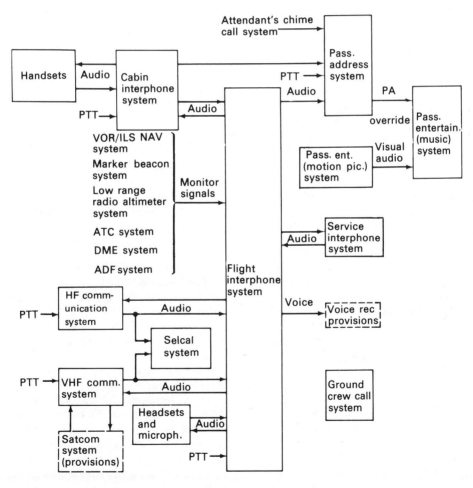

Fig. 2.15 Boeing 747: typical communications fit (courtesy Boeing Commercial Aeroplane Co.)

3. service interphone: allows ground staff to communicate with each other and also with the flight crew;
4. passenger address (PA): allows announcements to be made by the crew to the passengers;
5. passenger entertainment system: allows the showing of movies and the piping of music;
6. ground crew call system: allows flight and ground crew to attract each other's attention;
7. cockpit voice recorder: meets regulatory requirements for the recording of flight crew audio for subsequent accident investigation if necessary.

It should be noted that the above are not completely separate systems as illustrated in Fig. 2.15 and described below. The dividing lines between sub-systems of the total audio system are somewhat arbitrary, and terminology is varied; however the facilities described are commonplace.

Flight Interphone

This is really the basic and most essential part of the audio system. All radio equipments having mic. inputs or tel. outputs, as well as virtually all other audio systems, interface with the flight interphone which may, in itself, be termed the AIS.

A large number of units and components make up the total system as in Table 2.1 with abbreviated terms as listed in Table 2.2. Figure 2.16 shows the flight interphone block diagram, simplified to the extent that only one audio selection panel (ASP), jack panel etc. is shown. An ASP is shown in Fig. 2.17.

A crew member selects the tel. and mic. signals required by use of the appropriate controls/switches on an ASP. The various audio signals entering an ASP are selected by twelve combined push select and volume controls. Each ASP has an audio bus feeding a built-in isolation amplifier. The v.h.f. and h.f. comm. ADF, interphone and marker audio signals are fed to the bus via the appropriate select buttons and volume controls. The v.h.f. nav. and DME audio is fed to the bus when voice and range are selected with the Voice pushbutton; with voice only selected the DME audio is disconnected while the v.h.f. nav. audio is passed through a sharp 1020 Hz bandstop filter (FL1) before feeding the bus. With the fail-normal switch in the fail position only one audio channel can be selected (bypassing the amplifier) and the PA audio is fed direct to the audio-out lines. Radio altimeter audio is fed direct to the audio-out lines. The above audio switching arrangements are illustrated in Fig. 2.18. Note the series resistors in the input

Table 2.1 Flight interphone facilities

	CAPT	F/O	F/E	OBS1	OBS2	M.E.
ASP	X	X	X	X	X	X
Jack panel	X	X	X	X	X	–
Int – R-T p.t.t.	X	X	X	X	X	X
Handheld mic.	X	X	Jack	Jack	Jack	Jack
Headset	Jack	Jack	Jack	Jack	Jack	Jack
Boom mic. headset	X	X	X	X	X	–
Oxygen mask mic.	Jack	Jack	Jack	Jack	Jack	–
Interphone speaker	X	X	–	–	–	–

A 'X' indicates the particular unit or component is fitted at that station (column).

'Jack' indicates a jack plug is fitted to enable use of the appropriate mic. and/or tel.

Table 2.2 Abbreviations

CAPT – Captain	a.s.p. – Audio Selector Panel
F/O – First Officer	int. – Interphone
OBS – Observer	r/t – Radiotelephone
m.e. – Main Equipment Centre	p.t.t. – Press to Transmit
mic. – Microphone	tel. – Telephone

audio lines which, together with loading resistors in the interphone accessory box, form an anti-cross talk network; if one crew member has, say, h.f.1 selected on his ASP then the resistive network will greatly attenuate say h.f.2 which would otherwise be audible should another crew member have selected h.f.1 and h.f.2.

Six mic. select buttons are provided on an ASP; three v.h.f. comm., two h.f. comm. and PA. Additional switches associated with mic. select and transmission are the boom-mask and r.t.-int. p.t.t. on each ASP and also p.t.t. buttons on the hand-held microphones, jack panels and the captain's control wheel (R/T-int.).

To speak over interphone a crew member should select interphone using the r.t.-int. switch on the a.s.p. which will connect mic. high (boom or mask)

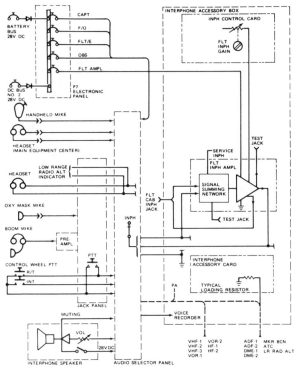

Fig. 2.16 Boeing 747: flight interphone (courtesy Boeing Commercial Aeroplane Co.)

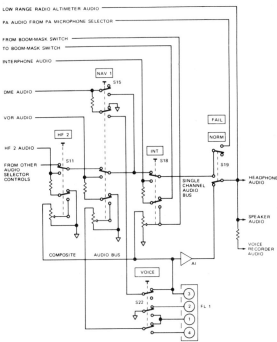

Fig. 2.18 Audio signal selection (courtesy Boeing Commercial Aeroplane Co.)

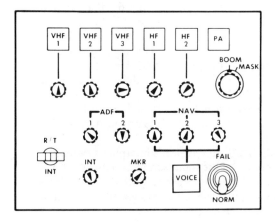

Fig. 2.17 Audio selection panel (courtesy Boeing Commercial Aeroplane Co.)

to the interphone mic. high output feeding the flight interphone amplifier in the interphone accessory box. Alternatively the captain can select interphone on his control wheel p.t.t. switch which will energize relay K2 thus making the mic. high connection as before. Note that the ASP r.t.-int. p.t.t. switch does not rely on power reaching the ASP for relay operation (*see*

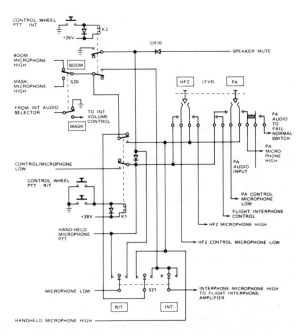

Fig. 2.19 Microphone signal selection (courtesy Boeing Commercial Aeroplane Co.)

Fig. 2.19). Interphone mic. signals from all ASPs are fed to the flight interphone amplifier which combines them and feeds the amplified interphone audio to all ASPs for selection as required.

Pressing a mic. select button on the ASP will connect the corresponding system mic. input lines to relay K2 and to contacts on the ASP r.t.-int. p.t.t. switch. Thus when a p.t.t. switch is pressed, the mic. lines will be made by either the contacts of K2 or by the ASP p.t.t. switch in the r.t. position. In Fig. 2.19 the h.f.2 select switch is shown as typical of all comm. select switches. When the PA select switch is pressed the flight interphone mic. circuit is interrupted and PA audio is applied to the fail-normal switch; in addition the mic. lines to the PA system are made. Operation of any p.t.t. switch mutes both interphone speakers to prevent acoustic feedback.

Cabin Interphone

The cabin interphone is a miniature automatic telephone exchange servicing several subscribers: the cabin attendants and the captain. In addition the system interfaces with the PA to allow announcements to be made.

Numbers are dialled by pushbuttons on the telephone type handsets or on the pilot's control unit. Eleven two-figure numbers are allocated to the subscribers, plus additional numbers for PA in various or all compartments, an 'all-attendants' call and an 'all-call'. Two dialling codes consist of letters: P-P is used by an attendant to alert the pilot (call light flashes on control unit and chime sounds once) while PA-PA is used by the pilot to gain absolute priority over all other users of the PA system. The directory is listed on the push-to-talk switch incorporated in each handset to minimize ambient noise.

All dialling code decoding and the necessary trunk switching is carried out in the central switching unit, CSU (automatic exchange). The CSU also contains three amplifiers, one of which is permanently allocated to the pilot on what is effectively a private trunk. Of the five other available trunks, two are allocated to the attendants, two to the PA system and one for dialling. (Note a trunk is simply a circuit which can connect two subscribers.)

The cabin interphone and service interphone systems may be combined into a common network by appropriate selection on the flight engineer's interphone switch panel, captain's ASP and cabin interphone control unit. Any handset may then be lifted and connected into the network (dial 'all-call'). In a similar way the flight interphone circuits may be used to make specific calls over the cabin interphone system.

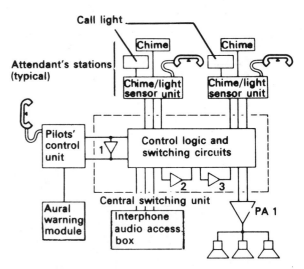

Fig. 2.20 Boeing 747: cabin interphone (courtesy Boeing Commercial Aeroplane Co.)

The system is more complex than has been suggested above but a basic description has been given, supported by Fig. 2.20.

Service Interphone

A total of twenty-two handset jacks are located in various parts of the airframe in order that ground crew can communicate with one another using the service interphone system. The system is rather simpler than those considered above. Mic. audio from all handsets, with 'press to talk' depressed, are combined in and amplified by the service interphone amplifier in the interphone audio accessory box. The amplified signal is fed to all handset tels. Volume control adjustment is provided by a preset potentiometer.

With the flight engineer's interphone switch selected to ON the input summing networks for both service and flight interphone systems are combined. All mic. inputs from either system are amplified and fed to both systems.

Passenger Address

The system comprises three PA amplifiers, tape deck, annunciator panel, attendant's panel, PA accessory box, control assemblies, speaker switch panel and fifty-three loudspeakers. The various PA messages have an order of priority assigned to them: pilot's announcements, attendant's announcements, prerecorded announcements and finally boarding music. All PA audio is broadcast over the speaker system and also, except for boarding music, overrides

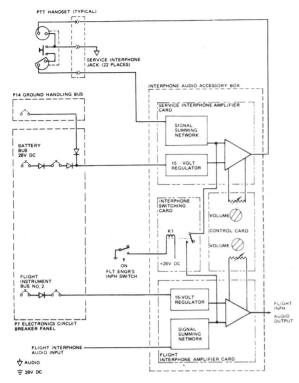

Fig. 2.21 Boeing 747: service interphone (courtesy Boeing Commercial Aeroplane Co.)

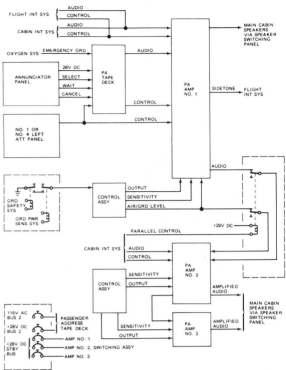

Fig. 2.22 Boeing 747: passenger address (courtesy Boeing Commercial Aeroplane Co.)

entertainment audio fed to the passenger stethoscope headsets. A prerecorded emergency announcement may be initiated by the pilot or an attendant, or automatically in the event of cabin decompression. A chime is generated when the pilot turns on 'fasten seat-belt' or 'no smoking' signs.

The passenger address amplifiers are fed via the flight or cabin interphone systems for pilot or attendant announcements respectively. Distribution of audio from the amplifiers to the speakers in various zones depends on the class configuration, since some announcements may be intended for only a certain class of passengers.

The necessary distribution is achieved by means of switches on the speaker switching panel. Audio is also fed to the flight interphone system for sidetone purposes.

Number 2 and number 3 amplifiers are slaved to number 1 for all-class announcements. Should separate class announcements be required the parallel control relay is energized, so separating the number 1 audio from that of number 2 and 3. The control assemblies in the PA accessory box contain potentiometers used to set the gain of the PA

amplifiers. When the aircraft is on the ground with landing gear locked down and ground power applied the level of speaker audio is reduced by 6 dB.

The tape deck contains up to five tape cartridges apart from the necessary tape-drive mechanism, playback head and a pre-amplifier. Boarding music is selected at an attendant's panel while prerecorded announcements are selected by means of twelve pushbuttons on the annunciator panel.

Passenger Entertainment System

The passenger entertainment system of the Boeing 747 and any other modern large airliner is perhaps the most complex of all airborne systems. It is also the system likely to cause most trouble and, fortunately, least likely to affect the safety of the aircraft unless bad servicing leads to a fire or loose-article hazard. Even on the same type of aircraft a variety of services will be available since different operators will offer different entertainment in a bid to capture more customers. In view of the above comments, the following description is particularly brief and does not do justice to the complexity involved.

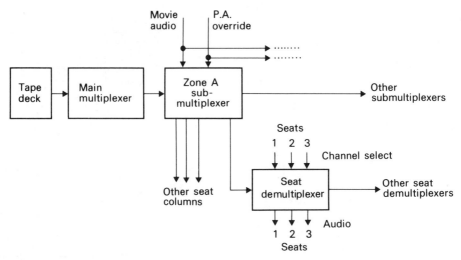

Fig. 2.23 Boeing 747: simplified passenger entertainment system

Both movies and music are provided, the movie audio being fed to individual seats via the music portion of the system. Ten tape-deck channels, four movie audio channels and one p.a. channel (total fifteen) are provided using time multiplexing. A time interval, termed a frame, is divided into fifteen channel times during which the signal amplitude of each channel is sampled. The audio signal amplitudes are binary coded (twelve bits) and transmitted, together with channel identification, clock and sync. pulses, over a co-axial cable running throughout the aircraft.

The music channels (five stereo, ten monaural or a mixture) are multiplexed in the main multiplexer, the resulting digital signal being fed to six submultiplexers in series, the final one being terminated with a suitable load resistor. Movie and PA audio are multiplexed with the music channels in the zone submultiplexers, each of which feeds three or four columns of seat demultiplexers. Channel selection is made by the passenger who hears the appropriate audio over his stethoscope headset after digital to analogue conversion in the demultiplexer. Alternate zone submultiplexers are used as back-up in the event of prime submultiplexer failure (class priorities exist if failures mean some passengers must have the entertainment service discontinued).

The controls necessary for activation of the entertainments system are located on attendants' control panels.

Ground Crew Call System
Ground crew call is hardly worthy of the title

'system', as can be seen from the schematic diagram in Fig. 2.24. The horn and flight-deck call button are located in the nose wheel bay while the ground-crew call (with illumination) and aural warning box are on the flight deck. Operation is self-explanatory from the diagram. Should horn or chime sound, the ground crew, or flight crew respectively, will contact each other using one of the interphone systems.

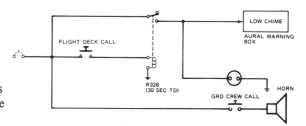

Fig. 2.24 Boeing 747: ground crew call (courtesy Boeing Commercial Aeroplane Co.)

Cockpit Voice Recorder
An endless tape provides 30 min recording time for audio signals input on four separate channels. The channel inputs are captain's, first officer's and flight engineer's transmitted and received audio and cockpit area conversation. Passenger address audio may be substituted for the flight engineer's audio in an aircraft certified to fly with two crew members.

The microphone inputs should be from so-called 'hot mics', i.e. microphones which are permanently live regardless of the setting of ASP or control column switches. The area microphone (which may

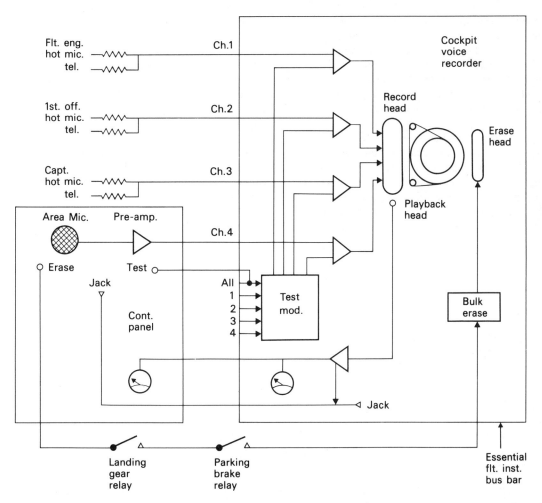

Fig. 2.25 Typical cockpit voice recorder block diagram

be separate from the control panel) is strategically situated so that it can pick up flight crew speech and general cockpit sounds.

While the control panel is situated in the cockpit, the recorder unit (CVR) is located at the other end of the aircraft where it is least likely to suffer damage in the event of an accident. The CVR is constructed so as to withstand shock and fire damage, and additionally is painted in a fire-resistant orange paint to assist in recovery from a wreck.

The recorded audio may be erased providing the landing gear and parking brake interlock relay contacts are closed. As a further safeguard against accidental erasure a delay is incorporated in the bulk erase circuit which requires the operator to depress the 'erase' switch for two seconds before erasure commences.

Test facilities are provided for all four channels,

separately or all together. A playback head and monitor amplifier allows a satisfactory test to be observed on meters or heard over a headset via jack plug sockets. Pressing the test button on the control panel or the all-test button on the CVR causes the channels to be monitored sequentially.

The power supply for the system should be from a source which provides maximum reliability. Since the tape is subject to wear and thus has a limited life, the CVR should be switched off when not in use. A suitable method would be to remove power to the CVR whenever external ground power is connected.

Testing and Trouble Shooting the Audio Systems

Various self-test facilities may be provided by which

tones may be generated and heard over headsets. However, to test properly all switches should be operated and all mic. and tel. jacks, as well as speakers, should be checked for the required audio. This should be sufficiently loud, clear and noise-free. Amplifier gain presets in accessory boxes may need to be adjusted. A full functional test is best done by two men, although it is not impossible for one man with two headsets and an extension lead to establish two-way contact between various stations.

Faults can be quite difficult to find owing to the complicated switching arrangements. However the wide range of switching can be used to advantage in order to isolate suspect units or interconnections. Disconnecting units provides a good method of finding short circuits or howls due to coffee-induced tel.-mic. feedback (i.e. spilt liquid providing a conducting path between tel. and mic. circuits). Where one has a number of units in series, e.g. demultiplexers in an entertainment system, disconnecting can be a particularly rapid method of fault-finding; it is usually best to split the run in half, then in half again, and so on until the faulty unit or connection is found. Continuity checks on very long cables can be achieved by shorting to earth at one end and then measuring the resistance to earth at the other. The resistance to earth should also be measured with the short removed in case a natural short exists.

3 Automatic direction finding

Introduction

Most readers will have come across the principle on which ADF is based when listening to a transistor radio. As the radio is rotated the signal becomes weaker or stronger, depending on its orientation with respect to the distant transmitter. Of course it is the antenna which is directional and this fact has been known since the early days of radio.

In the 1920s a simple loop antenna was used which could be rotated by hand. The pilot would position the loop so that there was a null in the signal from the station to which he was tuned. The bearing of the station could then be read off a scale on the loop. Tuning into another station gave rise to another bearing and consequently a fix. Apart from position-fixing the direction-finding loop could be used for homing on to a particular station. This primitive equipment represented the first use of radio for navigation purposes and came to be known as the radio compass.

The system has been much developed since those early days and in particular its operation has been simplified. Within the band 100-2000 kHz (l.f./m.f.) there are many broadcast stations and non-directional beacons (NDB). An aircraft today would have twin receivers which, when tuned to two distinct stations or beacons, would automatically drive two pointers on an instrument called a radio magnetic indicator (RMI) so that each pointer gave the bearing of the corresponding station. The aircraft position is where the two directions intersect. Since such a system requires the minimum of pilot involvement the name radio compass has come to be replaced by automatic direction finder (ADF).

Basic Principles

The Loop Antenna

The first requirement of any ADF is a directional antenna. Early loop antennas were able to be rotated first by hand and subsequently by motor, automatically. The obvious advantage of having no moving parts in the aircraft skin-mounted antenna has led to the universal use of a fixed loop and goniometer in modern equipments, although some older types are still in service.

The loop antenna consists of an orthogonal pair of coils wound on a single flat ferrite core which concentrates the magnetic (H) field component of the e.m. wave radiated from a distant station. The plane

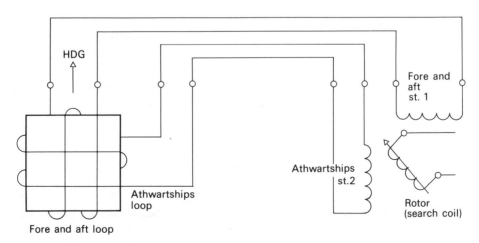

Fig. 3.1 Loop antenna and goniometer

of one coil is aligned with the aircraft longitudinal axis while the other is aligned with the lateral axis.

The current induced in each coil will depend on the direction of the magnetic field. When the plane of the loop is perpendicular to the direction of propagation, no voltage is induced in the loop since the lines of flux do not link with it. It can be seen that if one loop does not link with the magnetic field the other will have maximum linkage. Figure 3.1 shows that the loop currents flow through the stator winding of a goniometer (resolver) where, providing the characteristics of each circuit are identical, the magnetic field detected by the loop will be recreated in so far as direction is concerned. We now effectively have a rotating loop antenna in the form of the goniometer rotor or search coil. As the rotor turns through 360° there will be two peaks and two nulls of the voltage induced in it. The output of the rotor is the input to the ADF receiver which thus sees the rotor as the antenna. Such an arrangement is known as a Bellini-Tosi system.

Since we are effectively back with a rotating loop situation we should consider the polar diagram of such an antenna as we are interested in its directional properties.

In Fig. 3.2 we have a vertically polarized t.e.m. wave from the direction shown. That component of the H field linking with the loop will be H sin θ, so a plot of the loop current against θ produces a sine curve as shown. The polar diagram of such an antenna will be as in Fig. 3.3. It can be seen that because of the sinusoidal nature of the plot the nulls are far more sharply defined than the peaks.

The above has assumed a vertically polarized wave which is in fact the case with NDBs and most

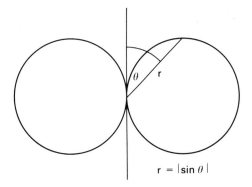

$r = |\sin \theta|$

Fig. 3.3 Loop aerial polar diagram

broadcast stations. However a vertically polarized signal travelling over non-homogeneous earth and striking reflecting objects, including the ionosphere, can arrive at the loop with an appreciable horizontally polarized component. The current in the loop will then be due to two sources, the vertical and horizontal components, which will in general give a non-zero resultant null, not necessarily in the direction of the plane of the antenna. This polarization error dictates that ADF should only be used with ground wave signals which in the l.f./m.f. bands are useful for several hundred miles. However, they are contaminated by non-vertically polarized sky waves beyond, say, 200 m at 200 kHz and 50 m at 1600 kHz, the effect being much worse at night (night effect).

The Sense Antenna
The polar diagram of the loop (Fig. 3.3) shows that the bearing of the NDB will be given as one of two

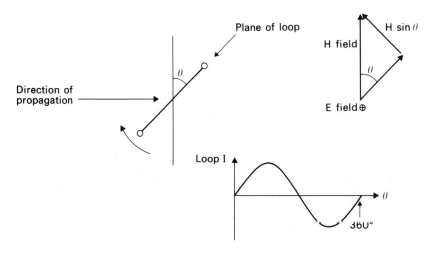

Fig. 3.2 To illustrate degree of coupling of loop aerial

figures, 180° apart, since there are two nulls. In order to determine the correct bearing further information is needed and this is provided by an omnidirectional sense antenna. In a vertically polarized field an antenna which is omnidirectional in the horizontal plane should be of a type which is excited by the electric (E) field of the t.e.m. wave i.e. a capacitance antenna. The output of such an antenna will vary with the instantaneous field strength while the output of a loop antenna varies as the instantaneous rate of change of field strength (Faraday's Law of induced e.m.f.). As a consequence, regardless of the direction of the t.e.m. wave, the sense antenna r.f. output will be in phase quadrature with respect to the search coil r.f. output. In order to sense the direction of the NDB the two antenna outputs must be combined in such a way as either to cancel or reinforce, and so either the sense or the loop signal must be phase shifted by 90°.

A composite signal made up of the search coil output phase shifted by 90° and the sense antenna output would appear as if it came from an antenna the polar diagram of which was the sum of those for the individual antennas. Now the figure-of-eight polar diagram for the loop can be thought of as being generated as we consider the output of a fixed search coil for various n.d.b. bearings or the output of a rotating search coil for a fixed n.d.b. bearing, either way the separate halves of the figure-of-eight will be 180° out of phase. As a consequence the sense antenna polar diagram will add to the loop polar diagram for some bearings, and subtract for others. The resultant diagram is a cardiod with only one null,

although not as clearly defined as the nulls for the figure-of-eight (Fig. 3.4).

Simplified Block Diagram Operation

Automatic direction finding (ADF) is achieved by means of a servo loop. The search coil is driven to a stable null position, a second null being unstable.

The search coil output, after amplification, is phase-shifted by 90° so as to be either in phase or out of phase with the sense antenna output, depending on the direction of the NDB. Prior to adding to the sense signal the phase-shifted loop signal is switched in phase in a balanced modulator at a rate determined by a switching oscillator, usually somewhere between a 50 Hz and 250 Hz rate. When the composite signal is formed in a summing amplifier it will be amplitude-modulated at the switching frequency since for one half period the two input signals will be in phase while for the next half period they will be in antiphase (see Figure 3.6).

The amplitude modulation is detected in the last stage of a superhet receiver. The detected output will be either in phase, or in antiphase, with the switching oscillator output and so a further 90° phase-shift is required in order to provide a suitable control phase for the servo motor. The motor will drive either clockwise or anticlockwise towards the stable null. When the null is reached there will be no search coil output hence no amplitude modulation of the composite signal so the reference phase drive will be zero and the motor will stop.

Should the servo motor be in such a position that the search coil is at the unstable null the slightest disturbance will cause the motor to drive away from this position towards the stable null. The sense of the connections throughout the system must be correct for the stable null to give the bearing.

A synchro torque transmitter (STTx), mounted on the search coil shaft, transmits the bearing to a remote indicator.

Block Diagram Detail

Tuning
Modern ADFs employ so-called digital tuning whereby spot frequencies are selected, as opposed to older sets where continuous tuning was usual. A conventional frequency synthesizer is used to generate the local oscillator (first l.o. if double superhet) frequency. The tuning voltage fed to the v.c.o. in the phase lock loop is also used for varicap

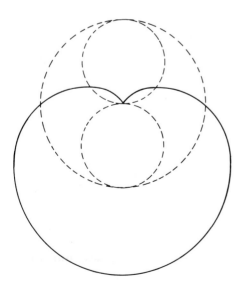

Fig. 3.4 Composite polar diagram

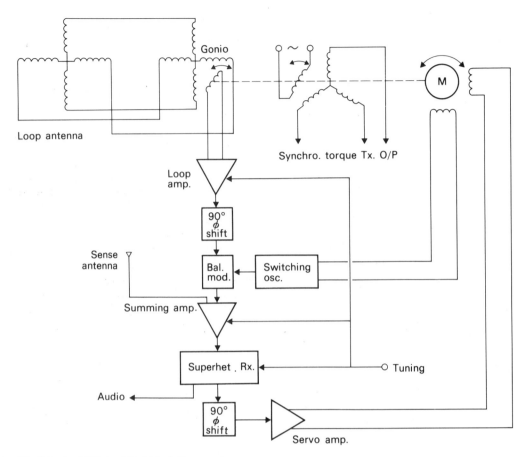

Fig. 3.5 An ADF simplified block diagram

tuning in the r.f. stages. Remote selection is by b.c.d. (ARINC 570) or some other code such as 2/5.

Balanced Modulator
Figure 3.7 shows the balanced modulator used in the King KR 85. Diodes CR 113 and CR 114 are turned on and off by the switching oscillator (Q 311 and Q 312) so alternately switching the loop signal to one of two sides of the balanced transformer T116. The output of T116 is thus the loop signal with its phase switched between 0° and 180° at the oscillator rate.

Receiver
A conventional superhet receiver is used with an i.f. frequency of 141 kHz in the case of the KR 85; i.f. and r.f. gain may be manually controlled but in any case a.g.c. is used. An audio amp, with normal gain control, amplifies the detected signal and feeds the AIS for identification purposes. A beat frequency oscillator (b.f.o.) can be switched in to facilitate the identification of NDBs transmitting keyed c.w. The

b.f.o. output is mixed with the i.f. so as to produce an audio difference frequency. Good sensitivity is required since the effective height of modern low-drag antennas gives a low level of signal pick-up. Good selectivity is required to avoid adjacent channel interference in the crowded l.f./m.f. band.

Indication of Bearing
In all indicators the pointer is aligned in the direction of the NDB. The angle of rotation clockwise from a lubber line at the top of the indicator gives the relative bearing of the NDB. If the instrument has a fixed scale it is known as a relative bearing indicator (RBI). More common is a radio magnetic indicator (RMI) which has a rotating scale slaved to the compass heading. An RMI will give the magnetic bearing of the NDB on the scale as well as the relative bearing by the amount of rotation of the pointer from the lubber line. Figure 3.8 illustrates the readings on RBI and RMI for a given NDB relative bearing and aircraft heading. An RMI normally provides for indication of

Assume search coil aligned with zero bearing

two magnetic headings from a combination of two ADF receivers and two VOR receivers. Figure 3.9 shows a typical RMI while Fig. 3.10 shows the RMI circuit and typical switching arrangements which may be internal or external to the RMIs.

Sources of System Error

Automatic direction finding is subject to a number of sources of error, as briefly outlined below.

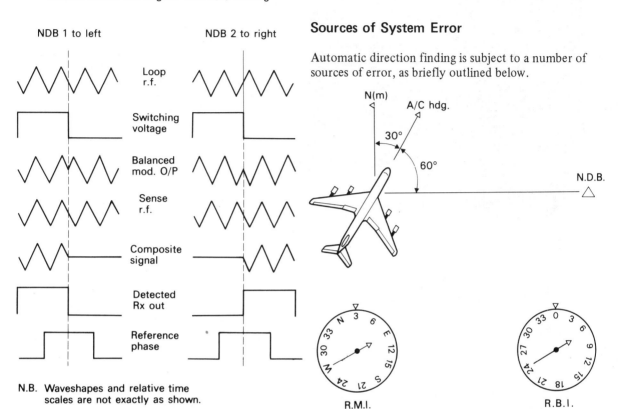

NDB 1 to left	NDB 2 to right	
	Loop r.f.	
	Switching voltage	
	Balanced mod. O/P	
	Sense r.f.	
	Composite signal	
	Detected Rx out	
	Reference phase	

N.B. Waveshapes and relative time scales are not exactly as shown.

Fig. 3.6 Diagram showing ADF phase relationships

R.M.I.   R.B.I.

Fig. 3.8 Diagram of RMI and RBI readings

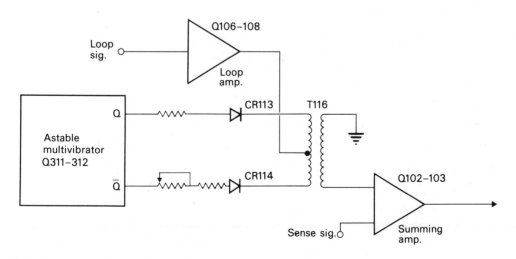

Fig. 3.7 King KR 85 balanced modulator — simplified

Fig. 3.9 KNI 581 RMI (courtesy King Radio Corp.)

Night Effect This is the polarization error mentioned previously under the heading of the loop antenna. The effect is most noticeable at sunrise or sunset when the ionosphere is changing most rapidly. Bearing errors and instability are least when tuned to an NDB at the low end of the frequency range of the ADF.

Coastal Refraction The differing properties of land and water with regard to e.m. ground wave absorption leads to refraction of the NDB transmission. The effect is to change the direction of travel and so give rise to an indicated bearing different from the actual bearing of the transmitter.

Mountain Effect If the wave is reflected by mountains, hills or large structures, the ADF may measure the direction of arrival of the reflected wave. The nearer the reflecting object is to the aircraft the greater the error by the geometry of the situation.

Static Interference Static build-up on the airframe

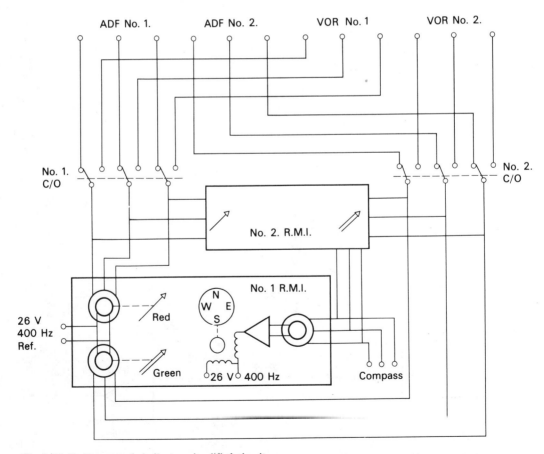

Fig. 3.10 Radio magnetic indicator: simplified circuit

and the consequent discharge reduces the effective range and accuracy of an ADF. Thunderstorms are also a source of static interference which may give rise to large bearing errors. The ability of ADF to pick up thunderstorms has been used by one manufacturer to give directional warning of storm activity (Ryan Stormscope).

Vertical or Antenna Effect The vertical limbs of the crossed loops have voltages induced in them by the electric component of the e.m. wave. If the plane of a loop is perpendicular to the direction of arrival of the signal there will be no H field coupling and the E field will induce equal voltages in both vertical limbs so we will have a null as required. Should, however, the two halves of the loop be unbalanced, the current induced by the E field will not sum to zero and so the direction of arrival to give a null will not be perpendicular to the plane of the loop. An imbalance may be due to unequal stray capacitance to earth either side of the loop; however in a well-designed Bellini-Tosi system, where each loop is balanced by a centre tap to earth, this is not a severe problem.

Station Interference When a number of NDBs and broadcast stations are operating in a given area at closely spaced frequencies station interference may result. As previously mentioned high selectivity is required for adequate adjacent channel rejection.

Quadrantal Error (QE) It is obvious that the two fixed loops must be identical in electrical characteristics, as must the stator coils of the goniometer. If the signal arrives at an angle θ to the plane of loop A in Fig. 3.11 the voltage induced in loop A will be proportional to $\cos\theta$ and in loop B to $\cos(90-\theta) = \sin\theta$. If now the search coil makes an angle ϕ with the stator P then the voltage induced in the search coil will be proportional to $(\cos\theta \times \cos\phi) - (\sin\theta \times \sin\phi)$ provided there is no mutual coupling between the interconnecting leads. So when the search coil voltage is zero:

$$\cos\theta \times \cos\phi = \sin\theta \times \sin\phi$$

or:

$$\cot\theta = \tan\phi$$

and:

$$\theta = \phi + 90 + N \times 180$$

where N is 0 or any integer. This is simply a mathematical model of the situation previously described under the heading of the loop antenna.

Now consider the two loops not electrically identical so that the ratio of the maximum voltages induced in the two loops by a given signal is r. The condition for zero voltage in the search coil is now:

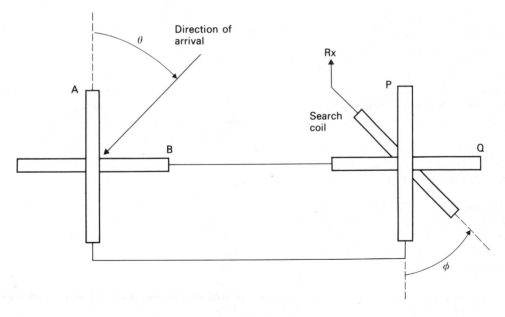

Fig. 3.11 Diagram showing search coil signal as a function of direction of arrival

$$\cot\theta = r \times \tan\phi'$$

when

$$\theta = 0 \qquad \cot\theta = \infty$$

therefore

$$\tan\phi' = \infty \quad \text{so} \quad \phi' = 90 + N \times 180$$

when

$$\theta = 90 \qquad \cot\theta = 0$$

therefore

$$\tan\phi' = 0 \quad \text{so} \quad \phi' = 0 + N \times 180$$

In these two cases (also when $\theta = 180$ or 270) we have the same situation as before i.e. $\phi = \phi'$, so no error.

At intermediate angles there will be an error, so the bearing indicated by the search coil will be incorrect. Since this type of error has a maximum value once in each quadrant it is called quadrantal error.

Now the t.e.m. wave from the NDB will cause r.f. currents to flow in the metal structure of the aircraft. Each of the loops will receive signals direct from the NDB and also re-radiated signals from the airframe. Since the aspect ratio of the aircraft fuselage and wings is not 1 : 1 the effect of the re-radiated energy on the two loops will be different; this is equivalent to making two physically identical loops electrically dissimilar. The resulting quadrantal error could be up to $20°$ maximum.

Fortunately, compensation can be made by using a QE corrector loop equalizer and possibly QE correction built into the loop. Normally the combined r.f. field produces a greater voltage in the longitudinal loop than in the lateral loop if the loops are identical. This being the case some loop antennas have more turns on the lateral loop than the longitudinal loop, typical correction being $12\frac{1}{2}°$ in the middle of the quadrants.

Loop Alignment Error If the longitudinal loop plane is not parallel to the aircraft longitudinal axis then a constant loop alignment error will exist.

Field Alignment Error If the loop antenna is offset from the aircraft centre line the maxima of the quadrantal error will be shifted, as will the zeros. Consequently the situation where the NDB is at a relative bearing of $0, 90, 180$ or $270°$ will not give zero error.

Loop Connector Stray Coupling Reactive coupling between the loop connections or between external circuits and the loop connections will lead to errors in the search coil position.

Installation

A typical transport aircraft ADF installation is shown in Fig. 3.12; No. 1 system only is shown, No. 2 being similar except that different power bus bars will be used. Main power is 28 V d.c., the 26 V, 400 Hz being used to supply the synchros. It is vital that the 26 V 400 Hz fed to the ADF receiver is from the same source as that fed to the RMI.

The loop antenna and its connecting cable form part of the input circuit of the receiver and so must have a fixed known capacitance (C) and inductance (L). This being so the length and type of loop cable is specified by the manufacturer of the loop. The length specified must not be exceeded, but it can be made shorter provided compensating C and L are correctly placed in the circuit.

The QE corrector loop equalizer contains the necessary reactive components to compensate for a short loop cable and to provide QE correction. A typical circuit is given in Fig. 3.13. C1, C2, L1, L2 and C3, C4, L3, L4 provide compensation (loop equalization) while L5, L6, L7 provide QE correction by attenuating the current in the appropriate stator of the goniometer. The QE corrector loop equalizer is mounted close to the loop.

Similar considerations apply to the sense antenna which is required to present a specified capacitance to the receiver. Again we have a given length of cable which must not be exceeded but can be made shorter provided an equalizer is fitted. Often both an equalizer and a suscepti-former are used to achieve the stated input capacitance to the receiver. The suscepti-former is a passive matching device which utilizes an auto transformer to increase the effective capacitance of the sense antenna. Typical units are shown in Fig. 3.14. As an alternative the necessary matching and equalization may be achieved in a single sense antenna coupler. The matching/equalizing unit(s) are mounted close to the antenna.

The loop antenna will consist of the crossed coils wound on a ferrite slab and encapsulated in a low-drag housing. On high-speed aircraft the loop will be flush with the skin but on slower aircraft the housing may protrude slightly, giving better signal pick-up.

The sense antenna can take many forms. On large jet transport aircraft a suppressed capacitive plate is common, whereas on slower aircraft a 'towel rail' type of antenna may be used. General aviation

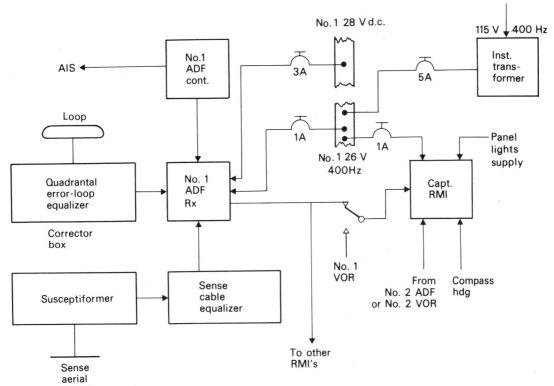

Fig. 3.12 Typical ADF installation

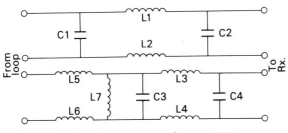

Fig. 3.13 Quadrantal error corrector/loop equalizer
(straight-through connections not shown)

aircraft might use a wire antenna or, as an alternative, a whip antenna. Some manufacturers now produce a combined loop and sense antenna for the general aviation market.

The position of both antennas is important. The loop should be mounted on, and parallel to, the centre line of the aircraft with no more than 0·25° alignment error. While the loop may be on top or

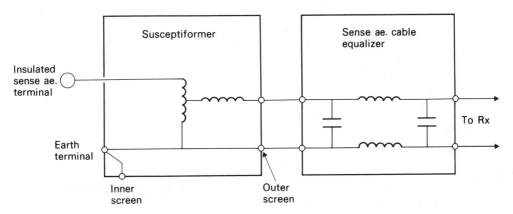

Fig. 3.14 Sense aerial matching

bottom of the fuselage it should not be mounted near the nose, tail, large or movable protuberances or near other system antennae. Similar considerations apply to the sense antenna, although being omnidirectional alignment is not a problem. Ideally the sense antenna will be mounted at the electrical centre of the aircraft in order to give accurate over-station turn-around of the bearing pointer.

The interconnections in the system must take into account that the phasing of voltages produced by sense and loop antennas will be different for top and bottom mounting. The method used will depend on the manufacturer but if the system conforms to ARINC 570 the synchro repeater connections will be as in Table 3.1. If, as in some light aircraft

Table 3.1 Synchro connections for alternate aerial locations. Indicator synchro receiver corrections

Aerial position		Bottom loop, bottom sense	Bottom loop, top sense	Top loop, top sense	Top loop, bottom sense
Synchro transmitter corrections	S1	S1	S1	S3	S3
	S2	S2	S2	S2	S2
	S3	S3	S3	S1	S1
	R1	R1	R2	R1	R2
	R2	R2	R1	R2	R1

installations, the goniometer is in the indicator and the bearing is presented directly rather than by synchro feed then the following corrections are necessary:

1. loop from top to bottom: longitudinal coil connections to goniometer stator reversed;
2. sense from top to bottom: search coil connections reversed.

Obviously one must check for which position, top or bottom, the connections are made in the supplied unit.

Protection from interference is of vital importance, and to this end adequate screening of cables should be employed. ARINC 570 calls for four individually shielded co-axial cables insulated and twisted, then jacketed. The sense antenna connector should use double shielding (tri-axial) cable. The cable runs should be clear of any high-level transmitting cables or a.c. power cables.

Controls and Operation

A standard ARINC 570 control panel is illustrated in Fig. 3.15.

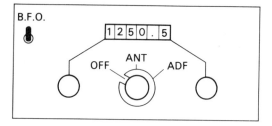

Fig. 3.15 ARINC 570 control panel (typical)

Function Switch. OFF-ANT-ADF In the antenna position (ANT) the receiver operates from the sense antenna only, the bearing pointer being parked at 90° relative bearing. This position may be used for tuning and NDB/station identification. In the ADF position signals from both loop and sense antenna provide normal ADF operation, the RMI indicating the bearing of the station.

Frequency Select Knobs Three knobs are used; one is mounted co-axially with the function switch, to select frequency in 0·5, 10 and 100 kHz increments. Digital type frequency display segments indicate the selected frequency. The information is passed to the receiver as parallel b.c.d.

Beat Frequency Oscillator Switch Selects the BFO for use when the NDB selected is identified by on-off keying of the carrier.

A number of other switches may be found on various controllers, as briefly described below.

Function Switch. OFF-ANT-ADF-LOOP An extra position of the function switch may be provided to operate the receiver from the loop aerial only. This position, LOOP, would be used in conjunction with a loop control.

Loop Control Spring loaded to off. When operated clockwise or anticlockwise the search coil rotates in the selected direction. This control can be used for manual direction-finding, the search coil being rotated until an audio null is achieved or, if provided, a visual tuning indicator indicates a null. Although not used in most modern equipments this does have the advantage over ADF that the nulls are sharper; ADF operation would have to be used to sense the correct null.

Gain Control An audio gain control is usually provided and may be annotated volume. On at least one system the gain of the R.F. amps is manually adjustable when ANT or LOOP is selected, whereas audio gain is controlled on ADF.

Beat Frequency Oscillator Tone A rotary switch, giving b.f.o. on-off, and a potentiometer may be mounted on the same shaft turned by the b.f.o. control. When switched on the frequency of the b.f.o. can be adjusted, so varying the tone in the headset.

Preselect Frequency Capability Provision can be made for in use and standby frequencies selected by means of a transfer switch. When frequency selection is made only the standby frequency changes. Switching the transfer switch (TFR) will now reverse the roles of in-use and standby frequencies. Both frequencies are displayed and clear annunciation of which is in use is required.

Characteristics

The following characteristics are selected and summarized from the ADF System Mark 3 ARINC 570.

Frequency Selection
Range: 190-1750 kHz; spacing: 0·5 kHz; channelling time less than 4 s; parallel b.c.d. frequency selection with provision for serial b.c.d.

ADF Accuracy
± 2° excluding q.e. for any field strength from 50 μV/m to 100 000 μV/m, assuming a sense aerial quality factor of 1·0. (Sense aerial quality factor = effective height × square root of capacitance, i.e. hi-root-cap).
± 3° excluding q.e. for a field strength as low as 25 μV/m.
± 3° after q.e. correction.

ADF Hunting
Less than ± 1°.

Table 3.2 Station interference conditions, with reference to desired frequency

Undesired frequency	Undesired signal strength
± 2 kHz	−4 dB
± 3 kHz	−10 dB
± 6 kHz	−55 dB
± 7 kHz	−70 dB

Sensitivity
Signal + noise to noise ratio 6 dB or better with 35 μV/m field strength modulated 30 per cent at 1000 Hz and hi-root-cap = 1·0.

Station Interference
An undesired signal from a source 90° to that of the desired signal at the frequencies and relative signal levels listed in Table 3.2 shall not cause a change in indicated bearing of more than 3°.

Receiver Selectivity
Passband at least 1·9 kHz at −6 dB points not more than 7 kHz at −60 dB points. Resonant frequency within ± 175 Hz of selected frequency.

Calibration and Testing on the Ramp

Loop Swing
The procedure for determining the sign and size of errors in an ADF installation is known as a loop swing. On initial installation a swing should be carried out at 15° heading intervals. Check swings should be carried out whenever called for in the maintenance schedule, after a lightning strike, when an airframe modification close to the ADF antenna is completed or when a new avionic system is installed. The check swing is carried out at 45° intervals. A swing should not be carried out within ± 2 h of sunset or sunrise to avoid night effect.

The loop swing may be carried out in the air or on the ground. The advantage of an air swing is that the aircraft is operating in its normal environment away from external disturbances but, in some ways, a ground swing is to be preferred, since readings may be taken more accurately. If the loop is mounted on the bottom of the fuselage the swing may be affected by the close proximity of the ground, in which case an air swing should be carried out. An installation should be checked by air test after q.e.s have been corrected.

Ground Swing A ground loop swing must be carried out at a site known not to introduce bearing errors. A base suitable for compass swings will not necessarily be suitable for loop swings. A survey using portable direction finding (D/F) equipment must be carried out if the site is doubtful.

The loop may be swung with reference to true or magnetic north. Using true north has the advantage that the loop swinging base may be permanently marked out. If the swing is with reference to magnetic north the loop should be calibrated using a datum compass, such as the medium landing compass, which should be aligned with the longitudinal axis of the aircraft and positioned about 100 ft from the aircraft. To sight the longitudinal axis, sighting rods or clearly visible plumb lines may be fixed to the aircraft centre line. Use of an upright nose-mounted propeller and the vertical stabilizer may suffice providing sighting is carried out carefully from a suitable distance. For a check swing the aircraft gyro magnetic compass may be used provided this has been recently swung, corrected and a calibration chart made out.

The aircraft must contain its full complement of equipment. Doors and panels in the vicinity of the ADF antennas must be closed. Internal power supplies should be used whenever possible since the external generator and lead may cause errors in the readings.

The ADF is tuned to a station or NDB within range and of a known magnetic bearing from the site. With the aircraft on the required number of headings the ADF reading and the aircraft magnetic heading are recorded on a loop swing record chart, a specimen of which is shown as Table 3.3.

The correction (D) is the signed angle which must be added to the indicated magnetic bearing of the station (B + C) in order to give the true magnetic bearing (A). So, for example, adding $-5 \cdot 5^\circ$ to 41° + 354° gives $389 \cdot 5^\circ = 29 \cdot 5^\circ$ as required.

When completed the values obtained in the final column should be plotted as a q.e. correction curve, as shown in Fig. 3.16. The average of the absolute values of the peaks gives the amount of correction required, the polarity being given by the sign of the correction in the first quadrant. So in the example given we have:

$$\frac{12 \cdot 5 + 12 \cdot 5 + 16 + 17 \cdot 5}{4} = +14 \cdot 625^\circ$$

as the required correction. The correction is made by suitable choice of components in the QE corrector loop equalizer as instructed by the manufacturer. The correction should be more or less the same for identical installations in a particular aircraft type. Once the prototype has had a calibration swing and the component values are chosen, subsequent swings on series aircraft should show the error bounded by $\pm 3^\circ$ as required.

Loop alignment error is given by the average of the peaks. So in the example we have:

$$\frac{12 \cdot 5 - 16 + 12 \cdot 5 - 17 \cdot 5}{4} = -2 \cdot 125$$

Since this is in excess of $\pm 0 \cdot 25^\circ$ this error should be taken out by re-alignment of the loop.

The line correction $= -2 \cdot 125$ has been drawn on Fig. 3.16. The correction curve should cross this line at 0, 90, 180 and 270° if there is no field alignment error. Within the limits of the accuracy of the plot and the scale we can see that this is the case in our example. If there were a field alignment error it would be measured along the horizontal axis.

Air Swing An air swing should be carried out in smooth air conditions in order to eliminate drift errors. There are various methods which may be employed but all involve flying a particular pattern over a clearly defined point or points some distance from the transmitter which is to be used for the swing. Magnetic heading and ADF relative bearing are noted for a number of headings, every 10° or 15°, depending on the pattern flown. The aircraft should be inland of the transmitter when readings are taken to avoid coastal refraction problems. Recording and plotting is as for the ground swing.

Table 3.3   Loop swing record chart

A/C Tail No ....   A/C Type ....
Date ....   Time 10.00   Base ....
Station − Droitwich   Freq. 200 kHz   Mag.Brg (A)029.5

Magnetic heading datum compass (B)	Automatic direction finding relative bearing (C)	Correction (D)
028	001·5	0
041	354	−5·5
054·5	346	−11·0
073	333	−16·5
089	318	−17·5
105·5	298	−14·0
122	272	−4·5
135	247	7·5
153	224	12·5
172	206	11·5
184	197	8·5
198	187	4·5
213	179	−2·5
230	169	−9·5
242	160	−12·5
257	148	−15·5
271·5	134	−16·0
286	115	−11·5
302	088	−0·5
317	063	9·5
332	045	12·5
345	032	12·5
358	021	10·5

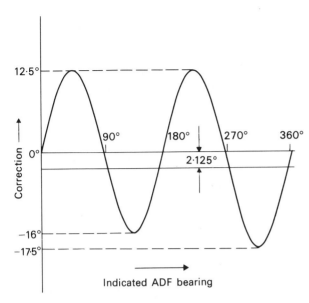

Fig. 3.16 Quadrantal error correction curve for Table 3.3

Two possible methods are position-line swinging and single-point swinging. With the first method a series of landmarks which give a ground reference line aligned with a distant transmitter are chosen. A zig-zag pattern is flown, both toward and away from the transmitter, the readings being taken as the aircraft crosses the line at various headings. With the second method a clearly defined point, some distance from the transmitter, is chosen. A clover-leaf pattern is flown centred on this point, readings being taken on various headings when overhead of the reference point.

Sense Antenna Capacitance Check
The total capacitance of the sense antenna and feeder should be checked when called for in the maintenance schedule, whenever the sense antenna or feeder is changed, upon initial installation or if a possible fault condition is suspected. A capacitance bridge or Q meter operating at 650 kHz should be used for the measurement.

Functional Test
Ideally there will be at least one station or NDB within range in each quadrant; in busy regions this will certainly be so, for example, at London Heathrow more than twenty beacons can be received under good conditions. The true magnetic bearing of those beacons to be used must be known. An accuracy check is performed by tuning into a beacon in each quadrant and ensuring that for each the pointer indicates the bearing to within the limits laid down in the procedure, say $\pm 5°$. The figure given will only be achievable if the aircraft is well away from large metal objects, and if the test is not carried out within 2 h of sunrise or sunset. Use of external power may also give erroneous readings.

All controls should be operated to ensure correct functioning. In particular if a loop control is provided the pointer should be displaced 170° first clockwise and then anticlockwise from the correct reading, to which the pointer should return without excessive hunting.

4 V.h.f. omnidirectional range (VOR)

Introduction

Prior to World War II it was realized that the propagation anomalies experienced with low- and medium-frequency navigation aids limited their usefulness as standard systems for a sky which was becoming ever more crowded. A system called four-course low-frequency range was widely implemented in the United States during the 1930s; this gave four courses to or from each ground station and fitted in quite nicely with a system of fixed airways. A problem with the four-course system is that each station only provides for two intersecting airways; a more complex junction requires more courses. The above, coupled with increased altitude of flying making line-of-sight frequencies useful at longer ranges, and the development of v.h.f. comms, led to the adoption of v.h.f. omnidirectional range (VOR) as standard in the United States in 1946 and internationally in 1949. The competition for an international standard system was fierce; the leading contender after VOR being Decca Navigator. It is debatable whether the technically superior system was chosen, but certainly VOR was cheaper, had the advantage of a large home market, and has done the job adequately ever since.

The VOR system operates in the 108-118 MHz band with channels spaced at 50 kHz. This band is shared with ILS localizer the VOR being allocated to 160 of the 200 available channels. Of these 160 channels 120 are allocated to VOR stations intended for en route navigation while the other forty are for terminal VOR stations (TVOR). The output power of an en route station will be about 200 W providing a service up to 200 nautical miles, its frequency will be within the band 112-118 MHz. A TVOR will have an output power of about 50 W providing a service of up to about 25 nautical miles, its frequency will be within the band 108-112 MHz, this being the part of the total band shared with ILS localizer.

The crew of an appropriately equipped aircraft can tune into a VOR station within range and read the bearing to the station and the relative bearing of the station. Should the flight plan call for an approach to, or departure from, a station on a particular bearing, steering information can be derived from the received VOR signals. It is this latter facility which makes VOR so useful in airways flying; stations can be placed strategically along so-called Victor airways and the pilot can then, by selection of the appropriate radials, fly from station to station either by obeying steering commands or by feeding the same to the autopilot.

To obtain a position fix from VOR one needs bearings to two separate stations; when used in this way VOR can be considered a theta-theta system. If a VOR station is co-located with a DME station an aircraft can obtain a fix using the pair as a rho-theta system. The VOR/DME system is currently the international short-range navigation standard. In recent years this system has become even more versatile with the advent of airborne equipment which can effectively reposition an existing VOR/DME station to give a 'phantom beacon' complete with radials which can be flown using VOR-derived steering information. This development is considered in Chapter 12.

Basic Principles

A simple analogy to VOR is given by imagining a lighthouse which emits an omnidirectional pulse of light every time the beam is pointing due north. If the speed of rotation of the beam is known, a distant observer could record the time interval between seeing the omnidirectional flash and seeing the beam, and hence calculate the bearing of the lighthouse. In reality a VOR station radiates v.h.f. energy modulated with a reference phase signal — the omnidirectional light — and a variable phase signal — the rotating beam. The bearing of the aircraft depends on the phase difference between reference and variable phases — time difference between light and beam.

The radiation from a conventional VOR (CVOR) station is a horizontally polarized v.h.f. wave modulated as follows:

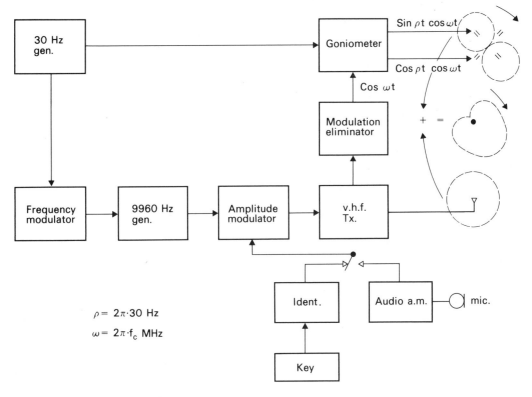

Fig. 4.1 Ground station block diagram, v.o.r.

$$\rho = 2\pi \cdot 30 \text{ Hz}$$
$$\omega = 2\pi \cdot f_c \text{ MHz}$$

1. 30 Hz a.m.: the variable phase signal.
2. 9960 Hz a.m.: this is a subcarrier frequency, modulated at 30 Hz with a deviation of ± 480 Hz. The 30 Hz signal is the reference phase.
3. 1020 Hz a.m.: identification signal keyed to provide morse code identification at least three times each 30 s. Where a VOR and DME are co-located the identification transmissions are synchronized (associated identity, *see* Chapter 7).
4. Voice a.m.: the VOR system can be used as a ground-to-air communication channel as long as this does not interfere with its basic navigational function. The frequency range of the voice modulation is limited to 300-3000 Hz.

The 30 Hz variable phase is space modulated in that the necessary amplitude variation in the received signal at the aircraft is achieved by radiating a cardioid pattern rotating at 1800 r.p.m. The frequency modulated 9960 Hz sub-carrier amplitude modulates the r.f. at source before radiation. It is arranged that an aircraft due north of the beacon will receive variable and reference signals in phase, for an aircraft

at $X°$ magnetic bearing *from* the station the variable phase will *lag* the reference phase by $X°$. Figures 4.1, 4.2 and 4.3 illustrate the basic principles.

The airborne equipment receives the composite signal radiated by the station to which the receiver is tuned. After detection the various modulating signals are separated by filters. The 30 Hz reference signal is

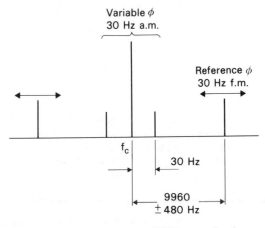

Fig. 4.2 Frequency spectrum: CVOR space signals

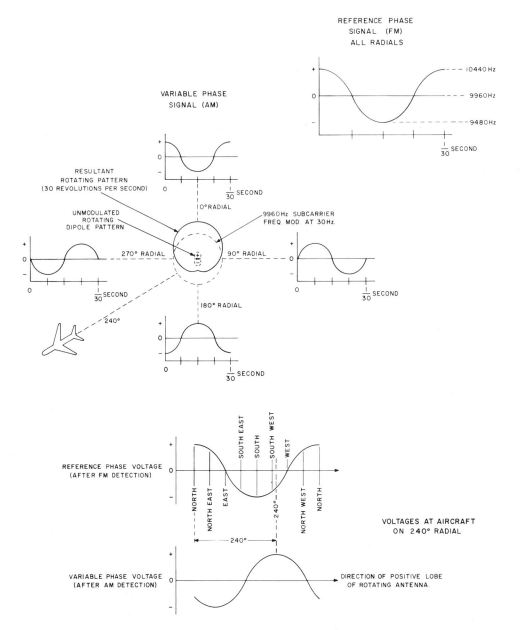

Fig. 4.3 Phase relationships, CVOR (courtesy King Radio Corp.)

phase compared with the variable signal, the difference in phase giving the bearing from the station. The actual reading presented to the pilot is the bearing to the station rather than from, so if the difference in phase between variable and reference signal is 135° the 'to' bearing would be 135 + 180 = 315°, as shown in Fig. 4.4.

If compass information (heading) is combined with the VOR-derived bearing the relative bearing of the station can be presented to the pilot. Figure 4.4 illustrates that the relative bearing to the station is the difference between the magnetic bearing to the station and the aircraft heading. An RMI is used to display the information. Such instruments are considered in Chapter 3. In this application the card is driven by the compass, as normal, so that the card reading at the lubber line is the aircraft heading. At the same time a pointer is driven to a position determined by

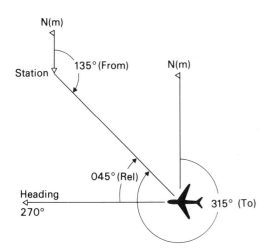

Fig. 4.4 To/from magnetic bearings and relative bearing

the difference between the bearing to the station and the heading. A differential synchro or resolver is used to give the required angular difference. Figure 4.5 shows the RMI presentation corresponding to the situation diagram shown in Fig. 4.4. Only one pointer is shown, for clarity.

The previous two paragraphs refer to 'automatic' VOR, so called since the pilot need do no more than switch on and tune in to an in-range station in order to obtain bearing information. 'Manual' VOR requires the pilot to select a particular radial on which he wants to position his aircraft. The actual radial on which the aircraft is flying is compared with the desired radial. If the two are different the appropriate

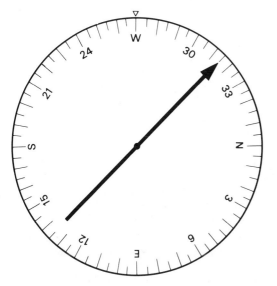

Fig. 4.5 RMI presentation

fly-left or fly-right signals are derived and presented to the pilot.

A complication is that radial information depends only on the phase difference between modulating signals and is independent of heading; hence the fly-right or fly-left information may send the aircraft the 'long way round'. Further, when an aircraft is on course, i.e. the steering command is nulled, the aircraft may be heading either toward or away from the station on the selected radial. A TO/FROM indication removes the ambiguity. With the aircraft heading, roughly, towards (away from) the station and the TO/FROM indicator indicating TO (FROM), the steering information gives the most direct path in order to intercept the selected radial.

If the reference phase (R) is phase shifted by the selected course (C) and then compared with the variable phase, a fly-right indication will be given if R + C lags V, while if R + C leads V, the command will be fly-left. If we now add 180 to the phase-shifted reference phase we have R + C + 180 which will, on addition, either cancel V, partially or completely, in which case a TO indication will be given, or reinforce V, partially or completely, in which case a FROM indication will be given.

Figure 4.6 shows two possible situations. In both cases the selected course is 042, i.e. the pilot wishes to fly towards the station on the 222 radial or away from the station on the 042 radial. With aircraft A we have a fly-left and a TO indication; with aircraft B we have a fly-right and a FROM indication. Note that if the headings of the aircraft were reversed, the indications would be the same, so sending them the 'long way round'. Figure 4.7 shows an electronic deviation indicator corresponding to aircraft B. The indication at top right shows the aircraft to be on the 022 radial from a second VOR station.

Doppler VOR (DVOR)

The use of CVOR leads to considerable site errors where the station is installed in the vicinity of obstructions or where aircraft are required to fly over mountainous terrain while using the station. The error is caused by multi-path reception due to reflections from the obstructions, and gives rise to course scalloping, roughness and/or bends when the aircraft is flown to follow steering commands. The terms used describing the course under these conditions refer to the nature of the departure from a straight line course. DVOR is relatively insensitive to siting effects which would render CVOR unusable.

Although the method of modulation is completely different DVOR is compatible with CVOR in that

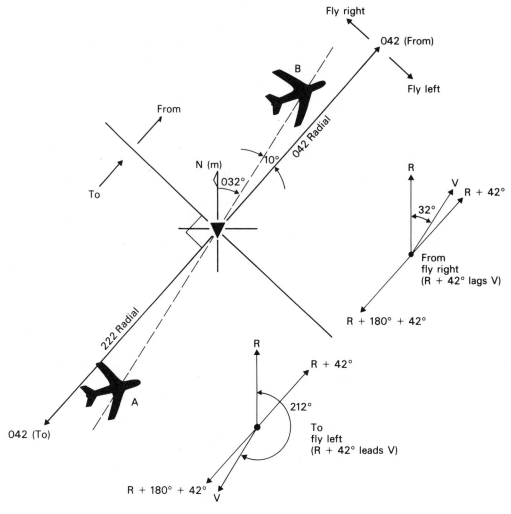

Fig. 4.6 Fly-left/fly-right and 'to/from' situation diagram

airborne equipment will give the correct indications when used with stations of either type. In the DVOR the reference signal is 30 Hz a.m. while the variable signal is 30 Hz f.m. on a 9960 Hz sub-carrier. Since the roles of the a.m. and f.m. are reversed with respect to CVOR the variable phase is arranged to *lead* the reference phase by X° for an aircraft at X° magnetic bearing *from* the station (cf. CVOR).

In a double sideband DVOR (DSB-DVOR) the carrier, f_c, with 30 Hz (and identification) a.m. is radiated from an omnidirectional antenna. Two unmodulated r.f. sideband signals, one 9960 Hz above f_c, the other 9960 Hz below f_c, are radiated from antennas diametrically opposite in a ring of about fifty antennas. These latter signals are commutated

at 30 Hz anticlockwise around the ring of antennas. To a receiver, remote from the site, it appears as if the signal sources are approaching and receding, and hence the received signal suffers a Doppler shift (*see* Chapter 10). With a diameter of 13·5 m and rotation speed of 30 r.p.s. the tangential speed at the periphery is $\pi \times 13·5 \times 30 \approx 1272$ m.p.s. At the centre frequency of the v.h.f. band, 113 MHz, one cycle occupies approximately 2·65 m, thus the maximum Doppler shift is 1272/2·65 = 480 Hz. In the airborne receiver the sidebands mix with the carrier at f_c to produce 9960 ± 480 Hz. Single sideband and alternate sideband DVOR are possible, but since they compromise the performance of the system they will not be discussed.

Fig. 4.7 IN-2014 electronic course deviation indicator (courtesy Bendix Avionics Division)

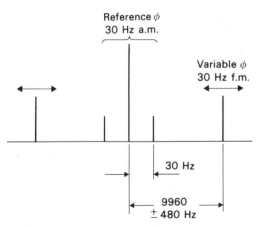

Fig. 4.8 Frequency spectrum – DVOR space signals

Aircraft Installation

Since VOR and ILS localizers occupy the same band of frequencies they invariably share the same receiver which will also contain the necessary circuits to extract the required information. It is not uncommon for v.h.f. comm. and v.h.f. nav. to share the same receiver, particularly with general aviation equipment. It is expected that the 'all v.h.f. in one box' trend will continue.

A large airliner, and indeed most aircraft from twins up, has a dual v.h.f. nav. installation. The instruments on which VOR information is displayed are multi-function hence quite complex switching arrangements are involved. Figure 4.9 shows one VOR/ILS system of a typical dual installation; only those outputs from VOR are shown.

The antenna may serve ILS as well as VOR but some aircraft have separate antennas, particularly if all-weather landing is a requirement when the optimum position for the localizer antenna may not suit VOR. If separate antennas are used with a common r.f. feed to the receiver the switching logic will be derived from the channel selection made at the control unit. The VOR antenna employs horizontal polarization with an omnidirectional radiation pattern. A horizontal dipole is often used with the dipole elements forming a 'V' shape to give a more nearly omnidirectional pattern. Since the dipole is a balanced load and the co-ax. feeder is unbalanced (with respect to earth) a balun (balanced to unbalanced line transformer) is used. The dipole may be mounted on the vertical stabilizer or on a stand-off mast, top-mounted on the fuselage.

The VOR/ILS receiver contains a conventional superhet, a filter for separation of signals and a converter to provide the required outputs which are

1. audio to AIS;
2. bearing information to two RMIs;
3. deviation from selected radial;
4. TO/FROM signal;
5. flag or warning signal.

The RMI feed is the result of the automatic VOR operation. Since the pointer on the RMI moves to a position giving relative bearing with respect to the lubber line the magnetic bearing (omnibearing) must be combined with heading information as previously described. The necessary differential synchro or resolver will be in the receiver or, in the case of equipment conforming with ARINC 579, in the RMI. In the former case magnetic bearing (mag.) is required by the receiver, this being obtained from the compass system via the RMI. The necessary switching for displaying VOR as opposed to ADF information, on either or both of the pointers, is on the RMI.

The deviation and TO/FROM signals are the result of manual VOR operation. These steering commands are displayed on a course deviation indicator (CDI) an electronic version of which is shown in Fig. 4.7. The CDI, however, may not be a stand-alone unit; it is likely to be part of a multi-function indicator known by a variety of names such as horizontal situation indicator (HSI) or pictorial navigation indicator PNI. In the installation shown in Fig. 4.9 an HSI is used

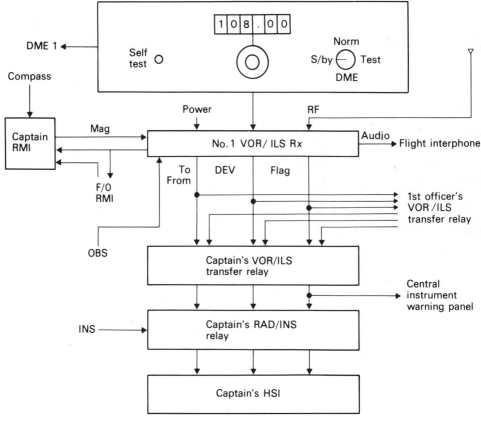

Fig. 4.9 Typical VOR installation

Fig. 4.10 KPI 552 pictorial navigation indicator (courtesy King Radio Corp.)

with remote course selection (o.b.s. − omnibearing selection) fitted, say, on an autopilot/flight director mode select panel. Figure 4.10 illustrates the King KPI 552 PNI where the built-in o.b.s., incorporated (course knob), has been set to 335°, a fly-right command is being given by the deviation bar and we have a TO indication (large arrow-head above aircraft symbol).

Various switching arrangements are possible; those shown illustrate the captain's choice of VOR/ILS1, VOR/ILS2 or inertial navigation system (INS) information being displayed on his HSI. Switching between VOR/ILS1 or 2 is achieved by means of the transfer relay (TFR/RLY) while VOR/ILS or INS switching is by means of the radio/INS (RAD/INS) relay. The first officer (F/O) has a similar arrangement at his disposal. Deviation signals from number 1 system to F/O's HSI and from number 2 system to captain's HSI may be via isolation amplifiers.

The flag signal is of vital importance since it gives

warning of unreliable data from the VOR/ILS receiver. It will be fed to all instruments selected to display VOR/ILS information and often to a central instrument warning system (CIWS). Should the deviation signal be fed to the automatic flight control system (AFCS), then obviously so must the flag or warning signal.

Controls and Operation

The controller is not particularly complicated. Frequency selection is achieved by rotation of two knobs, mounted co-axially or separately, so determining the appropriate 2/5 code fed to the receiver. It is normal for DME frequency selection to be made from the same controller with DME standby, normal and test switching also provided (see Chapter 7). Self-test switching facilities for the VOR/ILS are provided. Additional controls, other than those shown in Fig. 4.9, may be provided, namely VOR/ILS on-off and audio volume.

The location of display switches and the course selector has been mentioned previously, as has the interpretation of indications given to the pilot.

Simplified Block Diagram Operation

Received signals are selected, amplified and detected by a conventional single or double superhet receiver. The detected output is a composite signal which must be separated into its component parts by means of appropriate filtering circuits.

The audio signal, 1020 Hz identification, is routed via an amplifier and possibly a volume control on the v.h.f. nav. controller to the flight interphone sub-system of the AIS. The associated audio filter may be switchable to give a passband of 300-3000 Hz when the VOR system is being used as a ground-to-air communication link.

The reference phase channel (CVOR) consists of a 9960 Hz filter, a discriminator to detect the 30 Hz f.m. and, not shown, amplifier circuits. Limiting of the signal takes place before the discriminator to remove unwanted amplitude variations. The 30 Hz reference signal (R) then undergoes various phase shifts.

For manual VOR operation, as previously mentioned, we need to shift R by the selected course. This is achieved by the phase-shift resolver, the rotor of which is coupled to the course or OBS knob. A digital readout of the selected course is provided. The phase-shifted R is now compared with the variable phase signal. If they are in phase or 180°

out of phase there is no lateral movement of the deviation bar. Since it is simpler to determine when two signals are in phase quadrature (at 90°) a 90° phase shifter may be included in the reference channel prior to feeding the phase comparator where detection of phase quadrature will give no movement of the deviation bar. In the absence of either or both of the signals the flag will be in view.

'To' or 'from' information is derived by comparing the variable phase with the reference phase shifted by the OBS setting plus 180°. It follows that if the reference phase has been shifted by 90° before feeding the deviation phase comparator we only require a further 90° phase shift before feeding the 'to/from' phase comparator rather than a 180° phase shift as illustrated in Fig. 4.11. If the inputs to the 'to/from' phase comparator are within, say, ± 80° of being in phase then a TO indication is given; if within ± 80° of being in anti-phase a FROM indication is given; otherwise neither a TO nor a FROM indication is given.

For automatic VOR operation the reference channel is phase-shifted and compared with the variable phase. If the two inputs are in phase quadrature there is no drive to the motor, otherwise the motor will turn, changing the amount by which the reference phase is shifted until phase quadrature is achieved. The motor connections are arranged so that the stable null of the loop gives the required shaft position which represents the magnetic bearing to the station. Compass information is fed to a differential synchro, the rotor of which is turned by the motor following station magnetic bearing. The difference signal represents relative bearing which positions the appropriate RMI pointer via a synchro repeater. The RMI card is positioned by compass information.

Characteristics

The following characteristics are selected and summarized from ARINC characteristic 579-1. It should be noted that there are radical differences in outputs, between ARINC 579-1 and the older ARINC 547 with which many in-service systems conform.

Frequency Selection
160 channels, 50 kHz spacing, range 108-117·95 MHz.
Standard 2/5 selection system.
Channelling time less than 60 ms.

Receiver
Satisfactory operation with 1·5 μV signal.

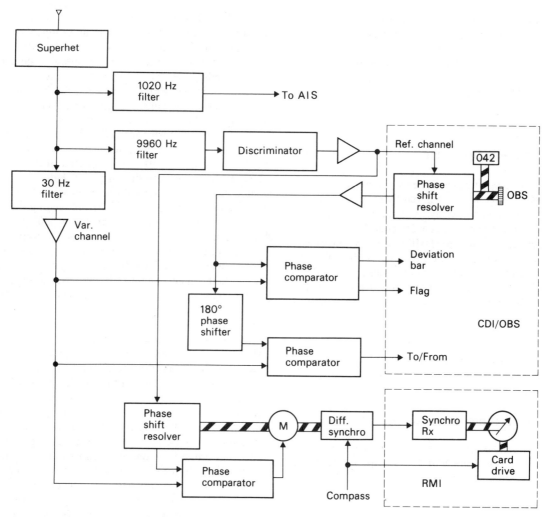

Fig. 4.11 Simplified block diagram, VOR

No more than 6 dB attenuation at $f_c \pm 17$ kHz; at least 60 dB attenuation at $f_c \pm 31\cdot5$ kHz.

Outputs
Audio: at least 100 mW into a load of 200-500 Ω from a 3 μV input signal modulated 30 per cent at 1000 Hz.
Omni-bearing: digital output in fractional binary form accurate to within $\pm 0\cdot4°$ under various specified conditions. Analogue output two 400 Hz a.c. voltages, one proportional to the sine of the bearing, the other to its cosine. The analogue output is designed to feed an OBS and a maximum of two parallel connected RMIs which are not interchangeable with RMIs used with ARINC 547.
Deviation: a high-level and low-level d.c. voltage

analogue signal proportional to perpendicular linear displacement. To compute this, distance from ground station is required from DME in the form of a pulse pair, the spacing of which is an analogue of the distance. The high-level output should give 2 V across a 200 Ω load for a course deviation adjustable within range ± 5 to ± 10 nautical miles. The corresponding low-level output should be 150 mV. The low-level output is provided to feed older CDIs (1000 Ω resistance, 150 μA f.s.d.), while the high-level output is to be used by the automatic flight control system (AFCS) and modern CDIs. In the event of loss of distance information from the DME the deviation output should automatically revert to an angular deviation mode of operation giving 2 V for 10° off course. (Note: prior to ARINC 579 deviation outputs

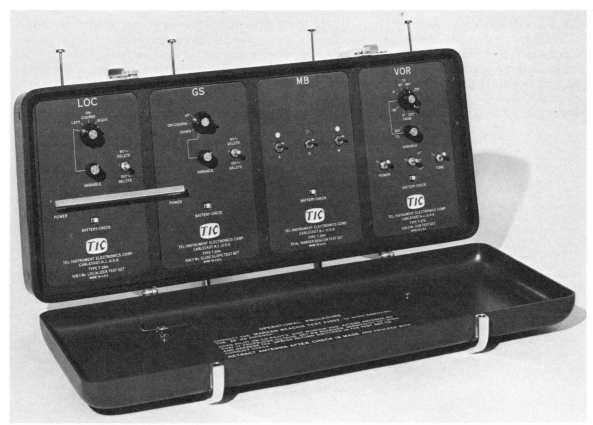

Fig. 4.12 TIC T-30B VOR/ILS test set (courtesy
Tel-Instrument Electronics Corp.)

represented angular displacement.)
TO/FROM: ground referenced providing 2 mA for
each of two 200 Ω loads in parallel. In addition a
low-level output of 200 μA may be provided to feed
older instruments.
Warning: high level, 28 V d.c. valid, absent invalid.
Low level, between 300 and 900 mV valid, less than
100 mV invalid. The low level signal should be
capable of driving from one to five 1000 Ω parallel
loads. The VOR digital output should also include
warning bits.

Ramp Testing

Testing of VOR should always be carried out with a
ramp test set capable of being tuned to any VOR
frequency, radiating sufficient energy to allow
satisfactory operation of the VOR and providing a
means of simulating various VOR radials. Most test
sets include provision for testing ILS as well as VOR.
Among those available are the Cossor CRM 555,
IFR NAV-401L.

The CRM 555 operates on any of the 160 VOR
channels with a frequency accuracy of
± 0·0035 per cent (−10°C to +30°C). Modulation of
the carrier is such that the simulated bearing may be
set to any reading between 0 and 360° with a
calibration accuracy of ± 1° or may be switched in
45° steps with an accuracy of ± 0·5°. Carrier power
can be attenuated in 1 dB steps between 0 dBm and
−120 dBm (0 dBm corresponds to an output of
1 mW). A self-test facility is provided. The
NAV-401L offers similar facilities but is more 'state
of the art' and so offers slightly more in the way of
performance.
The TIC T-27B is part of the T-30B test set
illustrated in Fig. 4.12. The facilities are not as
extensive as either of the previously mentioned test
sets but it has the advantage of ease of operation and
less cost. It is FCC type accepted. Operation is on
108·00 MHz radiated from a telescopic antenna.
Bearings of 0, 90, 180 and 270° can be simulated
both TO and FROM, alternately variation, 90-110°
'to' or 270-290° 'from', is available. A ± 1° switch

gives a useful sticky needle check.

Actual testing should be carried out in accordance with the procedures laid down, but briefly it would involve correctly positioning the test set antenna and radiating on sufficient frequencies to test frequency selection of the VOR. Sensitivity may be checked by reducing the r.f. level received either by use of the test set attenuator or moving the test set antenna further away. Various bearings should be simulated (check whether they are 'to' or 'from' station), the appropriate reading should be checked on the RMI and the OBS operated so as to check the manual mode of VOR.

5 Instrument landing system

Introduction

In order to be able to land the aircraft safely under visual flight rules (VFR), i.e. without any indication from instruments as to the aircraft's position relative to the desired approach path, the pilot must have at least 3 miles horizontal visibility with a ceiling not less than 1000 ft. Although most landings are carried out under these conditions a significant number are not; consequently, were it not for instrument aids to landing a considerable amount of revenue would be lost due to flight cancellations and diversions.

One method of aiding the pilot in the approach to an airport is to use a precision approach radar (PAR) system whereby the air traffic controller, having the aircraft 'on radar', can give guidance over the v.h.f.-r.t. The alternative method is to provide instrumentation in the cockpit giving steering information to the pilot which, if obeyed, will cause the aircraft to make an accurate and safe descent and touchdown. The latter, which may be complemented/monitored by PAR, is the method which concerns us here.

Early ILS date back to before World War II; the German Lorentz being an example. During the war the current ILS was developed and standardized in the United States. The basic system has remained unchanged ever since but increased accuracy and reliability have resulted in landing-minimum visibility conditions being reduced.

The ICAO have defined three categories of visibility, the third of which is subdivided. All categories are defined in terms of runway visual range (RVR) (*see* ICAO Annex 14) and, except Category III, decision height (DH), below which the pilot must have visual contact with the runway or abort the landing (*see* ICAO PANS-OPS). The various categories are defined in Table 5.1 where the standards are given in metres with approximate equivalents in feet (in parentheses). Sometimes categories IIIA and B are called 'see to land' and 'see to taxi'.

The ILS equipment is categorized using the same Roman numerals and letters according to its

Table 5.1   ICAO visibility categories

Category	d.h.	r.v.r.
I	60 m (200 ft)	800 m (2600 ft)
II	30 m (100 ft)	400 m (1200 ft)
IIIA	–	200 m (700 ft)
IIIB	–	30 m (150 ft)
IIIC	–	Zero

operational capabilities. Thus if the ILS facility is category II, the pilot would be able to land the aircraft in conditions which corresponded to those quoted in Table 5.1. An obvious extension of the idea of a pilot manually guiding the aircraft with no external visual reference is to have an autopilot which 'flies' the aircraft in accordance with signals from the ILS (and other sensors including radio altimeter) i.e. automatic landing.

Basic Principles

Directional radio beams, modulated so as to enable airborne equipment to identify the beam centres, define the correct approach path to a particular runway. In addition vertical directional beams provide spot checks of distance to go on the approach. The total system comprises three parts, each with a transmitter on the ground and receiver and signal processor in the aircraft. Lateral steering is provided by the localizer for both front-course and back-course approaches; the glideslope provides vertical steering for the front course only while marker beacons give the distance checks.

Localizer
Forty channels are allocated at 50 kHz spacing in the band 108·10-111·95 MHz using only those frequencies where the tenths of a megacycle count is odd; so, for example 108·10 and 108·15 MHz are localizer channels while 108·20 and 108·25 MHz are not. Those channels in the band not used for localizer are

allocated to VOR. The coverage of the beacon will normally be as shown by the hatched parts of Fig. 5.1, but topographical features may dictate a restricted coverage whereby the ± 10° sector may be reduced to 18 nautical miles range.

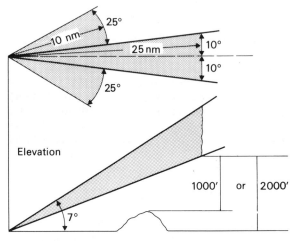

Fig. 5.1 Localizer front beam coverage

The horizontally polarized radiated carrier is modulated by tones of 90 and 150 Hz such that an aircraft to the left of the extended centre line will be in a region where the 90 Hz modulation predominates. Along the centre line an airborne localizer receiver will receive the carrier modulated to a depth of 20 per cent by both 90 and 150 Hz tones. Deviation from the centre line is given in d.d.m. (difference in depth of modulation), i.e. the percentage modulation of the larger signal minus the percentage modulation of the smaller signal divided by 100.

The localizer course sector is defined as that sector in the horizontal plane containing the course line (extended centre line) and limited by the lines on which there is a d.d.m. of 0·155. The change in d.d.m. is linear for ± 105 m along the line perpendicular to the course line and passing through the ILS datum point on the runway threshold; these points 105 m from the course line lie on the 0·155 d.d.m. lines, as shown in Fig. 5.2. The beacon is situated such that the above criterion is met and the course sector is less than 6°. Outside the course sector the d.d.m. is not less than 0·155.

The ICAO Annex 10 specification for the localizer-radiated pattern is more complicated than the description above indicates, in particular in the various tolerances for category I, II and III facilities; however we have covered the essential points for our purposes.

The airborne equipment detects the 90 and 150 Hz tones and hence causes a deviation indicator to show a fly-left or fly-right command. Full-scale deflection is achieved when the d.d.m. is 0·155, i.e. the aircraft is 2-3° off course. Figure 5.3 shows a mechanical and electronic deviation indicator both showing slightly over half-scale deflection of a fly-right command. Provided the pilot flies to keep the command bar at zero, or the autopilot flies to keep the d.d.m. zero, the aircraft will approach the runway threshold along the course line.

In addition to the 90 and 150 Hz tones the localizer carrier is modulated with an identification tone of 1020 Hz and possibly (exceptionally category III) voice modulation for ground-to-air communication. The identification of a beacon consists of two or three letters transmitted by keying the 1020 Hz tone so as to give a Morse code representation. The identification is transmitted not less than six times per minute when the localizer is operational.

Glideslope
Glideslope channels are in the u.h.f. band,

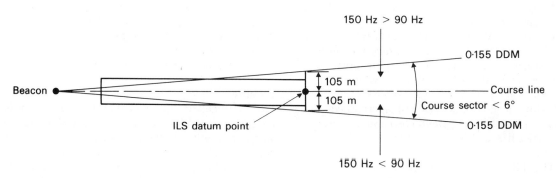

Fig. 5.2 Localizer course selector

Fig. 5.3 Electromechanical and electronic course deviation indicators (courtesy Bendix Avionics Division)

specifically 328·6-335·4 MHz at 150 kHz spacing. Each of the forty frequencies allocated to the glideslope system is paired with a localizer frequency, the arrangement being that localizer and glideslope beacons serving the same runway will have frequencies taken from Table 5.2. Pilot selection of the required localizer frequency on the controller will cause both localizer and glideslope receivers to tune to the appropriate paired frequencies.

Table 5.2 Localizer/glideslope frequency pairing (MHz)

Localizer	Glidepath
108·10	334·70
108·15	334·55
108·30	334·10
108·35	333·95
108·50	329·90
108·55	329·75
108·70	330·50
108·75	330·35
108·90	329·30
108·95	329·15
109·10	331·40
109·15	331·25
109·30	332·00
109·35	331·85

Localizer	Glidepath
109·50	332·60
109·55	332·35
109·70	333·20
109·75	333·05
109·90	333·80
109·95	333·65
110·10	334·40
110·15	334·25
110·30	335·00
110·35	334·85
110·50	329·60
110·55	329·45
110·70	330·20
110·75	330·05
110·90	330·80
110·95	330·65
111·10	331·70
111·15	331·55
111·30	332·30
111·35	332·15
111·50	332·90
111·55	332·75
111·70	333·50
111·75	333·35
111·90	331·10
111·95	330·95

The principle of glideslope operation is similar to that of localizer in that the carrier is modulated with 90 and 150 Hz tones. Above the correct glidepath the 90 Hz modulation predominates while on the correct glidepath the d.d.m. is zero, both tones giving a 40 per cent depth of modulation. The coverage and beam characteristics shown in Figs 5.4 and 5.5 are given in terms of the glidepath angle, typically $2\frac{1}{2}$-$3°$. Category I facilities may have asymmetrical upper and lower sectors, the figure of 0·0875 d.d.m. corresponding to an angular displacement of between 0·070 and 0·140 θ. By contrast a category III facility is as shown in Fig. 5.5 with a tolerance of $\pm$ 0·02 θ on the 0·12 θ lines.

Although d.d.m. = 0 lines occur at 2 θ, 3 θ and 4 θ they are not stable in the sense that if the pilot obeys the steering commands he will not maintain the corresponding angles of descent. The first stable null occurs at 5 θ which for a glidepath of $3°$ is at $15°$. This is sufficiently different from the desired descent angle to create few problems; however to avoid confusion the glideslope beam should be 'captured' from below.

Once in the correct beam fly-up and fly-down signals are indicated to the pilot in much the same way as with the localizer. Figure 5.3 illustrates a fly-up command of just over half-scale deflection. The glideslope output is more sensitive than localizer in that typically a $\frac{1}{2}°$ off the glidepath will give full-scale deflection (about 0·175 d.d.m.) compared with about $2\frac{1}{2}°$ off the course line for full-scale deflection.

Marker Beacons
A marker beacon radiates directly upwards using a carrier frequency of 75 MHz. The modulating signal depends on the function of the marker.

An airways, fan or 'Z' marker is a position aid for en-route navigation located on airways or at holding points. As such it is not part of ILS. The carrier is modulated with a 3000 Hz signal which causes a white lamp to flash in the aircraft while station identification in Morse code is fed to the AIS.

The outer marker is normally located $4\frac{1}{2}$ miles from the runway threshold. The carrier is amplitude-modulated by 400 Hz keyed to give two dashes per second which can be heard via the AIS and causes a blue (or purple) lamp to flash.

The middle marker is located 3500 ft from the runway threshold. The carrier is amplitude-modulated by 1300 Hz keyed to give a dot-dash pair 95 times per minute which can be heard via the AIS and causes an amber lamp to flash.

The ILS marker beam widths are sufficiently wide in the plane perpendicular to the course line to cover the course sector.

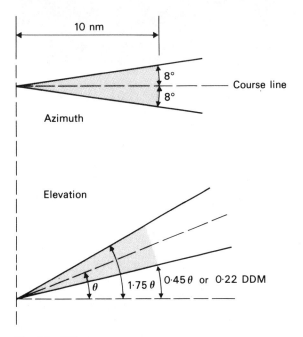

Fig. 5.4 Glideslope coverage

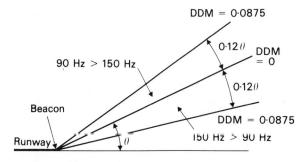

Fig. 5.5 Glideslope beam characteristics

Simplified Block Diagram Operation

Since the localizer and VOR frequencies occupy the same band it is normal to have a v.h.f. navigation receiver which selects, amplifies and detects signals from either aid, depending on the frequency selected.

Figure 5.6 illustrates the basic block diagram of a localizer receiver. A conventional single or double superhet is employed. A.g.c. is important since an increase in the 90 and 150 Hz output signals by the same factor would increase the magnitude of the difference, so giving more deflection of the deviation

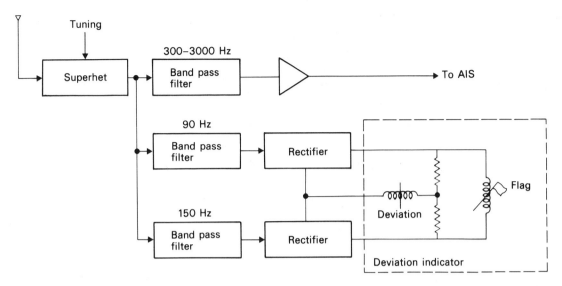

Fig. 5.6 Localizer simplified block diagram

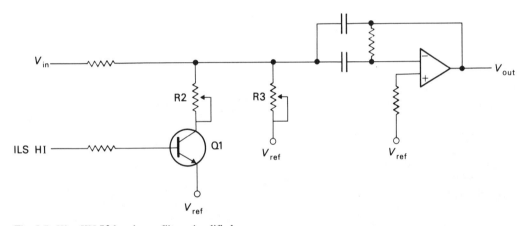

Fig. 5.7 King KN 72 band pass filter, simplified

indicator for the same d.d.m. Signal separation is achieved by three filters: audio, 90 and 150 Hz. The audio signal, identification and possibly voice, is passed via audio amplifiers (incorporating a noise limiter) to the AIS. The 90 and 150 Hz signals are full wave rectified, the difference between the rectifier outputs driving the deviation indication while the sum drives the flag out of view.

The 90 and 150 Hz filters, together with the rectifiers and any associated circuitry, are often part of the so-called VOR/LOC converter which may be within the v.h.f. navigation receiver or a separate unit. A combined converter will usually employ active filters which serve as either 30 Hz bandpass filters for VOR operation or 90/150 Hz band pass filters for

localizer operation. Figure 5.7 shows the circuit used in the King KN 72 VOR/LOC converter. When a VOR frequency is selected the ILS Hi line is low, so turning off Q1 which effectively disconnects R2 from the circuit, the centre frequency of 30 Hz is set by R3. Selection of a localizer frequency causes the ILS Hi line to go high, so turning on Q1 and placing R2 in parallel with R3. R2 is set to give a centre frequency of 90 or 150 Hz as appropriate.

The glidepath receiver converter block diagram is similar to that of the localizer except that the audio channel is not required. A separate receiver may be used or all navigation circuitry may be within the same unit. In any event separate antennas are used for localizer and glidepath.

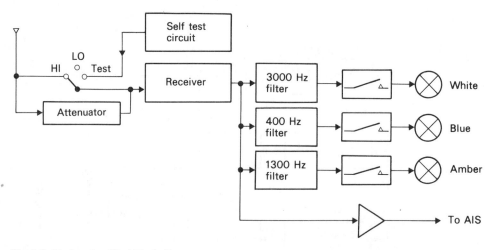

Fig. 5.8 Marker simplified block diagram

The marker is fixed tuned to 75 MHz and may employ a t.r.f. (tuned radio frequency) or superhet receiver. The detected audio is fed to three filters for tone separation and also amplified and fed to the AIS. The filter which gives an output causes the appropriate lamp-switching circuit to give an interrupted d.c. output to drive the associated lamp.

When switched to Hi the sensitivity of the receiver is such that it responds to airways marker beacons even though the aircraft is at a relatively high altitude. With high sensitivity there is a danger that when at lower altitudes, for example when flying over the outer and middle markers on approach, the lamps may be lit for longer than the maximum of 10 s. It is even possible for the outer and middle marker lamps to be lit simultaneously. To avoid this, low sensitivity is selected, whereby an attenuator (10 dB) is placed in line with the receiver input. Switching may take place at 10 000 ft.

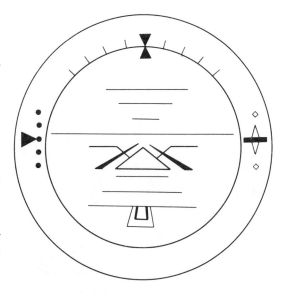

Fig. 5.9 Typical attitude director indicator

Installation

In Chapter 4 an installation incorporating a VOR/ILS receiver was discussed and illustrated (Fig. 4.9). In considering ILS we are interested in those outputs derived from the localizer, glidepath and marker receivers. Localizer and glideslope deviation (fly-left/fly-right, fly-up/fly-down respectively) will be fed to a conventional or electronic deviation indicator (Fig. 5.3) and/or an HSI (Fig. 4.10) and an attitude director indicator, ADI (Fig. 5.9). In the HSI the localizer drives a lateral deviation bar right and left of the course arrow while glideslope deviation is given by a deviation pointer

and scale conventionally on the left-hand side of the instrument. In the ADI the localizer drives a rising runway laterally to display deviation (vertical movement representing radio altitude) while the glideslope drives a pointer over a scale, again on the left-hand side of the instrument.

Localizer, glideslope and marker signals are also fed to an autoland system when fitted. The localizer deviation will be used to supply the appropriate demand signal to the roll (aileron) and yaw (rudder) channels. The pitch (elevator) channel will respond to glideslope. As the aircraft approaches touchdown the response of the pitch channel to glideslope deviation signals is progressively reduced; this reduction is triggered by the outer marker and thence controlled in accordance with the radio altimeter output. A modern ILS will provide dual parallel outputs for both localizer and glidepath deviation in order that the AFCS may accept information only when the same signal appears on each feed of a parallel pair.

A general aviation installation is illustrated in Fig. 5.10 incorporating King equipment. The KX 175B is panel-mounted and contains a 720-channel v.h.f. comms receiver, a 200-channel v.h.f. nav. receiver and all necessary controls with digital readout of comm. and nav. frequencies on the front panel. The KX 175B also provides tuning information for the DME and glideslope receiver.

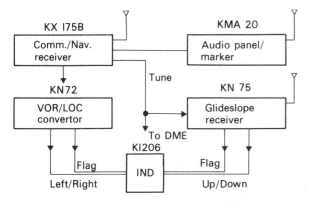

Fig. 5.10 King general aviation comm./nav. system

The KN 72 and KN 75 are remote-mounted VOR/LOC converter and glideslope receiver respectively. The KN 72 gives localizer deviation and flag signals (as well as VOR deviation, TO/FROM and flag), while the KN 75 gives glideslope deviation and flag. The KMA 20 is an audio control console providing speaker/phone selection for seven receive channels and mic. selection for two transmit channels as well as containing a marker receiver plus its controls and lamps. The indicator, KI 206, shows localizer deviation (vertical bar) and glideslope deviation (horizontal bar) as well as showing VOR deviation and TO/FROM indication if a VOR frequency is selected, the deviation relating to the OBS setting also on the KI 206. If a KI 204 is used instead of the KI 206 then the KN 72 may be omitted since a VOR/LOC converter is built in.

Typically a deviation indicator movement will be of 1000 Ω impedance and require 150 μA for full-scale deflection (f.s.d.), therefore the voltage across the deviation output of the receiver should be 150 mV for a d.d.m. of 0·155. If the receiver

deviation output circuit has an output impedance of 200 Ω and supplies the required current to five indicators in parallel then when less than five indicators are used the deflection will not properly correspond to the d.d.m. Consider a d.d.m. of 0·155, then 750 μA must be supplied for five loads in parallel from a generated deviation voltage of 300 mV. Now consider four loads fed from a 300 mV, 200 Ω source, the total current will be $300 \times 10^3/(200 + 250) = 666\cdot7$ μA divided equally among the four loads so that each load has $666\cdot7/4 = 166\cdot7$ μA, i.e. the indicators will over-read by about 11 per cent. Unless the receiver output is a constant voltage for a variety of loads (ARINC 578-3) we must compensate for loading variations.

Various methods have been used for loading compensation in the past. One possibility is to choose different receiver output impedances depending on the number of loads; in this case the receiver and the mounting rack should be suitably labelled. Another possibility is to fit a shunt resistor in an aircraft junction box through which the deviation signal is fed. With two indicators a 330 Ω shunt would be needed giving a 330 Ω and two 1000 Ω loads in parallel, i.e. total load of 200 Ω. Finally, but not exhausting the possibilities, five separate buffered outputs may be provided, each indicator being fed from one of the buffer amplifiers. Similar considerations apply to flag circuits where using four 1000 Ω loads in parallel is standard procedure.

Antenna arrangements vary between different types of aircraft. Mention of combined VOR/

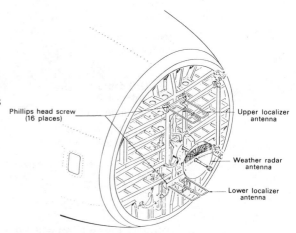

Fig. 5.11 Boeing 747 localizer aerials (note Bendix weather radar scanner with spoiler grid on parabolic reflector for mapping purposes – see Chapter 9). (Courtesy Boeing Commercial Aeroplane Co.)

Localizer antennas has been made in Chapter 4 but the glideslope and marker antennas will always be separate. As an example of a large passenger aircraft, consider the Boeing 747. Three VOR/ILS receivers are installed fed by one V-type VOR antenna at the top of the vertical stabilizer, two dual localizer antennas in the nose and a total of six glideslope antennas in the nose-wheel doors. One marker beacon receiver is installed, fed by a flush-mounted antenna on the bottom centreline of the aircraft.

The localizer antennas are mounted above and below the weather radar scanner. The lower antenna feeds receivers 1 and 2 while receiver 3 is fed from the upper antenna. Antenna switching between VOR and localizer aerials is achieved by either solid state or electromechanical switches mounted behind the VOR/ILS receivers.

The six glideslope antennas are split into two groups of three, one group in each nose-wheel door. A non-tunable slot (track antenna) dual unit is installed in each door leading edge while two tunable arrays (capture antennas) are mounted on the sides of each door. A total of four hybrid antenna couplers combine the r.f. outputs of the glideslope antennas providing suitable impedance matching.

Controls and Operation

Normally a combined VOR/ILS/DME controller is employed (Fig. 4.9). Such a controller is briefly described in Chapter 4. The marker receiver switching is likely to be remote from the combined controller and its action has been described above.

In use the glidepath should be captured from below, approaching from a direction determined by the approach procedures for the particular airfield. The marker sensitivity should be on low for the approach. The appropriate selection should be made on the audio control panel.

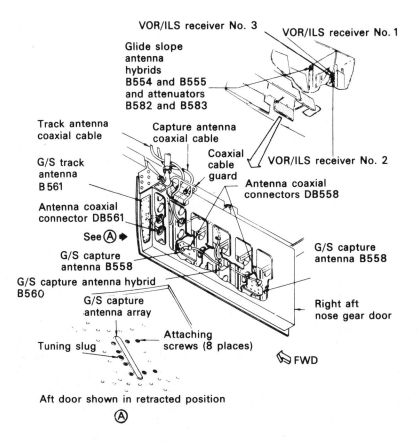

Fig. 5.12 Boeing 747 glideslope aerials (courtesy Boeing Commercial Aeroplane Co.)

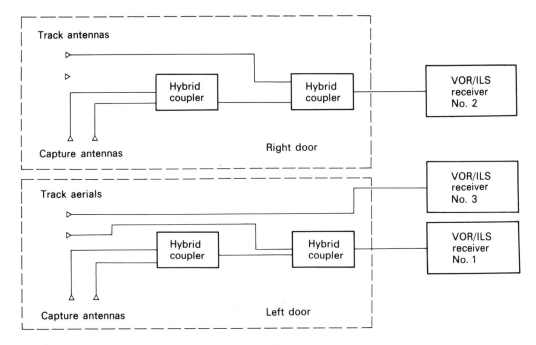

Fig. 5.13 Boeing 747 simplified glideslope aerial coupling arrangements

Characteristics

The basis for the following is ARINC Characteristic 578-3 although much of the detail has been omitted and not all sections covered.

Units The receiver should contain all the electronic circuitry necessary to provide deviation and flag signals for both localizer and glideslope. The control unit should provide for frequency selection of ILS, VOR and DME using 2/5 coding.

Antennas Separate localizer and glideslope antennas should be provided covering the appropriate frequency bands (108·00-112·00 MHz and 328·6-335·4 MHz respectively) and both having characteristic impedances of 50 Ω with a VSWR of less than 5 : 1.

Power Supply 115 V, 400 Hz, single phase.

Localizer Receiver Forty channels at 50 kHz spacing 108·00-111·95 MHz. Maximum channel time 60 ms. Selectivity is such that a carrier modulated 30 per cent at 1000 Hz should provide an output at least 60 dB down when separated from tuned frequency by ± 31·5 kHz; response should be within 6 dB when

carrier within ± 12 kHz of tuned frequency. Sensitivity is such that the flag should clear with a 5 µV 'hard' input signal ('hard' µV: the output of a signal generator calibrated in terms of open circuit load). The receiver should be protected against undesired localizer signals, VOR signals and v.h.f. comm. signals. The a.g.c. should be such that the receiver output should not vary by more than 3 dB with an input signal level range of 15-100 mV.

Glideslope Receiver Forty channels at 150 kHz spacing, 328·6-335·4 MHz. Channels to be paired with localizer channels for frequency selection purposes. The selectivity is specified in a similar way to localizer but the 60 dB points are at ± 80 kHz while the 6 dB points are at ± 21 kHz. The flag should clear with a 20 µV 'hard' signal. Protection against unwanted glideslope signals must be guaranteed. The a.g.c. should be such that the input signal level to the tone filters should not vary by more than $+\frac{1}{2}$ to -2 dB for an increase in input from 200 to 20 000 µV and should not vary by more than +3, -2 dB thereafter up to an input of 100 000 µV.

Deviation Outputs
Localizer: high-level 2 V for 0·155 d.d.m., low-level 150 mV for 0·155 d.d.m. Dual outputs in parallel for

AFCS. Output characteristics should not vary for loads between 200 Ω and no load. When 90 Hz predominates the 'hot' side of all deviation outputs should be positive with respect to the 'common' side; in this case 'fly-left' is given.
Glideslope: similar to localizer but high- and low-level outputs are 2 V and 150 mV respectively for 0·175 d.d.m.

Flag Outputs Two high-level warning signals (super flag) and one low-level warning signal should be provided by both localizer and glidepath receivers. The high-level flag characteristic is 28 V d.c. for valid status with current capabilities; 25 mA for AFCS warning; 250 mA for instrument warnings. The low-level flag should provide a voltage of between 300 and 900 mV into up to five parallel 1000 Ω loads.

Monitoring
Warning signals when: no r.f., either 90 or 150 Hz missing, total depth of modulation of composite 90/150 Hz signal is less than 28 per cent, etc.

Ramp Testing

A radiating test set must be used with a basic capability of simulating off-glidepath signals. In addition the test set should operate on one or more accurate spot frequencies and provide facilities for deleting either of the modulating frequencies.

TIC T-30B This test set was mentioned in Chapter 4 in connection with VOR testing. In addition to the VOR test set module we have the T-26B, T-28B and T-29B for testing the marker, localizer and glideslope receivers respectively. The T-26B provides at least 70 per cent modulation for the 400, 1300 and 3000 Hz tones. The T-28B operates on 108·1 MHz and can simulate 0 d.d.m., 0·155 d.d.m. left and right (switched) or 0 to ± 0·199 d.d.m. (variable). The T-29B operates on 334·7 MHz and can simulate 0 d.d.m., 0·175 d.d.m. up and down (switched) or 0 to ± 0·280 d.d.m. (variable). Either the 90 or the 150 Hz tones may be deleted with both the T-28B and the T-29B.

Cossor CRM 555 Forty localizer and forty glideslope channels may be selected, all crystal controlled. There are seven d.d.m. settings for localizer-simulated deviation and five for glidepath, the d.d.m. switch

being marked in decibels, e.g.:

> 6·6 dB fly-right (+ 0·1549 d.d.m.),
> 4·0 dB fly-left (– 0·0929 d.d.m.),
> 3·76 dB fly-up (+ 0·175 d.d.m.), etc.

Further switch positions on the d.d.m. switch allow for deleting one or other of the tones. In addition a variable 0 to ± 150 μA deviation is available. Stepped attenuators provide output levels variable between 0 dBm and −120 dBm in 1 dBm steps, in order that receiver sensitivity may be checked (test set aerial positioning will affect this check). Modulating tones of 400, 1300 and 3000 Hz are available for marker checks. Finally, 1020 Hz modulation is available for audio checks. As mentioned in Chapter 4 the CRM 555 can also be used to check VOR.

IFR NAV-402 AP Contains a modulated signal generator for marker, VOR, localizer, glideslope and communications testing. The output of the test set is variable between −7 and −110 dBm on all frequencies set by a variable frequency control (phase-locked at 25 kHz on each band except for glidepath where interval is 50 kHz). The localizer deviation can be switched to 0·093, 0·155 or 0·200 d.d.m. while glideslope d.d.m. offers 0·091, 0·175 and 0·400. Tone deletion can be selected. All three marker tones are available, as is 1020 Hz for audio check.

Fig. 5.14 NAV-402 AP test set (courtesy IFR Electronics Inc.)

Procedure The procedure for a functional check is straightforward if the operation of ILS is understood and full details of the test set are known. In practice, the procedure will be listed in the aircraft maintenance manual. Careful attention must be paid to test set antenna positioning if receivers with low sensitivity are not to be passed as serviceable. Self-test facilities on both the test set and the aircraft installation should be used if available.

6 Hyperbolic navigation systems

General Principles

The need for a co-ordinate system for navigation purposes is self-evident, the most important being the great circle lines of longitude and the lines of latitude parallel to the equator, itself a great circle. Figure 6.1 illustrates two alternative systems suitable for use in radio navigation.

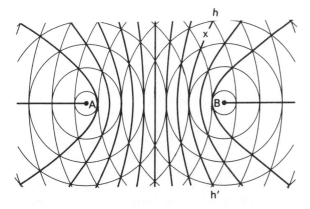

Fig. 6.1 Circular and hyperbolic co-ordinate systems

If two fixed points on earth have a sequence of concentric circles drawn around them, each circle representing a particular range from the fixed centre, then points of intersection are defined but ambiguous except on the line joining the two points (base line) where they are uniquely defined. Such a system is called rho-rho since two distance (rho) measurements are involved.

We can use the concentric circles to define hyperbolic lines. Where any two circles intersect we will have a difference in range defined; for example, the range to point A less the range to point B. The locus of points which have the same difference in range will describe a hyperbola. Thus in Fig. 6.1 the hyperbolic line hh′ is the locus of the point X such that AX − BX = constant. By plotting the lines for several different constants we obtain a family of hyperbolic lines. In the radio navigation systems to

be discussed we use the terms circular l.o.p. (lines of position) and hyperbolic l.o.p.

The patterns considered are not suitable for position fixing since two circular l.o.p. intersect at two places whilst knowing the difference in range to two points simply places one anywhere on one of two hyperbolic l.o.p. Knowing the starting position and subsequently the track and ground speed (or heading and true airspeed) will make it possible to use the rho-rho system, since a position calculated by dead reckoning will identify at which of the intersections the aircraft is. To use the hyperbolic l.o.p. we must generate another family of lines by taking a third fixed point, we then have the co-ordinate system shown in Fig. 6.2. A fix is given by the unique point where two hyperbolic l.o.p. cross. Of course the use of three fixed points gives the possibility of a rho-rho-rho system where three range circles intersect at a unique point.

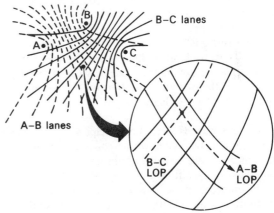

Fig. 6.2 Hyperbolic navigation position fix (courtesy Litton Systems International Inc., Aero Products Division)

The co-ordinate patterns described above are currently used in three radio navigation equipments, namely Loran C, Decca Navigator and Omega. Predecessors of these systems include GEE, a British World War II hyperbolic system developed to navigate bombers on missions to Germany.

It should be clear by now that the requirement of a hyperbolic system is that it can measure difference in range while a rho-rho-rho system must measure absolute range. Two methods are in use: time difference measurements for Loran C and phase measurements for Decca and Omega. These methods dictate that Loran C is a pulsed system while the other two are continuous wave (c.w.).

A basic problem with phase measuring systems is that range can only be determined if the whole number of cycles of e.m. radiation between the aircraft and the transmitting station are know. This is illustrated in Fig. 6.3. An aircraft at X measures the phase of the signal from station A which is

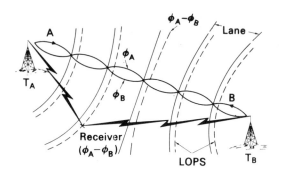

Fig. 6.4 Continuous wave hyperbolic navigation (courtesy Litton Systems International Inc., Aero Products Division)

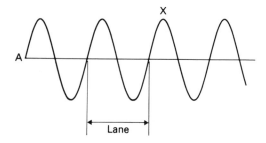

Fig. 6.3 Received signal phase measurement

transmitting at a frequency of 10 kHz. The wavelength, λ, is given by $C/10\,000$ where C is the speed of light; thus $\lambda \approx 16$ nautical miles. If the phase measured is, say $90°$, the distance AX is $(16N + 4)$ nautical miles where N is the number of whole cycles occupying the space between A and X. We say that the lane width is 16 nautical miles and the aircraft is $(N + \frac{1}{4})$ lanes from A.

Continuous Wave Hyperbolic Principles
With a hyperbolic system we are concerned with difference in range rather than absolute range; consequently the airborne equipment must measure the difference in phase between radio waves from two transmitting ground stations. Figure 6.4 shows that there will be zero phase difference between synchronized transmissions every half a wavelength.

An aircraft measuring a phase difference of $\phi A - \phi B$ could be on any of the dashed l.o.p.; i.e. in any of the lanes between transmitters A and B, each of which is half a wavelength wide at the base line. Since every lane is identical to the receiver on the aircraft a lane count must be established either from the aircraft's starting point or, during flight, from an independent position fix. Each lane may be

subdivided into say, centilanes (1/100th of a lane) and so determining on which l.o.p. the aircraft is flying is simply a matter of lane and centilane counting from some known point. A fix requires a separate count to be made of the lanes and centilanes between another pair of transmitters; one transmitter may be common to the two pairs. The two l.o.p. will intersect at the aircraft's position.

The possibility of lane slip exists; i.e. missing a lane in the count. If this happens the correct lane must be established, this process being termed laning. Obviously laning is easier when lanes are wider. Suppose the frequency of transmitter A is 10 kHz while that of B is 15 kHz, then we have a difference frequency of 5 kHz which corresponds to a lane width of 30 000 m as opposed to 15 000 m for 10 kHz and 10 000 m for 15 kHz. In this way lane width can be made wide without having to transmit impossibly low frequencies. While the use of wide lanes is of importance for the purposes of laning, narrow lanes give greater resolution and hence greater potential accuracy.

Measuring the difference in phase between signals from two transmitters will only be meaningful if the transmissions have a known and fixed phase relationship. Two possibilities exist:

1. one of the transmitters can be designated the master, the other the slave which, on receiving the transmission from the master, will ensure its own transmission is synchronized;
2. both transmitters are synchronized to some standard time scale such as provided by an atomic clock.

Pulsed Hyperbolic Principles
In such systems laning is not a problem since

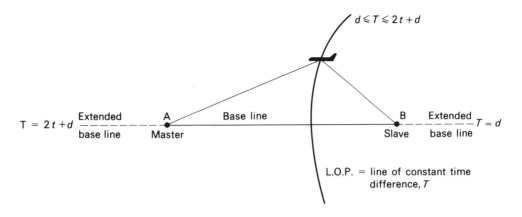

$d \leqslant T \leqslant 2t + d$

$T = 2t + d$ —— Extended base line / A Master / Base line / B Slave / Extended base line —— $T = d$

L.O.P. = line of constant time difference, T

Fig. 6.5 Pulsed hyperbolic navigation

unambiguous l.o.p.s are obtained. Consider the two transmitters at A and B in Fig. 6.5. One is designated the master; this transmits pulses of energy at a fixed published p.r.f. On receipt of the master pulse the slave will transmit, usually after some fixed delay, say d μs. If the propagation time from master to slave is t μs then we can see that an aircraft at the master station position, or anywhere on the extended base line outward from the master, will measure a time difference of $(2t + d)$ μs when comparing the time of arrival of the master and slave transmissions. An aircraft on the extended base line outward from the slave would record a time difference of d μs. Should an aircraft be anywhere other than on the extended base line the time difference will be some unique reading between d and $(2t + d)$ μs.

Disadvantages of hyperbolic systems are that lane width varies with distance from base line and that signal geometry is important. With a hyperbolic co-ordinate system the angle of cut between two l.o.p. can be such that the tangents to the lines at the aircraft position are almost parallel; for other aircraft positions the hyperbolic l.o.p. may cut almost at right angles. Of course if more than two l.o.p. are available the geometry problem is of little consequence since a most probable position can be computed. Figure 6.6 illustrates the various l.o.p. geometries.

Continuous Wave Rho-Rho and Rho-Rho-Rho Systems

To measure the phase of a received signal a suitable reference must be available, generated within the receiver. Let the phase of the reference signal be ϕ_r, the phase of the received signal be ϕ_a when the aircraft is at point A and ϕ_b when the aircraft is at

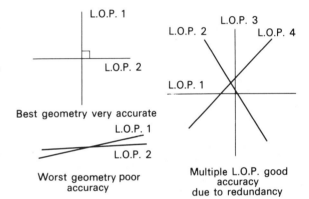

L.O.P. 1 / L.O.P. 2 / L.O.P. 2

Best geometry very accurate

L.O.P. 1 / L.O.P. 2

Worst geometry poor accuracy

L.O.P. 3 / L.O.P. 2 / L.O.P. 4 / L.O.P. 1

Multiple L.O.P. good accuracy due to redundancy

Fig. 6.6 Various geometries for hyperbolic systems

point B. The airborne equipment will measure the difference in phase between the received signal and the reference signal, i.e.:

$$\phi_m = \phi_a - \phi_r$$

when the aircraft is at point A, while:

$$\phi_m = \phi_b - \phi_r$$

when the aircraft is at point B. The change in phase as the aircraft moves will provide a measure of the change in range, we have:

$$\phi_m = (\phi_a - \phi_r) - (\phi_b - \phi_r)$$
$$= \phi_a - \phi_b \qquad (6.1)$$

These ideas are illustrated in Fig. 6.7.

The above working has assumed that the reference signal does not drift in the time it takes for the aircraft to travel from A to B. If the reference phase is ϕ_{ra} and ϕ_{rb} when the aircraft is at point A and B respectively, then equation (6.1) must be modified

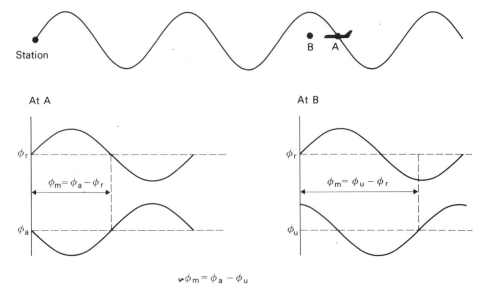

Fig. 6.7 Change in measured phase with aircraft movement

to account for this drift, it becomes:

$$\phi_m = (\phi_a - \phi_b) - (\phi_{ra} - \phi_{rb}) \quad (6.2)$$

Thus an equipment continuously monitoring the change in measured phase in order to calculate change in range will be in error by an amount depending on the reference oscillator drift.

At the moment of switch-on the reference signal on board the aircraft is not phase-locked to the ground transmitter's frequency. Further, since there is a signal phase shift due to the transmission path, there will be a phase or clock offset (ϕ_o) between received signal and the local reference. If at switch-on both the transmitter and receiver positions are known ϕ_o can be calculated, and if at subsequent aircraft positions this phase offset remains the same then by measuring phase difference as described earlier the change in range from the known starting point may be computed. Reference oscillator drift can be considered as a change in phase offset.

Errors arising due to a change in phase offset can be minimized in three ways:

1. use difference in phase between synchronized signals from two remote transmitters, in which case any change in reference phase cancels out (this is the hyperbolic approach);
2. a precision reference oscillator of atomic clock standard can be carried on the aircraft, in which case drift is negligible over the duration of the flight (this is the rho-rho approach);

3. estimate the phase offset throughout flight by utilizing signals from more than two transmitters (this is the rho-rho-rho approach).

The operation of a rho-rho system is illustrated in Fig. 6.8. As the aircraft flies from 1 to 2 the phase changes in the signals received from transmitters A and B are continuously measured; this allows the airborne equipment to count the number of range lanes and centilanes traversed with respect to both transmitters. Equation (6.1) applies, since reference oscillator drift is negligible. Thus if the aircraft position at point 1 is known it can be computed at 2.

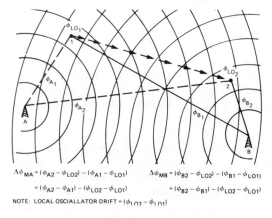

$\Delta\phi_{MA} = (\phi_{A2} - \phi_{LO2}) - (\phi_{A1} - \phi_{LO1})$
$\qquad = (\phi_{A2} - \phi_{A1}) - (\phi_{LO2} - \phi_{LO1})$

$\Delta\phi_{MB} = (\phi_{B2} - \phi_{LO2}) - (\phi_{B1} - \phi_{LO1})$
$\qquad = (\phi_{B2} - \phi_{B1}) - (\phi_{LO2} - \phi_{LO1})$

NOTE: LOCAL OSCILLATOR DRIFT = $(\phi_{LO2} - \phi_{LO1})$

Fig. 6.8 Rho-rho navigation (courtesy Litton Systems International Inc., Aero Products Division)

With a rho-rho-rho system two range (circular) l.o.p. give a position fix while a third can be used to eliminate error in phase offset, ϕ_e. In Fig. 6.9 it can be seen that a non-zero ϕ_e gives us the situation where three l.o.p. do not intersect at one point but form a triangle within which the aircraft is positioned.

hyperbolic and rho-rho-rho methods require three ground transmitters for a fix but the geometry of the aircraft and transmitters will degrade the accuracy of the hyperbolic system more so than either rho-rho-rho or rho-rho. A hyperbolic system has the most complex computer program, but is nevertheless

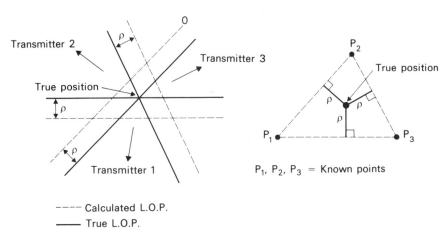

---- Calculated L.O.P.
—— True L.O.P.

Fig. 6.9 Rho-rho-rho navigation

Consideration of this position triangle shows that the perpendicular distances from the true position to the calculated l.o.p. are equal to each other and give a measure of ϕ_e. Sufficient information is available from the three l.o.p. to evaluate ϕ_e, assuming that reference oscillator drift is the only source of error. Should other errors contribute to the calculated l.o.p. the perpendicular distances from the true position to the calculated l.o.p. will not necessarily be equal and an approximate solution must be sought.

Comparison of Systems
There is no clear-cut best system to employ, and in fact all are in use as follows:

pulsed hyperbolic	Loran C
c.w. hyperbolic	Decca Navigator, Omega
c.w. rho-rho	Omega
c.w. rho-rho-rho	Omega

It is interesting to observe that manufacturers of Omega navigation systems have opted for different methods of calculating position, illustrating that there is no universally accepted best method.

The rho-rho method is certainly the simplest of the three, needing only two ground transmitters and employing a relatively simple computer program. It does, however, have the costly disadvantage of requiring a very stable reference oscillator. Both

probably the least costly since its local oscillator stability requirements are less stringent than even the rho-rho-rho system.

Omega Navigation System (ONS)

Omega is a very low-frequency, c.w., long-range navigation system. Three time-multiplexed signals of 10·2, 11·33 and 13·6 kHz are transmitted omnidirectionally from each of eight stations strategically located around the world. Although the concept was patented in 1923 it was not until the mid 1960s that the US Navy established the first experimental stations. By 1968 it was established that ONS was feasible and the setting-up of a worldwide network commenced. The USA is responsible for the stations in North Dakota, Hawaii, Liberia and a temporary station in Trinidad, while stations in Norway, Japan, Argentina, La Reunion and, by 1980, Australia are the responsibility of nations which have established bilateral agreements with the USA. Although the responsibility for co-ordination was originally allocated to the US Navy it has now been taken over by the US Coast Guard.

The Omega Stations and Broadcast Patterns
Each station has a transmitter power of 10 kW with

Table 6.1 Signal format, o.n.s.

Stations		0·9 s	1·0 s	1·1 s	1·2 s	1·1 s	0·9 s	1·2 s	1·0 s
		← 10 s →							
Norway	A	10·2	13·6	11·33					
Liberia	B		10·2	13·6	11·33				
Hawaii	C			10·2	13·6	11·33			
North Dakota	D				10·2	13·6	11·33		
La Reunion	E					10·2	13·6	11·33	
Argentina	F						10·2	13·6	11·33
Trinidad/Australia	G	11·33						10·2	13·6
Japan	H	13·6	11·33						10·2

the exception of the temporary station in Trinidad which has a 1 kW transmitter. Radiation is from an omnidirectional antenna which takes the form either of a vertical tower, approximately 450 m high, supporting an umbrella of transmitting elements, or a valley span typically 3500 m in length. Equipment redundancy ensures reliable operation 99 per cent of the time.

As mentioned above each station transmits three frequencies in a time-multiplexed pattern which is unique and provides identification. The transmission format is shown in Table 6.1. It can be seen that at any one time only three stations will be transmitting, each on a different frequency. There are short intervals (0·2 s) between transmission bursts. The pattern is repeated every 10 s.

All transmitters are phase-locked to a nearly absolute time standard provided by the use of atomic clocks at each of the station locations. The result is that the three frequencies in all transmitters simultaneously cross zero with positive slope at precise times every 15/17ths of a millisecond. This phase relationship is illustrated in Fig. 6.10. The net result is that the timing error between stations is at most 1 μs, leading to a maximum error in position fix of 300 m.

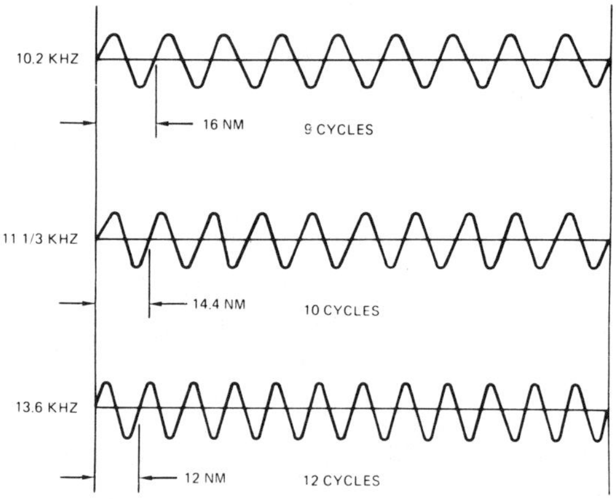

Fig. 6.10 Omega frequency relationships (courtesy Litton Systems International Inc., Aero Products Division)

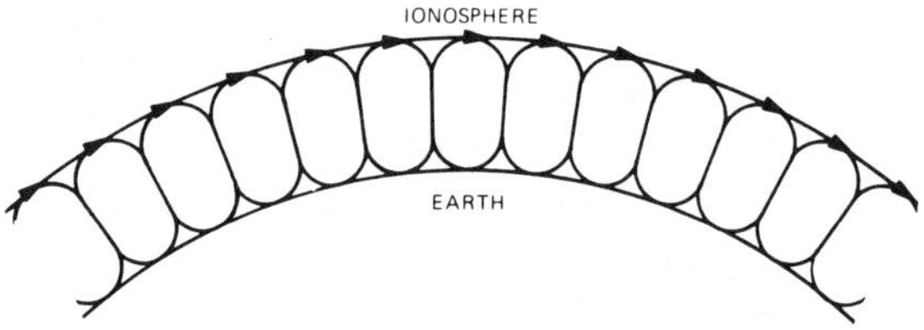

Fig. 6.11 Earth – Ionosphere waveguide (courtesy Litton Systems International Inc., Aero Products Division)

Propagation

The band of frequencies 10-14 kHz is an appropriate choice for a phase-measuring navigation system since e.m. radiation at these frequencies can travel thousands of miles with predictable phase-change characteristics. A natural waveguide is formed by the earth's surface and the D layer of the ionosphere, the dimensions of which are suitable for propagation of the ONS frequencies. This mode of propagation accounts for the range of the signals and the predictability of the changes in phase.

A requirement of the system is that four or more stations can be received everywhere. Account must be taken of the attenuation of the signal which varies with direction due to the rotation of the earth. Signals travelling in an easterly direction suffer approximately 2 dB/1000 km attenuation, while those on a westerly path suffer approximately

4 dB/1000 km. North and south attenuation is the same at 3 dB/1000 km. A further consideration is that signals cannot be used close to the source since the phase variations are unpredictable in this region. The implementation of ONS with eight stations, which are not equi-spaced around the world, leads to a situation where, under normal conditions, between four and seven stations are usable depending on the receiver location.

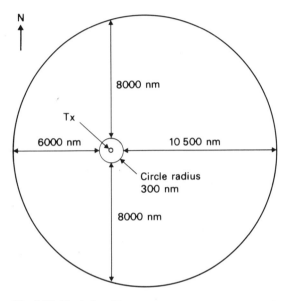

Fig. 6.12 Typical usable coverage

Factors Affecting Propagation

1. Diurnal Effect
The height of the ionosphere varies by approximately 20 km from day to night, being highest at night. The phase velocity of the propagated wave will be greatest during the day when the dimensions of the 'waveguide' are least; this leads to phase variations which fortunately are predictable and cyclic. Corrections to compensate for diurnal effect may be implemented by means of a software routine. The entry of GMT and date at switch-on is required by the routine.

2. Ground Conductivity
The different attenuating effects of the oceans and various types of landmass changes the phase velocity of the v.l.f. signal. The greatest loss of signal strength occurs in the ice-cap regions where the change in phase velocity is significant. Water has least effect. The effect of ground conductivity being well known

means that a conductivity map can be stored in the computer, so enabling a propagation-correction factor to be calculated for the path between the receiver and the known station location.

A complication arises in that it is possible to receive a direct signal and one which has gone the 'long way round', in which case we have a mutual interference problem. Automatic deselection of stations at ranges in excess of say 8000 nautical miles is used to minimize this effect.

3. Geomagnetic Field
The earth's magnetic (H) field alters the motion of ions and electrons in the lower region of the ionosphere, thus affecting v.l.f. propagation. Again the equipment software may be used to apply corrections.

4. Nonspheroidal Effects
The computation of aircraft position must take into account that the signal path from transmitting station to aircraft receiver is not on the surface of a sphere. Further, pressure differences at various latitudes effect the height of the ionosphere so compensation must be made for the effect on phase velocity.

5. Modal Interference
There are various modes of propagation in the earth-ionosphere waveguide. If one mode is dominant the phase grid produced will be regular; however in practice a competing mode can be almost equal to the dominant mode in which case irregularities appear in the phase pattern. The most serious case occurs when one mode is dominant at night and a second during the day. It follows that during sunrise and sunset the two modes will be equal. Some Omega receivers automatically deselect station B (Liberia) at critical times since signals from this station are particularly susceptible to modal interference at night.

6. Solar Effects
A solar flare gives rise to a large emission of X-rays which causes a short-term disturbance in a limited part of the ionosphere. Such an event is called a sudden ionospheric disturbance (SID) or a sudden phase anomaly (SPA) and may last for 1 h or more; l.o.p. in the affected regions may be shifted by up to say 5 nautical miles. These SIDs occur about 7 to 10 times per month, but during the peak of the 11-year sunspot cycle a major solar flare may product a shift in l.o.p. by up to 15 nautical miles. This latter event is predictable, and warnings may be issued.

Infrequently large quantities of protons are

released from the sun, producing a so-called polar cap disturbance (p.c.d.). The effect of a p.c.d., which is to shift l.o.p. from say 6 to 8 nautical miles, may last for several days. Only those transmission paths passing over the poles are affected. Since the p.c.d. is of long duration navigation warning messages may be broadcast.

Position Fixing

As previously discussed ONS may use hyperbolic, rho-rho or rho-rho-rho methods, a root mean square accuracy of 1-2 nautical miles being obtainable with all methods providing the computer software corrects for predictable errors.

Whatever method is used the lane in which the aircraft is flying must be established. Lane widths for the basic frequencies and difference frequencies are given in Table 6.2. It can be seen that the broadest lane for the direct ranging methods is 144 nautical miles while that for the hyperbolic method is 72 nautical miles. If it is known which broad lane the aircraft is in then it is possible to resolve lane ambiguity for the narrower lanes automatically, as shown in Fig. 6.13. In this example it is known in

Table 6.2   Frequencies and lane widths, o.n.s. (lane widths in nm)

		Direct ranging	Hyperbolic
Basic frequencies	10·2 kHz	16	8
	11·3 kHz	14·4	7·2
	13·6 kHz	12	6
13·6-10·2 =	3·4 kHz	48	24
13·6-11·3 =	2·3 kHz	72	36
11·3-10·2 =	1·1 kHz	144	72

which 3·4 kHz lane the aircraft is flying. Phase measurement of the 10·2 kHz signal gives three possible l.o.p. while the 13·6 kHz signal gives four possible l.o.p. Only one of the possible l.o.p. from each group is coincident, this being the unique l.o.p. on which the aircraft is positioned.

Rate Aiding

The ONS transmission pattern extends over a period of 10 s. If the phases of all usable signals are measured over this period and then l.o.p. are generated for position fixing, an error will result, since some of the phase information will be up to 10 s old. Aircraft direction and speed information may be used to update the phase information for l.o.p. calculations, this process being known as rate aiding. In practice we can generate l.o.p. at less than 10 s intervals, say every 1 s, thus ONS can be considered as a dead reckoning system with position-fixing updates every second or so.

Direction and speed information can come from a number of sources, for example compass heading and true air speed from an Air Data Computer or track and ground speed from Doppler or INS. Some Omega equipments generate track and ground speed internally from computed position changes.

If for any reason there is a loss of signal dead reckoning, data on direction and speed inputs or last-known internally generated track and ground speed can be used to continuously calculate the aircraft's position, so that on receipt of sufficient usable signals, lane ambiguity is easily resolved. Obviously if the internally generated last-known track and ground speed are used during dead reckoning then aircraft manoeuvre during this phase may cause laning problems when signals are received again.

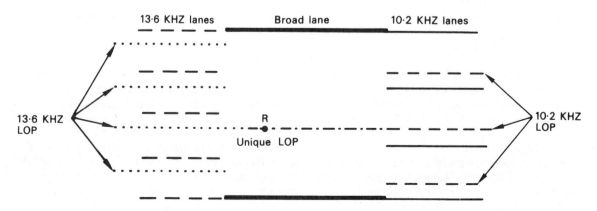

Fig. 6.13   Resolving lane ambiguity (courtesy Litton Systems International Inc., Aero Products Division)

In such a case aircraft approximate position would have to be entered by the pilot.

Most Probable Position

There is a redundancy in the Omega system in that normally more signals will be received than are necessary to compute the two l.o.p. needed for a fix. In this case, data from all receivable stations, and as many frequencies as possible, may be used to generate a number of l.o.p. If all frequencies are received from all stations there would be $3 \times 8 = 24$ phase measurements every 10 s, giving up to twenty-four l.o.p. for a single fix. The multiple l.o.p. will not cross at a point but will define a small polygon within which the aircraft is positioned. The computer will calculate the aircraft's most probable position within this polygon.

In practice there will be far fewer than twenty-four phase measurements available. Automatic deselection will take place for reasons of poor signal to noise ratio, poor geometry, susceptibility to modal interference or outside usable range (too close or too far). Manual deselection will be accomplished as a result of pre-flight or in-flight information received concerning station status or unusual ionospheric activity.

Communication Stations, v.l.f.

A worldwide high-power military communications network operating in the band 15-25 kHz is maintained by the US Navy. As a secondary purpose of the network is to provide worldwide synchronization of time standards, the carrier signals are precisely timed, and so may be used for navigation purposes. Since control of the stations is out of the hands of those bodies, either national or international, responsible for civil aircraft navigation, use of the network for navigation can only be considered as supplementary to other forms of navigation.

Hyperbolic navigation is not suitable for use with v.l.f. comms stations since absolute phase differences between two received signals cannot be determined due to each station operating on an unrelated frequency. A further disadvantage is that the diurnal phase shifts are not as predictable for v.l.f. signals as they are for ONS signals.

Several manufacturers offer equipment with v.l.f. and Omega capability; in some cases v.l.f. is optional. In such equipment Omega signals provide the primary navigation information while v.l.f. signals provide back-up should insufficient Omega signals be usable.

Installation

A typical simplified installation diagram is shown in Fig. 6.14. The ONS consists of a receiver processor unit (RPU), control display unit (CDU) and antenna coupler unit (ACU). Such a break-down of 'black boxes' conforms to ARINC Characteristic 599 but some manufacturers choose to separate the receiver and computer and also the antenna and coupling unit.

The RPU is fitted in a convenient location, the most important consideration being cooling arrangements, a forced downdraught or integral blower being typical. The CDU must of course be mounted in view, and in reach, of the pilot; normally special cooling arrangements are not required.

The antenna used may be of H field or E field type, the latter possibly employing a separate coupler unit with a supplied interconnecting cable. An E field system is sensitive to precipitation static discharge, thus good bonding and sufficient strategically spaced static wicks are essential. An H field system is sensitive to magnetic (a.c.) noise sources and a skin mapping should be carried out on initial installation to determine the optimum location for the antenna which may be on the top or bottom of the fuselage.

Skin Mapping Detailed procedure is given in manufacturer's literature, but basically the aircraft should be parked away from all power lines, both above and below ground, and away from all obstructions. Ambient signal plus noise is then initially recorded approximately 100 ft from the aircraft with a spectrum analyser set at 10·2, 11·3 and 13·6 kHz. Similar measurements are made with an ACU secured by tape at various airframe locations. Comparison of ambient and airframe measurements will identify several possible positions. The optimum position(s) can then be found by repeating the measurements under various on and off conditions of engines, lighting, electronics and fans. The final position should be checked out for signal to noise ratio with engines running at 90 per cent minimum.

Brief Description of Units

The descriptions which follow are based on the Litton LTN-211; other systems have similar units which vary in detail.

Receiver Processor Unit The RPU is the major part of any ONS. Omega broadcast signals from the ACU are processed together with inputs from other sensors to give present position and guidance parameters as required. The major parts of a RPU will typically be:

r.f. circuitry;

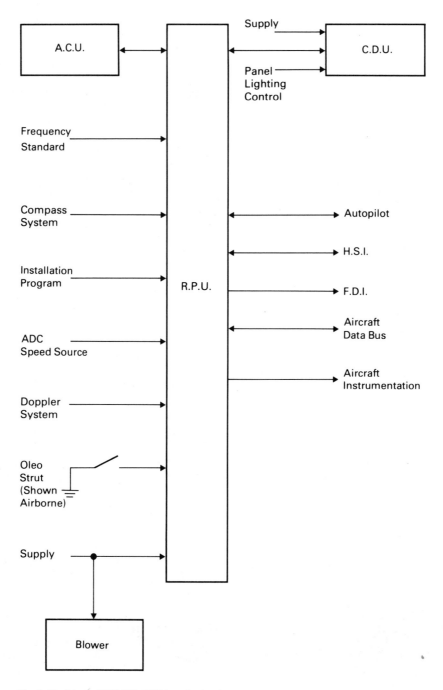

Fig. 6.14 Litton LTN-211 ONS installation (courtesy Litton Systems International Inc., Aero Products Division)

central processor for computing function;

scratch-pad RAM for temporary data storage;

special RAM in which pilot-entered data is saved during power interrupt;

ROM to store program which will incorporate corrections;

power supply assembly;

analogue interface;

digital interface;

BITE;

antenna switching;

chassis.

Control Display Unit The CDU provides the interface between the flight crew and the ONS. Data transmission between CDU and RPU is via two one-way serial digital data buses. The RPU transmits four 32-bit words to the CDU while the CDU transmits one 32-bit word to the RPU. The d.c. voltages for the CDU are provided by the RPU. The CDU annunciators are driven by signals from the RPU.

Antenna Coupler Unit Two H field bidirectional loop antennas are wound on ferrite rods arranged at right angles to each other. Pre-amplification of the signal takes place in the ACU. Provision is made for the injection of a test signal to each loop.

ONS Interface

Operator Inputs
1. Present position latitude and longitude: entered during initialization, i.e. during preparation of the system prior to take off;
2. waypoint latitude and longitude: up to nine entered as required during initialization; editing facility available for in-flight entry;
3. Greenwich Mean Time/date: entered during initialization.

External Sensor Inputs
1. Speed: from air data computer (ADC) or Doppler radar in a variety of signal formats;
2. heading: from compass system;
3. drift angle: from Doppler radar, optional;
4. speed valid signal;
5. heading valid signal;
6. compass free/slaved input;
7. oleo strut switch input;
8. drift angle valid signal.

Other Inputs
1. Frequency standard: rho-rho option;

2. 26 V a.c. 400 Hz reference: from external equipment accepting synchro feeds from ONS;
3. aircraft data bus: interface with digital air data system (DADS), inertial reference system (IRS), flight management computer system, etc.

Installation Programming
Various receiver processor unit connector pins, termed 'program discrete pins' are grounded by means of a link to earth in order to select:
1. Speed input format;
2. frequency standard;
3. magnetic/true heading   input/output;
4. oleo strut logic;
5. synchro output;
6. grid mode: local, Greenwich or two alternatives;
7. antenna mount: top/bottom.

System Outputs

Analogue/Discrete
1. Track angle;
2. cross track deviation;
3. track angle error;
4. drift angle;
5. track angle error plus drift angle;
6. true heading;
7. desired track angle;
8. track change alert;
9. track leg change;
10. steering signal (roll command);
11. To/from.

Digital
12. Present position (lat./long.);
13. heading (mag./true);
14. track angle;
15. ground speed;
16. distance to waypoint;
17. time to GO;
18. wind angle;
19. wind speed;
20. cross track distance;
21. track angle error;
22. drift angle;
23. desired track.

Warning
24. Cross track deviation failure;
25. true heading warning;
26. steering signal warning.

Figure 1.13 defines pictorially those outputs relating to angle and distance.

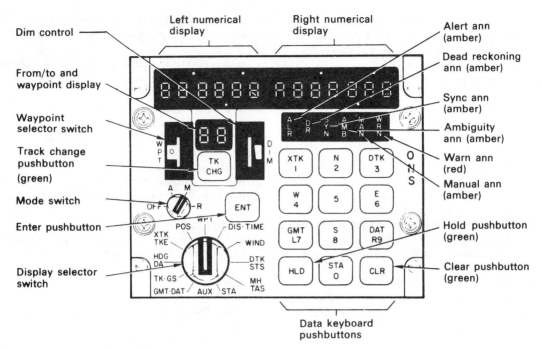

Fig. 6.15 Litton LTN-211 CDU (courtesy Litton Systems International Inc., Aero Products Division)

Controls and Operation

Figure 6.15 shows the Litton LTN-211 CDU which is similar to those of other manufacturers. A very comprehensive range of controls and displayed data is available. Brief details only are given here.

The pilot is able to enter his present position and up to nine waypoints defining a great-circle navigation flight plan which can be updated during flight. Information displayed to the pilot helps him to fly the specified route from waypoint to waypoint or fly parallel offsets from the flight plan. If the autopilot is engaged steering information from ONS causes the aircraft to automatically follow the flight plan, in which case the display is used for monitoring purposes.

The system also demands entry of GMT and date. A keyboard is used for all data entry which is checked for operator error, in which case a coded warning is given. System failure warning is given by the WRN annunciator when malfunction and action codes may be displayed. Several other annunciators give warning of track leg change imminent (ALR), system in dead reckoning mode (DR), synchronization of system with transmitted signal format taking place (SYN), lane ambiguity (AMB) and manually entered true airspeed, magnetic heading or cross track offset being displayed (MAN).

The following information may be displayed by appropriate positioning of the display selector switch:

GMT/DAT	Greenwich Mean Time and date
TK·GS	Track angle and ground speed
HDG/DA	Heading and drift angle
XTK/TKE	Cross track distance and track angle error
POS	Present position
WPT	Waypoint (selected)
DIS.TIME	Distance and time (to 'go')
WIND	Wind direction and velocity
DTK/STS	Desired track and status (malfunction)
MH/TAS	Magnetic heading and true airspeed
STA	Station status
FROM/TO	From and to waypoints for current leg.

System Software

The major tasks for the software employed in a rho-rho-rho Omega system are described briefly below.

Synchronization The transmission pattern must be identified in order that the ONS will know when each station is broadcasting. Since the Omega transmission pattern repeats every 10 s synchronization is attempted by sampling 10 s of data in order to try and find the start time (station A transmitting 10·2 kHz burst).

If synchronization is not successful a further 10 s period is sampled and so on.

Since before synchronization is complete signal direction is not known, the antenna is set to an omnidirectional mode.

The idea of the synchronization routine is to look for correlation in phase measurements from sample to sample for the three broadcast frequencies. Noise alone will of course appear with random phase, not correlated between samples.

Phase and Signal-to-Noise Measurements The phase difference between the received signal and a local reference is sampled at regular intervals throughout the burst. Forming sine and cosine sums of the sampled phase angles will allow a burst phase measurement (average of samples) and signal-to-noise measurement to be made. If no signal is being received during the sample then no contribution will be made to either the sine or cosine sums. We have:

$$\phi \text{ burst} = \tan^{-1}\left(\sum\left(\frac{\sin\phi}{\cos\phi}\right)\right) - \text{antenna phase shift} \quad (6.3)$$

$$R \text{ burst} = \left(\frac{\Sigma \sin\phi}{N}\right)^2 + \left(\frac{\Sigma \cos\phi}{N}\right)^2 \quad (6.4)$$

where the summations are of the samples over the burst, ϕ is the phase angle and R, which lies between 0 and 1, gives a measure of signal to noise ratio (s.n.r.).

The values of ϕ burst and R burst are fed to a tracking filter in order to give smooth values ϕ and R. There are a total of twenty-four tracking filters (three frequencies × eight stations). Rate aiding is applied to ϕ to compensate for known aircraft motion. Each tracking filter is updated after the appropriate burst, i.e. every 10 s, rate aiding values are calculated every 0·1 s.

Antenna Selection Every 10 s the bearing to the eight stations is computed and stored. Every second the difference between bearing and heading is computed and used to select the longitudinal loop, lateral loop or combination of loops to make the antenna directional, the main lobe being in the direction of the station to be received.

Station Selection For Omega rho-rho-rho navigation three stations must be received to calculate the three unknowns (latitude, longitude and clock or phase offset). Various criteria are used in the selection of stations to be employed:

1. eliminate manually deselected stations;
2. eliminate stations for which the aircraft is not within area covered (*see* Fig. 6.12);
3. eliminate stations with known modal interference problem at night in certain areas (Liberia);
4. eliminate stations on the basis of poor s.n.r.;
5. eliminate frequencies from particular stations whose phase difference between computed and measured exceeds a certain figure.

All qualifying frequencies are used for position determination. If less than minimum number of stations are available, the dead reckoning mode is entered.

Propagation Correction The computer must calculate a propagation correction ϕ_p, the value of which will depend on the path from station to aircraft, the time of day and the date. Factors affecting propagation have been discussed earlier and while complete understanding and quantification is not available, fairly accurate models are. The model used is simplified in order to save storage and computation time. Simplifications include:

1. increasing integration step size along path to say 1°;
2. using coarse memory map, i.e. subdividing earth into, say, 4° × 4° blocks and assigning a conductivity index to each corresponding to average conductivity in that area;
3. simplifying sub-routine which computes bearing of signal path to earth's magnetic field.

Computer comparisons of simplified and more accurate models have been carried out and show excellent agreement.

Current Least-Squares Error Calculation The measured phase ϕ is corrected for propagation shifts, ϕ_p, and estimated clock offset, ϕ_c, and then compared with the phase, ϕ_r, derived from the current calculated range between aircraft and station to give $\Delta\phi$, we have

$$\Delta\phi = (\phi - \phi_p - \phi_c) - \phi_r \quad (6.5)$$

There is one $\Delta\phi$ for each station frequency so there will be at most twenty-four. If there is no error, that is ϕ_p, ϕ_c and ϕ_r are all correct, then $\Delta\phi$ will be zero. In practice errors will exist, so the purpose of the least-squares error estimation routine is to find corrections to ϕ_c, and the computed position to minimize $\Delta\phi$ for the stations/frequencies in use.

Since the most reliable information comes from the strongest signal each $\Delta\phi$ is weighted by its s.n.r. (smoothed R from equation (6.4)). The squares of the $\Delta\phi$ are computed to prevent cancellation in the sum. We have:

$$\text{minimize } \Sigma R(\Delta\phi)^2 \qquad (6.6)$$

where the sum is taken over all the stations and frequencies in use.

The phase difference, $\Delta\phi$, can be expressed in terms of $\Delta\phi_c$, ΔN, ΔE and B where the first three terms are the corrections in clock offset, north position and east position respectively while B is the bearing to the station. If we consider the signal received from station I on frequency J, we have:

$$\Delta\phi(I,J) = \Delta\phi_c - \Delta N \cdot \cos B(I) - \Delta E \cdot \sin B(I) \qquad (6.7)$$

Thus equation (6.7) is used in (6.6), the minimization of the weighted sum of squares, giving a least-squares estimate of the current error which enables correction of clock offset and position.

The correction vector $X = (\Delta\phi_c, \Delta N, \Delta E)^T$ is smoothed by clock and position filters, rate aiding of speed, resolved north and east about aircraft heading, being applied to these filters. The output of the filters is wind (north and east), latitude and longitude. The wind is not computed when the aircraft is on the ground, as indicated by the oleo strut switch.

Summary The above notes on system softwave are by no means complete; some functions of the softwave have not been mentioned although have been implied elsewhere in the chapter. The major navigation tasks and their implementation are best summarized by a flowchart (*see* Fig. 6.16).

The Program

The actual program used in any ONS is proprietary and will vary greatly depending on the type of microprocessor used, the method of navigation and the ingenuity of the author.

In general there will be a main loop which checks for power interrupts, computes propagation correction, carries out self-testing, etc. The main loop will be interrupted when 10·2, 11·3 or 13·6 kHz information is available for processing and also when the CDU is ready to input or output data.

In the LTN-211 the phase data interrupts for the three frequencies occur regularly at 6·25 ms intervals. The 11·3 and 13·6 kHz interrupt loops simply serve to read the appropriate phase data while the

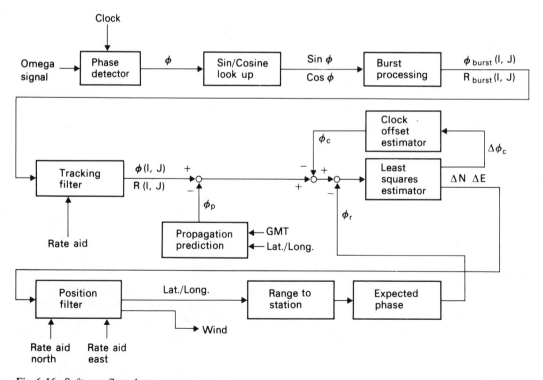

Fig. 6.16 Software flow chart

10·2 kHz interrupt loop processes all phase data and checks to see if it is time to start loops which occur regularly and perform various computations and checks. Briefly we have:

100 ms loop: update clock
                rate aid computation
                check synchronization
                antenna selection
                burst processing
                serve CDU
1 s loop: horizontal steering commands
10 s loop: least-squares estimator
                save key data

Hardware

Computer Inputs Figure 6.17 shows a simplified system block diagram of the LTN-211. Omega signals from the ACU are fed via an antenna switching matrix to three narrow-band receivers, one for each of the three Omega frequencies. Antenna switching is derived from the computed relative bearing of the station being received at that particular time. The amplified and limited signals are compared in phase with reference signals derived from a 4·896 MHz clock. A real-time interrupt is generated on completion of a phase measurement for each of the Omega frequencies. The 10·2, 11·3 and 13·6 kHz interrupts are each generated 160 times per second to inform the computer that phase data is available for 368 μs, during which time the appropriate interrupt routine is entered and the data read. The sensor phase data forms word 1 in a four-word, 16-bit digital multiplexer.

Heading and speed inputs enter the system in the form of three-wire synchro feeds. Scott-T transformers resolve this input into the sine and cosine components which are then demodulated and filtered to provide d.c. signals to an analogue multiplexer controlled by the computer. After analogue to digital conversion the heading and speed sine and cosine components are multiplexed as word 2 in the digital multiplexer. Words 3 and 4 contain data relating to various discretes, program pins, validities and source selectors.

ARINC 575 data from the CDU is converted to

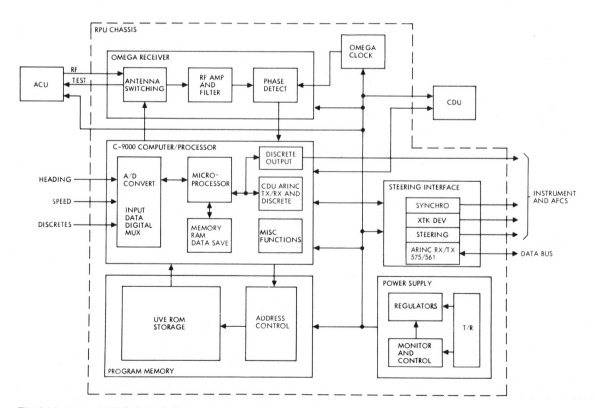

Fig. 6.17 Litton LTN-211 block diagram (courtesy Litton Systems International Inc., Aero Products Division)

TTL (transistor-transistor logic) levels and shifted into a serial to parallel shift register. When the input data is ready an interrupt is generated and the contents of the register are read by the computer.

A digital interface card, part of the steering interface, is a link between the ONS and other systems. There are four ARINC 575 receivers for DADS TAS (digital air data system true air speed), flight management, IRS (inertial reference system) and an inter-system b.c.d. or binary bus for interface with another ONS or possibly another type system. The address bus from the computer identifies the required receiver which stores the particular input word in a register and generates an interrupt. The computer acknowledges this interrupt, so requesting a transfer of data onto the 16-bit parallel data bus via a serial-parallel tri-state register. Since the ARINC 575 word is 32-bits long, transfer takes place in two sections.

Memory The navigation computer program is stored in a 20K × 16-bit word (K = 1024) UVEROM (ultraviolet erasable ROM) which can be programmed from cassette tape using a programming adapter. The data is retained in the UVEROM for an estimated 100 years unless erased by exposing all twenty chips to ultraviolet light.

Additional memory is provided on the computer/processor card in the form of a 2K word scratch pad RAM for temporary storage and a 128-word data save memory used to store present position, time/date, waypoints and additional data required to resume normal operations after a temporary power failure. Back-up power for data save is provided by a 4500 μF capacitor for at least 7 min.

The Computer The computer uses the input and stored data referred to in the above paragraphs to carry out the necessary navigation problem computations and to output the resulting information. The microprocessor employed is a TMS-9900, a 16-bit CPU (central processing unit) capable of addressing 32K words of length 16 bits.

Input/output (I/O) functions are treated in the same way as memory for addressing purposes, the address map being split into sixteen sections, twelve of which are assigned to UVEROM and two each to RAM, save data memory, steering interface I/O and other I/O. As an example F A 0 0 hexadecimal = $15 \times 16^3 + 10 \times 16^2 + 0 \times 16^1 + 0 \times 16^0 = 64\,000_{10}$, is the address of the digital multiplexer phase sensor word which will contain phase measurement data corresponding to 10·2, 11·3 or 13·6 kHz depending

on which interrupt is being serviced. Not all the available addresses are assigned in the LTN-211.

The computer can recognize sixteen interrupt levels with the highest priority level 0 and the lowest priority level 15. An interrupt mask is contained in a status register and continuously compared with the system-generated interrupt code. When the level of the pending interrupt is less than or equal to the current-enabling interrupt mask level (higher or equal priority) the processor recognizes the interrupt. On recognition the current instruction is completed, details of the position in current program stored, the appropriate interrupt service routine started, and the interrupt mask forced to a level that is one less than the level of the interrupt being serviced. When the interrupt routine is complete the interrupted program continues where it left off. In the LTN-211 seven interrupt levels are implemented:

0   reset (power on);
1   pending power fail or program cycle fail;
2   10·2 kHz sensor data input;
3   13·6 kHz sensor data input;
4   11·3 kHz sensor data input;
5   reserved for a sensor data input;
6   CDU ARINC data ready;
7   ARINC receiver data ready.

Computer Outputs A 16-bit word is transmitted to the receiver module for control of the antenna-switching matrix and the antenna-calibrate functions.

Various output functions respond only to the address bus state and do not require specific data to be placed on the output bus. These functions, with hexadecimal addresses are:

reset program cycle fail (F100), select analogue multiplexer address (F2X0), start analogue to digital converter (F300), acknowledge c.d.u. ARINC Rx (F600) and ARINC interrupt acknowledgement (CFAO).

The 'X' in address F2X0 can be any number from 0 to 7 depending on the function, e.g. heading sine, heading cosine, speed sine, etc.

Signals associated with other systems and instruments are output from the computer via the steering interface which is divided into three main sections: (1) analogue functions; (2) digital communications; (3) discrete flag drivers.

The analogue interface card provides four three-wire synchro outputs and both high- and low-level two-wire d.c. cross-track deviation. Digital data is fed to the analogue card on the data bus and converted to d.c.

in a digital to analogue converter. The analogue d.c. signal is fed in parallel to sample and hold circuits addressed by the computer via a decoder. Each of the synchro channels has a modulator for the sine and cosine d.c. inputs followed by a Scott-T transformer which provides the three-wire synchro output. The particular outputs are determined by the state of two synchro output select program pins, ground or open. In this way synchro number 1 will give heading or track, synchro number 2 will give ± drift angle or track angle error, synchro number 3 will give track angle error + drift angle, track angle error or desired track angle while synchro number 4 will give aircraft steering or track angle error.

The digital interface card has been referred to above in connection with its input function. In addition there are ARINC 575 and ARINC 561 serial digital outputs, two-wire b.c.d./binary for the 575 and six-wire (clock, sync and data) for the 561. The ARINC transmitters are selected when the appropriate data is on the data bus by suitable addressing from the computer. The output word is 32 bits long, and so must be entered into a register in two parts under the control of the address bus. Parallel to serial conversion takes place when the word is assembled in the register.

Flag signals at TTL levels are output from the computer and latched via drivers. The signals are then buffered, scaled and/or level shifted before output.

Characteristics

Much of this section on ONS has been based on the Litton-211 which is an ARINC 599 system. This being so, what follows is a particularly brief summary of the ARINC Mark 2 ONS since details such as input and output have already been covered.

The system comprises three units: a receiver processor, control/display and antenna/coupler unit which, together are capable of receiving and processing Omega ground station signals (v.l.f. not precluded) so as to provide minimum functional capabilities of present position readout and horizontal track navigation. The system should operate worldwide with a present position error of less than 7 nautical miles.

The power supply for the system is 115 V 400 Hz single phase fed via a circuit breaker. In addition a 26 V 400 Hz reference in accordance with ARINC 413A will need to be supplied via a circuit breaker from the appropriate instrumentation bus for excitation of synchros.

Ramp Testing

Little needs to be said here since the computing power of an ONS is such that comprehensive monitoring and self-test routines may be incorporated in the system software. Monitoring of system performance takes place virtually continuously during flight. In addition, operator error detection aids smooth operation and a reduction in reported defects due to 'finger trouble'. With a malfunction code readout and self-test display, turn-round delays for ONS. installation defect investigation and repair are minimized.

The Decca Navigator

Introduction

Decca navigator was invented in America by W. J. O'Brien but first used by the British in the closing stages of World War II. Since then a number of marks of the equipment have emerged from the continuous development of this, the most accurate of all the radio navigation aids. The system came second in the two-horse race for adoption by the ICAO as the standard short-range navigation system. That it survived is a credit to the Decca Navigator Company whose confidence in the basic merits of the system were such that it continued its airborne development program despite the setback in 1949.

Decca is a low-frequency c.w. hyperbolic navigation system. The service is provided for suitably equipped aircraft, ships and land vehicles by chains of transmitting stations. Each chain comprises a master station and normally three slave stations, all at known geographical locations (typically 70 miles apart), radiating phase-locked signals. The choice of frequency could give a ground wave coverage of 1000 nautical miles but c.w. operation prevents the separation of ground and sky wave signals so the usable range is limited to about 240 nautical miles by night and about twice that by day. There are chains in various parts of the world, in particular north-west Europe and the north-east seaboard of North America.

Phase differences between the master station and each of its slaves are displayed to the pilot on three phase meters or Decometers. The observed phase differences identify hyperbolic lines marked on specially prepared charts. By noting at least two phase readings the pilot can plot his position as the intersection of the corresponding lines. For ease of use the charts are printed with the three different families of hyperbolic lines in purple, red and green, hence the red slave station and the green Decometer, etc. Decometers are still used but for airborne systems, automatic and computer-based methods are usually found, with aircraft position being shown on a roller map (flight log display).

The Radiated Signals

Each chain is assigned a fundamental frequency f in the range 14-14·33 kHz. The stations each radiate a harmonic of f, namely $6f$ from the master and $5f$, $8f$ and $9f$ from the purple, red and green slaves respectively. Thus with $f = 14$ kHz we have radiated frequencies of $6f = 84$ kHz, $5f = 70$ kHz, $8f = 112$ kHz and $9f = 126$ kHz. Using different frequencies for the stations in a chain allows separation in the airborne receiver.

Decca chains are designed by an alphanumeric code. The basic codes are 0B, 1B, ..., 10B, the corresponding fundamental frequencies being separated by a nominal 30 Hz (separation is 29·17, 30 or 30·83 Hz). A subdivision of this basic allocation is provided by the so-called 'half frequencies' 0E, 1E, ..., 9E which have a nominal spacing of 15 Hz from the B fundamental frequencies. Additional subdivision is achieved by the use of frequencies 5/6 Hz above and below the B and E frequencies to give groups of six frequencies designated by the appropriate number and the letters A, B, C, D, E, F. An example of a group of frequencies is given in Table 6.3 showing code, fundamental and master ($6f$) frequencies; the slave frequencies are pro-rata.

Table 6.3 Decca frequencies — numerical group 5

Chain code	Fundamental 1f (Hz)	Master 6f (Hz)
5A	14 165·83	84 995
5B	14 166·67	85 000
5C	14 167·50	85 005
5D	14 180·83	85 085
5E	14 181·67	85 090
5F	14 182·50	85 095

Position Fixing

As with any hyperbolic system two hyperbolic lines of position must be identified, the fix being given by where they intersect. With Decca the hyperbolic patterns are divided into zones and lanes. Zones are designated by letters A to J starting at the master end of the master/slave base line. The sequence of letters repeats as necessary to cover the whole pattern (Fig. 6.18). Along the base line, zones have a constant width of between 10·47 and 10·71 km, corresponding to half a wavelength at the

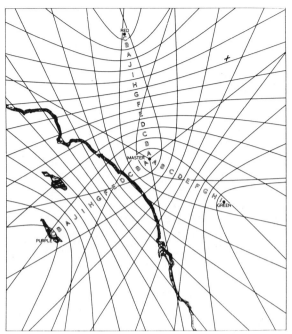

Fig. 6.18 Zone patterns (courtesy the Decca Navigator Co. Ltd)

fundamental frequency of the chain.

The zones are subdivided in two ways, depending on the method of phase comparison used in the aircraft. The transmitted signals cannot be compared in phase directly since they are of different frequencies; frequency multiplication or division may be used to bring the signals to a common frequency.

Since the transmitted frequencies are related to the fundamental by multipliers 5, 6, 8 and 9 (purple, master, red and green respectively) comparison can take place at the l.c.m. of any two of the multipliers which include 6. Thus purple and master transmissions can be phase compared at $30f$, i.e. at between 420 and 429·9 kHz. Similarly the red and green comparison frequencies are $24f$ and $18f$ respectively. A lane is defined as the region between hyperbolic lines with zero phase difference at the comparison frequency, i.e. every half-wavelength (Fig. 6.4). Thus there are 30 purple, 24 red and 18 green lanes per zone with baseline widths of approximately 352 m, 440 m and 587 m respectively.

Lane numbering starts from the master and runs 0-23 for red, 30-47 for green and 50-79 for purple. Decometers can be read to one or two hundredths of a lane. Figure 6.19 illustrates a position fix in terms of lanes: the red Decometer reads zone I (bottom window), lane 16 (outer scale), lane fraction 0·30

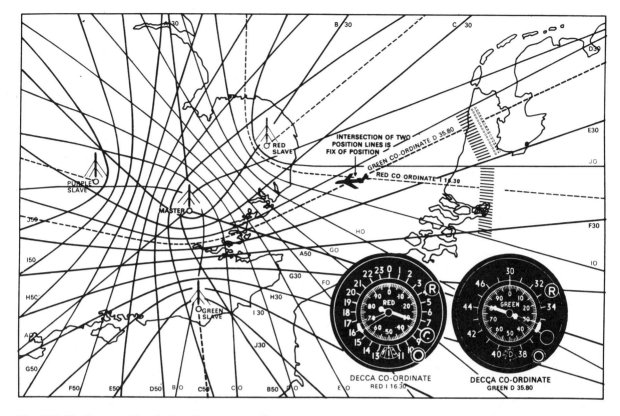

Fig. 6.19 Plotting a position fix from Decometer readings (courtesy the Decca Navigator Co. Ltd)

(inner scale) while the green Decometer reads zone D, lane 35, lane fraction 0·80. Thus the Decca co-ordinates are I 16·30 and D 35·80, intersecting as shown.

The accuracy obtained by using frequency multiplication is often not required for air navigation; furthermore a better s.n.r. can be achieved by dividing the received signals down to the fundamental. Since phase comparison is at f the zones are the 'lanes' for a dividing type receiver. Fractions of a zone are measured to a resolution of 1/1024, i.e. just over 10 m.

Resolving Lane Ambiguities
Since each lane appears to be the same, in so far as phase difference measurement is concerned, the pilot should know where he is, to within half a lane, in order to initially set the appropriate Decometer by hand. Thereafter, since through gearing the lane fraction pointer drives the lane pointer and zone read-out, the Decometer will record the correct co-ordinate by an integration process. Any interruption in reception would require a resetting of the Decometers.

Although the dividing type receiver does not measure lanes there is still ambiguity within a zone caused by the division process. For example dividing the master signal by six gives rise to an output which can start on any of six cycles, only one of which is correct. The ambiguous cycles are known as notches. The resulting ambiguity is the same as described in the previous paragraph since, for example, an error of +1 notch in the master divider output gives an error in the zone fraction reading of 1/6 while an error of −1 notch in the red divider output gives an error in the zone fraction reading of 1/8. The net error in the red zone fraction reading would be $1/6 − 1/8 = 1/24$ zone or 1 lane.

To resolve lane ambiguities most Decca chains operate in the MP (multipulse) mode (an older V mode will not be discussed here). Each station in turn, starting with the master, transmits all four frequencies ($5f$, $6f$, $8f$, $9f$) simultaneously. A sequence of transmissions lasts 20 s during which time each station transmits the MP signals for 0·45 s. In the receiver the four frequencies are summed, producing a composite waveform which has a

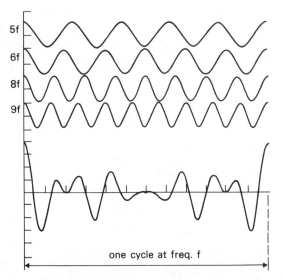

5f

6f

8f

9f

one cycle at freq. f

Fig. 6.20 Multipulse transmission – summation (courtesy the Decca Navigator Co. Ltd)

predominant spike or pulse occurring at the fundamental rate (Fig. 6.20).

In a receiver employing the multiplying method, with readout on Decometers, lane ambiguity is resolved by feeding a lane identification meter such that one arm of a six-armed vernier pointer, identified by a rotating sector, indicates the correct lane. The sector is driven in accordance with the phase difference between 1/6 of the master transmission (remembered during the MP transmission by a phase-locked oscillator) and the fundamental derived from an MP transmission. The vernier pointer is driven in accordance with the phase difference between the master transmission and six times the fundamental derived from an MP transmission, the drive being through 1 : 6 gearing. During the master MP transmission the lane identification meter should read zero and may be adjusted to do so if in error.

Fig. 6.21 Mk 19 Decca Navigation System (courtesy the Decca Navigator Co. Ltd)

As each MP transmission occurs the appropriate Decometer lane reading should correspond to the lane identification meter reading and may be adjusted if necessary. The current lane identification may be held to assist checking but will only be valid for a few seconds due to aircraft movement.

In a receiver employing the dividing method the MP transmissions provide a reference frequency f with which the phase of each divider output can be compared. The phase comparison and subsequent correction takes place automatically within the divider circuits. This process, known as notching, removes ambiguity from the zone fraction data.

Resolving Zone Ambiguity

We have seen how the particular lane (within a zone) in which the aircraft is flying can be identified but the possibility of an incorrect zone reading still exists since zones, like lanes, are indistinguishable by the normal phase measurements. A zone identification meter resolves the zone ambiguity, not completely but to within a group of five zones, i.e. a distance of over 50 km on the baseline.

An $8.2f$ signal is transmitted with the MP signals from each station in turn. A beat note between the $8f$ and $8.2f$ components of an MP transmission is produced having a frequency of $f/5$. The master beat frequency is 'remembered' and compared with each slave beat frequency in turn. The resulting hyperbolic pattern has zero phase differences on lines five zones apart, giving the required resolution.

Installation

Different options are available two of which are shown in Figs 6.21 and 6.22. The Mk 19 receiver is capable of driving Decometers (or digital readout) and/or a flight log; the multiplying method is used to drive the Decometers while the dividing method is used to drive the flight log through a computer unit. The Mk 15 receiver uses the dividing method only with readout on a flight log.

Where space is at a premium, a Dectrac position fixing unit (PFU) may be installed in conjunction with either a Mk 15 or Mk 19 receiver. The Dectrac PFU contains one indicator with four scales and a single pointer, effectively replacing the Decometers but not allowing the same degree of accuracy in reading, although this may be recovered by the addition of another small unit. A zone identity reading can be taken from the single indicator.

A capacitive type antenna is used, comprising a copper mesh within a fibreglass plate mounted flush with the aircraft skin. The mesh is at least 2 ft^2 in area. A pre-amplifier/matching unit allows a long

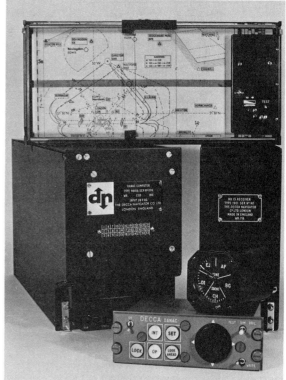

Fig. 6.22 Decca Mk 15/Danac navigation system (courtesy the Decca Navigator Co. Ltd)

feeder run. The antenna should be mounted as near to the centre of the aircraft as possible, either above or below the fuselage. If below a fixed 180° phase shift is applied in the pre-amplifier.

Mk 15/Danac Block Diagram Operation

Figure 6.23 shows a simplified block diagram of a Mk 15/Danac installation. A significant feature of the system is the degree of automatic control achieved.

The receiver output is fed to the computer as four pulse trains representing the received master, red, green and purple signals divided down to the fundamental frequency f. The master/slave phase differences at f are digitally measured in the computer, thus giving three hyperbolic lines of position each derived as a 10-bit binary number representing 1/1024 of a zone.

The computer converts the Decca co-ordinates into X and Y demand signals for the servos driving the laterally moving stylus and the vertically moving chart respectively. The major computing effort is carried out off-line on a more powerful computer which calculates constants to be used in the hyperbolic to X-Y conversion. These constants are written on a

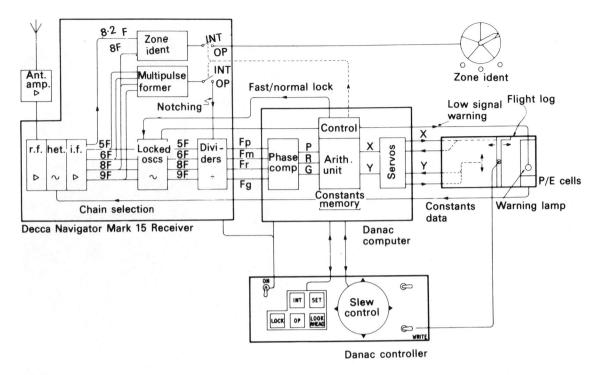

Fig. 6.23 Decca Mk 15/Danac navigation system block diagram (courtesy the Decca Navigator Co. Ltd)

non-visible part of the chart, among other data, in the form of a black and white ten-track digital Gray code read by a line of ten photoelectric cells.

The Y servo position feedback signal is in the form of a 9-bit word derived from nine of the digital tracks referred to above. The X servo position feedback signal is a 9-bit word derived from printed circuit tracks read by wiper contacts mounted on the stylus carriage. The servo drives are, of course, the differences between the demand and feedback signals.

Selection of the correct Decca chain is automatically achieved by including the code representing the frequency among the constants read by the photoelectric cells. Other data among the constants are the zone values for one or two checkpoints on the chart (to which the stylus goes initially) and the chart scale.

Setting up is largely automatic. If the required chart is in view the following sequence takes place when the system is switched on:

1. pushbutton lamps light for checking purposes, and the chart constants are read into the computer;
2. the stylus moves to a check point and receiver locks on to required signals;

3. zone fraction computation takes place using MP transmissions for notching;
4. stylus takes up a position within a zone on the chart corresponding to the aircraft position within the true zone. If the zone is correct the OP button is pressed and thereafter the stylus and chart should move so as to follow the aircraft's movements. If the stylus is in the wrong zone it may be manually set by pressing SET and operating the pressure-sensitive slewing control.

The correct zone is known from the zone identification indicator and the pilot's knowledge of his position to within five zone widths. When the aircraft 'flies off' the current chart and on to the next (on the same chart roll) the stylus goes straight to the aircraft position on the new chart except under certain conditions, e.g. chain change, in which case the above initial procedure relating to zone identification and slewing is carried out.

The pilot may bring another chart into view by pressing LOOK AHEAD and operating the slewing control. Pressing the LOOK AHEAD button a second time causes the new chart to remain in view, otherwise the stylus is returned to the aircraft's present position (still calculated during LOOK AHEAD) on the previous chart.

Pressing the INT button causes the system to go into the integration only mode where the MP and zone identification facilities are switched off. It may be desirable to select INT when flying in a fringe area since spurious or imperfect notching signals may cause the warning lamp to come on, indicating a discrepancy between displayed position and receiver output. On some charts covering fringe areas or chains without MP transmissions, INT is selected automatically by a suitable chart constant.

The LOCK button has several functions, one of which is to put the receiver phase-locked oscillator into a fast lock condition, providing the warning lamp is on. It may also be used to initiate the automatic setting-up routine when a new chart, brought into view by LOOK AHEAD, does not have the same colours as the previous chart.

The stylus may be prevented from marking the chart by selecting WRITE off, otherwise the track of the aircraft will be traced out on the chart. The TEST-DIM-BRIL switch is the only control not previously mentioned, it may be used for lamp test or to select the brightness level of the lamps.

The above description is sketchy to say the least, but I hope it will give the reader an idea of how one Decca Navigator system configuration performs its function.

Loran C

Introduction
Loran A was proposed in the USA in 1940, had trials in 1942 and was implemented over much of the north and west Atlantic in 1943. Since then coverage has been extended to many of the oceanic air routes of the world, but some time in 1980 the last Loran A transmitter should be switched off. Since the implementation of Loran A the family has been extended to B, C and D. Loran B was found to be impractical and Loran D is a short-range, low-altitude system intended for use where line-of-sight system coverage is inadequate.

Loran C is a long-range, pulsed hyperbolic navigation aid with accuracy approaching that of Decca under favourable circumstances. It was introduced in 1960 and now provides a valuable service in many parts of the world, in particular the north and east Pacific and Atlantic. The system is used by many ships and aircraft and would appear to have an indefinite future.

Chain Layout
A transmitter, designated the master, has associated with it, up to four slave transmitters designated W, X, Y and Z. The master occupies a central position surrounded by the slaves so far as the geography allows. Base lines are of the order of 500-1000 nautical miles over sea but are reduced over land.

The range of the system is about 1000 nautical miles (from master) using groundwaves and up to about 2000 nautical miles using skywaves. The accuracy depends on the geometry of the chain but may be in the order of about 400 ft at 350 nautical miles range to 1700 ft at 1000 nautical miles range provided groundwaves are used. With skywaves the accuracy would be in the order of 10 nautical miles at 1500 nautical miles range.

The Radiated Signals
Pulses of 100 kHz r.f. are transmitted from all stations. The slave transmissions are synchronized with those of the master either directly (triggered by master groundwave) or by use of atomic clocks. The delay between the time of transmission of the master and each slave (coding delay) is fixed so that wherever the aircraft receiver is located in the area covered, the slave signals will always arrive in the same order after the master.

Since all chains transmit the same r.f., mutual interference must be avoided by use of different pulse repetition periods (p.r.p.) for each chain. There are a total of six so-called basic rates, each of which have eight specific rates as given in Table 6.4. The chains are identified by their p.r.p., thus chain SS7 (Eastern seaboard of North America) has a basic rate period of 100 000 μs (SS) which is reduced by 700 μs since the specific rate is 7, hence the period between transmissions from the master (and from each slave) is 99 300 μs, i.e. fractionally over 10 transmissions per

Table 6.4   Basic and specific rates for Loran C

Basic repetition period (μs)		Specific periods (subtract) (μs)	
H	30 000	0	0
L	40 000	1	100
S	50 000	2	200
SH	60 000	3	300
SL	80 000	4	400
SS	100 000	5	500
		6	600
		7	700
		8	800

second. Not all the basic rates are in use and indeed some may never be used since 6 X 8 = 48 chains are unlikely to be needed.

Groups of eight pulses of r.f. are transmitted from each station once during a repetition period. With synchronous detection in the receiver the eight pulses are combined to give a much better s.n.r. than one would obtain with a single pulse. The spacing between pulses within a group is 1 ms. The master transmits a ninth pulse in its group, 2 ms after the eighth, for identification.

Some types of interference (e.g. skywave contamination) can be discriminated against by use of phase coding. The r.f. of certain pulses within a group has its phase reversed; unless this is properly decoded in the receiver synchronous detection will give a loss of signal power. Additionally, since master and slave phase coding is different for a particular chain, decoding can be used to separate the received master signals from the slave signals.

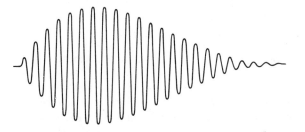

Fig. 6.24 Loran C pulse and pulse format

The pulse duration is approximately 270 μs, i.e. a total of about 27 cycles of r.f. in each pulse. To radiate a pulse of short rise-time leads to problems in frequency spectrum spreading and transmitting antenna design at the low carrier frequency involved. In fact 99 per cent of the radiated energy must be in the band 90-110 kHz, hence the slow rise and decay time illustrated in Fig. 6.24 (in which the signal format, master and three slaves, is also shown). The maximum amplitude occurs by the eighth cycle.

Principles of Operation
The basic principles of a pulsed hyperbolic navigation aid have been given earlier in the chapter.

To measure the time difference between master and slave transmissions corresponding 'events' must be identified in each. Obviously from Fig. 6.24 it is impractical to measure from leading edge to leading edge or even to use the lagging edges, consequently one of the cycles must be chosen in master and slave transmissions and the time between them measured. Such a process is known as cycle matching or indexing.

From the point of view of s.n.r. the eighth cycle is the obvious one for indexing; however it may be subject to skywave contamination and therefore difficult to identify. The minimum difference in propagation times between skywave and groundwave is 30 μs, so up to and including the third cycle the pulse is clear. For this reason the third cycle is usually chosen for indexing, particularly in fully automatic equipment.

An automatic receiver would select the third cycle by looking for the unique change of amplitude between the second and fourth cycle; in this way the indexing circuits are able to lock on. The transmission of the first eight pulses must be accurate and consistent since an error in indexing of one cycle would give a 10 μs time difference error.

If indexing is carried out manually using a c.r.t. to display the pulses, on time-bases of decreasing duration as the process proceeds, use of up to the eighth cycle may be possible with a skilled operator.

Installation
A Loran C system may consist of up to five units, namely antenna, antenna coupler, receiver, c.r.t. indicator and control unit. A c.r.t. display is used where the indexing procedure is manual or where, if automatic, it is thought necessary to provide the operator with monitoring of the procedure. On some systems indexing is manual but thereafter the third cycle is tracked automatically.

Figure 6.25 shows the Decca ADL-81 Loran C/D receiver and control indicator; an aerial and coupler would be needed to complete the installation. The ADL-81 is fully automatic providing digital time difference readouts with a resolution of 100 ns on the control indicator and 50 ns via a computer interface. Synchronization provides third cycle indexing in groundwave cover and optimum cycle indexing during skywave working. Three time-differences are computed, two of which may be displayed. Tunable automatic notch filters provide rejection of the strongest interfering signals. Overall system performance checks may be performed using built in test equipment (BITE).

The antenna is usually a capacitive type, sometimes

Fig. 6.25 ADL-81 Loran C/D (courtesy the Decca Navigator Co. Ltd)

serving both ADF sense and Loran, in which case an antenna coupler would provide the necessary impedance matching and isolation for the two receivers served. A pre-amplifier may be included for the Loran feed.

Block Diagram Operation

The received signals are separated into master and slave groups by the phase decode circuits, the groups being fed to the appropriate master and slave phase lock loops (p.l.l.). In Fig. 6.26 only one slave p.l.l. is shown but in practice there will be a minimum of two, to provide the two hyperbolic l.o.p. required for a fix. Three slave p.l.l.s would enable an automatic system to select the two which gave the best angle of cut, although the calculations involved would probably be carried out by a computer to which the three time-difference readings would be fed.

Gate pulse formers feed the p.l.l.s with a series of eight pulses spaced by 1 ms and of, say, 5 μs duration. The object of the p.l.l. is to provide a signal to the appropriate oscillator, driving the corresponding gate pulse former, so that the phase of the oscillator, and hence timing of the gate pulse, is altered such that each gate pulse is coincident with some specific point on the third cycle in any received pulse. The rate at which the gate pulse groups are generated is set to equal the rate of the required chain.

The basic idea of indexing, as carried out by the p.l.l.s, is as follows. In Fig. 6.27 line 1 is a representation of the leading edge of a received pulse. Line 2 is a representation of the leading edge of a

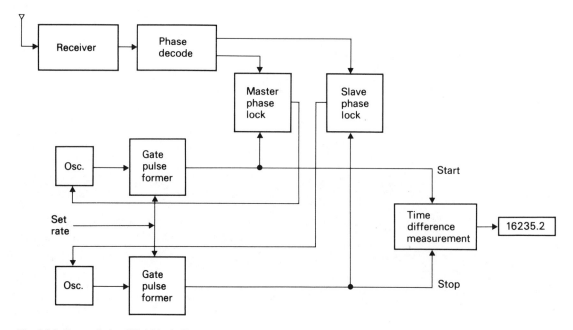

Fig. 6.26 Loran C simplified block diagram

16235.2

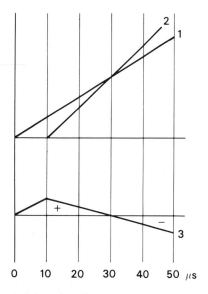

Fig. 6.27 A method of indexing

received pulse after it has been delayed by 10 μs and amplified by a factor of 1·5. It can be seen that lines 1 and 2 cross at a time 30 μs after the pulse leading edge. Line 3 is a representation of the result of subtracting the delayed and amplified received pulse from the received pulse. Since the crossover point of this difference signal is at 30 μs it can be used as a servo signal to set the gate pulse timing for coincidence with the third cycle. The full bandwidth of 20 kHz is required to preserve pulse shape during the indexing process, although initial signal acquisition may take place with a restricted bandwidth in order to improve the s.n.r.

Once phase lock is established, time-difference readout is easily achieved by starting and stopping a counter with the master and appropriate slave gate pulse group respectively.

Acquisition of the received master and slave pulses, i.e. the initial alignment to a point where the p.l.l. can take over, may be carried out by the operator or automatically. With manual acquisition both received pulses and gate pulses are displayed on a c.r.t.; a slewing control allows the operator to align the gate pulses with the third cycle of the received pulses by use of different time-base selections for the A-type display (time-base horizontal deflection, signal vertical deflection). With automatic acquisition the gate pulse groups must be slewed or swept automatically until the p.l.l. can track successfully.

7 Distance measuring equipment

Introduction

Distance measuring equipment (DME) is a secondary radar pulsed ranging system operating in the band 978-1213 MHz. The origins of this equipment date back to the Rebecca-Eureka system developed in Britain during World War II. International agreement on the characteristics of the current system was not reached until 1959 but since then implementation has been rapid.

The system provides slant range to a beacon at a fixed point on the ground. The difference between slant range and ground range, which is needed for navigation purposes, is small unless the aircraft is very high or close to the beacon. Figure 7.1 shows the relationship between slant range, ground range and height to be:

$$S^2 = G^2 + (H/6080)^2 \qquad (7.1)$$

ignoring the curvature of the earth. To see the effect of this consider an error in range of 1 per cent, i.e. $S = 1 \cdot 01G$. Substituting for G, rearranging and evaluating we have:

$$S \doteq H/853$$

for a 1 per cent error. Thus at 30 000 ft if the DME readout is greater than about 35 nautical miles the error is less than 1 per cent, while at 5000 ft greater than about 6 nautical miles readout will similarly give an error less than 1 per cent.

Giving range, DME alone can only be used for position fixing in a rho-rho scheme, three readings being needed to remove ambiguity. With the addition of bearing information, such as that derived from VOR, we have a rho-theta scheme; DME and

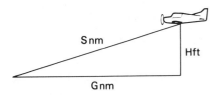

Fig. 7.1 Slant range/ground range triangle

VOR in fact provide the standard ICAO short-range navigation system. A DME beacon may also be located on an airfield equipped with ILS, thus giving continuous slant range readout while on an ILS approach, such use of DME is limited at present.

TACAN is a military system which gives both range and bearing with respect to a fixed beacon. The ranging part of TACAN has the same characteristics as civil DME. There are, however, more channels available with TACAN since it utilizes an extended frequency range of 962-1213 MHz. Thus a civil aircraft equipped with DME can obtain range measurement from a TACAN beacon provided the DME can be tuned to the operating frequency of the TACAN concerned. Many civil aircraft carry a DME which covers the full frequency range.

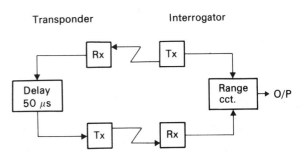

Fig. 7.2 The d.m.e. system

Basic Principles

The airborne interrogator radiates coded r.f. pulse pairs at a frequency within the band 978-1213 MHz from an omnidirectional antenna. A ground transponder (the beacon), within range of the aircraft and operating on the channel to which the interrogator is selected, receives the interrogation and automatically triggers the beacon transmitter after a fixed delay of 50 μs. The omnidirectional radiation from the beacon is coded r.f. pulse pairs at a frequency 63 MHz below or above the interrogation frequency. This reply is received by the suitably tuned interrogator receiver and after processing is fed to the range circuits where the round trip travel time is computed. Range is given by:

$$R = (T - 50)/12 \cdot 359 \qquad (7.2)$$

where: R is the slant range distance in nautical miles to or from the beacon; T is the time in microseconds (μs) between transmission of the interrogation and reception of the reply. The constants in the equation are 50 μs corresponding to the fixed beacon delay, $12 \cdot 359$ μs being the time taken for r.f. energy to travel 1 nautical mile and return.

Both beacon and transponder use a single omnidirectional antenna shared between transmitter and receiver in each case. This is possible since the system is pulsed, and diplexing is simple since the transmit and receive frequencies are different.

Once every 30 s the beacon transmits its identity which is detected by the pilot as a Morse code burst of three letters at an audio tone of 1350 Hz. It should be noted that the r.f. radiated from the beacon during identification is of the same form as when transmitting replies, i.e. pulse pairs. The difference is that when replying there are random intervals between transmissions whereas during identification the intervals are constant at 1/1350th of a second.

Further Principles and Terminology

By now the reader may have identified several problems with the principles of system operation as described. With DME, many aircraft will be asking the beacon 'what is my range?', the beacon will reply to all of them, the problem being how each is to identify its own reply. Another problem is how to prevent the airborne DME interrogating an out-of-range beacon since this would be wasteful of equipment life.

It is obvious that the DME operation must be in at least two phases since we cannot expect an instantaneous readout of the correct range the moment we select a beacon. There must be some period when the DME is acquiring the range followed by a period, hopefully much longer, during which the indicator continuously displays the correct reading. In this latter period we must consider the eventuality of a temporary loss of reply such as occurs during the transmission of the identification (ident) signal by the beacon, or perhaps during 'manoeuvre' when all signals might be lost.

We have assumed that the r.f. energy will travel in a straight line from aircraft to beacon and back. This of course will be the case unless there are any obstructions intervening; however, it is possible that there may be more than one path to or from the beacon if there are reflecting objects inconveniently placed with respect to the aircraft and the beacon. This possibility arises since the antennas at both ends of the link are omnidirectional. Should such a 'dog leg' path occur, the round-trip travel time T in equation (7.2) may be that for the long way round and thus lead to a readout in excess of true short range.

To describe the way in which the system design copes with this it is necessary to introduce several new terms which are defined and explained below.

Jitter Deliberate random variation of the time interval between successive interrogations. Each interrogator produces a 'jittering pulse (pair) repetition frequency (p.r.f.)' which, over a period of several interrogations, describes a unique pattern since the variations are random. With an interrogation rate of, say, 100, the average interval between interrogations will be 10 ms, with any particular interval being between say 9 and 11 ms. The unique interrogation pattern enables the DME to recognize replies to its own interrogation by stroboscopic techniques.

Automatic Standby Often referred to as signal-activated search. When the aircraft is out of range of the beacon to which the airborne DME is tuned, no signals will be received. This state inhibits interrogations until such time as the aircraft is within range and signals are received.

The implementation of this feature determines whether interrogations commence as a result of mean signal level exceeding some predetermined level or the rate of signals being received exceeds some predetermined rate. The two alternatives are equivalent as the aircraft approaches the beacon from beyond maximum range, and typically interrogations commence when the received signal count is in excess of 300-400 per second. They are not equivalent when the aircraft is close to the beacon since the mean signal level will be raised due to signal strength; consequently the required rate is much reduced for the former alternative. This is of little consequence when the aircraft is well within range; one would not expect the DME to be on auto standby. When ground testing, however, an auto standby circuit which monitors mean signal level can give unexpected, but not unexplainable, results since the test set (beacon simulator) will normally output constant-strength signals regardless of range simulated.

Squitter The auto standby circuit will not allow interrogations to commence until it detects signals from the beacon. When a sufficient number of interrogating aircraft are within range of the beacon there is no problem, since another aircraft coming within range will receive all the replies and thus begin to interrogate. If, however, we consider the beacon having just come on line or the first flight, after a quiet period, approaching the beacon, we have a chicken-and-egg situation: the beacon will not reply unless interrogated; the interrogator will not interrogate unless it receives signals.

From the explanation thus far there are in fact signals available, namely ident, but this means an aircraft may have to wait 30 s, perhaps more in weak signal areas, before coming out of auto standby. This is unacceptable; consequently the beacon is made to transmit pulse pairs even in the absence of interrogations. Such transmissions from the ground beacon are known collectively as 'squitter' to distinguish them from replies. When the random squitter pulse pairs are received the airborne equipment starts to interrogate.

A beacon must transmit randomly distributed pulse pairs at a repetition rate of at least 700; this minimum rate includes distance replies as well as squitter. Beacons which supply a full TACAN service, i.e. range and bearing, must maintain a rate of 2700 pulse pairs per second. In order to achieve this during ident an equalizing pair of pulses is transmitted 100 μs after each identity pair. A range-only DME beacon at a constant duty cycle of 2700 pulse pairs per second is not ruled out.

If we consider the case of a beacon with a constant duty cycle in a quiet period all transmitted pulse pairs are squitter, apart from during the dots and dashes of the ident signal transmission. With one aircraft using the beacon interrogating at a rate of, say, 27 then the number of squitter pulse pairs will be $2700 - 27 = 2673$ s^{-1} while the reply pulse pairs will number 27 s^{-1}. Two aircraft would lead to a squitter rate of 2646 s^{-1} and a reply rate of 54 s^{-1} and so on until we arrive at a condition of beacon saturation with a nominal maximum of 100 aircraft interrogating. We can see that all the squitter pulse pairs have become synchronized with received interrogations. From the interrogator's point of view all received pulse pairs appear to be squitter except those identified by the range circuits as being replies to its own interrogations.

Maintaining a constant duty cycle for the beacon is achieved by varying the receiver sensitivity. When no interrogations are received sensitivity is sufficiently high for noise to trigger the beacon modulator 2700 times per second. As interrogations are received the sensitivity decreases so maintaining the duty cycle.

Should more than 2700 interrogations per second be received the sensitivity is reduced still further, thus maintaining the service for those aircraft closest to the beacon.

In fact the nominal maximum of 100 aircraft is exceeded since interrogation rates on track (*see below*) are considerably less than twenty-seven for modern equipment, and further the interrogator does not need 100 per cent replies in order to maintain readout of range. The beacon capability of 100 aircraft may be reduced if peak traffic is much less than this figure.

Search During search the range-measuring circuits of the interrogator have not recognized those pulses amongst the total received which have the same jittering pattern as the interrogation. The interrogation rate is high so as to decrease search time, the maximum rate allowed being 150 s^{-1}. The search time in a modern equipment is typically less than 1 s. A p.r.f. of 135 is avoided since it may cause interference with the bearing measurement function of TACAN. The readout will be obscured by a 'flag' if of the mechanical type, or will be blanked if electronic. The counter drums of an electro-mechanical indicator can be seen to be rotating when the interrogator is searching; an electronic indicator may have a lamp or l.e.d. which illuminates during search.

It is an ICAO recommendation that if after 15 000 pairs of pulses have been transmitted without acquiring indication of distance then the p.r.f. should not exceed 60 until a change in operating channel is made or a successful search is completed. In practice use of automatic standby circuits and search p.r.f.s as low as, say, 40 in modern equipments makes this recommendation redundant.

Track During track the range-measuring circuits, having acquired the reply pulses, follow their early or late arrival as the aircraft moves towards or away from the beacon. Continuous range readout is given with the 'flag' out of view. The p.r.f. is low. In order to optimize beacon capability a maximum average p.r.f. of 30 is laid down. This assumes that 95 per cent of the time is occupied by tracking, thus:

$$95T + 5S \leqslant 3000 \tag{7.3}$$
where: T is the track p.r.f. and S the search p.r.f.

In practice modern equipments may have track p.r.f.s of less than 10.

In some equipments the transition from search to track, during which the range measuring circuits check they have in fact acquired the correct signals, is known as acquisition. It is convenient to identify this event by a separate term since it takes a finite, though short, time and the equipment is neither searching nor tracking.

Memory If replies are lost an interrogator will not immediately revert to search or auto standby but will enter its memory condition; this may be one of two types, either static or velocity. With static memory the readout is maintained steady, whereas with velocity memory the readout continues to change at its last known rate. Memory time will normally lie between 4 and 12 s.

If, during memory, replies are re-acquired, the equipment will continue tracking; thus the pilot will have been spared a false warning. At the end of memory, if there are no signals at all being received, auto standby will ensue; otherwise the equipment will commence searching.

Echo Protection The possibility of the interrogator tracking replies which have suffered reflection must be guarded against, both on the ground, for the interrogation path, and in the air, for the reply path.

On the ground, depending on the geography of the terrain, the reflected or echo interrogation will arrive a short time after the line-of-sight interrogation. Thus if the ground receiver is suppressed for long enough after reception of an interrogation the echo will not trigger a reply. Normally a suppression period, or dead time, of up to 60 μs is sufficient; exceptionally up to 150 μs may be necessary.

A similar situation exists in the air but a different solution is normally employed. The line-of-sight and the echo replies will both exhibit the same jittering p.r.f. as the interrogator; however, the line-of-sight reply arrives before the corresponding echo. To achieve echo protection the interrogator is arranged to search outbound. If the search commences at zero nautical miles and moves out, then the first set of replies satisfying the range circuit's search for the jitter pattern will be those corresponding to the true range. To guarantee echo protection on changing channel or before commencing search after memory or auto standby, the range circuits should be returned to the zero nautical miles condition. This is done in some equipments where the reverse movement towards zero may be known as a reciprocal search, although no interrogation takes place. In other equipments, where search is outbound from the last reading, echo protection is likely but not guaranteed. In this latter situation use of the self-test switch or button will give full echo protection since virtually all interrogators have a self-test facility which simulates a range of zero, or near zero, nautical miles. Thus after self-test the outbound search commences from at or near zero.

Percentage Reply We can see from the above that not all interrogations will give rise to replies even if the aircraft concerned is well within range. It may happen that an interrogation arrives during the ground receiver dead time. Other causes of loss of replies are ident transmission from the beacon and suppression of the interrogator receiver by other airborne L band equipment. Every time an L band equipment, i.e. ATC transponder or DME interrogator, transmits, a suppression pulse is sent on a common line to all other L band equipment. This may well be when a reply would otherwise have been received.

Ignoring, for the moment, ident transmission from the ground and suppression due to ATC transponder replies we can calculate a worst-case percentage reply figure. Assuming a beacon dead time of 60 μs and maximum capability operating conditions of 2700 interrogations per second, we have a total dead time of $60 \times 2700 = 162\,000$ μs s^{-1}; i.e. dead time constitutes 16·2 per cent of total time. The maximum p.r.f. (average) of No. 2 DME is 30 with a suppression pulse width of not greater than 60 μs; thus No. 1 DME will be suppressed for at most $30 \times 60 = 1800$ μs s^{-1}; i.e. 0·18 per cent of the time. Thus we are left with $100 - 16·38 = 83·62$ per cent as the reply rate expectation.

The ident transmission occurs once every 30 s when the total key-down time will be less than 4 s. The code group transmitted consists of dots and dashes of time duration 0·1-0·125 s and 0·3-0·375 s respectively. The time between dots and dashes is available for replies. We have the situation where about three replies will be lost during a dot, and about ten during a dash, assuming a track p.r.f. of about 27. For a modern equipment with a lower p.r.f., reply losses will be even less. Under these circumstances it is not sensible to calculate the expected percentage reply since the effect of the ident is possibly to make the interrogator go into memory, particularly when a dash is transmitted. Since the memory time is at least as long as the total key-down time the momentary switch between track and memory and back to track will not be noticed by the pilot.

It should be noted by the maintenance engineer that in simulating ident during a ramp test the ident signal will be continuous, rather than keyed, as long as the appropriate switch on the test set is held on. Thus if ident is simulated for longer than the memory time the interrogator will start to search. This is useful since operation of one switch on the test set allows the checking of ident tone with its associated volume control, memory time and search p.r.f.

The ATC transponder produces replies, and hence suppression pulses, only when interrogated. If an aircraft is within range of one interrogator it will only be interrogated about thirty times per sweep. With a sweep rate of say 12 r.p.m. and a beam width of say 5° these thirty interrogations will occur during a time interval given by the product of 5/360 and 60/12, i.e. about 0·07 s. For thirty interrogations the p.r.f. would need to be $30/0.07 \approx 430$ which is close to the maximum p.r.f. of 450. We have a similar situation to the reply loss during ident transmission, i.e. the occurrence is relatively infrequent; for example 0·07 in 5 s. If the aircraft is within range of more than one interrogator the total interrogation time in, say, 5 s is increased.

Considering the effect on DME only during the time the ATC transponder is replying we have, assuming an ATC interrogation rate of 450 and a suppression pulse duration of 30 μs, percentage suppression time = 450 × 30 × 100/1 000 000 = 1·35 per cent. If we also take into account the worst-case percentage reply for the DME system of 83·62 per cent we have during this short time 83·62 − 1·35, 82 per cent replies. In fact the DME interrogator should cope with this and remain on track.

The above is not quite the whole story. The intention is to allay the fears of students who, on finding out how many ways replies can be lost, wonder how on earth DME works at all. The few simple calculations given show that the situation is in fact quite satisfactory. It can, however, be worse than suggested since the ICAO specification only requires that the DME beacon have a 70 per cent reply efficiency; one of the reasons, not previously mentioned, being that time must be allowed for self-monitoring. Even so most DME interrogators will cope with percentage replies as low as or lower than 50 per cent.

Ground Speed and Time To Station The interrogator continuously monitors the slant range to the beacon which, of course, will change as the aircraft flies towards or away from the beacon. Measurement of the rate of change of slant range gives the speed of approach or departure to the beacon. Such measurement is carried out by most airborne DMEs and presented as so-called ground speed. It is important that the pilot realizes that the readout can only be considered as ground speed when the aircraft is flying directly towards or away from the beacon and is some distance from it. An aircraft flying a circular path centred on the beacon would register a ground speed of zero on the DME indicator!

If the airborne equipment has calculated ground speed, it is a simple matter to give time to station (beacon) since TTS = DST/KTS where TTS is time to station, DST is slant range and KTS (knots) is the ground speed. Again this is only a useful indication when the aircraft is on course to/from the beacon and some distance from it.

The time constant of the ground speed measuring circuit is long but can cope with aircraft acceleration. In ground testing, however, one must wait some time for the ground speed reading to take up the simulated value of velocity selected on the ramp test set, since in switching-in a velocity one is simulating an infinite acceleration.

Interrogation

The full TACAN interrogation frequency range is 1025-1150 MHz with 1 MHz spacing. Thus the interrogation will be one of 126 possible frequencies depending on the channel selected. The r.f. is keyed by pulse pairs. The timing, which is dependent on channel selection, X or Y, is illustrated in Fig. 7.3.

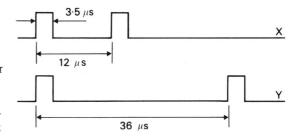

Fig. 7.3 Interrogation pulse spacing

The p.r.f. is dependent on the mode of operation of the DME:

Search	40-150	Average
Track	10-30	Average

The actual p.r.f. depends on the equipment design and may be lower than minimum figures given. There will be a small variation in the average p.r.f. due to jitter. The average p.r.f., assuming that 95 per cent of the time is spent on track, must be less than 30. The radiation is omnidirectional with vertical polarization.

Reply

The r.f. at one of 252 frequencies between 962 and

1213 MHz is keyed by pulse pairs the timing of which is similar to that given in Fig. 7.3, the difference being that Y channel spacing is 30 μs, not 36 μs. The radiation is omnidirectional with vertical polarization.

X and Y Channel Arrangements

There are 126 interrogation and 252 reply frequencies in the full TACAN frequency range. The reply frequency is 63 MHz above or below the interrogating frequency, as shown in Fig. 7.4. The channel spacing is 1 MHz for both interrogation and reply. The TACAN channels are numbered $1X$, $1Y$, ... $126X$, $126Y$.

Using Fig. 7.4 we see that channel $20X$, say, corresponds to an interrogation at 1044 MHz and a reply at 981 MHz, while channel $116Y$, say, corresponds to an interrogation at 1140 MHz and a reply at 1077 MHz.

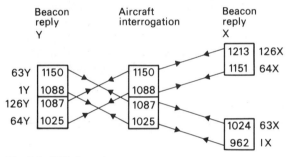

Fig. 7.4 X/Y channel arrangements

For civil DME beacons the 52 channels 1-16, X and Y, and 60-69, X and Y, are avoided for two reasons. Firstly DME is meant to be used in conjunction with VOR and ILS, which occupy 200 channels rather than 252. Secondly, having fifty-two redundant channels, the gaps are chosen to overlap the ATC transponder frequencies of 1030 and 1090 MHz to avoid any possible interference, although different codes and mutual suppression are also used for this purpose.

The use of the fifty-two missing channels is, however, not precluded by the ICAO; they may be allocated on a national basis. The fact that civil aircraft may wish to use TACAN beacons means that many DME interrogators have the full 252 channels.

The Link With v.h.f. Navigation

As stated previously DME is meant to be used in conjunction with VOR and, largely as a future requirement, ILS. To achieve this, DME beacons are co-located with VOR or ILS beacons, there being prescribed maximum separation limits (Annex 1 to the convention on International Civil Aviation). Where we have co-location constituting a single facility the two systems should operate on a standard frequency pairing (Table 7.1) and transmit an associated identity signal.

Table 7.1 Frequency pairing

v.h.f. nav. freq.	v.h.f. allocation	TACAN channel
108·00	VOR	17X
108·05	VOR	17Y
108·10	ILS	18X
108·15	ILS	18Y
108·20	VOR	19X
....	....	....
111·95	ILS	56Y
112·00	VOR	57X
112·05	VOR	57Y
112·10	VOR	58X
....	....	....
112·25	VOR	59Y
112·30	VOR	70X
....	....	....
117·95	VOR	126Y

With standard frequency pairing the need for separate DME and v.h.f. nav. control units is eliminated. It is normal practice for a combined controller to be used, the selected frequency indication being given in terms of the v.h.f. nav. frequency. Thus a selection of 108·05 MHz would tune the v.h.f. nav. receiver to that frequency and the DME to the paired channel 17Y.

Some equipments have a hold facility whereby, when engaged, a change in the selected v.h.f. nav. frequency will not cause the DME channel to change. When using hold, range and bearing information is given but not to a common point. This could lead to pilot navigation error, to avoid this a warning light is illuminated when hold is selected; nevertheless, some national authorities frown upon the availability of such a facility.

In Table 7.1 the frequency pairing arrangements are shown. The frequencies shown as being allocated to ILS are, of course, localizer frequencies the highest of which is 111·95 MHz. The glidepath/localizer frequency pairing is not affected by DME pairing.

Those TACAN channels not paired with v.h.f. nav.

channels may nevertheless still be required. In this case the pairings for channels $1X$ to $16Y$ are 134·40-135·95 MHz and for channels $60X$ to $69Y$ are 133·30-134·25 MHz solely for the purpose of selection on combined controllers. Selection of one of these channels would only give range information to an aircraft not equipped with full TACAN.

Associated identity is the term given for synchronization of the ident signals from co-located beacons. Each 30 s interval is divided into four or more equal parts with the DME beacon ident transmitted during one period only and the associated v.h.f. facility ident during the remaining periods. Associated identity would also be used with a Vortac beacon which provides bearing and range information to both civil and military aircraft. A TACAN (or DME) beacon not co-located with VOR would use independent identity.

Installation

The DME interrogator comes in many forms; airline standard equipment is rack-mounted whereas general aviation interrogators may be panel-mounted with integral controls and digital readout. King have gone one better with their KNS 80 integrated nav. system since one panel-mounted box contains the DME interrogator; v.h.f. nav. receiver and converter, glideslope receiver, RNAV computer plus integral controls and readout of range, ground speed, and time to station (*see* Fig. 1.10).

Figure 7.5 shows a single DME installation with a combined v.h.f. nav./DME controller, an output to an

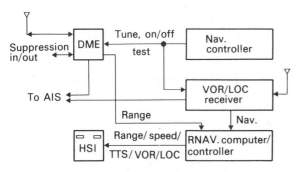

Fig. 7.5 DME installation with RNAV tie-in

RNAV computer/controller and with slant range and ground speed or time to station displayed on an HSI (Fig. 7.6). All larger aircraft would have a dual installation, possibly with changeover relays for HSI feeds. A combined controller is usually found, but it is possible (not advised) to have separate DME and

v.h.f. nav. controllers. The RNAV facility (*see* Chapter 12) may not be available, in which case slant range would be fed direct to the HSI or often, a separate DME indicator in which speed and time is computed. With a DME indicator fitted the HSI may still act as a repeater for slant range.

Fig. 7.6 KPI 533 pictorial navigation indicator (courtesy King Radio Corp.)

Co-axial cables are used for antenna feeder and suppression. With a dual ATC transponder and dual DME installation all four sets will be connected in parallel for suppression purposes, so that when one transmits they are all suppressed. The antenna is mounted on the underside of the fuselage in an approved position. Sufficient spacing between all L-band equipment antennas must be allowed to help prevent mutual interference, although suppression, different frequencies, p.r.f.s and pulse spacing all contribute to this.

Tuning information to both DME and the v.h.f. nav. receiver is likely to be 2/5, although b.c.d. and slip codes may be found. Screened cables, preferably twisted and screened, are used for transfer of analogue or digital data and also for audio identification to the audio integrating system. The audio may be routed through the controller if a volume control is incorporated in the system. Other controller/DME interconnections are for self-test, off, standby and on.

Controls and Operation

A drawing of a combined controller is shown in Chapter 4 (Fig. 4.9). Controls for DME are minimal. Frequency selection is usually by rotary click stop knobs, the digital readout of frequency on the controller being the v.h.f. nav. frequency, e.g. 108·00 MHz. The DME on/off switching may incorporate a standby position. Usually 'standby' indicates that VOR/ILS is on, while DME is on standby i.e. transmitter disabled. Such a switch is often marked 'off'-v.h.f. nav. and DME off; 'receive' – v.h.f. nav. on, DME standby; 'transmit' – both v.h.f. nav. and DME on. A self-test switch will be provided on the controller or, rarely, be panel-mounted. Further switching takes place on the indicator for ground speed (KTS or SPD) or time-to-station (TTS or MIN). A hold switch may also be found (see previous note on 'hold').

Operation is simple: just switch on, tune to required beacon and ensure lock-on after a brief search. If the indicator employs a mechanically driven digital readout a flag will obscure the reading during search, whereas with an electronic digital readout the display will be blanked. When tuning to a different beacon the ident signal should be checked to ensure the correct channel has been selected. Also if the DME is of a type which searches out from its last-known reading the self-test must be operated to return the dials to near zero so that an outbound search will result in lock-on to a line-of-sight reply and not an echo. Even with DMEs which automatically search out from zero after a channel change the self-test should be operated occasionally.

Simplified Block Diagram Operation

The block diagram of Fig. 7.7 can be used to explain the operation of virtually all DME interrogators. Naturally variations will occur when comparing types of DME; in particular the range-measuring circuits will reflect the ingenuity of the designer and further, as one would expect, have in recent years made the transition from analogue to digital techniques.

A jitter generator divides the p.r.f. of a timing oscillator output by a variable divisor. For example with a basic p.r.f. of 400 a divisor of approximately 20 would provide a track p.r.f. of 20, while a divisor of approximately 4 would provide a search p.r.f. of 100. Of vital importance to the operation of DME is that the divisor varies randomly, so that if on track then between, say, 15 and 25 timing pulses may occur between successive output pulses t_0 from the jitter generator.

The pulses t_0 are fed to the modulator and thus decide the time of transmission. The modulator produces pulse pairs of the appropriate spacing which in turn key the transmitter power amplifiers. The r.f. is generated by a frequency synthesizer the output of which serves as receiver local oscillator as well as transmitter master oscillator. The amplified r.f. is fed to and radiated from an omnidirectional antenna. The peak power output of a modern airline standard DME will be about 700-800 W nominal.

Received pulses are fed to the receiver mixer via a tuned preselector which gives image rejection and some protection from the transmitted signal. In addition duplexing action will normally be employed to ensure receiver mixer protection during transmission. Since the transmit and received frequencies are always 63 MHz apart, the frequency synthesizer can be used as described above and the i.f. amplifier is tuned to 63 MHz. A dual superhet may be employed. The receiver output will be the detected video signal.

The decoder gives an output pulse for each correctly spaced pair of pulses. The decoder output consists of replies to all interrogating aircraft plus squitter or pulses at the identification p.r.f. of 1350 Hz, in which case a band pass filter gives a 1350 Hz tone output to the audio integrating system. The auto standby circuit counts the pulses coming from the decoder and if the rate exceeds a predetermined figure (say 400 per second) enables the jitter generator. If the rate is low there will be no modulator trigger and hence no interrogation. A third decoder output is fed to the range gate.

The zero time pulses t_0 are effectively delayed and stretched in the variable delay which is controlled either by the search or track circuits. The output of the variable delay, often termed the range gate waveform, opens the range gate T μs after every interrogation. If a reply or squitter pulse is received at a time when the range gate is open, a pulse is fed to the coincidence counter. Assume the DME is searching with an interrogation rate of 100, and further, assume the range gate waveform gating pulses are 20 μs in duration, then on average during a period of $1/100 = 10\,000$ μs the range gate will be open for only 20 μs, i.e. 1/500th or 0·2 per cent of the time. Now squitter and unwanted replies occur randomly so the chance of full coincidence at the range gate is roughly 1 in 500 for each of the decoder output pulses. Since there are 2700 received pulse pairs per second we will have, on average, 2700/500, i.e. 5-6 pulses per second from the range gate.

During search the variable delay is continuously increased at a rate corresponding to anything from

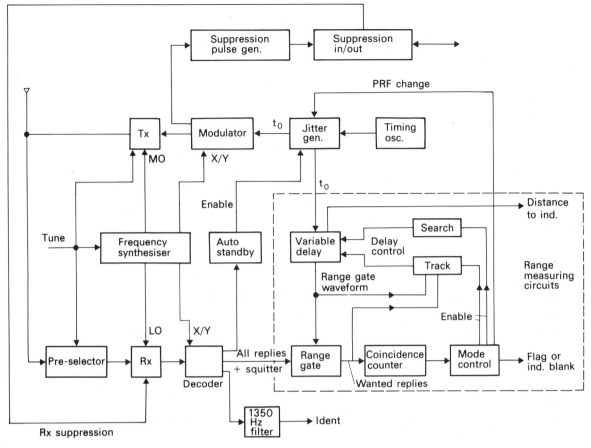

Fig. 7.7 Interrogator block diagram

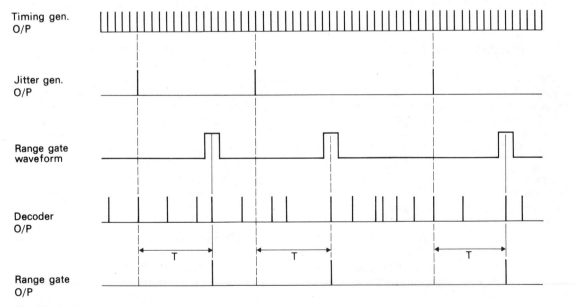

Fig. 7.8 Stroboscopic principle

20 to 400 nautical miles per second, depending on the vintage of the design. While in search the range gate, output rate, as detected by the coincidence counter, is low. When the delay T μs is equal to the round trip travel time plus the 50 μs beacon delay the range gate output rate increases by a significant amount. Assuming as above a search p.r.f. of 100, and also a 50 per cent reply rate, then the output of the range gate will jump from say 5 pulses per second to 50 pulses per second. This is the situation shown in Fig. 7.8. When this easily detected increase in rate occurs the mode control circuit will: (a) enable the tracking circuit; (b) inhibit the search circuit; (c) send a p.r.f. change signal to the jitter generator; and (d) lift the indicator blanking or flag as appropriate.

During track the variable delay is controlled by the tracking circuits so as to keep each wanted reply in the centre of the corresponding range gate waveform pulse. Should the aircraft be flying towards the beacon, successive replies will appear early within the gate pulse, so causing the delay to be reduced. The opposite occurs when the aircraft is flying away from the beacon. The variable delay represents the slant range and so a signal proportional to or representing this delay is fed to the indicator and/or RNAV computer.

If wanted replies are lost, the coincidence counter output registers a zero rate and hence the mode control switches to memory. With static memory the tracking circuits are 'frozen', whereas with velocity memory the tracking circuits continue to change the variable delay at the last known rate.

Range Measuring and Mode Control

Analogue
Typically in an older analogue DME the variable delay takes the form of a phase shifter resolver, the rotor of which is fed from the timing oscillator and is mechanically coupled to a distance measuring shaft. The tracking circuits in such equipment often employ a ramp generator. Figure 7.9 illustrates a block diagram and waveforms which may be used to explain the operation of such a DME but is not meant to represent any particular equipment.

The timing generator output is sinusoidal and so must be fed to a pulse former (zero crossing detector) before the jitter generator. The timing signal is also fed to a phase shift resolver where it is phase-shifted (delayed) by an angle depending on the position of the distance-measuring shaft which also drives the readout. Pulses coincident with the positive-going

zero crossings of the delayed sine wave turn on ($Q = 1$) a bistable which is turned off ($Q = 0$) by the zero time pulses from the jitter generator. The bistable output is connected to the positive-going trigger input of a monostable; in this way the resulting 30 μs pulses occur at a time determined by those delayed timing pulses which occur T μs after transmission. The elapsed time T represents the range readout which will be obscured by a flag during search.

In the logic employed in Fig. 7.9 a low rate output from the range gate will give a logic zero output from the coincidence counter, so enabling the search circuit but disabling the early and late gates. When T μs corresponds to the actual slant range of the beacon the range gate output rate is high, hence the search circuit is disabled and a logic one is fed to the early and late gates. The other inputs to the early and late gates are the decoded pulses and a ramp waveform symmetrical about zero volts and coincident with a 30 μs range gate waveform pulse. The ramp input to the late gate is inverted so that the late gate is open for almost all of the latter half of the 30 μs period, while the early gate is open for almost all of the first half. The slope of the ramp waveform is chosen so as there is a period (equal in duration to the decoder output pulse width) when neither early nor late gate is open. Thus when on track the wanted replies are steered to the decrease or increase range circuits, depending on whether the replies arrive early or late within the range gate waveform pulse respectively.

The motor drive circuits supply the motor so that when in search the readout and delay progressively increases. While in track the motor will turn in a direction dependent on which of the decrease and increase circuits gives an output. It can be seen that in track we have a servo system which maintains the wanted replies in the centre of the range gate waveform pulses.

The memory circuit is enabled with the early and late gates when it clears the flag. Subsequently, should there be a loss of replies, search will be inhibited and the motor held (static memory) or made to continue rotating with the same sense and speed (velocity memory) for the memory time.

Digital
What follows is an explanation of the principles of a first-generation digital DME based on, but not accurately representing, the RCA AVQ 85. Currently the trend is to use a special purpose l.s.i. chip to perform the range measurement and mode control tasks.

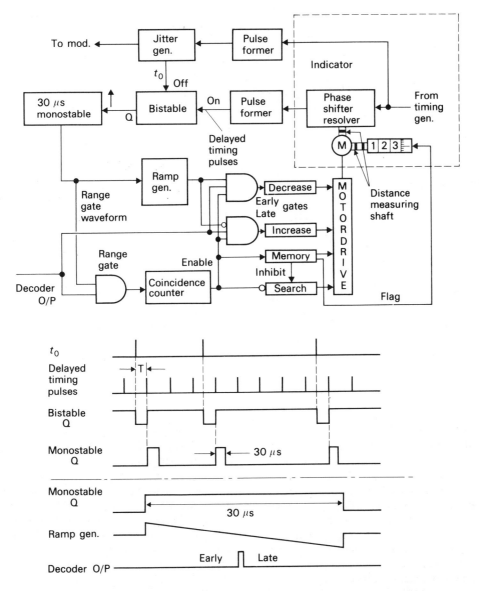

Fig. 7.9 Analogue range measuring and mode control block diagram

The AVQ 85 has a search p.r.f. of 40, a track p.r.f. of 12 and a maximum range of 400 nautical miles, which corresponds to a two-way travel time of 5000 μs. During this time the number of pulse pairs received from a beacon will be, on average:

$$5000 \times 10^{-6} \times 2700 = 13 \cdot 5.$$

Of the thirteen or fourteen pulse pairs received one will, hopefully, be a wanted reply.

During the search mode the elapsed time between t_0 and the time arrival of a particular decoded pulse is measured. If t_n is the time measured after the nth interrogation then t_{n+1} is the time to the first decoded pulse to arrive such that $t_{n+1} \geqslant t_n$, where $n = 0, 1 \ldots$, and $t_0 = 0$. When we have equality, i.e. $t_{n+1} = t_n$, then t_n is, subject to further checking, the round trip travel time to the beacon. It can be seen that if the aircraft is at maximum range we shall need, on average, 13-14 successive interrogations to complete the search time. At a search rate of 40 this will take say $13 \cdot 5/40$ s, i.e. about one-third of a second. The acquisition time of the AVQ 85 is quoted as less than 1 s.

115

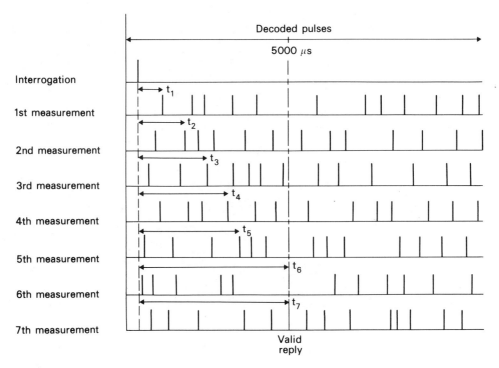

Fig. 7.10 Digital range measurement — search

With the above operation only one time measurement needs to be stored in a register. With a modest amount of memory the wanted reply could be identified within two successive interrogations, provided that such a reply was received after each of the interrogations. If we assume a 50 per cent reply rate then four interrogations would be needed. During a 5000 μs interval less than eighty-four pulse pairs will be received, assuming a minimum spacing of 60 μs between beacon squitter transmissions and allowing for a 60 μs dead time. Each time measurement would need 12 bits if a resolution of one-tenth of a nautical mile is required. Thus a faster search time could be achieved if a RAM of 12 × 84 × 4 = 4032 bits were provided. A practical circuit would consist of 4 × 1K bit (1K = 1024) RAMs, the pulse arrival times, expressed as distances, after each of four interrogations being recorded successively in each RAM chip. The first chip would thus record the arrival times after the first, fifth, ninth, etc. interrogations, similarly for the second, third and fourth chips. Of course only one 4K bit chip is needed, provided it can be organized into four linear arrays of 12-bit words. With a search p.r.f. of 40 there is a period of 30 000 μs (= 1/40) less 5000 μs in which to check for equal arrival times

which, when detected, signal the end of search.

In Fig. 7.11 we return to the one measurement per interrogation situation. Initially the distance measuring circuit counters and registers are cleared. Time measurement from t_0 is carried out by the distance counter which counts 809 kHz clock pulses, thus giving a range resolution of one-tenth of a mile. The sequence of events following the $(n+1)$th interrogation of a search cycle is as follows:

1. $t_0 + 20$ μs
   Distance counter clears.
   Blanking counter loaded with contents of distance storage register $\equiv t_n$.
2. $t_0 + 47$ μs
   Blanking counter starts to count down.
3. $t_0 + 50$ μs
   Distance counter starts to count up towards maximum range.
4. $t_0 + t_n$
   Blanking counter reaches zero and hence enables blanking gate and triggers range gate waveform generator.
5. $t_0 + t_{n+1}$
   A decoded pulse arrives and passes through enabled blanking gate to stop distance counter

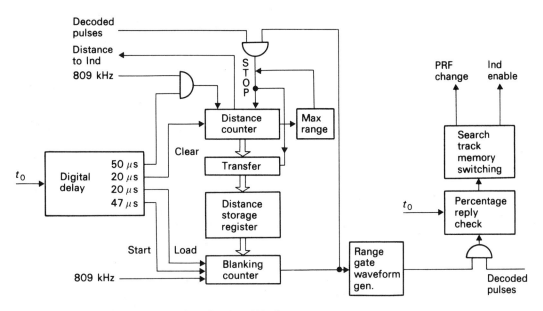

Fig. 7.11 Digital range measuring and mode control block diagram

and trigger transfer of data to distance storage register; n becomes $n+1$ and circuit waits for next t_0.

The above sequence is repeated after each interrogation. Within, on average, fourteen interrogations the time to a wanted reply will be counted and the distance storage register will contain the number of tenths of a nautical mile actual range. After the next interrogation the blanking counter will enable the blanking gate 3 μs before the arrival of the wanted reply, since the blanking counter start is 47 μs after t_0 while the distance counter start is 50 μs after t_0. It therefore follows that the distance counter will record the same distance, subject to aircraft movement, thereafter.

The pulse from the range gate waveform generator is of 6 μs duration, its leading edge being X μs after t_0 where X is the time of arrival of the previously measured decoded pulse less 47 μs. This gating pulse is fed to the range gate together with the decoder output. Coincidence indicates that the two latest pulses to be measured have arrived with the same time delay $\pm$ 3 μs with respect to t_0 and are thus probably wanted replies. The percentage reply checking circuit then checks that two of the next eight interrogations give rise to a decoded pulse within the track gate and if so the mode switches to track. On track the p.r.f. is reduced and the indicator gives a readout of the range as measured by the distance counter. After switching to track, at least four of any sixteen successive

interrogations must give rise to a range gate output; failure initiates a switch to memory. Five seconds after memory is entered the mode will revert to search, subject to auto standby, unless the four-from-sixteen check indicates success, in which case track resumes.

Characteristics

The following summary is drawn from the ARINC Characteristic 568-5 for the Mk 3 airborne DME, it is not complete and does not detail all the conditions under which the following should be met.

Channels
252 channels selected by 2/5 switching.

Pulse Spacing
Interrogation 12 $\pm$ 0·5 μs mode X; 36 $\pm$ 0·5 μs mode Y.
Decoder output if 12 $\pm$ 0·5 μs mode X; 30 $\pm$ 0·5 μs mode Y.
Decoder: no output if spacing of received pulse pairs more than $\pm$ 5 μs from that required.

Range
0-200 nautical miles with override to extend to 300 nautical miles.

Tracking Speed
0-2000 knots.

Acquisition Time
1 s or less.

Memory
4-12 s velocity memory.

r.f. Power Output
> 25 dBW into 50 Ω load.

Interrogation Rate
Overall less than 30, assuming on track 95 per cent of time, searching 5 per cent of time.

Auto Standby
At least 650 pulse pairs per second received before interrogations allowed.

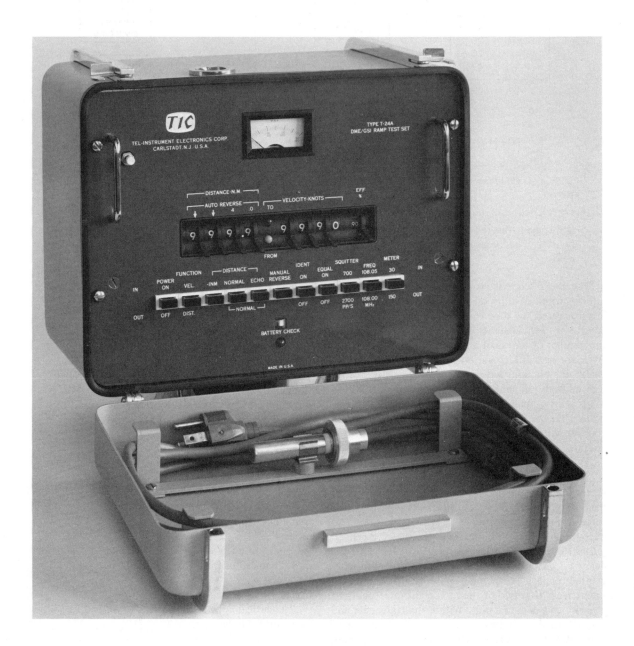

Fig. 7.12 TIC T-24A (courtesy Tel-Instrument Electronics Corp.)

Tx Frequency Stability
Better than ± 0·007 per cent.

Rx Sensitivity
−90 dBm lock-on sensitivity.

Suppression Pulse Duration
Blanket: 19 μs mode *X*; 43 μs mode *Y*.
Pulse for pulse: 7 μs.

Antenna v.s.w.r.
1·5 : 1 over 962-1213 MHz referred to 50 Ω.

Antenna Isolation
> 40 dB between L-band antennas.

Outputs
1. Digital: 32-bit serial b.c.d. word at least five times
   per second, resolution 0·01 nautical miles.
   Buffers in utilization equipment.
2. Analogue: pulse pairs 5-30 times per second with
   spacing, in μs, 50 + 12·359*d* (*d* being slant
   range). Each load 12K in parallel with less than
   100 pF.

3. Range rate pulse transmitted for each 0·01 nautical
   mile change in range.
4. Audio > 75 mW into 200-500 Ω load.
5. Output impedance < 200 Ω.
6. Warning flag < 1 V d.c. for warning, 27·5 V d.c.
   satisfactory operation.

Range Output Accuracy
From ± 0·1 to ± 0·3 nautical miles, depending on
signal strength and time since acquisition.

Ramp Testing

A DME installation should be tested using a ramp test
set which will test by radiation, simulate various
ranges and velocities, operate on at least one spot
frequency for mode *X* and mode *Y*, and provide for
simulation of identification. Two such test sets are
the TIC T-24A (Fig. 7.12) and the IFR ATC-600A
(Fig. 8.23).

TIC T-24A
A battery-operated, one-man test set operated from

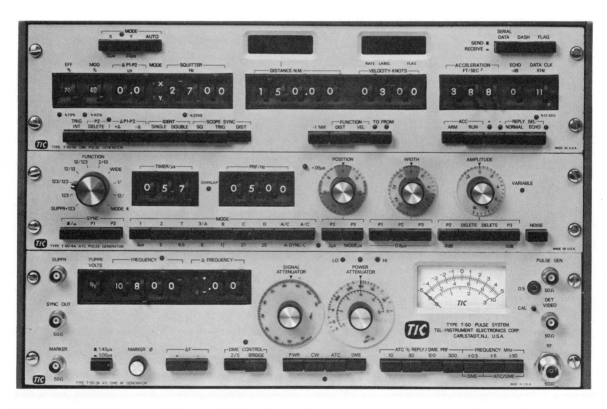

Fig. 7.13 TIC T-50A (courtesy Tel-Instrument Electronics
Corp.)

the cockpit and testing by radiation. Channels $17X$ and $17Y$ are available (108·00 and 108·05 MHz VOR frequencies) with range simulation from 0 to 399·9 nautical miles in 0·1 nautical mile increments. The velocity, inbound or outbound, can be selected in 10-knot increments from 0 to 9990 knots. Squitter is selectable at 700 or 2700 pulse pairs per second. Identity is available as 1350 or equalized 1350 pulse pairs per second. An additional pulse pair 10 nautical miles after the reply pulse pair can be selected, to enable a check of echo protection. The p.r.f. meter has two ranges 0-30 and 0-150. Finally the percentage reply may be selected in 10 per cent increments from 10 to 100 per cent.

ATC 600A

This test set does not have all the facilities of the T-24A but does offer comprehensive testing ability for the ATC transponder (Chapter 8). Like the T-24A the ATC 600A operates on channels $17X$ and $17Y$. The range can be set from 0 to 399 nautical miles in 1 nautical mile steps. Twelve different velocities may be simulated in the range

50-2400 knots inbound or outbound. The identity is equalized 1350 pulse pairs per second. The percentage reply is either 50 or 100 per cent by selection. Features of the ATC 600A not available with the T-24A are an interrogator peak r.f. power readout, accuracy ± 3 dB (± 50 per cent) and interrogation frequency check.

Bench Testing

Various test sets exist for the bench testing of DME, one of these is the TIC T-50A (Fig. 7.13) which also provides facilities for ATC transponder bench testing. This is not the place to detail all the features of such a complex test set; suffice it to say that the test set is made up of optional modules so that the customer can choose the most suitable package. One feature which must be mentioned is the ability to measure the pulsed r.f. from the DME interrogator with a resolution of 10 kHz. TIC have found that many units change their output frequency, sometimes beyond allowable limits, when a change in pulse spacing occurs; i.e. X to Y mode or vice versa.

8 ATC transponder

Introduction

With the rapid build-up of international and domestic civil air transport since World War II, control of air traffic by means of primary surveillance radar (PSR) and procedures is not adequate to ensure safety in the air.

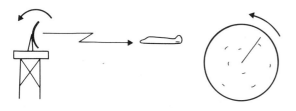

Fig. 8.1 Primary surveillance radar

A PSR does not rely on the active co-operation of the target. Electromagnetic (e.m.) radiation is pulsed from a directional antenna on the ground. Provided they are not transparent to the wavelength used, targets in line with the radiation will reflect energy back to the PSR. By measuring the time taken, and noting the direction of radiation, the range and bearing of the target are found. Display is by means of a plan position indicator (*see* Chapter 9). Such a system has the following disadvantages:

1. Sufficient energy must be radiated to ensure the minimum detectable level of energy is received by the p.s.r. after a round trip to a wanted target at the maximum range. Range is proportional to the 4th root of the radiated energy.
2. Targets other than aircraft will be displayed (clutter). This can be much reduced by using Doppler effect (*see* Chapter 10) to detect only moving targets.
3. Individual aircraft cannot be identified except by requested manoeuvre.
4. An aircraft's altitude is unknown unless a separate height-finding radar is used.
5. No information link is set up.

Recognition of these disadvantages, in particular No. 3, led to the development of a military secondary surveillance radar (SSR) known as identification friend or foe (IFF). With this system only specially equipped targets give a return to the ground. This system has since been further developed and extended to cover civil as well as military air traffic; the special equipment carried on the aircraft is the air traffic control (ATC) transponder.

Basic Principles

Secondary surveillance radar forms part of the ATC radar surveillance system; the other part being PSR. Two antennas, one for PSR, the other for SSR, are mounted co-axially and rotate together, radiating directionally. The SSR itself is capable of giving range and bearing information and would thus appear to make PSR redundant; however we must allow for aircraft without ATC transponder fitted or a possible failure.

We can briefly explain SSR in terms of Fig. 8.2. The SSR transmitter radiates pulses of energy from a directional antenna. The direction and timing of the SSR transmission is synchronized with that of the PSR. An aircraft equipped with a transponder in the path of the radiated energy will reply with specially coded pulsed r.f. provided it recognizes the interrogation as being valid. The aircraft antenna is omnidirectional.

The coded reply received by the ground is decoded, and an appropriate indication given to the air traffic controller on a p.p.i. display. The reply will give information relating to identity, altitude or one of several emergency messages. Figure 8.3 shows a typical data presentation. As can be seen, a variety of symbols and labels are used to ease the task of the controller.

Interrogation

One interrogation consists of a pair of pulses of r.f. energy, the spacing between the pulses being one of four time intervals. Different modes of interrogation

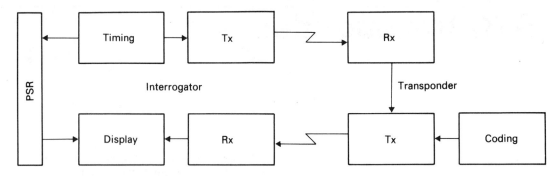

Fig. 8.2 Secondary surveillance radar

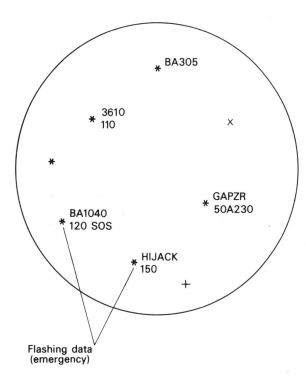

Fig. 8.3 Typical data presentation

are coded by the different time intervals, each mode corresponding to a different ground-to-air 'question'. For example mode A — 'what is your identity'? Figure 8.4 illustrates the modes of interrogation.

Many transponders have only mode A and C capability; this is sufficient to respond to an interrogator operating on mode interlace whereby mode A and C interrogations are transmitted in sequence, thus demanding identification and altitude information. Mode D has yet to be utilized.

The maximum interrogation rate is 450 although, in order to avoid fruiting (*see below* — False Targets), the rate is as low as possible consistent with each target being interrogated twenty to forty times per sweep. The pulses of r.f. are 0·8 μs wide and at a frequency of 1030 MHz (L band) this being the same for all interrogations.

Reply

A transponder will reply to a valid interrogation, the form of the reply depending on the mode of interrogation. A valid interrogation is one received from the interrogator mainlobe (*see below* — Side Lobe Suppression), the time interval between pulses being equal to the mode spacing selected by the pilot.

In every reply two pulses of r.f. 1090 MHz, spaced 20·3 μs apart are transmitted, these are the frame or bracket pulses, F1 and F2. Between F1 and F2 there are up to twelve code pulses designated and spaced as shown in Fig. 8.5; a thirteenth pulse, the X pulse, may be utilized in a future expanded system.

The presence of a code pulse in a reply is determined by the setting of code selector switches on the pilot's controller when the reply is in response to a mode A (or B) interrogation. If the interrogation is mode C the code pulses transmitted are automatically determined by an encoding altimeter.

A pulse 4·35 μs after F2 may be transmitted. This is the special position indicator (SPI) pulse, otherwise known as the indicate position (I/P) or simply ident pulse. If the reply is in response to a mode A interrogation the SPI pulse is selected by a spring-loaded switch or button on the pilot's controller. A brief depression of the switch will cause the SPI pulse to be radiated with every reply to a mode A interrogation received within 15-30 s. Some older transponders will transmit a SPI pulse in reply to a mode C interrogation when the reply code contains a D4 pulse; this corresponds to an altitude in excess of 30 700 ft.

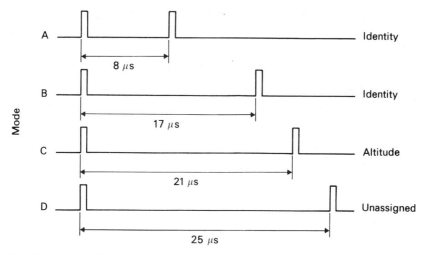

Fig. 8.4 Interrogation pulse spacing

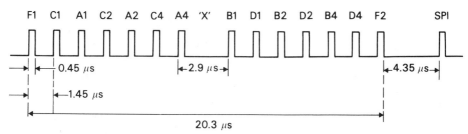

Fig. 8.5 Reply train format

Coding: Identification

The code pulses transmitted depend on four code selector switches, each of which controls a group of three pulses in the reply and may be set to one of eight position, 0-7. The code groups are designated A, B, C and D, the pulses within each group having suffixes 4, 2 and 1 (*see* Fig. 8.5). The resulting code is binary coded octal, the most significant octal digit being determined by the group A pulses, the least significant by the group D.

Selection of the A pulses gives the familiar binary code, as shown in Table 8.1. Similarly with selection of the B, C and D pulses.

The number of possible code combinations is easily arrived at since we have four octal digits giving $8^4 = 4096$. Some of the code combinations are given special significance; we have:

7600   Radio failure   7700   Emergency

There is also a special code for hijack.

Coding: Altitude

The flight level of the aircraft referenced to a pressure

Table 8.1 Group A code selection (similarly for groups B, C and D)

A4	A2	A1	Selection
0	0	0	0
0	0	1	1
0	1	0	2
0	1	1	3
1	0	0	4
1	0	1	5
1	1	0	6
1	1	1	7

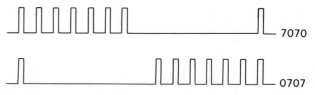

Fig. 8.6 Examples of pulse trains for particular selected codes

of 1013·25 mbar (29·92 inHg) is encoded automatically in increments of 100 ft, the code used being laid down by the ICAO. The maximum encoded range is from −1000 to 126 700 ft inclusive. With 100 ft increments this requires 1278 different code combinations, with 4096 available we see there is considerable redundancy. It is impractical to use more of the available codes since the accuracy of barometric altimeters is such that it is not sensible to have, say, 50 ft increments; in any case the objective is to indicate flight levels which are in hundreds of feet.

To accommodate the redundancy the D1 pulse is not used and, further, at least one C pulse is transmitted but never C1 and C4 together in a single reply. Thus for each eight possible A group combinations of pulses we have eight B group, five C group and four D group, giving $8 \times 8 \times 5 \times 4 = 1280$ possible code combinations; two more than necessary. The extra two, if assigned, would correspond to −1100 and −1200 ft.

The C pulses form a unit distance reflected binary code giving the 100 ft increments. As shown in Table 8.2 the reflected pattern, starting at C1 = C2 = 0, C4 = 1, begins when $Mod_{10}(A) = 8$; i.e. when the remainder on dividing the altitude (in hundreds of feet) by 10 is 8. Thus to find the C pulses in the code for, say, 25 400 ft we have A = 254, $Mod_{10}(A) = 4$, so C1 and C2 are in the reply.

Table 8.2　100-Foot increment coding

$Mod_{10}(A)$	C_1	C_2	C_4	
8	0	0	1	
9	0	1	1	
0	0	1	0	
1	1	1	0	
2	1	0	0	Reflection
3	1	0	0	
4	1	1	0	
5	0	1	0	
6	0	1	1	
7	0	0	1	

The A, B and D pulses form a Gray code giving a total of 256 increments of 500 ft each, i.e. 128 000 ft, commencing at −1000 ft. In order of frequency of bit change we have B4, B2, B1, A4, A2, A1, D4, D2; thus B4 changes every 1000 ft whereas D4 does not enter the code until 30 800 ft and D2 until 62 800 ft. Needless to say aircraft in the general aviation category will not need to employ encoding altimeters giving D4 and D2 selection.

To find the A, B and D pulses we can use Table 8.3. Since the entries in the table commence with zero, whereas the altitude commences at

Table 8.3　500-Foot increment coding

				B4	0	1	1	0	0	1	1	0	0	1	1	0	0	1	1	0
				B2	0	0	1	1	1	1	0	0	0	0	1	1	1	1	0	0
				B1	0	0	0	0	1	1	1	1	1	1	1	1	0	0	0	0
				A4	0	0	0	0	0	0	0	0	1	1	1	1	1	1	1	1
D2	D4	A1	A2																		
0	0	0	0		0	1	2	3	4	5	6	7	8	9	10	11	12	13	14	15
0	0	0	1		31	30	29	28	27	26	25	24	23	22	21	20	19	18	17	16
0	0	1	1		32	33	34	35	36	37	38	39	40	41	42	43	44	45	46	47
0	0	1	0		63	62	61	60	59	58	57	56	55	54	53	52	51	50	49	48
0	1	1	0		64	65	66	67	68	69	70	71	72	73	74	75	76	77	78	79
0	1	1	1		95	94	93	92	91	90	89	88	87	86	85	84	83	82	81	80
0	1	0	1		96	97	98	99	100	101	102	103	104	105	106	107	108	109	110	111
0	1	0	0		127	126	125	124	123	122	121	120	119	118	117	116	115	114	113	112
1	1	0	0		128	129	130	131	132	133	134	135	136	137	138	139	140	141	142	143
1	1	0	1		159	158	157	156	155	154	153	152	151	150	149	148	147	146	145	144
1	1	1	1		160	161	162	163	164	165	166	167	168	169	170	171	172	173	174	175
1	1	1	0		191	190	189	188	187	186	185	184	183	182	181	180	179	178	177	176
1	0	1	0		192	193	194	195	196	197	198	199	200	201	202	203	204	205	206	207
1	0	1	1		223	222	221	220	219	218	217	216	215	214	213	212	211	210	209	208
1	0	0	1		224	225	226	227	228	229	230	231	232	233	234	235	236	237	238	239
1	0	0	0		255	254	253	252	251	250	249	248	247	246	245	244	243	242	241	240

−1000, we must add 1000 to the altitude before entering the table. The table records the altitude in increments of 500 ft. The following algorithm will give the required code:

(i) add 1000 to the altitude;
(ii) enter table with the integer part of the result of (i) divided by 500;
(iii) read the code: row, column.

As an example we will find the complete code for 110 200 ft:

(i) 110 200 + 1000 = 111 200;
(ii) Int. (111 200/500) = 222;
(iii) 10110001 = D2 D4 A1 A2 A4 B1 B2 B4.

To find the C pulses:

Mod_{10} (1102) = 2, therefore 100 = C1 C2 C4.
Complete code is 10110001100.

False Targets

There are several causes of unwanted returns being displayed on the air traffic controller's p.p.i., one of which is interrogation by side lobes. This is discussed in some detail below under the heading side lobe suppression.

Since the transponder antenna is omnidirectional the reply pulses meant for one interrogator may also be received by another, providing it is within range and its antenna is pointing in the direction of the aircraft concerned. Such unwanted returns will not be synchronized with the transmission of the interrogator suffering the interference and would appear as random bright dots on the p.p.i. This type of interference, known as fruiting, can be dealt with by making use of the fact that different interrogators work on different interrogation rates;

replies may thus be sorted on this basis.

A reply from a transponder lasts for a period of 20·3 μs, thus the transmitted pulse train will occupy a distance of $163\,000 \times 20 \cdot 3 \times 10^{-6} = 3 \cdot 3$ nautical miles in space (speed of propagation being 163 000 nautical miles per second). As a consequence any two aircraft in line with the interrogator, and with a difference in slant range of less than 1·65 nautical miles, will transmit replies which overlap in space and consequently mutually interfere at the interrogator receiver. Such replies are said to be garbled. Secondary surveillance radar is most useful when traffic densities are greatest. These circumstances, of course, give increased garbling.

Reflections of the transmitted energy, either interrogation or reply, from mountains, hills or large structures will give an indicated reply at an incorrect range. Since the direct path is shorter than the reflected path echo protection may be used; i.e. the receiver may be suppressed or desensitized for a limited period on receipt of a pulse.

Side Lobe Suppression (SLS)

When a reply is received its angular position on the controller's p.p.i. is determined by the direction of the main lobe radiation from the interrogator. If the reply is due to an interrogation from a side lobe then the indicated bearing will be incorrect. Two systems have been designed to suppress replies to side lobe interrogation: they are the ICAO 2 pulse and the FAA 3 pulse SLS systems. Some older transponders have circuitry applicable to either system; however three-pulse SLS has advantages over its virtually obsolete rival and is the only system considered.

The polar diagram for the interrogator antenna system is shown in Fig. 8.7. P1 and P3 are the interrogation pulses spaced at 8, 17, 21 or 25 μs radiated from the directional antenna. P2 is the SLS control pulse radiated from an omnidirectional

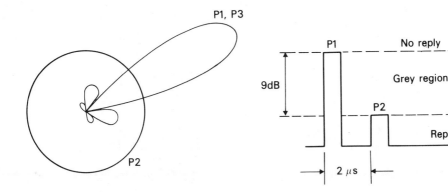

Fig. 8.7 Three-pulse s.l.s.

antenna. The field strength for P2 is such that an aircraft within the P1/P3 main lobe will receive P2 at a lower amplitude than P1/P3 whereas elsewhere P2 will be greater. The condition for a reply/no reply are:

$$P2 \geqslant P1 \qquad \text{no reply}$$
$$P2 \leqslant P1 - 9 \text{ dB} \qquad \text{reply}$$
$$\text{otherwise may reply}$$

In the grey region the probability of a reply increases with decreasing P2 amplitude relative to P1.

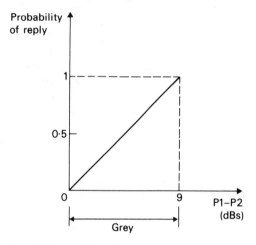

Fig. 8.8 Probability of a reply

Installation

Figure 8.9 shows a typical transport category aircraft dual installation. Two transponders are mounted side by side in the radio rack mating with back plate connectors in the mounting tray junction box. Two encoding altimeters and the control unit have their connectors routed through the back plate to the transponders while direct connections to the front of the transponders are made from two L-band antennas and the suppression line interconnecting all L-band equipments. Power supplies are routed through the back plate.

The encoding altimeters may be blind (no altitude indication) or panel-mounted. On larger transport aircraft encoded altitude information may be derived from a static pressure-activated capsule mechanism in a central air data computer (CADC).

The transponders are fitted on a shock-mounted tray. Cooling is by convection and radiation. Most transponders designed for the general aviation market combine transponder and control unit in one box, which is panel-mounted. To ensure adequate cooling sufficient clearance must be allowed around each unit.

A common co-axial cable interconnects the transponders and DME interrogators. A transmission by any one 'black box' will cause the receivers of the

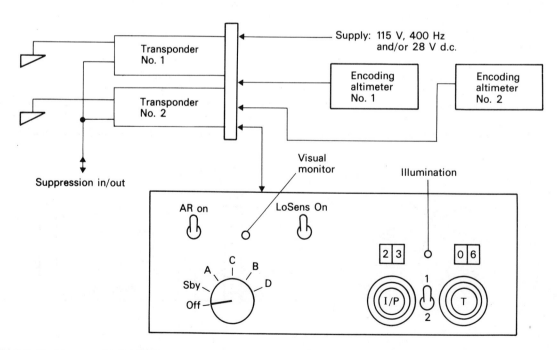

Fig. 8.9 Dual transponder installation

other three to be suppressed for a period depending on the source; a transponder suppression pulse will be about 30 μs.

The control unit is, of course, panel-mounted in the cockpit and provides the pilot with complete control over the transponders. Only one transponder at a time is in use while the other is on standby.

Controls and Operation

Function Switch Off-Standby-A-B-C-D. Mode C operation will depend only on the position of the altitude reporting (a.r.) switch; hence if the function switch has a 'C' position such a selection would serve to switch modes A, B and D off but have no effect on the selection of mode C. Many transponders have only A and C capability in which case the function switch might have positions Off-Standby-A.

Code Switches Rotary switches mounted co-axially in pairs; thumbwheel switches are a common

alternative. The code selected appears in a window above the switches and will determine the code pulses present in the reply in response to a mode A (or B) interrogation. Some transponders have a facility for remote automatic keying for modes A and B; this may be selected by setting the code switches to 8888. In fact the necessary extra equipment has never been introduced.

I/P Switch Spring-loaded to off pushbutton or toggle switch for selection of the SPI pulse. May be labelled SPI or Ident.

Lo Sense Switch When selected to 'on' reduces the transponder receiver sensitivity by 12 dB. This feature was introduced as an interim measure for reducing side lobe response. Subsequent developments have made this facility unnecessary.

A.R. Switch On-off selection for altitude reporting.

Test (T) Switch Spring-loaded to off pushbutton or

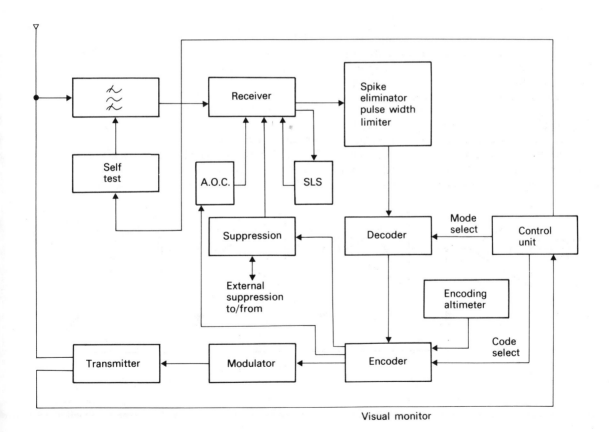

Fig. 8.10 Transponder block diagram

toggle switch which energizes the self-test circuitry. Indication of a successful self-test is given by a green visual monitor lamp which also illuminates when a reply is sent in response to a valid interrogation. The self-test switch and visual monitor may be repeated on the transponder unit for the use of the maintenance engineer.

Transfer Switch Selects either transponder No. 1 or No. 2 in a dual installation.

Pilot work load with transponder is minimal, there being no indication other than the monitor lamp while control switch changes are initiated on ATCs instructions either by r.t. or through standard procedures.

Simplified Block Diagram Operation

The interrogating pulses of r.f. energy are fed to the receiver by way of a 1030 MHz band pass filter. The pulses are amplified, detected and passed as a video signal to the spike eliminator and pulse-width limiter circuits; these only pass pulses greater than $0.3 \ \mu s$ in duration and limit long pulses to less than that duration which will cause triggering. The decoder examines the spacing of the interrogation pulses P1 and P3, if it is that for the mode selected an output will be given to the encoder. If the P1-P3 spacing is $21 \ \mu s$ an output will be given regardless of the mode selected.

The encoder, on being triggered by the decoder, produces a train of pulses appropriate to the required reply which is determined by code switches (mode A) or encoding altimeter (mode C). The encoder output triggers the modulator which keys the 1090 MHz

transmitter. Radiation is by an omnidirectional antenna.

The side lobe suppression circuits are fed with the receiver video output. In the event of an interrogation by side lobe, the receiver will be suppressed for about $35 \ \mu s$ commencing at a time coincident with the P2 pulse, thus blocking the passage of P3.

The suppression circuit is triggered whenever there is a reply. The suppression pulse so produced is used to suppress the receiver and is also fed to other L-band equipment for the same purpose. The suppression feature between L-band equipments is mutual.

Automatic overload control (a.o.c.) otherwise known as group countdown, progressively reduces the receiver sensitivity after the reply rate exceeds typically 1200 groups per second. Assuming 15 pulse replies, $0.45 \ \mu s$ pulse widths and a maximum reply rate of 1480 groups per second we have a typical airline requirement of a 1 per cent duty cycle to handle multiple interrogations.

Self-test facilities are provided. On being activated, a test signal is injected into the front end of the receiver. A successful self-test is indicated by the visual monitor lamp which lights whenever there is an adequate transmission. Some transponders have an audio monitor facility in addition to the visual monitor.

Block Diagram Details

Transmitter Receiver
The r.f. sections will employ normal u.h.f. techniques suitable for processing signals in the region of 1000 MHz. Interconnecting internal co-axial leads

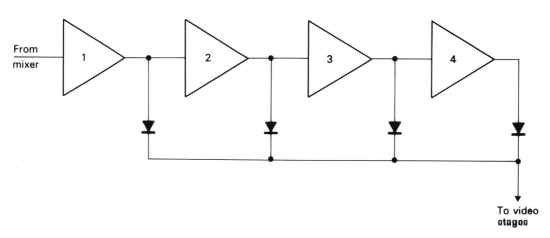

Fig. 8.11 Logarithmic i.f. amplifier

must be of a length laid down by the manufacturer as they play a part in the circuit action; in particular the lead to the transmitter will be of a length such that received signals will see the transmitter feed as a high impedance, thus assisting in the duplexing action.

In flying from maximum range towards the interrogator a large dynamic range of signal strength is received, at least 50 dBs from minimum triggering level. Providing adequate amplification for the weak signals can result in saturation of the last stage(s) of the i.f. amplifier when stronger signals are received. Such saturation may give rise to the suppression of valid interrogations by the SLS circuit since the stronger P1 main lobe pulses will be limited.

Successive detection of the video signal can overcome the saturation problem. Figure 8.11 shows a logarithmic amplifier using successive detection. Assuming a gain of A for each stage and a maximum stage input signal V before saturation of that stage, an input to the i.f. amp. of V/A^3 will cause stage 4 to saturate. In this event the detected output to the video stage will be $(V/A^2) + (V/A) + (V) + (AV)$ which is approximately equal to AV for a reasonable gain A. Table 8.4 illustrates the difference between a conventional and logarithmic amplifier.

Decoder
Many transponders still in service use multi-tapped delay lines in both decoder and encoder; however all modern transponders employ monostables and shift registers, in the form of integrated circuits, which will be the only type of transponder considered here.

The detected video signals are applied to the spike eliminator and pulse width limiter in series. The action of the 0·3 μs delay and AND gate is to prevent any pulses or noise spikes less than 0·3 μs in duration

Table 8.4 Comparison of conventional and logarithmic amplifiers

Input signal	Output signal	
	Conventional	*Logarithmic*
$\dfrac{V}{A^3}$	AV	AV
$\dfrac{V}{A^2}$	AV	2AV
$\dfrac{V}{A}$	AV	3AV
V	AV	4AV

being passed to the decoder. Long pulses which might cause a reply are reduced in duration by the pulse-width limiter monostable, the output of which is a pulse about 0·5 μs in duration regardless of the width of the input pulse.

The decoder input monostable ensures that only the leading edge of P1 (positive-going ↑) triggers the mode A and C delay circuits each of which consists of a monostable and a differentiating circuit. The mode A and C AND gates will give an output if the delayed P1 pulses from the differentiators are coincident with the undelayed P3. An output from either AND gate will give a trigger ('T') output from the OR gate.

Encoder
In the example of an encoder shown, two 10-bit shift registers are used (e.g. Signetics 8274). The operating

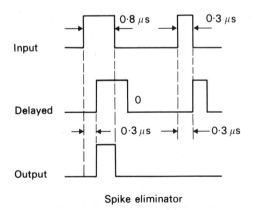

Spike eliminator

Fig. 8.12 Spike eliminator and pulse width limiter waveforms

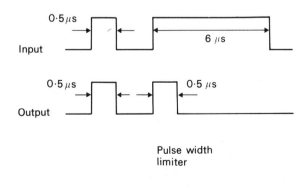

Pulse width limiter

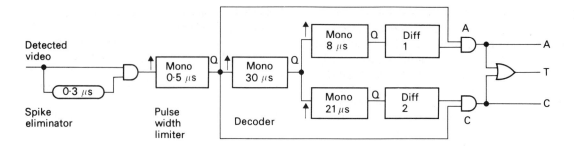

Fig. 8.13 Decoder

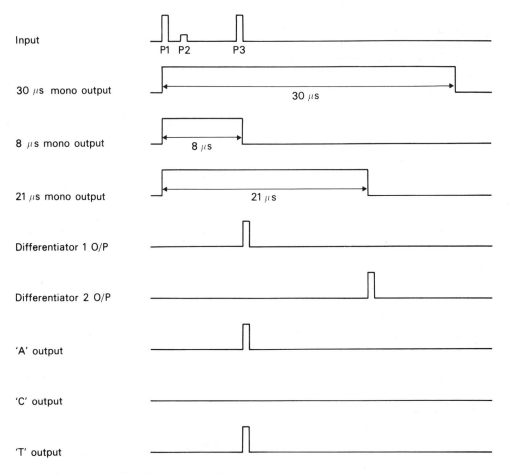

Fig. 8.14 Decoder waveforms – mode A interrogation

mode is controlled by inputs S0 and S1, hold, clear, load and shift being selected by the input values shown in the truth table (Fig. 8.15). These two control waveforms are produced by two monostables, one triggered by the positive-going edge of the 'T' output from the decoder, the other by the negative-going edge. This arrangement gives us the

sequence load, shift, clear, hold. The S0 waveform is also used to gate a clock generator, period 1·45 μs.

Load The leading edge of T triggers the controlling monostables so that S0 = 1, S1 = 0 and the shift register elements will be loaded with the binary information present on the input lines. Since F1 and

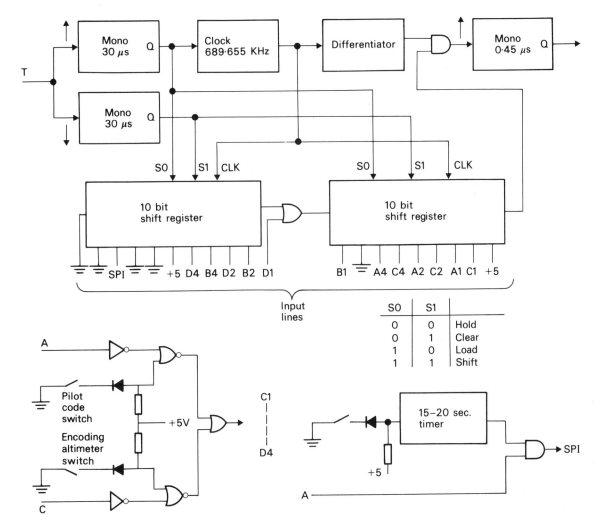

Fig. 8.15 Encoder

S0	S1	
0	0	Hold
0	1	Clear
1	0	Load
1	1	Shift

F2 are required in all replies, the appropriate inputs are high (+5 V). The one time-slot between A4 and B1 and the two time-slots between F2 and SPI are never used; consequently their input lines, together with the two spare after SPI, are low (earth). The dynamic input lines C1 to D4 will be high or low depending on the code switch selection (mode A interrogation) or the altitude (mode C interrogation). Assuming a valid mode A interrogation has been received there will be a pulse present on the 'A' line from decoder to encoder coincident in time with the pulse on the 'T' line. After inversion this A pulse is applied in parallel to one of twelve NOR gates, the other inputs of which are connected individually to the twelve pilot code switches. Those code pulses selected result in a ground on the appropriate NOR gate input. Since the other input in each case is also

low for the duration of the load mode, the NOR gate outputs corresponding to selected codes go high and thus set the appropriate shift register element. Similar action occurs whenever mode C interrogations are received although D1 selection is not involved. Noise filtering is employed (r.c. networks) within the transponder for each of the altitude information input leads. SPI loading occurs when the A pulse is coincident with the 15-30 s output pulse from the SPI timer produced on depression of the SPI switch.

Shift The trailing edge of pulse T triggers the S1 monostable thus S0 = S1 = 1 and the shift registers are in the shift operating mode. Shifting occurs with a high to low transition of the clock pulses, thus in the 1·45 μs after the first transition the shift register output is high (F1); after the next transition the

131

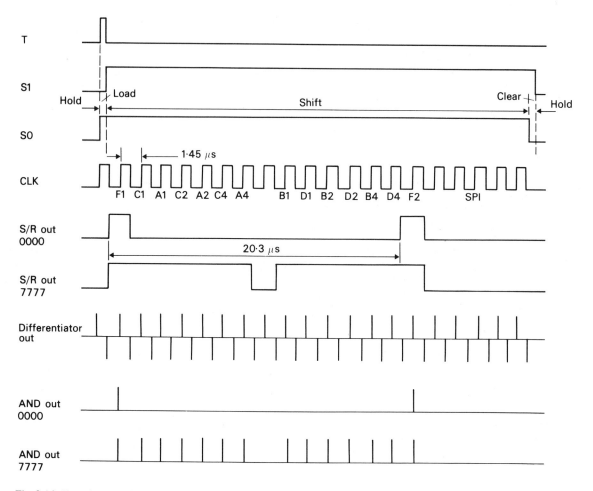

Fig. 8.16 Encoder waveforms

output will be high or low depending on how the C1 element was loaded, and so on.

Clear and Hold S0 and S1 pulses are each of approximately 30 μs duration, thus S0 goes low first giving S0 = 0, S1 = 1 when all the elements clear. In fact during shift all elements will have cleared so this clear mode of operation is not vital. What is important is that S0 goes low first, since we do not want to load again until just before the next transmission. At the end of S1 we have S0 = S1 = 0, the hold mode which is maintained until the next valid interrogation.

The output of the shift register contains the coded information but not in the form required, i.e. a train of pulses. Differentiated clock pulses are fed to an AND gate which is enabled by the shift register output, thus positive pulses appear at the output of the AND gate in the appropriate time-slots. The final

monostable is to provide pulses of the correct duration to the modulator.

Encoding Altimeter

As the aircraft ascends, the decrease in static pressure causes expansion of the capsule and consequent movement of a position-sensing device, an optical or magnetic transducer (Fig. 8.17). The resulting servo-assisted drive, through appropriate gearing, drives the altitude display and encoding disc. The pressure reference for the indicated altitude can be changed by the baroset control. It should be noted that this does not affect the encoding disc position which is always referred to 1013·25 mbar (29·92 in.Hg) the standard mean sea-level pressure. As a result all aircraft report altitude referenced to the same level; an essential requirement for ATC purposes.

Variations on the above are encoding altimeters which give no indication of altitude, blind altimeters,

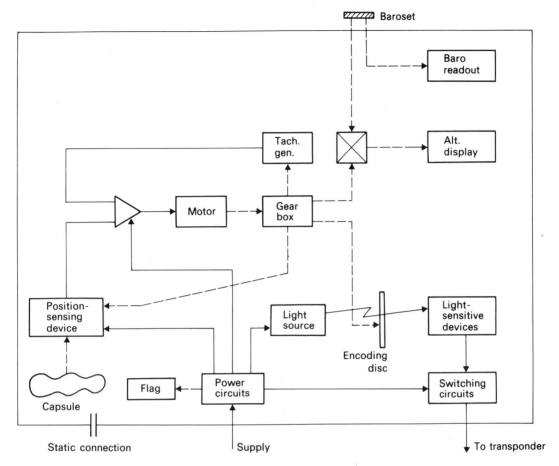

Fig. 8.17 Servo encoding altimeter

and those which do not have servo-assisted drives but do employ a vibrator to give smooth movement of pointer and encoding disc.

Altitude Encoding

A transparent disc, usually glass, is divided into tracks and segments. Each concentric track represents one of the code pulses, the outer track being C4, while a segment represents a particular altitude. An opaque pattern is formed on the disc so that on a particular segment the area of intersection with each track will be either opaque or transparent depending on the code assigned to the altitude represented by that segment.

The disc rotates between a light source and photosensitive devices, one for each track, aligned along the 'reading line'. As the disc is driven by the barometric altimeter the appropriate segment is read.

Referring back to Tables 8.2 and 8.3 we see that the code changes by 1 bit for each 100 ft increment. This use of a 1-bit change or unit distance code

minimizes the error when the reading line is aligned with the junction of two segments.

In the simplified encoder circuit shown in Fig. 8.20 with A/R switch ON Zener diode VR2 is shorted and emitter of Q2 returned to earth. When light from LED VR1 falls on photo transistor Q1, via a transparent part of the encoding disc, current is drawn through R switching on Q2. Thus collector of Q2 falls to a low value, i.e. input 2 to NOR gate is low. If input 1 is driven low by an output from the decoder a high output from the NOR gate is available for loading into the encoder shift register.

If no light falls on Q1 we have no volts drop across R, thus Q2 is off and input 2 to NOR gate is high. Under these conditions a 'zero' will be loaded into the appropriate shift register element. The circuitry described is repeated for each track of the disc.

Side Lobe Suppression

Of the several possible ways of designing an SLS circuit one is illustrated in Fig. 8.21, with the

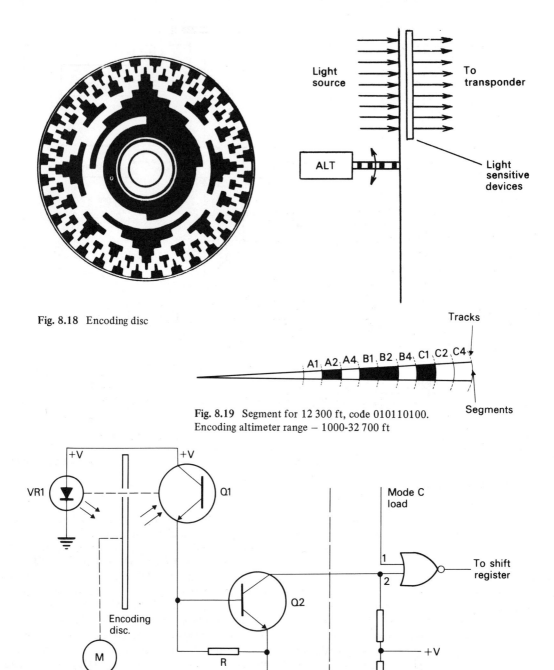

Fig. 8.18 Encoding disc

Fig. 8.19 Segment for 12 300 ft, code 010110100.
Encoding altimeter range – 1000-32 700 ft

Fig. 8.20 Simplified altitude encoder circuit

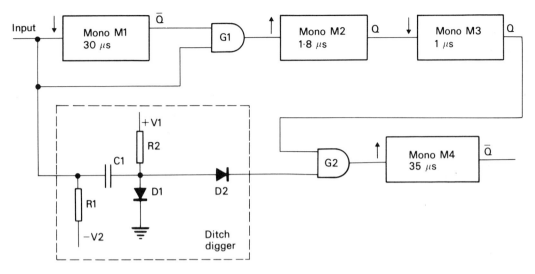

Fig. 8.21 Side lobe suppression circuit

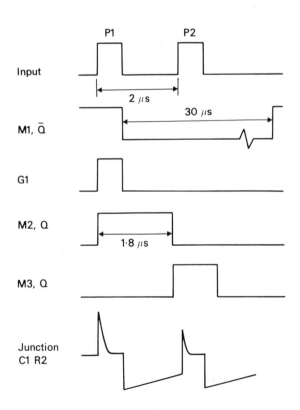

Fig. 8.22 Side lobe suppression waveforms

associated waveforms in Fig. 8.22. Monostable M1 and AND gate G1 separate the P1 pulse from P2 and P3 so that M2 will be triggered by P1 only and will not be triggered until the next interrogation. M2 and M3 provide a gating waveform about 1 μs wide in the P2 pulse position.

The input pulses are also applied to a 'ditch-digger' circuit. Prior to P1, D1 is forward biased and the junction of C1/R2 is low. Both inputs to G2 are low. The leading edge of P1 causes D1 to conduct charging C1 rapidly. The lagging edge of P1 causes D1 to cut off, since the junction C1/R2 falls by an amount equal to the amplitude of P1. C1 now discharges through R1 and R2. When P2 arrives D1 will conduct providing the amplitude of P2 is sufficient. The time constant C1R1R2 and the bias voltages V1 and V2 are chosen so that if P2 $\geqslant$ P1 AND gate G2 will receive an input via D2 which will be coincident with the gating waveform from M3. Thus the SLS pulse generator M4 will be triggered if and only if P2 $\geqslant$ P1, the subsequent suppression pulse being used to inhibit the receiver video output to the spike eliminator.

Characteristics

The following summary is drawn from ARINC Characteristic No. 572.1 for the Mk 2 ATC transponder. It is worth pointing out that several features on the Mk 1 transponder are not required for the Mk 2, however the engineer will find many transponders still in service which have some or all of the following:

1. two-pulse SLS;
2. SLS countdown — receiver desensitized when the number of SLS pulses exceeds a limiting figure;
3. low sensitivity selection;
4. receiver video signal output socket;
5. remote automatic keying;
6. external transmitter triggering position;
7. audio monitor;
8. transmission of SPI pulse whenever D4 is one bit of the altitude reporting code.

Receiver

Minimum Triggering Level (MTL)
−77 to −69 dBm at antenna or
−80 to −72 dBm at transponder.

Dynamic Range
MTL to 50 dBs above m.t.l.

Frequency and Bandwidth
Centre frequency 1030 MHz.
−3 dB points at ± 3 MHz.
−60 dB points at ± 25 MHz.

Decoding Facilities
Decoder output for pulses spaced 8, 17 and 21 μs tolerance ± 0·2 μs on spacing. Automatic mode C decoding regardless of mode selection switch. Space provision for 25 μs decoding.

Side Lobe Suppression Facilities
P1 ⩾ P2 + 6 dBs should give 90 per cent reply rate. 6 dBs rather than ICAO 9 dBs ensures adequate margin to allow for performance rundown in service.

SLS Pulse Duration
25-45 μs.

Transmission

Transmitter Frequency
1090 ± 3 MHz.

Minimum Peak Power
500 W.

Reply Pulse Characteristics
Duration 0·45 ± 0·1 μs measured between 50 per cent amplitude points.
0·05-0·1 μs rise time, 10-90 per cent.
0·05-0·2 μs delay time, 90-10 per cent.

Reply Delay
3 ± 0·5 μs.

Reply Rate Capability
1200 replies per second.

Reply Pulse Interval Tolerance
± 0·1 μs for spacing of any pulse, other than SPI, with respect to F1; ± 0·15 μs for spacing of any pulse with respect to any other except F1; ± 0·1 μs for spacing of SPI with respect to F2.

Mutual Suppression Pulse
25-33 μs duration.

Monitor Lamp
To light when five replies are detected at a rate greater than 150 replies per second. To stay illuminated for 15 s after last reply detected.

Antenna
Polarization: vertical.
v.s.w.r.: better than 1·42 : 1 at 1030 and 1090 MHz.

Ramp Testing

A transponder can be tested *in situ* using one of several portable test sets. A suitable ramp test set will test by radiation, be capable of interrogating on at least modes A and C, be capable of simulating a side lobe interrogation, display the transponder reply and provide a means of measuring the transponder transmitter frequency.

ATC 600A

A popular test set is the IFR ATC 600A illustrated in Figure 8.23. A reason for its popularity is the fact that it can test both DME and ATC transponder with a comprehensive range of checks, making it suitable for functional tests on the ramp or bench.

P1, P2 and P3 pulses are generated and used to key a crystal-controlled 1030 MHz oscillator. The interval between P1 and P3 is switched to simulate a mode A/C interlace, two mode A interrogations being transmitted for each mode C. The following characteristics may be varied by front panel controls:

1. P1-P3 interval — to check decoder;
2. P2 amplitude — to check SLS;
3. Transmitter power output — to check MTL.

The reply is displayed by a bank of lamps, one for each code pulse and one for the SPI pulse. There is

Fig. 8.23 ATC 600A (courtesy IFR Electronics Inc.)

also a numerical readout which shows either the pilot code or the altitude in thousands of feet. In addition to this basic information the following can be checked:

1. F2 timing;

2. power output of transponder (± 50 per cent accuracy);
3. frequency of the transponder transmitter;
4. percentage reply;
5. invalid altitude code, i.e. no C pulses or C1 and C4 together;
6. absence of code pulses in reply to mode C interrogation.

Supply is by rechargeable battery or a.c., battery operation is limited by a timer. Further features are direct connection to the transponder via an external 34 dB pad, self-testing of display, lamps and battery and direct connection of encoding altimeter.

TIC T-33B and T-43B

The TIC approach to ramp testing is to use separate test sets for L band equipments, the T-33B and T-43B being those for ATC transponder.

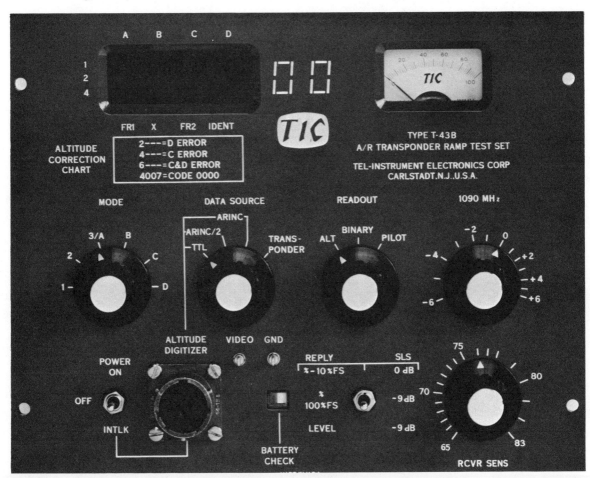

Fig. 8.24 TIC T-43B (courtesy of Tel-Instrument Electronics Corp.)

Specifications for the two test sets are identical except for the added facility of direct connection of an encoder which is available on the T-43B.

The capabilities of these test sets and the ATC 600A are similar in so far as ATC transponder ramp testing is concerned, in that they both meet the FAA requirements. Differences are largely due to the use of the ATC 600A as a bench test, although it should be noted that a particular ATC 600A is best used as either a bench test set or a ramp test set but not both.

To detail the differences, the TIC test sets do not have facilities for continuously varying P1-P3 spacing or strobing the F2 pulse, and do not indicate invalid or 'no altitude' information or transmitter power.

Features of the TIC test sets not available on the ATC 600A are provision of all military and civil modes of interrogation and change of scale for percentage reply meter (0-10 per cent SLS on; 0-100 per cent SLS off). There are other minor differences, and one other major difference, in that the TIC test sets are designed for use in the cockpit on the ground or in flight, the antenna being mounted on the test set as opposed to the ATC 600A where the antenna is mounted on a tripod near the aircraft antenna. The antenna arrangements for the TIC test sets necessitate the use of direct connection to the transponder for receiver sensitivity checks.

9 Weather avoidance

Introduction

Weather forecasting is by reputation and, until the introduction of satellites, in fact, notoriously unreliable. Even with modern techniques rapidly changing conditions and lack of detailed information on the exact location and severity of bad weather results in diversions or cancellations of flights where the forecast is the only available information. What is required is an airborne system capable of detecting the weather conditions leading to the hazards of turbulence, hail and lightning.

Attention has been concentrated on developing systems which will 'detect' turbulence. If an aircraft passes through regions of severe turbulence it is obviously subject to mechanical stress, which may cause damage, possibly leading to a crash. On commercial flights, passenger comfort is also important since the number of customers would soon decline if the discomfort and sickness which turbulence may bring became commonplace. Unfortunately the phenomenon of rapidly and randomly moving air currents is not amenable to detection by any currently realizable technique; however, some progress may be made by utilizing a pulsed Doppler system.

As a consequence of our inability at present to detect the turbulence directly, systems have been developed which detect either water droplets or electrical activity, both of which are associated with convective turbulence in cumulonimbus clouds. Clear air turbulence has no detectable associated phenomena which can give a clue to its presence.

To detect water droplets or raindrops a conventional primary radar is used with frequency and special features chosen to optimize the presentation of signals which would, in a normal search radar, be unwanted. Weather radar has been used for many years, and is mandatory for large aircraft. There has been a steady move into the general aviation market by radar manufacturers but here a relatively recent innovation is the Ryan Stormscope, a patented device which detects electrical activity.

The maximum diameter of a water droplet which can remain in a cloud without falling to earth is dependent on the speed of the up-draught of air. In the appendix to this chapter it is shown that the signal in a weather radar is proportional to the sixth power of the droplet diameter, so strong signals are associated with a rapid up-draught. If a small volume of the cloud results in strong signals from one part and weak from an adjacent part we have a steep 'rainfall gradient', most probably due to a down- and up-draught close to one another. The region around this vertical wind shear is likely to be highly turbulent.

The corresponding argument for associating electrical activity with turbulence goes as follows. A wind shear will result in the separation of positive and negative electrical charges in the air due to the friction of the moving air currents. An electrical discharge occurs after sufficient charge of opposite polarity has accumulated in distinct parts of the cloud. These discharges occur repetitively, most being hidden from view but occasionally seen as lightning. Each discharge is accompanied by a large burst of e.m. radiation which can be received at some distance. In most radio applications the 'noise' received due to lightning is a nuisance but its association with turbulence is put to good use in a Ryan Stormscope in a way similar to that in which a weather radar uses the 'nuisance' signals of weather clutter.

We can summarize and combine the above arguments by saying: convective turbulence occurs where we have large shear forces which imply: (a) an up-draught supporting large raindrops formed from the water vapour in the warm moist air rising from ground level; (b) a nearby down-draught which cannot support large raindrops; (c) frictional forces giving rise to charge separation; and (d) electrical discharge due to charge separation and a saturated intervening medium.

Cause and effect are very much bound up in this argument, the various phenomena being interdependent. However reasonable the theory, the ultimate justification for the association between turbulence, steep rainfall gradient and electrical activity is recorded correlation during many flights. Weather radar is certainly well proven with many years in service, while the Stormscope, although only available since 1976, has been independently evaluated and shown to be a useful aid.

Weather Radar

Basic Principles

Weather radar operation depends on three facts:

1. precipitation scatters r.f. energy;
2. the speed of propagation of an r.f. wave is known;
3. r.f. energy can be channelled into a highly directional beam.

Utilizing these facts is fairly straightforward in principle. Pulses of r.f. energy are generated by a transmitter and fed to a directional antenna. The r.f. wave, confined to as narrow a beam as practicable, will be scattered by precipitation in its path, some of the energy returning to the aircraft as an echo. The elapsed time between transmission and reception is directly proportional to range R, in particular $R = ct/2$ where c is the speed of propagation (= 162 000 nautical miles per second); t is the elapsed time; and the divisor 2 is introduced since travel is two-way. The direction of the target is simply given by the direction in which the beam is radiated.

Since the pilot needs to observe the weather in a wide sector ahead of the aircraft the antenna is made to sweep port and starboard repetitively, hence we use the term scanner for a weather radar antenna. Any storm cloud within the sector of scan will effectively be sliced by the beam so that a cross-section of the cloud is viewed.

Display of three quantities for each target is required: namely range, bearing and intensity of echo. A plan position indicator (p.p.i.) display is invariably used since this allows the simultaneous display of the three quantities and is easy to interpret.

A cathode ray tube (c.r.t.) is used in which the beam of electrons is velocity modulated in accordance with the received signal strength. Wherever the beam strikes the phosphor coating on the back of the viewing screen a glow occurs, the intensity of which is dependent of the velocity of the electrons. Thus a strong signal is associated with a bright spot on the screen; hence the term intensity modulation. The beam is made to sweep across the screen in synchronism with both the time of transmission and the antenna position.

In a conventional (rho-theta) display the beam strikes the screen at bottom centre (origin) at the instant the transmitter fires. Subsequently the beam will be deflected across the screen in a direction dependent on the scanner azimuth position, e.g. if the scanner is pointing dead ahead the beam is deflected vertically from the origin. In this way a time-base line is traced out on the screen and is made to rotate in synchronism with the scanner.

The duration of the time-base, i.e. the length of time it takes to traverse the screen, depends on the range selected by the pilot. Every microsecond of round trip travel time corresponds to a range of 0·081 nautical miles, thus for a selected range of 20 nautical miles the time-base will be about 250 μs in duration. An echo received 125 μs after transmission would cause a bright spot to appear half-way up a 250 μs time-base, so indicating to the pilot that the range of the target is 10 nautical miles.

The net result of the above is that a cross-section of the targets within the selected range and scanned sector of the radar are viewed in plan. The position of the bright patches on the screen relative to the origin is representative of the position of the targets relative to the aircraft. Figure 9.1 illustrates the situation.

Choice of Characteristics and Features

Frequency

The higher the frequency (smaller the wavelength) the larger is the backscatter cross-section per unit volume of the target (see A9.12) hence the greater the echo power. However, high frequencies suffer more atmospheric absorption than do low, and further cannot penetrate clouds to the same extent. Thus the choice of frequency is a compromise. An additional consideration is the beamwidth; for a given scanner diameter a narrower beam is produced with a higher frequency.

Practically, taking into account availability of standard components, the choice comes down to either about 3·2 cm (X-band) or 5·5 cm (C-band). The majority of radars in service and currently manufactured are X-band.

Pulse Width

The volume of the target giving rise to an echo is directly related to the pulse width (see A9.8) thus use of long pulses will give improved range.

There are two arguments against long pulses.

1. Since there is only one antenna and a common

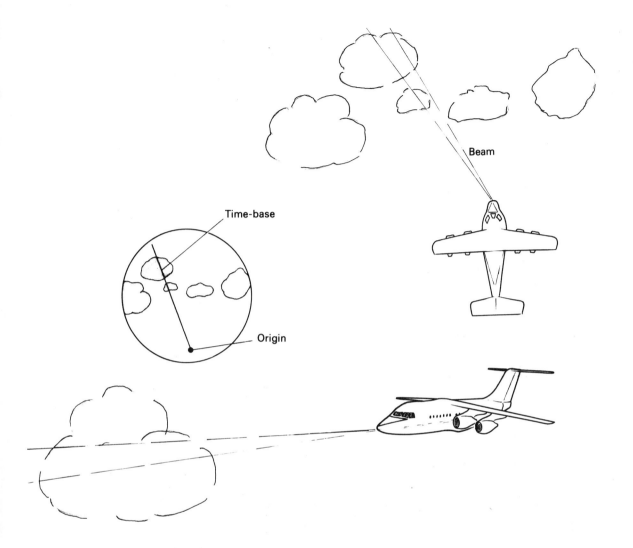

Fig. 9.1 Display principles

frequency for transmit and receive, the antenna must be switched to the transmitter for the duration of the pulse; thus the pulse width determines minimum range. For a 2 μs pulse no return can appear for the first 2 μs of the time-base, giving a minimum range = $2c \times 10^{-6}/2 \approx$ one-sixth of a nautical mile.

2. Range resolution deteriorates with increasing pulse width. A pulse of 2 μs duration occupies about 2000 ft in space. If two targets are on the same bearing but within 1000 ft of one another the echo from the nearest target is still being received when the leading edge of the echo from the furthest target is received. The result is that both targets merge on the p.p.i. display. The range of the targets does not affect the resolution.

Since range resolution and minimum range are not critical in a weather radar, pulses tend to be longer than in other radars, say 2-5 μs. A shorter pulse width, say 1 μs, may be switched in when a short displayed range is selected.

A technique is available which realizes the advantages of both long and short pulses. The transmitted pulse can be frequency modulated so that the r.f. increases over the duration of the constant amplitude pulse. The frequency modulated return is passed through a filter designed so that the velocity of propagation increases with frequency. Thus the higher frequencies at the trailing edge of the echo 'catch up' with the lower frequencies at the leading edge. In this way, the duration of the echo is compressed. It should be noted that the bandwidth

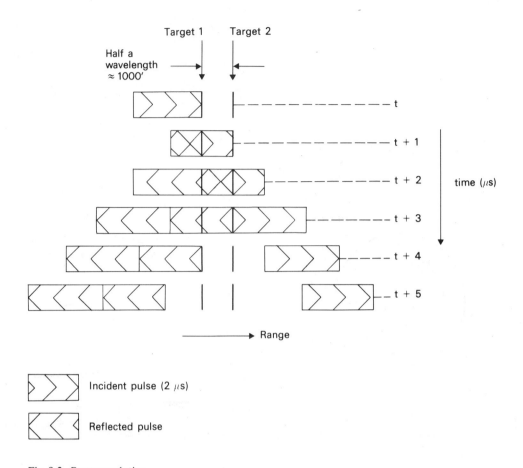

Fig. 9.2 Range resolution

requirements are increased by using frequency
modulation of the pulsed r.f., this being the penalty
for obtaining better range resolution. This technique
is known as pulse compression but, so far as the
author is aware, is not used on existing airborne
weather radars.

Pulse Repetition Frequency, p.r.f.

Changing the p.r.f. will affect the number of pulses
striking a given volume of the target in each sweep
and hence change the display integration factor
(*see* A9.17). However in order to maintain a constant
duty cycle (pulse width × p.r.f.) an increase in p.r.f.
must be accompanied by a decrease in pulse width, so
keeping average power and hence heat dissipation
constant. Alternatively an increase in p.r.f.
accompanied by a reduction in peak power will also
keep heat dissipation constant. The net result is that
for constant average power a change in p.r.f. does not,
in theory, affect the maximum range of the radar.

Limits are imposed on the choice of p.r.f. since if
it is too low the rate at which information is received

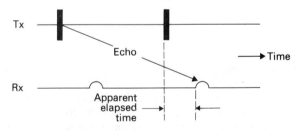

Fig. 9.3 Second trace echoes

is low, while if it is too high the serious problem of
second trace echoes may arise. If the characteristics
of the radar are such that the maximum range from
which echoes can be detected is, say, 200 nautical
miles then the round trip travel time for a target at
maximum range would be about 2500 μs. In such a
system a pulse repetition period p.r.p. (= 1/p.r.f.) of
2000 μs would mean that the time-base start would
occur 500 μs before the return of an echo of the
previous transmitted pulse from a target at 200
nautical miles. This second trace echo would appear

to be at about 40 nautical miles range. It follows that in the above example the maximum p.r.f. would be 400 and in general p.r.f. $< c/2R$ where R is the maximum range.

A popular choice for older radars was a p.r.f. of 400 synchronized to the supply frequency. With improved performance leading to increased range, a submultiple of the supply frequency, e.g. 200, was used. In modern systems internal timing is independent of the supply frequency and one finds p.r.f.s from about 100 to 250.

Power Output

In older radars peak power outputs of about 50 kW or even higher were common, while maximum range was modest. In modern radars, peak power is about 10 kW with increased range compared with previous systems. This apparent spectacular improvement is put in perspective by considering the range equation (*see* A9.7) where we see that maximum range is proportional to the fourth root of the peak power. Thus reducing power by four-fifths reduces maximum range by about one-third. This shortfall of one-third has been more than made up by improvements in aerial design, receiver design and sophisticated signal processing.

Beam Width

Although the larger the beam width the greater the volume of the target contributing to the echo this effect is more than cancelled out due to the inverse relationship between aerial gain and beamwidth $(G \propto 1/\theta^2)$. A narrow beam is always preferred, since the net effect is to increase range and improve bearing resolution. Simple geometric considerations show that with a 4° beamwidth two targets separated by about $3\frac{1}{2}$ nautical miles, at a range $\geqslant 50$ nautical miles, will appear as one on the p.p.i. Bearing resolution, unlike range resolution, is dependent on the target range. An equally important consideration is that ground returns will appear at closer ranges for wider beamwidths, thus masking the cloud returns.

Tilt and Stabilization

The reason for requiring stabilization is related to the previous paragraph. A weather radar may scan up to 300 nautical miles ahead of the aircraft within azimuth scan angles of typically ± 90°. Unless the beam is controlled to move only in or above the horizontal plane part or all of the weather picture may be masked by ground returns. Imagine the aircraft rolling with port wing down. If the swept region is in the same plane as the aircraft's lateral and longitudinal axes, then when the scanner is to port the beam will be pointing down towards the ground, while when to starboard the beam will be pointing up, possibly above the weather. Figure 9.4 illustrates this problem.

In fact stabilization holds the beam not in the horizontal plane but at a constant elevation with respect to the horizontal. This constant elevation is determined by the tilt control as set by the pilot. Details of stabilization and tilt are discussed later.

Contour

The pilot will be interested in those regions where the precipitation is greatest. In order to make the situation clearer, those signals which exceed a certain predetermined level are inverted so as to show the cells of heavy precipitation as dark holes within the bright 'paint' caused by the cloud surrounding the cell. The width of the 'paint' around the cell is an indication of the rainfall gradient. The narrower the width the steeper the gradient, and hence the greater the probability of encountering turbulence. This technique is known as iso-echo (equal echo) contour presentation.

Sensitivity Time Control, s.t.c.

For correct contour operation the signal strength

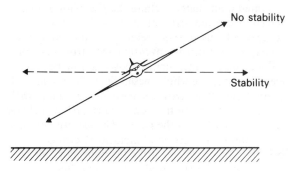
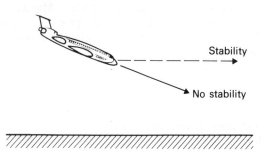

Fig. 9.4 Scanner stabilization

should depend only on the characteristics of the target, but of course the range also affects the received power. As a consequence if the contour inversion level is set so as to indicate storm cells at a certain range then innocent targets closer than that range may cause inversion while storm cells beyond that range may not. In order to solve the problem the receiver gain is made to vary with range, being minimum at zero range and increasing thereafter (i.e. with time), hence sensitivity time control or swept gain, as it is sometimes called.

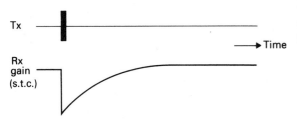

Fig. 9.5 Sensitivity time control

The aim is to make the receiver output independent of range. Unfortunately the received power decreases as the square of the range for targets which fill the beam, but as the fourth power of the range otherwise (*see* Appendix). To achieve the aim would require a complex gain control waveform which would, even then, only be correct for a certain sized target. Many systems have been designed assuming a 3 nautical mile diameter cloud as standard; among such systems, s.t.c. has operated to a range where such a target would fill the beam; beyond that gain is constant with time. It has been observed that it is uncommon for water droplet returns to come from a region which fills the beam vertically except at close ranges.

Following from the above, s.t.c. may be arranged to compensate for the range squared law out to about 30 nautical miles for a 6° beam. A change in scanner size would lead to a change in maximum s.t.c. range since the beamwidth would alter. Alternatively, a modified law may be compensated for out to, say, 70 nautical miles, ignoring the possibility of beam filling.

Automatic Gain Control, a.g.c.

It is neither practical nor indeed desirable with contour operation to have a.g.c. determined by signal level as in receivers for other systems. The normal arrangement is to have a.g.c. noise-derived. During the time immediately before transmission the output from the receiver is noise only, since the p.r.f. will have been chosen to avoid second-trace echoes, i.e. the time corresponding to maximum range expires well before the next pulse. The a.g.c. circuit is gated so that the receiver output is connected to it only for a short time before transmission.

The result of having such a.g.c. is to keep the receiver noise output constant, which under normal conditions means the gain is constant. If, for any reason there is excessive noise generated or received, the gain will fall, so keeping the background noise displayed at a constant level, although signals will fade and contour will not highlight all storm cells.

An alternative arrangement is to keep the receiver gain constant regardless of how the receiver output may change. This has the virtue of keeping the conditions for inversion in the contour circuit unchanging. Such preset gain is found in modern digital systems, whereas noise-derived a.g.c. is found in older analogue systems.

Display

A problem in display design for cockpit use is the large range of ambient lighting conditions. Some storage of the information received is inevitable if it is to be viewed, owing to the relatively low refresh rate of the fleeting basic information.

In older and simpler radars the c.r.t. screen is coated with a long-persistence phosphor which continues to glow some time after the electron beam has passed on its way thus storing the information over the scan interval. Unfortunately, such phosphors are not very efficient and very high shielding is required for adequate viewing in bright conditions.

The direct view storage tube (d.v.s.t.) is a solution to the problems of a conventional c.r.t. A mesh is mounted immediately behind the phosphor-coated screen. Electrons arrive at the mesh from two sources: a focused beam, velocity-modulated by the signal, comes from a conventional electron gun while a flood gun provides, continuously, a wide beam of electrons over the whole mesh. Since the modulated beam is deflected across the mesh in accordance with scanner position and time since transmission, a charge pattern is written on the mesh. The pattern determines where and what fraction of incident electrons penetrate the mesh and strike the phosphor. Since each glowing element of phosphor is excited continuously, very bright displays are possible. A slow discharge path for the mesh must be provided to prevent saturation; the possibility of changing the discharge rate exists and a pilot-adjustable control may be provided. On changing range the mesh will be 'instantly' discharged to prevent confusion between new and old screen positions of the targets. If the discharge path is broken and updating inhibited we have a frozen picture.

The modern approach to information storage is to digitize the signal which is then stored in an intermediate memory at a location depending on the scanner azimuth angle and the time of arrival measured with respect to the time of transmission. The p.p.i. time-base scan format can be either rho-theta or X-Y as per a conventional television. In either case memory can be read at a much higher rate than that at which information is received. With many more pictures per second painted we have a bright, flicker-free display without the need for long-persistence phosphors of low efficiency or the expensive d.v.s.t.

In the case of a rho-theta display the scan format is the same for receipt and display information but, as explained, the repetition rate is different, so only scan conversion in time is required. With a television-type display both the scan format and repetition rate are different, so complete scan conversion is required from input (received) format to readout (displayed) format. Use of the television-type display makes multiple use of the weather radar indicator relatively simple so we find such indicators able to display data from other sensors (e.g. Area nav.) or alphanumeric data such as checklists.

Digitizing the signal involves the recognition of only discrete values of signal intensity. The standard practice is to have three levels of non-zero intensity, the highest corresponding to the contour inversion level. Although these three levels correspond to different degrees of brightness of the paint, with the use of a colour tube they can be made to correspond to three colours. While there is no standardization of the colour code as yet (1979) red is the obvious choice for contourable targets.

Perhaps the most significant virtue of a digital weather radar is the absence of noise on the display. The output of the receiver, the video signal, is digitized and then averaged in both time and position, i.e. the video output occurring ρ μs after a transmission is averaged with that occurring ρ μs after the next transmission and the video data which would appear at adjacent positions on the screen are subject to a weighted averaging process. With a suitable choice of minimum signal level for a 'paint' uncorrelated noise is virtually eliminated from the display with the exception of a few noise spots per memory update.

Scanner

There are two types of scanner employed to obtain the required narrow beam, namely a directly fed parabolic reflector or a flat plate planar array. Of the two, for a given diameter and wavelength, the flat plate has the higher gain/narrower beam/least side lobe power, but is most expensive. Since the flat plate is almost twice as efficient as the parabolic reflector it is invariably used with a modern system except where cost is an overriding factor or the space available in the nose of the aircraft allows a large parabolic reflector to be used.

The flat plate antenna consists of strips of waveguide vertically mounted side by side with the broad wall facing forward. Staggered off-centre vertical slots are cut in each waveguide so as to intercept the wall currents and hence radiate. Several wavelengths from the antenna surface, the energy from each of the slots will be summed in space, cancellation or reinforcement taking place depending on the relative phases. In this application the phase of the feed to each slot, and the spacing between slots, is arranged so as to give a resultant radiated pattern which is a narrow beam normal to the plane of the plate. The greater the number of slots the better the performance; since the spacing between the slots is critical we can only increase the number of slots by increasing the size of the flat plate.

The parabolic reflector works on a similar principle to a car headlamp reflector. Energy striking the reflector from a point source situated at the focus will produce a plane wave of uniform phase travelling in a direction parallel to the axis of the parabola. The feed in a weather radar parabolic antenna is usually a dipole with a parasitic element which, of course, is not a point source. The consequence of a dipole feed is that the beam departs from the ideal and there is considerable spill-over, giving rise to ground target returns from virtually below the aircraft, the so-called height ring.

In both types of antenna, scanning is achieved by rotating the complete antenna assembly, thus a rotating waveguide joint is required. An electronically steered beam is possible with the flat plate but the considerable complications of arranging the correct phasing of the feed to all slots have made this impractical for airborne weather radar systems. Some of the simpler, cheaper weather radars employing a parabolic reflector rotate the reflector only, leaving the feed fixed and so eliminating the need for an azimuth rotating joint. A disadvantage of this latter system is that the feed is not at the focus except when the reflector axis is dead ahead; the resulting deterioration of the beam shape means the angle through which the beam is scanned must be restricted.

Installation

Figure 9.6 illustrates a typical installation in block form as represented by the Bendix RDR 1200, a digital weather radar designed with the upper end of the general aviation market in mind. The installation will be discussed in terms of the RDR 1200 first, and then variations and refinements will be described.

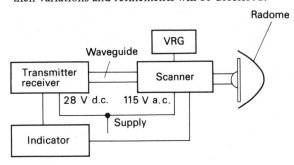

Fig. 9.6 Bendix RDR 1200 installation

The transmitter receiver (t.r.) contains all the r.f. circuitry and components as well as the modulator, duplexer, IF stages, analogue to digital (a/d) converter and power supply circuits. Unlike older systems, the basic timing circuitry is in the indicator rather than the t.r. This timing controls the p.r.f., scanner

rotation, memory write/read and all display circuitry. Thus in a modern weather radar we see that the 'brain' of the system is situated in the indicator while the 'heart' remains in the t.r. This view is reinforced by the fact that the pilot/system interface is achieved completely through the indicator, both for display and control.

The scanner is a flat plate array plus associated circuitry for scanner stabilization and azimuth drive. The flat plate is mounted on a gimballed surface which allows rotation in response to pitch and roll signals from the aircraft vertical reference gyro (VRG). Radiation is through a radome which ideally is transparent to the X-band energy but at the same time provides protection for the scanner, preserves the aerodynamic shape of the aircraft and has adequate structural strength.

Most of the interconnections are made using standard approved cables with signal and control lines screened. The interconnection between t.r. and scanner is, of necessity, by way of waveguide, losses in co-axial cable being unacceptable at X-band (or even C-band).

While the above is a simplified description of the Bendix RDR 1200 the units and their contents are very much the same for all modern digital systems. A trend in lightweight systems for general aviation aircraft is to combine the transmitter and scanner in one unit. The main advantage of a two unit system, t.r./scanner plus indicator, is that the waveguide run is eliminated, so reducing capital and installation costs and waveguide losses. The argument against combining the t.r. and scanner is that the unit

Fig. 9.7 Primus 200 multifunction colour weather radar. Two-unit sensor on the left, multifunction accessories on the right (courtesy RCA Ltd)

installed in the nose is costly in terms of maintenance should it require regular replacement; thus reliability assumes even greater importance in such systems.

Single-engined aircraft have not been neglected, the problem having been tackled in two different ways, both of which involve a combined t.r./scanner unit. Bendix have gone for an under-wing pod-mounted unit, while RCA have developed a wing leading edge mounted unit in which a section of a parabolic reflector is used, as well as a pod-mounted unit.

Corrosion due to moisture collection is a problem in the waveguide run, which may be eased by pressurization. The ideal is to have a reservoir of dry air feeding, via a pressure-reducing valve, a waveguide run which has a slow controlled leak at the scanner; this method is not used on civil aircraft. Several installations allow cabin air to pressurize the waveguide run via a bleeder valve, desiccant and filter. If the cabin air is not dried and filtered more problems may be created than solved. Two interesting cases that have been brought to the author's attention are: a nicotine deposit on the inner wall of the waveguide causing excessive attenuation, and rapid corrosion caused by fumes from the urine of animals transported by air. If no active pressurization is employed the pressure within the waveguide may still be higher than static pressure if all joints are tightly sealed. A primary aim of waveguide pressurization is to reduce high-altitude flash-over.

Fig. 9.8 Installation of Weather Scout 1 t.r./scanner unit (courtesy RCA Ltd)

The waveguide run should be kept as short as possible. Inaccessibility or inadequate cooling may mean that the t.r. cannot be situated so as to minimize the length of the run. Straight rigid waveguide should be used, avoiding bends, twists, corners and flexible sections, except where necessary, so reducing costs and losses. A choke flange to plain flange waveguide joint is normal practice, the choke flange having a recess to take a sealing ring.

The radome is usually a covered honeycomb structure made of a plastic material reinforced with fibreglass. The necessity for mechanical strength, small size and aerodynamic shape may compromise the r.f. performance. Lightning conductors on the inside surface of the radome will obstruct the beam, but their effect is minimized if they are perpendicular to the electric field of the wave. Horizontal polarization is normal since there is less sea clutter, although with moderate to rough seas the advantage is minimal.

On large aircraft a dual installation is used. Obviously the scanner cannot be duplicated but both t.r. and indicator can be. In some cases only the indicator is duplicated, thus eliminating the need for a waveguide switch. Unless one indicator is purely a slave with no system controls other than, say, brilliance, a transfer switch will be necessary to transfer control from one indicator to another. Even if two t.r.s are fitted a transfer switch is still necessary for scanner stabilization on-off and tilt control.

Controls

The following list of controls is quite extensive; most will be found on all radars but some are optional. The nomenclature varies but alternative names for some of the controls are listed where known.

Range Switch Used to select displayed range. Will also change the range mark spacing. Selection may be by pushbutton or rotary switch, the latter possibly incorporating 'OFF', 'STANDBY' and 'TEST' positions.

Off/Standby Pushbutton or incorporated in the range switch. With standby selected there will be no transmission while indicator extra high tension (e.h.t.) may or may not be on.

Function Switch Selects mode of operation 'NORMAL', 'CONTOUR', 'CYCLIC', 'MAPPING', 'BEACON'. The last two of these modes are described later. Normal operation allows the use of a.g.c. (preset gain) or variable gain; s.t.c. is usually active. Contour operation selection causes blanking of strongest signals, a.g.c. and s.t.c. automatically selected. Cyclic operation causes normal and contour presentations to alternate. Pushbutton or rotary control may be used. 'NORMAL' switch may be omitted, this mode of operation automatically being selected when a range switch incorporating 'OFF' and 'STANDBY' is selected to any range while 'CONTOUR' or 'CYCLIC' switches are off. (*See also* 'gain control'.)

Gain Control Used to set gain of receiver manually. A continuously rotatable or click-stop control is normal. The control may incorporate contour on-off; by rotating the knob past the maximum gain position contour plus preset gain will be selected. In this latter case a separate spring return pushbutton may be used to turn contour off momentarily. In other systems the gain control may simply incorporate a preset gain on-off switch at its maximum position.

Test Switch A special pattern specified by the manufacturers replaces weather (or mapping) picture when test is selected.

Scanner Stab Switch On-Off Switching.

Tilt Control Adjustment of scanner elevation angle typically ± 15°.

Brilliance or Intensity Control Adjusts brightness of display to suit ambient lighting.

Freeze or Hold Switch Data update of display stopped, last updated picture displayed. Transmission and scanner rotation continues. Warning lamp may be provided. Only available on digital system or where d.v.s.t. is employed.

Erase or Trace Control Spring return switch to rapidly discharge mesh in d.v.s.t., so wiping picture clean or continuously variable control which alters discharge rate.

Range Mark Control Alters intensity of range marks.

Azimuth Marker Switch Electronically generated; azimuth marks may be turned on or off.

Target Alert Switch On-off. When activated flashes an alert on the screen if a contourable target is detected in a 'window' ahead of the aircraft (window size for RCA Primus 200 is 7·5° either side of heading at a range of 60-150 nautical miles). Warning given regardless of selected range also when in 'freeze' mode.

Sector Scan Switch Allows selection of one of two

(usually) sector scan angles, e.g. Bendix RDR 1200 has ± 30° or ± 60° options.

Contrast Control Adjusts video amplifier gain and hence allows some control of picture as opposed to display brightness even when i.f. amps are operating under a.g.c. Sometimes called intensity.

Manual Tune Control Associated with automatic frequency control (a.f.c.) on-off switch. When a.f.c. is selected to off, local oscillator may be tuned manually for best returns. Generally not used on modern systems.

Operation

The actual operation of a weather radar is quite straightforward, but to get the best use of the system a considerable amount of experience and expertise is required on the part of the pilot. Beginners are advised to avoid by a wide margin any contourable target within s.t.c. range and any target at all outside that range.

With experience the pilot is able to distinguish between safe and unsafe targets to the extent that he may be able to penetrate, rather than just avoid, weather. Several words of warning are in order when attempting penetration: one should always select one of the longer ranges before attempting to fly between storm cells since the way through may be blocked further ahead; weather conditions can change rapidly; the limitations of X-band radar in so far as signal penetration is concerned should be remembered.

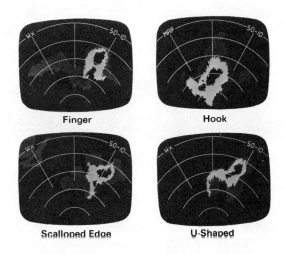

Fig. 9.9 RDR 1100 displays (courtesy Bendix Avionics Division)

It has already been mentioned that a narrow paint around a storm cell is a good indication of severe turbulence but whatever the width the cell should be avoided; the only question is by what margin. The shape of the return on the screen is also a pointer to the type of weather ahead. Targets with fingers, hooks, scalloped edges or that are U-shaped have been observed to be associated with hail. Long hooks or crescent-shaped indentations may indicate a tornado, but there are no guarantees either way.

This chapter, and its appendix, have thus far been concerned mainly with rain, so a word is in order here about returns from other types of precipitation. Dry snowfall will not be seen but wet snowfall may be seen with difficulty. Fog and mist will not be detected. Hail may give strong or weak returns: if it is dry and small compared with the wavelength, returns are weak; if it is water-coated, returns are strong; if it is dry and of a size comparable with the wavelength (an extreme condition with 3 cm radar) the echo is very strong. The increase in scattering for water-coated ice particles, hail or snow, may give rise to a 'bright band' at an altitude where the temperature is just above $0°C$. Lightning creates an ionized gaseous region which may, if oriented correctly, backscatter the radar energy.

Several things may affect the weather picture on the p.p.i. Icing on the radome will cause attenuation of the transmitted and received signal, so targets which would have been displayed may, under these circumstances, remain undetected until very close; 'innocent' precipitation will also attenuate the signal. Ground or sea returns may mask a storm cell; the tilt control should be used to separate weather and ground targets, a difficult task in mountainous regions.

Interference, which takes the form of broken, curved or straight lines on the p.p.i. display, is caused by other radar systems. The exact effect varies with the type of video signal processing and scan conversion (if any) and with the p.r.f. of the interfering radar. The older type of weather radar with no scan conversion and no averaging of the video output is particularly susceptible to interference. High p.r.f. interfering signals, such as GCA, give many fine broken radial lines on the screen. If the interfering p.r.f. is close to a harmonic of the p.r.f. of the radar being interfered with, then curved broken lines, apparently moving into or away from the origin, will result. Where motion is apparent, the interference is commonly referred to as 'running rabbits', another commonly encountered term is 'rabbit tracks'. Selection of contour may alleviate interference problems.

Abnormal p.p.i. presentations will be observed if scanner stabilization faults exist. With the scanner tilted down and stabilization on a bright circular band of terrain targets centred on the origin should be presented. If the band is not circular but is severely distorted, then most probably the gyro is 'toppled' or 'spilled', i.e. the spin axis is not vertical. The gyro will be in such a condition if its rotor is running slow, as will be the case if it has just been switched on or there is a supply or gyro motor defect. A gyro fast erect switch may be provided which, when depressed, increases the supply voltage so accelerating the run up to operating speed. The switch should not be held on for more than half a minute or so, otherwise the rotor speed may exceed that for which it was designed, so causing damage.

To complete an airborne check of stabilization, the aircraft should be banked and pitched, within the stabilization limits, satisfactory operation being indicated by an unchanging circular terrain band. Note that with tilt down selected, the amount of nose up pitch that the stabilization circuits can deal with is limited.

Spoking is any p.p.i. presentation which resembles the spokes of a wheel. It is almost certainly caused by a fault within the weather radar system, although it can be caused by unshielded electromagnetic devices producing strong changing magnetic fields. There are two main classes of fault which cause spoking: (a) video signal and noise spokes due to abnormal video output amplitude variations such as might be caused by the automatic frequency circuits (a.f.c.) sweeping through the local oscillator frequencies and (b) sweep spokes due to faulty display circuitry such as damaged slip rings in the time-base resolver employed in an older all-analogue radar. To determine which of (a) or (b) is the cause, the gain may be turned down and the antenna tilted to maximum up; if the spoking persists, the fault is in the display circuitry.

The above is only a brief discussion of some of the factors one must consider when operating weather radar. Because of the degree of skill involved, a pilot new to weather radar should study the manufacturer's pilot's guide carefully; they are usually very good. Equally important, he should learn each time he uses the system; for example, if a detour is made to avoid an unusually shaped return, a simple sketch and a phone call on landing to enquire about the weather associated with that target will add to his experience. Remember that to a large extent the body of knowledge concerning weather returns is empirical. What better way to learn than to collect one's own results?

A final and most important point needs to be

made, and that is that weather radar presents a considerable hazard when operated on the ground. Details are given later in this chapter.

Block Diagram Operation

We shall consider both analogue and digital systems: the former since it illustrates the principles of weather radar directly and systems of this type are still very widely used; the latter since it is the current approach of all manufacturers. Two types of digital system will be considered: rho-theta display and X-Y display.

All Analogue System
The p.r.f. generator provides time synchronization for the complete system; the output is often called the

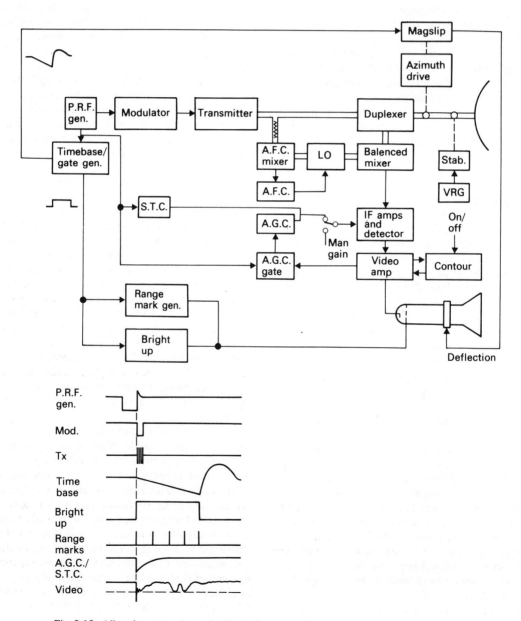

Fig. 9.10 All analogue weather radar block diagram and waveforms

150

pre-pulse, since the lagging edge is used to trigger the modulator. The transmitter is a magnetron keyed by the modulator which determines the pulse width. The burst of r.f. energy (main bang) is fed from the transmitter to the scanner via a duplexer and waveguide run. The duplexer allows common aerial working in that it is an electronic switch which automatically connects the scanner to the transmitter for the duration of the transmitted pulse, thus protecting the receiver.

A sample of the transmitted frequency is fed to the a.f.c. (automatic frequency control) mixer along with an output from the l.o. (local oscillator). If the difference frequency is not equal to the required i.f. the a.f.c. circuit applies a control signal to the l.o., so adjusting its frequency until we have equality. If the difference frequency is outside the bandwidth of the a.f.c. circuit, the control signal is made to sweep until such time as the a.f.c. loop can operate normally.

The main receiver mixer is balanced to reduce l.o. noise. The i.f. amplifier chain is broad band (bandwidth $> 2 \times$ reciprocal of pulse width) with gain controlled by the a.g.c./s.t.c. circuits or the manual gain control. The video envelope is detected and after further amplification is used to intensity modulate (Z-modulation) the c.r.t.

With contour on, the video signal is sampled, and if above a preset inversion level the video fed to the c.r.t. is effectively removed.

The pre-pulse is fed to the a.g.c. gate which thus allows the video output through to the a.g.c. circuit only for the duration of the pre-pulse (say 10 μs). In this way the gain control line voltage level is made a function of receiver noise. The lagging edge of the pre-pulse triggers the s.t.c. circuit which reduces i.f. gain at zero range and returns it to normal after, typically, 30 nautical miles (about 370 μs).

The lagging edge of the pre-pulse also initiates the start of the time-base and gate waveforms, the duration of which depend on the range selected. The time-base waveform $I(t)$ is fed to a magslip (synchro resolver) in the scanner; since the rotor of the magslip is driven in synchronism with the scanner azimuth movement the outputs are $I(t) \sin \theta$ and $I(t) \cos \theta$ where θ is the azimuth angle measured with reference to the aircraft heading. Using the cosine output for vertical deflection and the sine output for horizontal deflection provides the necessary rotating time-base.

The start of the time-base run-down must correspond to zero deflection of the c.r.t. spot. Since the magslip, being basically a transformer, removes any d.c. level a balancing half-cycle is required immediately after the time-base flyback to make the average (zero) value of the composite time-base

waveform coincide with the start of the run-down. If the balancing half-cycle is made larger than necessary we have an open centre whereby zero range is represented by an arc, of non-zero radius, on the p.p.i. display.

The gate waveform is fed to the marker and bright-up circuits which provide the necessary feeds to the c.r.t. for the duration of the time-base. Range marks are produced at equally spaced intervals during the gate, and are used to intensity modulate the c.r.t. electron beam. The bright-up waveform provides a bias which prevents the velocity of the beam being sufficient to excite the phosphor coating on the screen, except during the time-base rundown.

Pitch and roll stabilization is provided by a gyro-controlled servomechanism.

Digital Weather Radar – Rho-Theta Display

The radio and intermediate frequency part of the block diagram is much the same for analogue and digital systems, so here only the video, timing and control blocks will be considered. The following is based on the RCA Primus 40.

Analogue video data from the receiver is digitized in an analogue to digital (a/d) converter. The range selected is divided into 128 equal range cells, for example, with 300 nautical miles selected each cell is $300/128 = 2.344$ nautical miles, or, in terms of time, 3607 μs is divided into 128 time-slots of 28.96 μs. During each time-slot the video level is first integrated then encoded as a 2-bit word, thus giving four discrete representations from zero to maximum signal. In the Primus 40 a complemented Gray code is used for the conversion but is then changed to standard binary.

The scanner is driven by a stepper motor such that 1024 steps are taken for $120°$ of scan. The transmitter fires on every other step so providing 512 azimuth directions from which echoes may be received. Thus on each of 512 azimuth angles data is acquired in 128 range increments.

The averaging/smoothing circuits reduce the number of lines (azimuth directions) by a factor of 4 to 128 (= 512/4) and apply a correction to the gradient of the signal in range and azimuth. The 4 to 1 line reduction is achieved by averaging the sum of four adjacent azimuth time cells as shown in Fig. 9.13 and Table 9.1. After averaging we have 128 lines with 128 range cells per line giving $128 \times 128 = 16\,384$ data cells. The data is then corrected first in range then in azimuth as follows: if in a series of three adjacent cells the outer two cells are the same but the inner is different, then the inner is corrected so as all three are the same; for example,

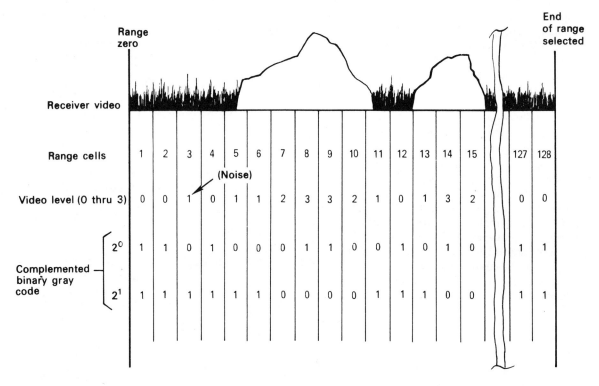

Fig. 9.11 Analogue to digital conversion in the Primus 40 (courtesy RCA Ltd)

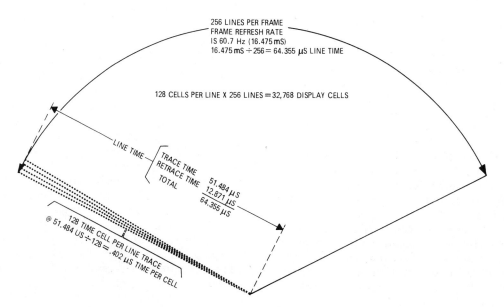

Fig. 9.12 Rho-theta raster scan format in the Primus 40; 512 transmissions per scan, 128 lines in memory, 256 displayed lines (courtesy RCA Ltd)

Table 9.1 Four to one line averaging

Sum of four azimuth adjacent time cells	Average
0-1	0
2-5	1
6-9	2
10-12	3

313 would be corrected to 333 while 012 would remain the same (*see* Fig. 9.14). The above processes, together with the integration of the video signal within each range cell prior to digitization, reduce the displayed noice to negligible proportions.

Each of the 128 lines of 128 cells is placed in memory as it is received. Since the signal level within each range cell is coded as a 2-bit word the memory capacity must be $2 \times 128 \times 128 = 32\,768$ bits. The memory comprises sixteen 2×1024-bit shift registers, so application of clock pulses causes the circulation of data provided the output is connected to the input which is the case when new data are not being loaded. New data must be loaded into memory at the correct time in the sequence of circulating data; this timing control is provided by the new data line control circuit which synchronizes the loading with scanner position. Loading is inhibited when the freeze button is pressed but circulation of data continues. The data is continuously read out as it circulates at a rate of about 7772 lines per second compared with loading every fourth main bang, a rate of $121 \cdot 4/4 = 30 \cdot 35$ lines per second. The different load and read rates give the scan conversion in time, leading to a flicker free bright picture.

Although 128 lines of video are stored, 256 lines are displayed, so it is necessary to double the stored lines. The line-doubling circuit averages two adjacent stored video lines to generate a middle line, so giving the required 256 lines each of 128 cells (i.e. a total of 32 768 displayed cells). In the averaging process the rule is to average up if an integer average is not possible. The following example, considering part of

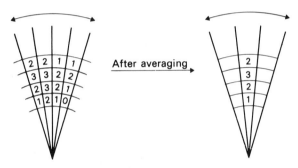

Fig. 9.13 Four to one line averaging in the RCA Primus 40

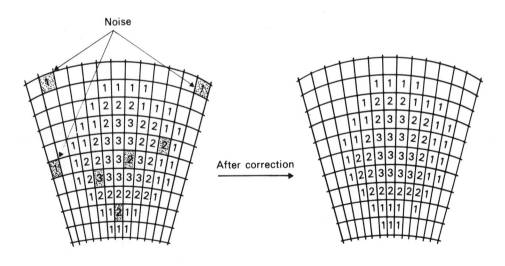

Noise

After correction

Corrected

Fig. 9.14 Range and azimuth smoothing and correction in the RCA Primus 40

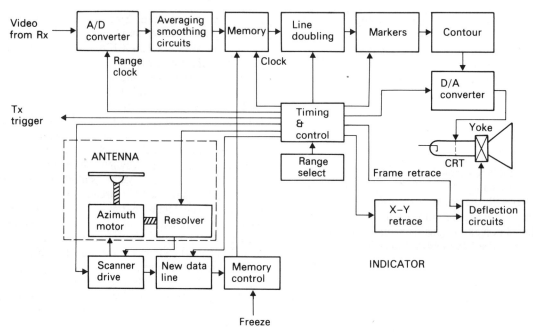

Fig. 9.15 Video processing and rho-theta display block diagram

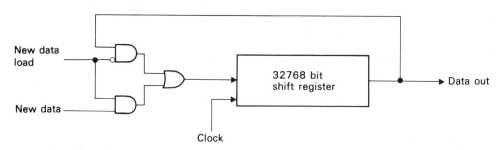

Fig. 9.16 Simplified memory

three adjacent stored lines, illustrates the process:

```
stored line ...3   3   2   2   1 ...
middle line ...3   3   2   2   1 ...
stored line ...3   2   2   1   0 ...
middle line ...2   1   1   1   0 ...
stored line ...0   0   0   0   0 ...
```

Range marks are obtained by raising the appropriate range cell level for each of the 256 lines by 1, i.e. 0 becomes 1, 1 becomes 2, 2 becomes 3 while 3 remains at 3. Thus range marks appear slightly brighter than target returns except for level 3 targets. Identification of the appropriate range cell in each line is achieved by a counter. For example on the 25 nautical mile range there are five range marks 5 nautical miles apart. Since there are 128 range cells per line each nautical

mile is represented by $128/25 = 5 \cdot 12$ cells, so the first mark is located at cell 26 (= $5 \times 5 \cdot 12$) with subsequent marks at cells 51, 77, 102 and 128.

Azimuth marks are obtained by raising all 128 cells of the appropriate lines by 1 in a similar way to that described above. The sweep is $120°$, so for $15°$ azimuth markers we require $1 + 120/15 = 9$ lines to be enhanced in intensity. With 256 lines those chosen are line 2 and line $256 N/8 = 32N$ where $N = 1$-8. Line 2 is used for the $-60°$ marker since blanking is applied to the first trace line, thus the leftmost azimuth marker is in fact at $-59 \cdot 0625°$.

The contour circuit converts a video 3 level to a video 0 level. If we had a range sequence of cells 0 2 3 0 0, say, then the contoured cell of level 3 would not be bordered, the sequence being

154

0 2 0 0 0. To avoid this, the range cell adjacent to a contoured level 3 cell is raised to level 2 if necessary, thus in our example 0 2 3 0 0 would become 0 2 0 2 0 after contouring. Bordering is guaranteed in azimuth as a result of the line-doubling process since, for example, if we have adjacent azimuth cells with video levels 1 3 0 from memory, then line-doubling will give 1 2 3 2 0 and after contouring 1 2 0 2 0 as required. This bordering feature is necessary where the video gradient is steep, such as when we receive returns from mountains or distant weather targets.

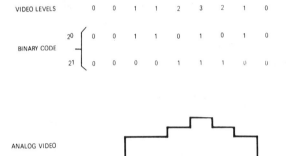

Fig. 9.17 Digital to analogue conversion (uncontoured) (courtesy RCA Ltd)

The c.r.t. is intensity modulated by one of four d.c. levels applied to its control grid. Since the output from the contour circuit is digital we must employ a digital to analogue (D/A) conversion circuit.

The rho-theta raster is generated by the deflection circuits which are triggered by the frame and X-Y retrace waveforms. A linear ramp current waveform needs to be generated for both the Y (vertical) deflection coils and the X (horizontal) deflection coils which form the yoke. The duration of the ramp is 53·89 μs with a 10·46 μs retrace (flyback) giving a total line time (time-base period) of 64·35 μs. The amplitudes of the ramp waveforms determine the amount of deflection in the X and Y directions and thus the particular line which is traced on the screen; line 1 is at $-60°$, line 256 is at $+60°$. In practice, since on the completion of one frame at line 256 on the right we start the next frame on the left after frame retrace, line 1 is blanked in order to allow the deflection circuits to settle down. The frame rate is 60·7 Hz.

The X and Y ramp waveforms are initiated by the X-Y retrace pulses. The amplitude of the Y ramp must be a minimum at the beginning and end of the frame and a maximum half-way through the frame; its polarity is constant throughout. The amplitude of the X ramp must be a maximum at the beginning and end of the frame and zero half-way through the frame, when the polarity reverses. To achieve the amplitude variations described the X and Y ramp waveforms are amplitude-modulated by appropriately shaped waveforms triggered by the frame retrace pulse.

It should be evident that timing and synchronization are all-important. We see from the simplified block diagram that the timing and control circuits are connected to virtually all parts to ensure the

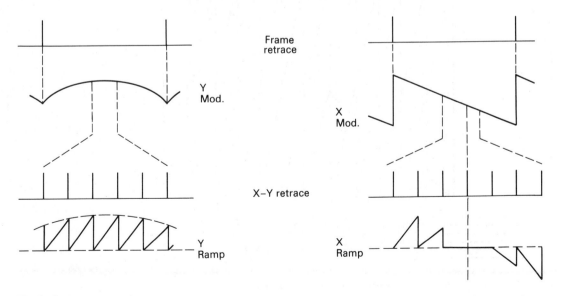

Fig. 9.18 Ramp generation

necessary synchronization. All timing signals are derived from a 4·972 459 MHz crystal-controlled oscillator (period 0·201 107 7 μs). Of particular significance is the scanner position when new data is loaded into the memory. A counter in the scanner drive circuits counts every eighth step in the sweep, first clockwise then counterclockwise and so on. The counter thus gives the memory line number from 1 to 128 (= 1024/8) which is used by the new data load circuit. It is possible that the scanner stepping motor may miss a few beats, in which case the count referred to above will not represent the scanner position correctly. In order to prevent cumulative errors the count is 'jammed' at 64 whenever the scanner crosses the dead ahead position going clockwise. The information required for 'jam centre' operation is derived from the X-axis stator output of a resolver, the rotor of which is driven by the azimuth motor. This output varies in amplitude, and phase-reverses when the scanner passes through the dead ahead position.

The above is a much-simplified description of the essential features of the Primus 40; many details have been omitted. Other digital weather radars with rho-theta displays such as the Bendix RDR 1200 will differ in detail but will operate in a similar way.

Digital Weather Radar — Television (t.v.) Display
In the previous section we saw that a digital weather radar with a rho-theta display required scan conversion in time only. This follows since the data are collected in the same order as they are presented; only the rates are different. With a t.v. display this is not so, therefore we need scan conversion in both position and time. Since the basic differences between the two types of digital radar are the rasters, scan conversion, and the organization of memory we shall concentrate on these topics. What follows is based on the RCA Primus 30.

The raster is similar to a standard t.v. display except that the field and line directions of displacement are reversed and it is quantitatively different. The raster consists of 256 vertical lines each with 256 cells, thus we have 256 × 256 = 65 536 displayed data cells. Each frame of 256 lines is displayed in two interlaced fields each of 128 lines. The field rate is approximately 107·5 per second so the interlace gives approximately 53·75 frames per second (faster than conventional t.v.), which gives a flicker-free picture.

Azimuth drive is similar to the Primus 40, the angle of scan being 120° achieved in 1024 steps. An azimuth counter counts every fourth step so that when the count has gone from 0 to 255 there is a phase reversal of the drive signal causing the scanner to reverse direction. When switching from standby to a transmit mode (normal, contour, cyclic or mapping) the scanner is driven counterclockwise to the

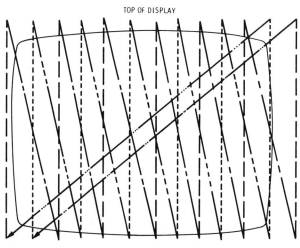

TOP OF DISPLAY

— — — — FIRST FIELD RASTER LINE, ONE OF 128 LINES WRITTEN AT RATE OF 107.5 Hz*
– ‑ – ‑ – ‑ FIRST FIELD BLANK RETRACE LINE, ONE OF 128 GENERATED AT RATE OF 107.5 Hz*
——— ·· — BLANK FLYBACK LINE FROM END OF FIRST FIELD TO BEGINNING OF SECOND FIELD AT RATE OF 107.5 Hz
‑‑‑‑‑‑‑ SECOND FIELD RASTER LINE, ONE OF 128 LINES WRITTEN AT RATE OF 107.5 Hz*
‑ ‑ ‑ ‑ ‑ ‑ ‑ SECOND FIELD BLANK RETRACE LINE, ONE OF 128 GENERATED AT RATE OF 107.5 Hz*
——— ··· — BLANK FLYBACK LINE FROM END OF SECOND FIELD TO BEGINNING OF FIRST FIELD AT RATE OF 107.5 Hz
*13760 LINES PER SEC

Fig. 9.19 Simplified raster for the Primus 30 (only eleven lines shown) (courtesy RCA Ltd)

leftmost position, and 'chatters' there until the azimuth counter reaches 255 when clockwise rotation is initiated; this ensures synchronization of counter and position.

Digitized data is written into a random access memory (RAM) consisting of eight 4096-bit RAM chips giving a total of 32K bit storage (1K bit = 1024 bits). Thus with a cell containing a 2-bit word there is provision for 16K cells (= 128 × 128). Conceptually the memory is arranged as a grid with orthogonal axes, so the address at which data is to be stored must be in X-Y format. Scan conversion is required to provide the correct address given that the data is being received in a rho-theta format.

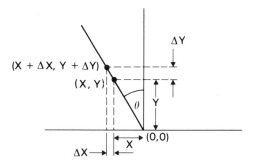

Fig. 9.20 Rho-theta to X/Y scan conversion

Assume a word has been correctly stored at address (X, Y) the next word, assuming a unit range step, must be stored at $(X + \Delta X, Y + \Delta Y)$ where $\Delta X = \sin \theta$ and $\Delta Y = \cos \theta$, θ being the scanner azimuth angle given by the azimuth counter (*see* Fig. 9.20). The rate of generation of new addresses is determined by the rate of generation of new data cells, of which there are 128 for each azimuth count. The first data cell in each group of 128 corresponds to the address $(0, 0)$. A read only memory (ROM) is

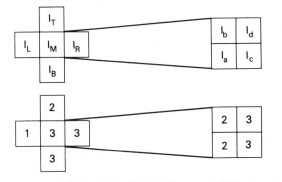

Fig. 9.21 A RAM cell to display cell conversion in the RCA Primus 30

used as a lock-up table to give the values of $\cos \theta$ and $\sin \theta$.

The 128×128 = 16K RAM cells must be converted to 256×256 = 64K display cells; this is achieved by a data smoothing circuit. Each RAM cell is converted into four display cells, the video level in each display cell being determined by a weighted and biased average of levels in the corresponding RAM cell and some of its neighbours. With the cells designated as shown in Fig. 9.21 we have:

$$Ia = \text{int. } [(2I_M + I_B + I_L + 1)/4]$$
$$Ib = \text{int. } [(2I_M + I_T + I_L + 1)/4]$$
$$Ic = \text{int. } [(2I_M + I_B + I_R + 1)/4]$$
$$Id = \text{int. } [(2I_M + I_T + I_R + 1)/4]$$

where int. $[\ldots]$ means integer part of $[\ldots]$.

An example of the process for one RAM cell is given in the figure.

Four concentric arcs, with centre at the middle of the bottom edge of the display, serve as range marks. The addresses of the display cells to be illuminated for range mark purposes are stored in a ROM. The 8K bit ROM is time-shared with the scan converter which utilizes it as a sin/cos look-up table, as stated previously.

The rho-theta sector of target returns occupies only part of the X-Y display. The unused area of the screen is used for alphanumerics identifying the operating mode and the range marks. A ROM, used only for alphanumerics, contains the position code for the bottom of each character on any given line of the raster.

Each of the circuits providing the functions of raster generation, azimuth drive, digitization, RAM and ROM addressing and transmission must be synchronized in time. All timing signals are derived from a 10·08 MHz crystal oscillator. Suitable sub-multiples of the basic frequency are fed throughout the system as triggers and clocks which keep everything in step.

Scanner Stabilization

The need for scanner stabilization has already been stated; here we shall review the implementation. There are basically two types of stabilization: platform and line-of-sight. With the former the moving part of the scanner can be considered as being mounted on a platform controlled, independently in pitch and roll, by a vertical reference gyro (VRG). With the latter, pitch and roll signals are combined,

157

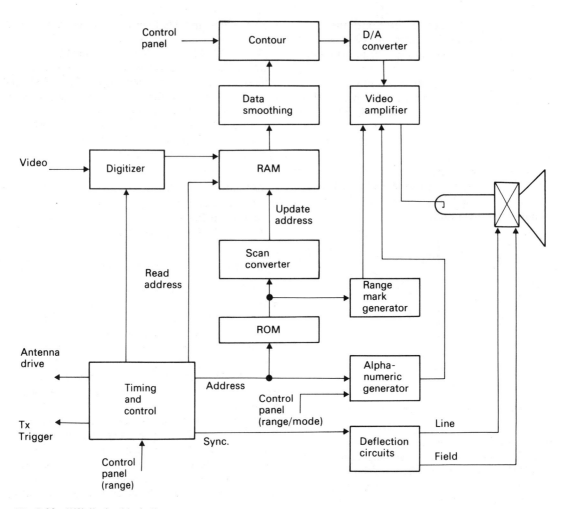

Fig. 9.22 *X/Y* display block diagram

taking into account the azimuth angle of the scanner, the composite signal being used to control the beam tilt angle. Since the platform system requires rotating waveguide joints for azimuth, pitch and roll movement plus pitch and roll motors, the line-of-sight system is preferred in most modern weather radars. Only the line-of-sight system will be explained below.

While the scanner is pointing dead ahead, aircraft movement in roll will have no effect on the beam direction since the axis about which the aircraft is rotating is in line with the beam axis. With the scanner pointing 90° port or starboard pitch movement will have a negligible effect since the axis about which the aircraft is rotating is parallel and close to the beam axis. Conversely with the scanner dead ahead, aircraft pitch must be corrected in full while the scanner at ± 90° aircraft roll must be corrected in full by pitching or tilting the scanner.

The above paragraph is the basis for line-of-sight stabilization. Pitch and roll signals from the VRG are combined in an azimuth resolver, the rotor of which is driven by the azimuth motor. The stators of the resolver are connected to the pitch (P) and roll (R) outputs of the VRG, in such a way that the rotor output is $P \cos \theta + R \sin \theta$, where θ is the azimuth angle.

The composite demand signal is fed to a servo amplifier which also has position and velocity feedback inputs. If the sum of the inputs is non-zero, an error signal from the servo amplifier will drive the motor so as to reduce the error to zero. The position feedback from the tilt synchro is modified by the tilt control so that the angle of the beam above or below the horizontal may be set by the pilot. Velocity feedback is provided by a tachogenerator to prevent excessive overshoot.

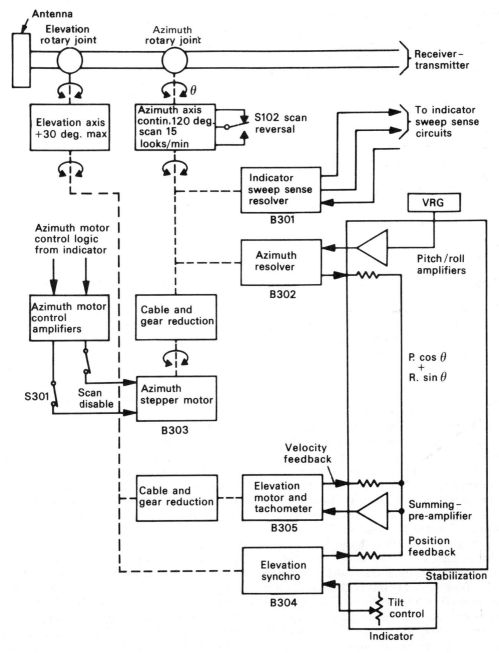

Fig. 9.23 RDR 1200 scanner block diagram (courtesy Bendix Avionics Division)

The components used in the stabilization system can vary. The position feedback transducer and tilt control may be two- or three-wire synchros or indeed potentiometers. Some equipments use a d.c. rather than a.c. motor although a.c. is normal for demand and feedback signals. On some systems no roll correction is employed if the scanner azimuth angle is restricted to say ±45°, as on various general aviation systems.

Unless an azimuth stepper motor is used the azimuth angular velocity of the scanner is not constant. Reversal of direction at the extremities means that the scanner accelerates towards the dead ahead position and slows down going away from dead ahead.

It follows that less time is available to make stabilization corrections at the dead ahead position. If the servo loop response is fast enough to cope with the most rapid movement in azimuth it will be too fast at the extremities. In order to vary response time the velocity feedback may be modified so that it is greatest in amplitude when the azimuth angle is a maximum.

With a flat plate aerial the beam is tilted by pitching the plate, thus a pitch-rotating waveguide joint is needed. There is a choice when the system uses a parabolic reflector, either the reflector and feed move in pitch or the reflector only. In the latter case no pitch-rotating joint is used but the beam shape deteriorates since the feed point is displaced from the focus with tilt applied.

Other Applications for Weather Radar

Although the primary function of a weather radar is to detect conditions likely to give rise to turbulence, various other uses for the system or part of the system have been, and continue to be, found. These will be briefly described.

Mapping

Virtually all weather radars offer a mapping facility. At its most crude, selection of mapping merely removes s.t.c., whereupon the pilot can tilt the beam down to view a limited region of the ground. At its best the beam is changed to a fan-shaped beam, whereby received echo energy is constant from all parts of the illuminated ground region. In the Appendix it is shown that the received power is inversely proportional to the square of the range for a beam-filling target (A9.9), also if the beam is depressed at an angle ϕ to the horizontal the range $R = h \csc \phi$ where h is the aircraft height. So for equal returns from ground targets at different depression angles (hence range) the transmitted power needs to be distributed on a $\csc^2 \phi$ basis, since we will then have $(P_r) \propto (P_t/R^2) \propto (\csc^2 \phi/h^2 \csc^2 \phi) = (1/h^2)$, i.e. P_r is independent of range.

With a parabolic reflector an approximate $\csc^2$ beam can be obtained by use of a polarization-sensitive grid ahead of the reflector surface. In the weather mode the grid is transparent to the beam since the E field is perpendicular to the conducting vanes of the grid while in the mapping mode the grid reflects part of the beam energy downward since the E field is parallel to the vanes and therefore does not satisfy the boundary conditions. To achieve remote switching between weather and mapping, either the

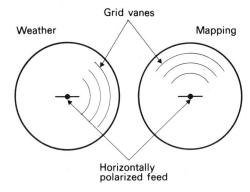

Fig. 9.24 Weather-mapping facility using a parabolic reflector

reflector is rotated through 90° (as in Fig. 9.24) or the direction of polarization is rotated by using a waveguide rotating joint or a ferrite polarization twister.

The $\csc^2$ beam is difficult to achieve with a flat plate array designed specifically for a pencil beam. However, a fan-shaped beam can be obtained by reversing the phase of the r.f. energy fed to the slots in the top half of the plate.

When selected to mapping, rivers, lakes and coastlines are clearly identified, so allowing confirmation of position. Built-up areas and mountains will give strong returns. An interesting phenomenon may be noticed over the plains of the United States: since fences, buildings and power lines tend to be laid out with a north-south or east-west orientation, returns from the cardinal points are strongest, thus giving noticeable bright lines on the radar corresponding to north, south, east or west.

Drift Indication

With downward tilt the returned echo is subject to a Doppler shift due to the relative velocity of the aircraft along the beam. The spectrum of Doppler shift frequencies is narrowest when the beam is aligned with the aircraft track. The Doppler signal can be displayed on a suitable indicator (A-type display) where, due to the spectrum, it appears as noise elevated onto the top of the return pulse. With manual control of the azimuth position of the scanner the pilot can adjust until the Doppler 'noise' (spectrum) is at a minimum, when the drift angle can be read off the control. This option is rarely found.

Beacon Interrogation

The transmitted pulse from the weather radar can be used to trigger a suitably tuned beacon (transponder) on the ground. The beacon replies on 9310 MHz, so a weather radar with a local oscillator frequency of 9375 MHz and a transmit frequency of 9345 MHz will produce a difference frequency of 30 MHz for normal returns and a difference frequency of 65 MHz for the beacon reply. Two differently tuned i.f. amplifiers can be used to separate the signals. As an alternative two local oscillators may be used.

On some systems the selection of beacon eliminates the normal returns from the display; on others it is possible to show weather and the beacon response.

The ease with which this facility can be used to find offshore oil rigs makes radars offering beacon operation an attractive proposition for helicopters supplying the rigs. Such radars usually have a short-range capability; for example, the Primus 50 offers 2 nautical mile range using a 0·6 μs pulse, thus giving good range resolution.

Multifunction Display

The weather radar indicator is increasingly used for purposes other than the display of weather or mapping information. *X-Y* rasters in particular make the display of alphanumeric data straightforward, hence all the major manufacturers now offer a 'page-printer' option with one or more of the radars in their range. Similarly display of navigation data is available as an option with the latest colour weather radars.

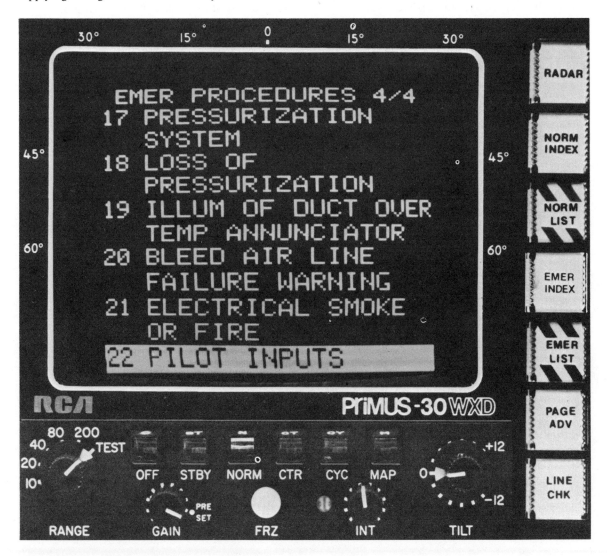

Fig. 9.25 Primus 30 with page-printer option (courtesy RCA Ltd)

A page-printer option is normally used to display checklists. The alphanumeric data is arranged and stored in pages on EPROMs, either in the indicator or in an external auxiliary unit. Each page may be called up in turn using a page-advance button. Pages containing the normal checklist index and emergency checklist index are particularly important, and usually have dedicated buttons used to call them up for display. Having displayed a page of one of the indexes a line-check button may be used to advance a cursor (line highlighted by displaying, say, black alphanumerics on green background rather than green on black as for the other lines). With the cursor set, the chosen checklist can be displayed using a list button.

Apart from checklists other alphanumeric information which may be listed includes waypoints, or indeed any pilot-entered data if pages are allocated to this facility. One method of allowing the pilot to enter data is to use a calculator keyboard; Hewlett-Packard and Texas Instruments make calculators which can be modified to interface with the page-printer system.

Display of navigation data from external sensors such as VORTAC, Omega, INS or Loran is achieved through an interface unit. Typically the pilot is able to display waypoints joined by track lines, together with the weather data. As an example the RCA Data Nav. 11 system allows the display of current VORTAC frequency, range and bearing to current waypoint and up to three correctly positioned waypoint symbols from twenty which can be stored. An additional feature of the Data Nav. 11 is a designator symbol which may be set to any desired location on the screen; this location can then be entered as a new waypoint to replace the current one, so providing an alternative route if storms are observed on original intended course.

Progress in this area is rapid. In 1979, with the appropriate interface, the weather radar could display projections of aircraft position on straight or curved paths, ETA at waypoints and warnings of sensor data failure in addition to the data referred to above.

Weather Radar Characteristics

ARINC Characteristic 564-7 allows the designer more freedom than do most other such documents; however it is quite clear what performance and facilities are to be made available. The following is a summary of some of the more significant and/or interesting items.

Range
At least 180 nautical miles for subsonic aircraft and

300 nautical miles for s.s.t. is usually demanded by customers.

Range marks at 25 nautical mile intervals up to 100 nautical miles are suggested, as are the available range selections of 30/80/180 or 30/100/300 or 30/80/180/360. The advantages of a continuously variable displayed range from 30 nautical miles to maximum are stated.

Displayed Sector
At least ±90° but not more than ±120°. Displayed range at ±90° to be not less than 60 per cent of maximum range. The scan may be reciprocating or circular. (Note in the case of the latter, since the scanner rotates through 360° RAM (radar absorbent material) screening is needed on the nose bulkhead to prevent excessively strong received signals.)

Radio Frequency
C-Band   5400 MHz ± 20 MHz (nominal)
X-Band   9375 MHz ± 20 MHz (nominal), or
          9345 MHz ± 20 MHz (nominal)

Bandwidth
Minimum bandwidth = $1 \cdot 2/\delta$ where the pulse width δ must be less than 10 μs.

Display Accuracy
Azimuth angle: ± 2°.
Range: the greater of ± 5 per cent or 1 nautical mile.

Sensitivity Time Control
Range^2 law from 3 nautical miles to the point where a 3 nautical mile target ceases to be beam filling. Two-wire logic from scanner to set s.t.c. maximum range in accordance with antenna gain (and hence beamwidth).

Scanner Stab and Tilt
Two-wire pitch and roll signals each $(E/2300)$ V ± 2 per cent per degree where E is nominal 115 V 400 Hz reference phase (50 mV per degree but expressed in terms of supply). The phase of signals is specified. Dummy load of 20 kΩ where signal not used.
Pitch and roll rate capability 20° per second.
Line-of-sight (two-axis system): combined roll, pitch and tilt freedom ± 35° with accuracy ± 1°, manual tilt ± 14°.
Split axis (three-axis system): roll ± 40°, pitch ± 20°, manual tilt ± 14°, combined pitch and tilt ± 25°, accuracy ± 0·5°.
Droop nose signal $(E/575)$ V per degree, same phase as nose down. (Two-wire signal, 20 mV per degree

Enroute Navigation.

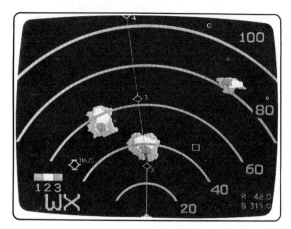

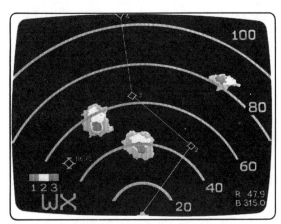

1) The intended track line originating from the aircraft symbol displays the programmed route of flight. Waypoints and their numbers can be displayed on the track line. When DataNav is utilized with RNAV, the associated VORTAC symbol is displayed along with its frequency as illustrated. When used with a VLF/OMEGA or INS system, the DataNav will display similar information. When weather is encountered the current Waypoint may be offset by using RCA's exclusive Designator feature. The Designator can be moved to any location on the screen by means of the Waypoint

offset control showing the Designator symbol at 35° right, 46 nm.

2) When the Designator is at the desired position, the new Waypoint can be entered into the Navigation System by means of the "ENTR" button on the DataNav control panel. The current Waypoint will be moved to the new location and a new track line established. The Range and Bearing of the aircraft to the VORTAC station will always be displayed in the lower right hand corner of the display.

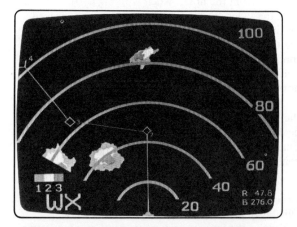

W/P	1	2	3
FREQ	116.70	116.70	112.80
RADL	141.5	101.0	144.2
RNG	52.0	39.1	50.7
ALT	41000.	41000.	41000.
ELEV	3650.	3650.	9040.
VERT	0.0	0.0	0.0
CRS	11.0	10.0	07.0
DIST	1949.	1949.	1949.

WAYPOINT LISTING

3) The aircraft has now completed the turn and intercepted the new track line which will safely circumnavigate the dangerous weather. If desired, you can return to the original Waypoint and track line by pressing the cancel button on the DataNav control panel.

4) Waypoint Listing Mode can be selected by means of the "MODE" button on the DataNav control panel. Information for 3 Waypoints can be displayed on the screen. The current Waypoint will be displayed in yellow with all other data in green. All the Waypoints can be displayed in groups of three by moving the "Waypoint Offset Control" left or right.

Fig. 9.26 En-route navigation with the (colour) Primus 200 (courtesy RCA Ltd)

for SST aircraft where scanner mount is dropped with nose.)
Scale required on scanner whereby tilt angle may be read.

Waveguide
C-Band type ARA 136 or WR 137. X-Band type RG-67U. Ridged waveguide rejected; v.s.w.r. maximum 1·1 : 1.

Magnetron Magnetic Field
No more than 1° compass deviation with sensor 15 ft from the t.r. The t.r. should be mounted at least 2 ft from the indicators, other t.r. units and other devices sensitive to magnetic fields.

Maintenance and Testing

Safety Precautions
There are two hazards when operating weather radar, namely damage to human tissue and ignition of combustible material.

The greater the average power density the greater the health hazard. A figure of 10 mW cm² is a generally accepted maximum permissible exposure level (m.p.e.l.). Among the most vulnerable parts of the body are the eyes and testes.

The greater the peak power the greater the fire hazard. Any conducting material close to the scanner may act as a receiving aerial and have r.f. currents induced. There is obviously a risk, particularly when aircraft are being refuelled or defuelled.

An additional hazard, which does not affect safety but will affect the serviceability of the radar, is the possibility of very strong returns if the radar is operated close to reflecting objects. The result of these returns is to burn out the receiver crystals which are of the point contact type.

The following rules should be observed when operating the weather radar on the ground:

1. ensure that no personnel are closer to a transmitting radar scanner than the m.p.e.l. boundary, as laid down by the system manufacturer;
2. never transmit from a stationary scanner;
3. do not operate the radar when the aircraft is being refuelled or defuelled, or when another aircraft within the sector scanned is being refuelled or defuelled;
4. do not transmit when containers of inflammable or explosive material are close to the aircraft within the sector scanned;
5. do not operate with an open waveguide unless r.f. power is off; never look down an open waveguide; fit a dummy load if part of the waveguide run is disconnected;
6. do not operate close to large reflecting objects or in a hangar unless r.f. energy absorbing material is placed over the radome (RAM cap).

The safe distances for radars vary widely, depending on average power transmitted and beam width. It is normal to calculate the m.p.e.l. assuming a stationary scanner and a point source, in which case an average power of $\delta \times F \times P_t$ is spread over an area of $\pi \times D^2 \times \tan^2(\theta/2)$; thus the distance D in metres for an exposure level of 10 mW/cm² is given by:

$$D = \frac{1}{100} \left[\frac{\delta F P_t}{10\, \pi \tan^2(\theta/2)} \right]^{0.5} \text{m}$$

where: δ is pulse width in seconds;
$\quad\quad$ F is pulse repetition frequency in pulses per second;
$\quad\quad$ P_t is peak power in milliWatts;
$\quad\quad$ θ is beam width.

Thus consider an older airline standard weather radar (Bendix RDR IE/ED) using manufacturers' nominal figures for the longest range option, i.e. $\delta = 5\ \mu s$; $F = 200$; $P_t = 75$ kW; $\theta = 3°$; we have D = 18·66 m (≈ 60 ft), while for a modern general aviation radar (RCA Primus 20) where $\delta = 2·25\ \mu s$, $F = 107·5$, $P_t = 8$ kW, $\theta = 8°$ we have $D = 1·12$ m ($\approx 3\frac{1}{2}$ ft).

To ensure safety precautions are observed consult manufacturers' data for safe distances then, if operating the radar for maintenance purposes, place radiation hazard warning notices the appropriate distance from the nose. When working by the scanner with the radar on standby a notice should be placed by the controls stating 'do not touch', or better still the transmitter should be disabled or the waveguide run broken and a dummy load fitted. If the radar is switched on prior to taxiing, the transmitter should not be switched on until clear of the apron.

X-ray emission is a possible hazard when operating the transmitter with the case removed, such as might be done in a workshop. The likelihood of danger is small but the manufacturers' data should be consulted.

Check for Condition and Assembly
Obviously the weather radar system as a whole is subject to the same requirements as all other airborne equipment in respect of security of attachment and condition; however, certain points need to be highlighted.

The waveguide run should be the subject of fairly frequent inspections and should be suspected if poor performance is reported. When inspecting the waveguide, corrosion and physical damage such as cracks and dents are obvious things to look for. Flexible waveguide coverings are subject to perishing, cracking and a detached mechanical bond at the flanges. Internal damage in flexible waveguide can be found by gently flexing while listening and feeling for clicks. There should be no more than minor bends in the H plane of flexible waveguide and the radius of bends in the E plane should be greater than about $2\frac{1}{2}$ in.

If it is thought necessary to dismantle the waveguide run to carry out an internal inspection, or if a piece of waveguide needs to be replaced, care must be taken when re-installing. Choke joint flanges must mate to plain flanges. Sealing or O-rings must be fitted to achieve a pressure seal. The E planes of adjoining waveguide pieces should be parallel. Undue force should not be used in aligning waveguide, either within the run or at the ends of the run. All waveguide supports should be secure and undamaged.

If an internal inspection using a probe light reveals dirt or moisture it may be possible to clean by pulling through a clean soft cloth and/or blowing out with an air pressure line. Care must be taken not to scratch the inside surface of the waveguide since this would render it scrap, as would signs of corrosion or deposits which cannot be removed as suggested above.

Any drain trap in the waveguide run should be checked for blockage, and accumulated moisture should be removed. Filters and desiccators in the pressurization feed, if fitted, should be inspected for cleanliness (filter) and colour (if desiccator is pink it is unserviceable).

The scanner should be checked for freedom of movement as well as general condition and security of attachment. In carrying out scanner inspections the dish or plate should not be turned directly by hand but through the gearing. Backlash in the gears can be checked by gently applying forward and backward movement to the edge of the dish or plate in both azimuth and pitch directions: in a 30 in. diameter antenna, movement of $\frac{1}{4}$ in. at the edge indicates a total backlash of nearly $1°$. No chafing of cables should occur due to scanner movement.

When replacing the scanner, ensure shims or washers are used for the replacement, in the same positions as they were used for the item removed; this ensures the azimuth scan axis is mutually perpendicular to the roll and pitch axis of the aircraft. Some scanners may be mounted with input waveguide flange up or down, but polarized connections will be correct for only one orientation; failure to check this point may result in an incorrect sense of rotation in azimuth and pitch.

The t.r. is likely to have an internal cooling fan, in which case the filter should be secure and free from obstruction. It may be possible to clear a blocked filter by air blast in the opposite direction to normal airflow, which should be into the unit.

Functional Ramp Check – Radar
Observe Safety Precautions

1. Check warm-up time for magnetron.
2. Check fan motor (a light piece of paper should 'stick' to the filter).
3. Check internal power supply voltages and currents with built-in meter, if fitted, or test meter connected to test socket, if supplied.
   NB: when disconnecting a test meter from the test socket it is vital that the shorting plug should be replaced, otherwise crystal earth returns, broken for current measurement, will not be made.
4. Check test facility: pattern should be as specified by manufacturer. In particular check the pattern is centred and neither overfilling or underfilling screen, and that the range marks are equally spaced (linear deflection, rho-theta), symmetrical arcs (linear deflection, X-Y) and correct in number (time-base duration, rho-theta). A rho-theta raster may show a small open centre (about $\frac{1}{8}$ in.) but no tail.
5. Observe ground returns on all ranges. Operate all controls and ensure the desired effect is achieved.

Notes
The above is only a brief outline of the checks to be carried out. One should always use the manufacturers' recommended procedures when testing. When carrying out item (5) above, experience is necessary if one is to state, with any certainty, the condition of the system. The picture obtained will depend on the heading of the aircraft; as an extreme example an aircraft pointing out to sea will give very different ground returns on its radar when compared with an aircraft pointing in the direction of a range of hills. The technician should be aware of the form of the target/noise picture expected at a particular airfield on a particular heading.

The test facility varies from system to system. At its simplest a ramp or triangular voltage is generated which varies from signal level zero to a maximum of signal level three. If such a waveform is applied to the digitizer then all three levels of illumination and contour operation can be checked. Additional tests which have been provided include a gated noise source for checking s.t.c. and comparing with normal receiver noise, reflected power monitor, a.f.c. monitor and a.g.c. monitor.

Radar Systems Tester
Because of the possible misinterpretation of the system condition when judged on returns from ground targets a systems tester is sometimes used to give more control over the features of the target.

A pickup horn is attached to the radome at dead

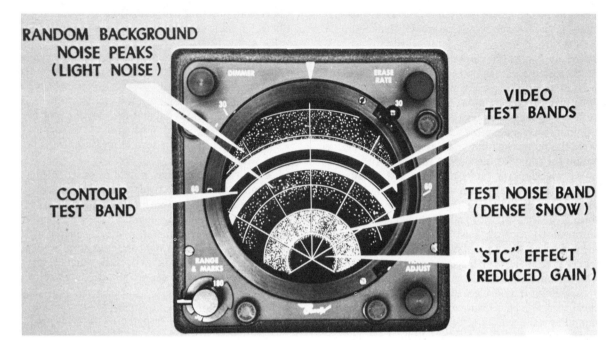

RANDOM BACKGROUND
NOISE PEAKS
(LIGHT NOISE)

CONTOUR
TEST BAND

VIDEO
TEST BANDS

TEST NOISE BAND
(DENSE SNOW)

"STC" EFFECT
(REDUCED GAIN)

Fig. 9.27 RDR IE/F test pattern (courtesy Bendix Avionics Division)

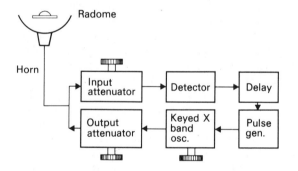

Fig. 9.28 Simplified radar systems tester

centre position. A co-axial cable connects the horn to the tester which is inside the cockpit. The tester serves as a beacon and returns a signal which should appear at zero degrees on the p.p.i. display at a range determined by the tester delay. An input attenuator can be adjusted so if the tester just fails to be triggered, the attenuator will give a measure of the radiated power. An output attenuator can be adjusted so that the 'echo' is just visible (radar on preset gain with standardized brilliance setting), thus the attenuator will give a measure of system sensitivity. The output attenuator may also be used to check the contour inversion level setting.

Note the tester will check the waveguide run,

scanner and radome as well as the t.r. If both attenuators read less than normal then the fault must be in the common r.f. components; if only the input attenuator reads low then transmitter power output is down; while a low output attenuator setting indicates poor receiver sensitivity.

Functional Test — Scanner Stabilization
Observe Safety Precautions
1. Remove radome. Switch to standby with stabilization on and tilt zero. Check, using a spirit level, that the flat plate or the plane across the rim of the reflector dish is vertical with the scanner dead ahead and at the extremities of the sector scan.
2. Remove VRG from its mounting and fit on a tilt table adjusted so that its surface is horizontal along both axes.
3. Inch scanner to the dead-ahead position. With stabilization on, adjust tilt control until scanner is vertical.
4. Simulate a suitable pitch angle ϕ nose up. Using a protractor spirit level ensure scanner elevation changes by ϕ degrees down. Repeat for nose down.
5. Simulate aircraft roll, ensure no change in scanner elevation.
6. Inch scanner to port extremity, azimuth angle θ.

Simulate a suitable roll angle α port wing down and ensure scanner elevation changes by $\alpha \sin \theta$ up. Repeat for starboard wing down.

7. Simulate aircraft pitch angle ϕ and ensure scanner elevation change is $\phi \cos \theta$ in opposite sense.
8. Repeat (6) and (7) but with scanner at starboard extremity noting sense of roll correction is reversed.
9. Inch scanner to dead ahead. Simulate suitable pitch angle. Switch stabilization from on to off and back to on, and ensure scanner moves in elevation without excessive overshooting.
10. Switch stabilization off replace gyro in aircraft mounting.
11. Carry out final check of tilt control before switching off and replacing radome.

Notes:

The above applies to a typical line-of-sight system. For any particular equipment the manufacturers' procedure should be followed, observing stated tolerances.

A platform system checkout varies from the above in that changes in elevation are independent of azimuth angle.

In items (6), (7) and (8) an azimuth angle of 90° should be chosen if possible, since this will make $\cos \theta = 1$ and $\sin \theta = 0$, so simplifying checking.

Pitch and roll correction potentiometers are often accessible in which case pitch correction should be carried out with the scanner dead ahead and roll correction carried out to balance any errors at the extremities.

A gyro simulator may be used for a checkout of the complete system less the VRG. The VRG is disconnected and the simulator connected in its place. The procedure is then similar to that above, with the appropriate pitch and roll angles being selected on the simulator. Since the VRG is not tested this is not a full functional test but is useful for fault-finding. The signals from the simulator should correspond to the VRG output signal standards (e.g. ARINC).

Check of v.s.w.r.

If the waveguide run or scanner is suspect, v.s.w.r. checks can be carried out to find the faulty item. To carry out such a check a directional coupler must be fitted in the run, and power in the forward and reverse directions measured using, for example, a thermistor bridge power meter. The check should be carried out at both ends of the waveguide run so that

a measure of waveguide losses can be obtained from the differences in forward power at either end.

Practical difficulties occur in fitting the directional coupler in a rigid waveguide run. In some installations a coupler may be permanently fitted at one end, usually at or close to the t.r.

In order to measure the v.s.w.r. of the waveguide the scanner should be disconnected and a dummy load fitted in its place. ARINC 564-7 specifies a maximum v.s.w.r. of 1·1 : 1 for a new installation.

When measuring the v.s.w.r. of the scanner the radome should be removed and the scanner tilted up to maximum to avoid returns. Figures obtained should be checked against manufacturers' data. On fitting the radome the v.s.w.r. at the antenna will deteriorate, measurement at various azimuth and tilt angles will give an indication of the radome performance.

The most likely cause of loss of radome efficiency as a transparent material to r.f. is ingress of moisture through small pinholes and cracks which may appear on the outside surface of the radome. Such pinholes and cracks may be seen by shining a light on the outside surface and viewing from the inside. A moisture detector can be used to measure the resistance between two adjacent points on the radome. The detector has two probes which are pressed firmly against the inside surface of the radome. Where the resistance measured is lower than normal it may be due to an ingress of moisture.

Bench Testing

There is not space here to consider bench testing in depth, but mention should be made of a special

Fig. 9.29 RD-300 weather radar test set (courtesy IFR Electronics Inc)

weather radar test set, the IFR RD-300 which, together with an oscilloscope, can be used to perform all the common radar tests without the proliferation of signal generators and other instruments normally found on a radar test bench.

Ryan Stormscope

Being a relatively new development the Stormscope is, as yet, not to be found in service in anything like as many aircraft as is weather radar. Since space is at a premium the coverage of the Stormscope in this book has been limited to allow a more detailed coverage of radar. The number of pages allocated here reflects the importance of each of the systems to maintenance staff and aircrew today. The situation may well be reversed in the future or, more likely, equalized.

As stated in the introduction to this chapter, the Ryan Stormscope depends for its success on detecting electrical activity which is associated with turbulence. Since the radiating source is natural only a receiver is required; an immediate advantage over weather radar. To obtain directional information, use is made of an ADF loop and sense antenna, both either dedicated to the Stormscope installation or time-shared with ADF. The rest of the installation comprises a display unit and a computer/processor unit.

Care must be taken in installation planning since Stormscope is prone to interference from generators, motors, strobe lights, etc. Interference from communication transceivers is avoided by inhibiting the Stormscope whenever a transceiver is keyed.

measurement possible and reasonably accurate. For range measurement the received signals are compared with a 'standard' to give so-called pseudo range. The method used to determine range means that particularly strong signals appear to be closer than they actually are, which is not really a disadvantage since the source of such signals is a region of severe electrical activity and hence turbulence.

Each discharge appears as a bright green dot on the circular display screen at a position representative of the source position relative to the aircraft. An aircraft symbol is located at the centre of the display with radial lines marked at $30°$ intervals and two equally spaced range rings. The range of the outer ring is as selected on the panel-mounted receiver: 40, 100 or 200 nautical miles. Since the outer ring is not at the periphery of the display the maximum range available is of the order of 260 nautical miles.

Each discharge is only a momentary event so storage in memory is required. The memory can store the position of 128 dots, these being displayed to form a map-like picture. When the 129th discharge occurs the oldest dot in memory is replaced; in this way the image is continuously updated. If the aircraft heading changes or a new range is selected the dot positions are incorrect until all 128 have been updated, a process which can take up to 25 s on a

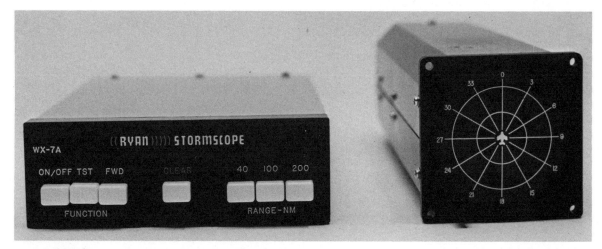

Fig. 9.30 Ryan Stormscope display unit and computer/processor (courtesy Ryan Stromscope)

Operation

Signals from the two orthogonal loops and the sense antenna are utilized to give range and bearing of the source of electrical activity received. The properties of the loop and sense antenna make bearing

stormy day (only 5-10 s with tornado activity within range). On quiet days a dot may remain a long time but after 5 min it is automatically erased. A 'clear' button allows the pilot to erase the display starting with the oldest data and progressing to the newest in a total erase time of 1 s. Another button allows the display of that activity which is forward of the aircraft with, of course, the full memory dedicated to these signals.

The 128 dots appear in clusters on the display, indicating where bad weather can be expected. As the weather becomes more severe there is a spreading inward towards the centre due to the pseudo range reducing as a result of the stronger signals. With increasing storm intensity the display becomes very animated.

A test facility is built in whereby when the appropriate button is pressed a dot cluster appears near to a position of 45°; 100 nautical miles. In addition, a test set is available which can simulate signals at various ranges and azimuth angles for system checkout and calibration.

Comparison of Stormscope and Radar

It would appear that, purely from a functional point of view, i.e. ability to avoid turbulence, there is little to choose between the two systems. Some advantages of Stormscope over radar are:

1. no moving parts and no transmitter, hence mean time between failures (m.t.b.f.) should be higher;
2. simpler antenna installation which keeps down installation costs;
3. only the cheapest radars compare in capital cost;
4. fully operational on the ground with 360° field of view.

Some disadvantages of Stormscope compared with radar are:

1. sensitive to interference;
2. limited rate and accuracy of data acquisition although it would appear from operational evidence that this does not prevent the Stormscope from being used for efficient and safe weather avoidance;
3. lacking in any other applications such as mapping, navigation data display or page printer option.

Two things should be pointed out here; firstly the extras with weather radar have to be paid for; secondly the Stormscope is a relatively new development by a company small in comparison to the giants of weather radar. It should not be beyond the ingenuity of the designers to develop the system so as to eliminate some, if not all, of the disadvantages.

Appendix

Factors Affecting Weather Radar Performance

The Radar Equation

If power P_t is radiated from an omnidirectional antenna then the power density (power per unit area) decreases with range. At a range R a sphere of surface area $4\pi R^2$ is illuminated by the e.m. wave, thus:

$$\text{Power density from omni antenna} = \frac{P_t}{4\pi R^2} \quad (A9.1)$$

Since a directional antenna is used with gain G (over an isotropic antenna, i.e. perfectly omnidirectional) we have:

$$\begin{matrix} \text{Power density from} \\ \text{directional antenna} \end{matrix} = \frac{P_t G}{4\pi R^2} \quad (A9.2)$$

The target will intercept part of the radar beam, the size of the part depending on the radar cross-section of the target σ. Since the reflected power is subject to the same spreading out in space as the incident power we have:

$$\begin{matrix} \text{Power density of} \\ \text{echo at aircraft} \end{matrix} = \frac{P_t G \sigma}{(4\pi R^2)^2} \quad (A9.3)$$

The radar antenna intercepts part of the echo signal, the size of the part depending on the effective capture area A, so received echo power P_r is given by

$$P_r = \frac{P_t G A \sigma}{(4\pi R^2)^2} \quad (A9.4)$$

The relationship between antenna gain and effective capture area can be shown to be

$$G = \frac{4\pi A}{\lambda^2} \quad (A9.5)$$

where λ is the wavelength of the e.m. wave. So equation (A9.4) becomes:

$$P_r = \frac{P_t G^2 \lambda^2 \sigma}{(4\pi)^3 R^4} \quad (A9.6)$$

Replacing P_r by the minimum detectable signal power m and rearranging, we have the well-known radar range equation:

$$R_{\max}{}^4 = \frac{P_t G^2 \lambda^2 \sigma}{(4\pi)^3 m} \quad (A9.7)$$

The Radar Equation for Meteorological Targets

With meteorological targets we have a large number of

independent scatterers of radar cross-section σ_i so, providing the target fills the beam, we may represent the total radar cross-section by:

$$\sigma = V_m \Sigma \sigma_i \qquad (A9.8)$$

where: $\Sigma \sigma_i$ is the average total backscatter cross-section of the particles per unit volume;

V_m is the volume occupied by the radiated pulse which can be approximated by $(\pi/4)R^2\theta^2 c\delta/2$;

θ is the beamwidth (equal in horizontal and vertical planes for a pencil beam);

c is the velocity of propagation:

δ is the pulse duration.

Substituting for σ in (A9.6) we have:

$$P_r = \frac{P_t G^2 \lambda^2 \theta^2 c\delta \Sigma \sigma_i}{512\pi^2 R^2} \qquad (A9.9)$$

Equation (A9.9) is applicable where the target is beam-filling, for example a spherical cloud of 3 nautical miles diameter will fill a 4° beam up to about 43 nautical miles. For a target outside the beam-filling range the proportion of beam filled can be shown to be $(D/\theta R)^2$ where D is the target diameter. So equation (A9.9) would become, for such a target:

$$P_r = \frac{P_t G^2 \lambda^2 c\delta D^2 \Sigma \sigma_i}{512\pi^2 R^4} \qquad (A9.10)$$

an equation in which the fourth power of R occurs as in the basic radar equation (A9.6) and contrasting with equation (A9.9) where we have the square of R. Again we can produce a range equation assuming non-beam-filling targets:

$$R_{max}^4 = \frac{P_t G^2 \lambda^2 c\delta D^2 \Sigma \sigma_i}{512\pi^2 m} \qquad (A9.11)$$

If the wavelength is long compared with the diameter d of a scattering particle then it can be shown that:

$$\Sigma \sigma_i = \frac{\pi^5 1k1^2 \Sigma d_i^6}{\lambda^4} \qquad (A9.12)$$

where $1k1^2$ is related to the dielectric constant and has a value of about 0·9 for water and 0·2 for ice.

It is helpful to replace Σd_i^6 by an expression involving rainfall rate, such an expression is provided by $\Sigma d_i^6 = 200r^{1·6}$ where r is the rainfall rate in mm/h. It should be noted that this is an empirical relationship, the constants being subject to variability from one experimental observation to another. Replacing $\Sigma \sigma_i$ in equation (A9.9) and using the relationship between $\Sigma d_i r$ we have

$$P_r = \frac{180r^{1·6} P_t G\theta^2 c\delta \pi^3}{512\lambda^2 R^2} \qquad (A9.13)$$

as the echo power received from a beam-filling rain cloud. (Note that $180 \approx 200\ 1k1^2$).

Minimum Detectable Signal

Equation (A9.11) gives the maximum range of a weather radar in terms of the minimum detectable signal from a non-beam-filling target. A threshold level must be chosen which is greater than the r.m.s. value of the noise occupying the same part of the frequency spectrum as the signal. If the signal exceeds the threshold it is detected; if not it is missed. Too low a threshold will give rise to false alarms.

In choosing the threshold level the interpretation of the operator is significant, particularly in conventional (analogue) weather radars. In digital weather radars the choice of threshold is taken out of the hands, or eyes, of the operators. Noise spikes which do not occur in the same time-slot after several successive transmissions are not displayed; they are said to be averaged out. As a result in a digital weather radar a lower threshold, or minimum signal to noise ratio (s.n.r.), can be tolerated with consequent improvement in maximum range.

In introducing the factors relating to noise into the radar equation it is convenient to use the noise figure F given by

$$F = \frac{S_i/N_i}{S_o/N_o} \qquad (A9.14)$$

where: S_i/N_i is the input s.n.r.;

S_o/N_o is the output s.n.r.

The input noise can be taken as kTB

where: k is Boltzmann's constant, $= 1·38 \times 10^{-23}$ joules/degree;

T is temperature in degrees Kelvin;

B is the noise bandwidth (different from 3 dB bandwidth but often approximated by it).

So rearranging equation (A9.14) and substituting for N_i we have:

$$S_i = kTBF\ S_o/N_o \qquad (A9.15)$$

Substituting for m in equation (A9.11) gives:

$$R_{max}^4 = \frac{P_t G^2 \lambda^2 c\delta \Sigma \sigma_i}{512\pi^2\ kTBF\ (S_o/N_o)_{min}} \qquad (A9.16)$$

Equation (A9.16) results from considering a single pulse; however many pulses are normally received from a target during one sweep of the aerial. The number of pulses returned from a point target is

$$n = \frac{\theta \times \text{p.r.f.}}{\omega} \qquad (A9.17)$$

where ω is the scanning rate in degrees per second;
p.r.f. is the pulse repetition frequency.

We can utilize some or all of the n pulses to improve detection in a process known as integration. Use of a c.r.t., together with the properties of the eye and brain, constitutes an integration process. Digital techniques, whereby the signal occurring in successive corresponding time-slots is averaged, is also a form of integration in this sense. We can define the integration efficiency as follows:

$$E_n = \frac{(S/N)_1}{n(S/N)_n}$$

where $(S/N)_1$ = s.n.r. of a single pulse for a given probability of detection;
$(S/N)_n$ = s.n.r. per pulse for the same probability of detection when n pulses are integrated.

The integration improvement factor nE_n can be included in the range equation.

The average power P of the radar is related to the peak power P_t by:

$$P = P_t \times \delta \times \text{p.r.f.} \qquad (A9.18)$$

Substituting for P_t in equation (A9.16) and incorporating the integration improvement factor we have:

$$R_{\text{max}}^4 = \frac{PG^2 \lambda^2 \theta^3 c E_n \Sigma \sigma_i}{512\pi^2 kTBF \omega (S/N)_1} \qquad (A9.19)$$

In an effort to simplify the range equation EUROCAE and RTCA have derived a Performance Index, PI, from the basic radar equation. Details of the calculations involved are given in ARINC Characteristic 564 together with an empirical formula relating PI and maximum range. The primary purpose of the PI is to enable a comparison to be made between different radars rather than effect the accurate calculation of maximum range.

Atmospheric Effects

There are three effects, namely attenuation, refraction and lobing, which can degrade or even enhance the performance of a radar operating in the earth's atmosphere.

Attenuation due to absorption by gases, primarily oxygen and water vapour, will reduce the maximum range attainable. Precipitation particles also absorb the e.m. energy and cause scattering. The scattering is essential for the operation of weather radar but absorption will decrease the range and reduce the ability of the radar to penetrate clouds in order to 'see' what is beyond. Empirical results are available but we may simply state that degradation increases with frequency, hence the descriptions of C-band equipment as weather-penetration radar and X-band as weather-avoidance radar.

Since the density of the atmosphere is not uniform, refraction or bending of the radar waves may take place. Water vapour is the main contributor to this effect. The radar waves will normally be bent around the earth since the atmospheric density usually increases with decreasing altitude, thus leading to an increase in radar range.

Lobing is the arrival at the target of two radar waves, one via the direct path and one by way of reflection from the earth's surface. Depending on the relative phases range may be enhanced or degraded. In an airborne weather radar with small side lobes this does not create the same problem as with ground-based radars.

10 Doppler navigation

Introduction

A Doppler navigator is a self contained dead-reckoning system giving continuous readout of aircraft position usually related to waypoints. Military aircraft have made use of such equipment since the mid-1950s while civil use for transoceanic navigation commenced in the early 1960s. In recent years the use of Doppler navigators in long-range commercial aircraft has largely been superseded by inertial navigators, triple systems being fitted to airliners such as the 747 and Concorde. Military developments include composite Doppler and inertial systems and we may expect to see such systems 'go civilian' in the future.

There are still many civil aircraft carrying Doppler navigators but these are older, long-range airliners and as such they are fitted with equipment which, although not in any way primitive, does not employ the very latest techniques. A class of civil aircraft for which there is a continuing need for Doppler navigators is survey aircraft which, by the very nature of their work, operate in areas not covered by ground-based navigation aids (except Omega) and require accurate positional information. Use of Doppler navigators in helicopters is not unusual; there is equipment specifically designed for such aircraft.

The advantage of Doppler navigation lies in the fact that it is a self-contained system which does not rely on ground-based aids and can operate in any part of the world. This advantage is shared by inertial navigation which also shares the disadvantage of degradation of positional information as distance flown is increased. The degradation of information arises from the fact that starting from a known position subsequent positions are computed by sensing the aircraft velocity and integrating with respect to time. Errors, once they are introduced, can only be eliminated by a position fix.

A simplistic example will illustrate the build-up of error. An aircraft takes off from A to fly to B, 3000 nautical miles away in a direction due west from A. Using heading information from a directional sensor such as a gyromagnetic compass the Doppler navigator senses that the aircraft is flying due west at 300 knots. Thus after 1 min the system gives a readout of position as being 2995 nautical miles from B on track; after 1 h 2700 nautical miles from B; after 10 h the indicated position is B.

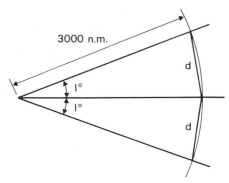

Fig. 10.1 Effect of heading error

With a ± 1 per cent error in computed speed, the tolerance on the position readout after 1 min, 1 h and 10 h will be ± 0.05, ± 3 and ± 30 nautical miles respectively. With a ± 1° error in the heading information we have the situation given in Fig. 10.1. We can see that $d = 2 \times 300t \times \sin 0.5$, thus after 1 min, 1 h and 10 h the aircraft may be up to 0.087, 5.24 and 52.4 nautical miles away from the indicated position. In both cases the absolute error increases with distance flown. In practice it is the heading information which usually limits the accuracy of the system.

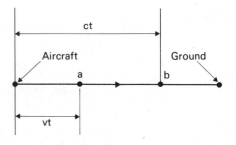

Fig. 10.2 Doppler effect – transmission

Doppler Effect

In 1842 the Austrian scientist Christian Doppler predicted the Doppler effect in connection with sound waves. It was subsequently found that the effect is also applicable to e.m. waves. The Doppler effect can be described as the change in observed frequency when the source (transmitter) and observer (receiver) are in motion relative to one another. The noise of moving trains and road traffic is a demonstration of the effect commonly observed. The applicability to e.m. waves is illustrated by the use of police radar speed traps, to the cost of offenders.

In an airborne Doppler radar we have a transmitter which, by means of a directional antenna, radiates energy towards the ground. A receiver receives the echo of the transmitted energy. Thus we have the situation where both transmitter and receiver are moving relative to the ground; consequently the original frequency transmitted is changed twice. The difference between transmitted and received frequencies is known as the Doppler shift and is very nearly proportional to the relative motion between the aircraft and the ground along the direction of the radar beam.

Consider the transmission of e.m. energy towards the ground. Let the relative velocity of the aircraft in the direction of the beam be v, the frequency of the radiation f and the speed of the electromagnetic waves c ($= 3 \times 10^8$ ms^{-1}). Referring to Fig. 10.2 we see that in t seconds the wave will have moved a distance ct to b while the aircraft will have moved a distance vt to a. The waves emitted in time t will be bunched up in the distance between a and b which is $ct - vt$. The number of waves emitted will be ft cycles. Thus the wavelength observed at the target, λ', is given by:

$$\lambda' = (ct - vt)/ft = (c - v)/f \qquad (10.1)$$

We can see that if the transmitter is stationary with respect to the ground then $v = 0$ and equation (10.1) reduces to the familiar relationship $c = f\lambda$. If the transmitter is moving away from the ground target, that is the beam is directed towards the rear, then v in equation (10.1) becomes $-v$ and we have $\lambda' = (c + v)/f$.

Now consider the received signal. In a time t the aircraft would receive all the waves occupying space ct in Fig. 10.3. However in this time the aircraft moves a distance vt and hence will receive the number of waves occupying $ct + vt$ in t seconds or $(c + v)/\lambda$ waves in 1 second. Thus the received frequency, f_r, is given by:

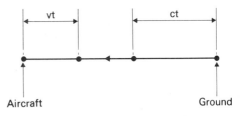

Fig. 10.3 Doppler effect – reception

$$f_r = (c + v)/\lambda \qquad (10.2)$$

Again we see $v = 0$ leads to $c = \lambda f$ and the aircraft moving away from the ground target gives $f_r = (c - v)/\lambda$.

We must now consider both effects simultaneously. The wavelength λ in equation (10.2) is the wavelength of the echo which must be λ' in equation (10.1). Thus substituting λ' for λ we have:

$$f_r = \frac{(c + v)}{(c - v)} f.$$

We are interested in the Doppler shift, f_D, which is the difference between transmitted and received signals thus:

$$f_D = f_r - f = f \left\{ \frac{(c + v)}{(c - v)} - 1 \right\} = \frac{2v}{c - v} \cdot f.$$

Now $c = 186\,000$ miles per second so v is obviously very small compared with c, so with negligible error we may write:

$$f_D = 2vf/c. \qquad (10.3)$$

This equation is the basis of a Doppler radar. Observing, as above, the convention that v is positive for movement towards, and negative for movement away, the ground target gives an increased received frequency on a forward beam and a decreased received frequency on a rearward or aft beam.

From Figs 10.4 and 10.5 we see that the relative velocity of the aircraft in the direction of the beam centroid is $v = V \cos \theta \cos \alpha$ where V is the magnitude of the aircraft velocity with respect to the ground. So equation (10.3) becomes:

$$f_D = (2Vf \cos \theta \cos \alpha)/C. \qquad (10.4)$$

It is at this stage that the student is often convinced that a Doppler radar could not possibly work due to the smooth earth paradox and the mountain paradox, which are hopefully dispensed with below.

It is falsely argued that if an aircraft is moving parallel to flat ground then there is no change in range between the aircraft and the ground and therefore no Doppler shift. That this is false can be seen by

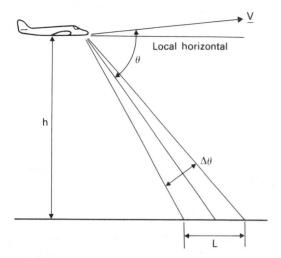

Fig. 10.4 Airborne Doppler single-beam geometry in the vertical plane

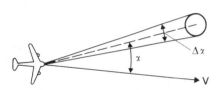

Fig. 10.5 Airborne Doppler single-beam geometry in the horizontal plane

considering the actual targets which produce backscattering of the energy. These targets are irregularly shaped scattering objects such as pebbles and there is, of course, relative motion between the aircraft and individual targets — hence a Doppler shift. If the illuminated area were perfectly smooth no reflected energy would be received at the aircraft.

The other false argument concerns sloping terrain. If the aircraft is flying horizontally above a slope then its range to the ground along the beam is changing and therefore the Doppler shift will be affected. Again this falsehood is exposed by the fact that the actual targets are individual objects whose 'slope' with respect to the aircraft is random and hence is not related to the slope of the ground.

Antenna Mechanization

The aircraft velocity has three orthogonal components:

V_H' the heading velocity component;
V_A' the lateral velocity component; and

V_V' the vertical velocity component

as shown in Fig. 10.6. These velocities are in antenna co-ordinates which, with an antenna fixed rigidly to the aircraft, are airframe co-ordinates. As the aircraft pitches and rolls the antenna moves with it and hence V_H', V_A' and V_V' will not be the velocities in earth co-ordinates required for navigation.

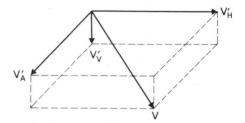

Fig. 10.6 The resolved velocity vector

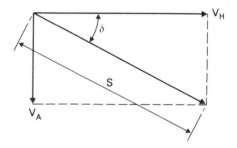

Fig. 10.7 Drift angle and ground speed

One conceptually simple solution is to stabilize the antenna in pitch and roll, in which case the earth co-ordinate-related velocities V_H, V_A and V_V are equal to V_H', V_A' and V_V' respectively. If the lateral velocity V_A is non-zero it means that the movement of the aircraft is not in the direction of the heading and a non-zero drift angle, δ, exists as in Fig. 10.7. The resultant of V_H and V_A is the velocity vector with magnitude equal to ground speed s, and direction that of the aircraft's track. It is convenient for navigation purposes to present the pilot with ground speed and drift angle information rather than V_H and V_A.

With moving antenna systems, the antenna is stabilized in pitch and roll and also aligned in azimuth with the track of the aircraft, that is to say track-stabilized. The drift angle is given by the angle between the antenna and aircraft longitudinal axes measured in the horizontal plane. Some Dopplers use pitch but not roll stabilization since error due to roll is small for small drift angles and furthermore tends to average out over the flight.

Fixed antenna systems must compute the velocities V_H, V_A and V_V each being a function of V_H', V_A', V_V', R and P, where R and P are roll and pitch angles appearing in the expressions as trigonometric functions. The relationships are derived in the Appendix.

Doppler Spectrum

The beams are of finite width, hence energy will strike the ground along directions of different relative velocities. As a consequence a spectrum of Doppler shift frequencies is received as shown in Fig. 10.8 where the effects of side lobes are ignored.

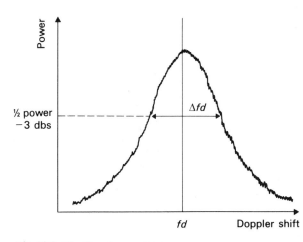

Fig. 10.8 The Doppler spectrum

Such a phenomenon is undesirable but providing the spectrum is reasonably 'peaky' the mean Doppler shift is easily measured. If γ is the angle between the beam centroid and the aircraft velocity vector then equation (10.3) becomes:

$$f_D = \frac{2Vf}{c} \cos \gamma. \tag{10.5}$$

Differentiation with respect to γ gives a first approximation to the half-power bandwidth of the spectrum:

$$\Delta f_D = \frac{2Vf}{c} \Delta \gamma \cdot \sin \gamma \tag{10.6}$$

where $\Delta \gamma$ is the half-power beam width. The ratio of Δf_D to f_D is thus given by dividing equation (10.6) by (10.5).

$$\frac{\Delta f_D}{f_D} = \Delta \gamma \cdot \tan \gamma. \tag{10.7}$$

With $\Delta \gamma$ typically 0·07 radians (4°) and γ typically 70° we have $\Delta f_D / f_D$ typically 0·2.

Since backscattering from the illuminated target area is not constant over the whole area there is a random fluctuation of the instantaneous mean frequency f_D. To determine the aircraft's velocity accurately the time constant of the velocity-measuring circuits must be sufficiently long to smooth this fluctuation, but not so long as to be unable to follow the normal accelerations of the aircraft.

Beam Geometry

Since there are three unknowns V_H', V_A' and V_V', a minimum of three beams are required to measure them. In practice three or four beams are used in a configuration involving fore and aft beams; as such it is known as a Janus configuration after the Roman god who could see both behind and in front.

The beams radiated can be either pencil, as in Fig. 10.10 or narrow in elevation ($\Delta \theta$) but wide in azimuth ($\Delta \alpha$) as in Fig. 10.9. The hyperbolic lines f_a, f_b, f_{-a}, f_{-b} are lines of constant Doppler shifts called isodops and are drawn assuming a flat earth. When wide azimuth beams are used a fixed antenna system would lead to the beam crossing a wide range of isodops under conditions of drift, resulting in an excessively wide Doppler spectrum. Consequently such beams virtually dictate a track-stabilized antenna. A wide azimuth beam has advantages in that smaller antenna areas are required and roll performance is improved in the case where no roll stabilization is employed.

Figure 10.9 shows that for a fully stabilized system the Doppler shift on all four beams is the same. Without roll stabilization small errors are introduced which tend to average out. Stabilization can be achieved by servo loops which drive the antenna so as to equalize the Doppler shifts. Alternatively pitch information (and possibly roll) can be fed to the Doppler from a vertical reference such as a gyro or even a mercury switch leaving azimuth stabilization to be achieved by equalization of Doppler shifts. Typically in such radars ground speed and drift angle are the only outputs where ground speed is given by equation (10.4) and drift angle by the amount of azimuth rotation of the antenna. Heading information is usually added to the drift angle to give aircraft track.

Figure 10.10 shows that for a fixed aerial system the Doppler shifts on all four beams are, in general, not equal. It is shown in the Appendix to this

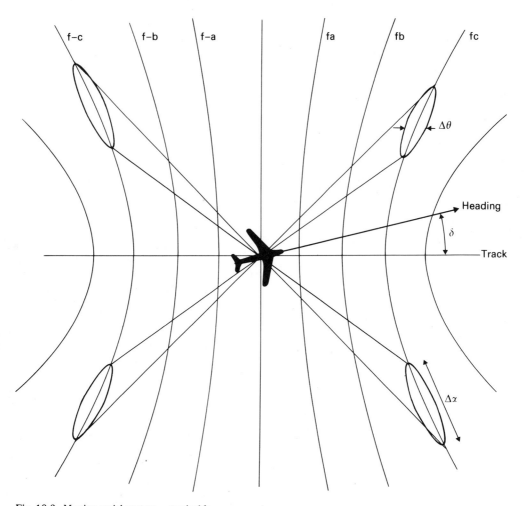

Fig. 10.9 Moving aerial system – typical beam geometry

chapter that the velocities in airframe co-ordinates, V_H', V_A' and V_V', depend on $(f2-f1)$, $(f2-f3)$ and $(f1+f3)$ respectively, where $f1$, $f2$ and $f3$ are the Doppler shifts on beams 1, 2 and 3. Relationships for these velocities can also be derived using $f4$ and two other Doppler shifts. With this redundancy we have the possibility of self-checking or continued operation after one beam failure.

Computation of ground speed and drift angle in a fixed antenna system can be divided into three parts: firstly computation of V_H', V_A' and V_V', using the Doppler shifts from three of the four beams; secondly computation of V_H, V_A and V_V using pitch and roll information and the previously computed airframe co-ordinate velocities; and lastly, drift angle = arctan (V_A/V_H) and ground speed = $(V_H{}^2 + V_A{}^2)^{0.5}$ (*see* Figure 10.7).

Transmitter Frequency

The choice of r.f. is, as ever, a compromise. The advantage of using a high frequency is that the sensitivity of the radar in Hertz per knot is high, as can be seen from equation (10.3); furthermore, for a given antenna size, the higher the frequency the narrower the Doppler spectrum. If, however, the radiated frequency is too high atmospheric and precipitation absorption and scattering become more of a problem. Another consideration is the availability of components for the various frequency bands which might be considered. Most Doppler radars operate in a band centred on 8·8 GHz or 13·325 GHz, the former, to date, being perhaps the most common for civil aircraft use.

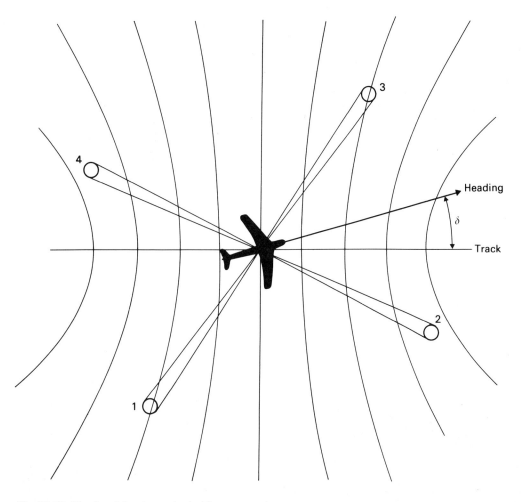

Fig. 10.10 Fixed aerial system – typical beam geometry

Modulation

At first sight it would appear that no modulation is necessary, indeed c.w. Doppler radars have been built and operated, a great attraction being simplicity. Difficulties, however, arise in transmitter receiver isolation and discrimination against reflections from nearby objects in particular the dielectric panel (radome) covering the airframe opening for the antenna. At other than low altitudes unwanted reflections are comparable in amplitude to ground returns. Noise like variations in vibrating radome echoes will more than likely be in the same frequency band as the expected Doppler shifts, and thus indistinguishable except where the s.n.r. is sufficiently high at low altitudes.

To overcome the above problems both pulsed and frequency modulated (f.m.c.w.) radars have been used. The earliest Dopplers were pulsed so that echoes from nearby objects were received during the recovery time of the diplexer and hence were not processed. In the so-called incoherent pulse systems a Doppler signal is obtained by mixing received signals from fore and aft beams; this has two undesirable consequences. Firstly the returns on the fore and aft beams must overlap in time if mixing is to take place, this means stabilization and/or wide beams must be used. Secondly, the Doppler shift on the individual beams is not available, hence the sense of direction of the velocity vector (forward or backward) and the vertical velocity cannot be computed.

With modern radars f.m.c.w. is the most common type of transmission. The spectrum of the transmitted signal consists of a large number of sidebands as well as the carrier. Theoretical analysis of f.m.c.w. reveals an infinite number of sidebands spaced by the modulation frequency f_m amplitude of individual sidebands being determined by Bessel functions of the first kind of order n and argument m where n is the sideband concerned (first, second, third, etc.) and m is the modulation index, i.e. ratio of deviation to f_m. By using the Doppler shift of a particular sideband, and choosing an appropriate value of m to give sufficient amplitude of the sideband concerned, suppression of noise due to returns from the radome and other nearby objects is achieved.

A problem common to both pulsed and f.m.c.w. Doppler radars is that of altitude holes. In a pulsed system if the echo arrives back at the receiver when a subsequent pulse is being transmitted then it is gated out by the diplexer and no Doppler shift can be detected. Similarly with f.m.c.w., if the round-trip travel time is nearly equal to the modulation period a dead beat will occur when mixing transmitted and received signals, and again no Doppler shift will be detected.

If a low modulating frequency is used the first altitude hole may appear above the operating ceiling. However low p.r.f. in pulse system leads to low efficiency and the possibility of interference if the p.r.f. is in the range of Doppler frequencies expected (audio). For f.m.c.w. given a choice of sideband used, typically third or fourth, and modulation index, typically $2\frac{1}{2}$ or 3, such as to avoid radome noise, the modulating frequency must be fairly high to allow a reasonable deviation. A fairly high modulating frequency is usually varied either continuously (wobble) or in discrete steps to avoid altitude holes at fixed heights.

Over-Water Errors

Doppler navigators measure the velocity of the

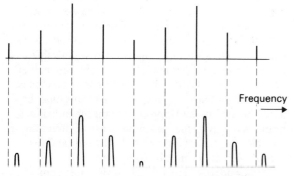

Fig. 10.11 Frequency modulated continuous wave transmitted signal and received ground echo spectrum

aircraft relative to the surface below them. When flying over water that surface itself may be moving due to sea currents or wind-blown water particles. Random sea currents are of speeds usually a good bit less than half a knot, and this small effect averages out since the currents are in random directions. Major sea currents do not exceed, say, 3 knots and since direction and approximate speed are known they can be compensated for. Wind-blown droplets would give an error less than the wind speed, about 3 knots error for 10 knots wind with the error varying as the third root of the wind. On long flights such an error will be reduced by averaging.

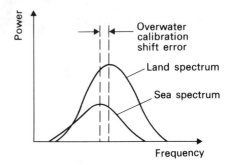

Fig. 10.12 Over-water calibration shift

When flying over land the beams illuminate an area containing many scattering particles. Generally the backscattering coefficients over the whole illuminated area will be of the same order giving rise to the Doppler spectrum shown in Fig. 10.8. Over smooth sea the situation is different; a larger fraction of the incident energy will be returned on the steepest part of the beam since the surface backscattering coefficient will depend on the angle of incidence. The net result is to shift the Doppler spectrum as shown in Fig. 10.12, so that the mean Doppler shift is less than it should be for the aircraft velocity.

The error introduced, which could be up to 5 per cent, is known as over-water calibration shift error. The narrower the beam width the less significant the error, so some Dopplers are designed to produce beams narrow enough to keep the error within acceptable limits. Other Dopplers have a manual land-sea or sea bias switch which, when in the sea or on position respectively, causes a calibration shift in the opposite sense by weighting the response of the Doppler shift frequency processing in favour of the higher frequencies. For a carefully chosen compensation shift the error can be reduced by a factor of about ten.

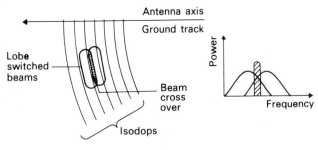

Fig. 10.13 Lobe switching

Lobe switching is a more successful method of reducing calibration shift error. The beam angle of incidence to the ground is switched by a small amount periodically. The illuminated areas for the two switched angles overlap, as do the Doppler spectra. The Doppler shift frequency used for velocity measurement is where the spectra cross. This crossover point corresponds to the return from the same group of scatterers at the same angle of incidence and is thus not affected by over-water flight. Figure 10.13 illustrates the technique, which works far better when track-stabilized antennas since then the lobe switching is at right angles to the isodops.

Navigation Calculations

The ground speed and drift angle information is normally presented to the pilot but in addition is used, together with heading information, to give the aircraft position relative to a destination or forthcoming waypoint. To achieve this the pilot must set desired track and distance to fly before take off. In Fig. 10.14 the pilot wishes to fly from A to B, a distance of 50 nautical miles, with desired track 090. The aircraft has flown for 6 min at a speed of 500 knots on a heading of 100 with a drift of $27°$ starboard, thus the total distance is 50 nautical miles and the aircraft is at point C. The track error is $37°$, the along distance to go is $X = 10$ nautical miles; the across distance is $Y = 30$ nautical miles.

In order to see how the Doppler navigator arrives at the along and across distances indicated to the pilot we must consider the information available:

Ground speed (s) and
drift angle (δ)   — Doppler radar
Heading (H)   — gyromagnetic compass
Desired track (Td) and
Distance (D)   — pilot

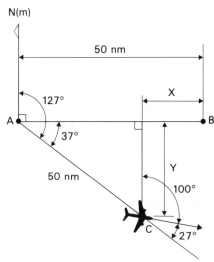

Fig. 10.14 Navigation calculations

To arrive at along distance to go (X) and across distance (Y) the true track (T) and track error angle (E) are needed. We have, assuming drift to starboard as positive:

$$T = H + \delta \qquad (10.8)$$

$$E = T - Td \qquad (10.9)$$

$$X = D - \int_0^t S \cos E \, dt \qquad (10.10)$$

$$Y = \int_0^t S \sin E \, dt \qquad (10.11)$$

where t is the time of flight, and the sense of the across distance is positive to the right.

Block Diagram Operation

Moving Antenna System
Figure 10.15 illustrates a block diagram based on the Marconi AD 560, a system introduced in the mid-1960s and used on a variety of civil aircraft. It is still to be found in service.

The sensor is an f.m.c.w. type employing wobbulation of the modulating frequency f_m to avoid altitude holes and using the Nth sideband ($N = 3$ in the AD 560) to avoid unwanted interference due to radome vibrations. For the choice of the third sideband a suitable modulation index is $2·5$, obtained by using a deviation of ± 1 MHz on the 8800 MHz carrier and a modulating frequency of 400 kHz.

Two mixer stages give the Doppler shift frequency

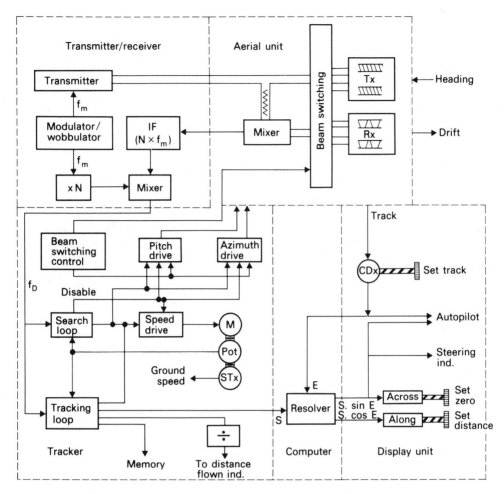

Fig. 10.15 Moving aerial Doppler block diagram based on
the Marconi AD 560

f_D. The first mixes the received signal with a sample
of the transmitted signal, the required sideband
(1200 kHz in the AD 560) being selected by the
intermediate frequency amplifiers. The second mixes
N times f_m with the selected sideband to extract f_D
by means of a low pass filter with a cut-off frequency
of about 20 kHz.

There are two transmit and two receive linear
slotted arrays. Anti-phase and in-phase arrays are
used for transmit and receive, an arrangement which
can be shown to compensate for changes in
wavelength. The arrays are connected to appropriate
inlets/outlets by an r.f. switch (varacter diodes in the
AD 560). Fore and aft beams are obtained by
providing for connection to either end of each array,
while port and starboard deflection is achieved by use
of side reflectors. The beam-switching sequence is
important where pitch and azimuth drive of the aerial
is concerned; the AD 560 sequence is port forward,
starboard aft, starboard forward, port aft, a complete
cycle taking 1 second.

The Doppler spectrum is fed to two loops: one
coarse and one fine. The search loop provides for
coarse adjustment of a ground-speed measuring shaft
which determines the frequency of a voltage controlled
oscillator (v.c.o.) in the tracking loop through a
feedback potentiometer. With the search loop nulled
the v.c.o. frequency is approximately equal to the
mean Doppler shift frequency, a discriminator within
the tracking loop is then able to apply an error signal
to the speed drive so as to position the ground-speed
shaft accurately. The Doppler can then be said to be
locked on, and any change in ground speed will be
tracked by the fine tracking loop.

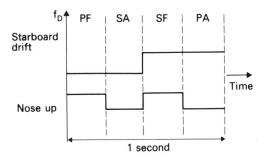

Fig. 10.16 Change in Doppler shift with aerial misalignment

If the antenna axis is not aligned with the track of the aircraft, either in pitch or in azimuth, the Doppler shift will change with beam-switching. With misalignment in azimuth the change in Doppler occurs at a rate of 1 Hz, while if the misalignment is in pitch the rate is 2 Hz. This follows from the beam-switching sequence and rate (*see* Fig. 10.16). Reference waveforms of 2 and 1 Hz are fed to the pitch and azimuth drive circuits respectively; any misalignment of the antenna will be detected by the drive circuits, resulting in the antenna rotating so as to align itself with the aircraft track. At this stage the Doppler shift is the same on all four beams and accurately represents ground speed, also the angle between the aircraft and antenna longitudinal axes is equal to the drift angle.

The s.n.r. is measured in both the search and tracking loops. If the search loop check is not satisfactory for three out of the four beams the three servodrive circuits are disabled. The signal to noise check in the tracking loop causes the system to go to memory if it is not satisfactory. In memory the antenna and ground-speed shaft are fixed and a memory flag appears in a ground-speed and drift angle indicator. The sensor continues to give the last-measured ground-speed and drift angle for as long as the poor s.n.r. continues.

Ground-speed output from the sensor is in two forms. A synchro rotor is mechanically coupled to the ground-speed shaft giving a three-wire feed. The tracking v.c.o. frequency, which is proportional to ground speed, is fed to a sine-cosine resolver in the computer and also to a frequency divider which scales and shapes the signal so that one pulse per nautical mile is fed to a distance flown indicator (integrating counter).

A synchro transmitter in the antenna unit gives a drift angle output since the body is bolted to the fixed part of the antenna and the rotor is driven by the azimuth motor. A differential synchro transmitter is used to add heading (from compass) to

drift angle (azimuth drive) and so give track to another differential synchro in the display unit. The rotor of the second differential synchro is set by the operator at the desired track angle, hence the output is the difference between track and desired track, i.e. track angle error E.

The resolver in the computer unit resolves ground speed S into its along and across speed components $S \cos E$ and $S \sin E$ respectively. In the AD 560 a ball resolver is used, thus giving mechanical analogue computing. The ball is driven by a tracking oscillator-fed stepper motor, hence the rate of rotation is proportional to ground speed. The axis of rotation depends on the angle of the drive wheel which is set by a servo position control system to be equal to the track error angle. Two pick-off wheels mounted with their axes at right angles rotate at a rate depending on the along and across speeds. These rotations are repeated in the display unit by means of servo drives and cause the counters to rotate. The along distance counter is arranged to count down from the initial distance to the waypoint until it reaches zero when the aircraft will be on a line perpendicular to the desired track and passing through the waypoint. If both along and across distances read zero simultaneously the aircraft is over the waypoint.

Fixed Antenna System
Figure 10.17 may be used to explain the principles of a fixed antenna system to block diagram level. The antenna consists of planar arrays of slotted waveguide or printed circuit, separate arrays being used for transmission and reception. Beam-switching is achieved using varactor diode or ferrite switches to couple the transmitter and receiver to the appropriate port.

The received signal is mixed with a sample of the f.m.c.w. transmitted signal and the wanted sideband filtered out and amplified. If only ground speed and drift angle are required further mixing may take place to extract the Doppler frequencies as in the moving antenna case; however the sense of the shift (positive or negative) is lost. If the three velocity vectors in the direction of the aircraft co-ordinates are required, an intermediate frequency f_0 is retained which will be reduced or increased by an amount depending on which beam is being radiated.

The time-multiplexed Doppler shifted f_0 signals are separated by a demultiplexer driven by the beam-switching control and feeding four tracking loops. Voltage-controlled oscillators become locked to the incoming frequencies $f_0 \pm f_D$ by sweeping through their range until they lock on. The four tracker outputs are then summed and differenced, as

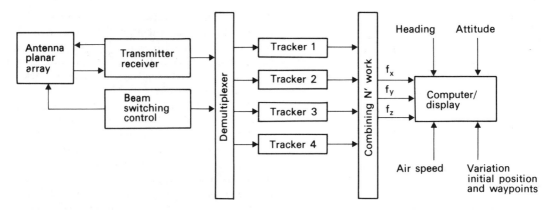

Fig. 10.17 Fixed aerial Doppler block diagram

appropriate, in a combining network to provide signals f_x, f_y and f_z proportional to aircraft co-ordinate velocities (*see* Appendix, A10.3).

Within the computer/display unit (CDU) the aircraft referenced velocity components are transformed into track-orientated earth-referenced components using attitude signals (pitch and roll) from a vertical reference gyro (*see* Appendix, A10.4). With a heading input and waypoints, in terms of desired track and distance, set in by the pilot the computer can integrate the along and across velocities to give distance to go and across-track error (distance) respectively.

The CDU may offer latitude and longitude readout of position by transforming the aircraft velocities into north-orientated horizontal components. True north, as opposed to magnetic north, may be used as the reference if the pilot is able to enter the variation. With attitude, heading and true air speed inputs the output from an airspeed transformation circuit or routine may be compared with the velocity transformation to give wind speed and direction.

Installation

The Doppler navigator system illustrated in Fig. 10.15 requires five units as indicated; i.e. antenna, transmitter-receiver, tracker, computer and display unit. The Marconi AD 560 comprises the five units mentioned plus a junction box, ground-speed and drift-angle indicator, distance-flown indicator and a control unit (or simply a panel-mounted switch). The weight of the AD 560 is about 30 kg which should be compared with Marconi's latest Doppler the AD 660 which weighs 5 kg (sensor only).

The AD 660 is a single-unit Doppler sensor giving

ground-speed and drift-angle outputs and, with a compass input, will provide navigation data to a CDU giving a two-unit Doppler navigation system. Digital outputs are provided in accordance with ARINC 429 (DITS) and ARINC 582, there is also an optional synchro output for drift angle. This unit, introduced in 1979, may herald a comeback for Doppler in airline service since it has been ordered by Boeing for installation in their 727s and 737s, to be used in conjunction with Lear Siegler's performance and navigation computer system (PNCS).

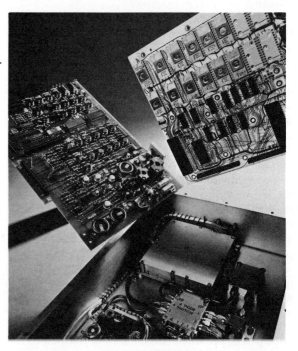

Fig. 10.18 AD 660 (courtesy Marconi Avionics Ltd)

Fig. 10.19 Doppler 71 antenna/electronics unit (courtesy the Decca Navigator Co. Ltd)

Figure 10.18 shows the AD 660 with cards removed. Note the use of large-scale integrated circuits common in all modern systems as we approach the 1980s. The antenna is a printed circuit microstrip producing four beams transmitted sequentially. The transmitter is a f.m. Gunn diode oscillator generating over 200 mW at a carrier frequency of 13·325 GHz. Computation and control is achieved through a microprocessor.

The Decca Doppler 71 and 72 are designed for v./s.t.o.l. (vertical/short take-off and landing) aircraft operating below 300 knots and fixed-wing aircraft operating up to 1000 knots respectively. These systems have had civilian sales limited to aircraft with special needs such as certain helicopter operations and surveying. Figures 10.19-10.22 show units of a typical Decca Doppler 71 installation. Interconnections are simple; all three indicators being driven directly from the antenna/electronics unit. A heading input is required for the PBDI which, together with the antenna/electronics unit, forms a basic two-unit system, the two meters being optional. Another optional unit is an automatic chart display driven by the PBDI or a more sophisticated replacement, a TANS computer.

Fig. 10.20 Doppler 71 position, bearing and drift indicator (PBDI) (courtesy the Decca Navigator Co. Ltd)

Fig. 10.21 Doppler 71 ground-speed and drift meter (courtesy the Decca Navigator Co. Ltd)

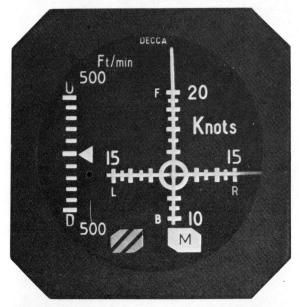

Fig. 10.22 Doppler 71 hovermeter (courtesy the Decca Navigator Co. Ltd)

The Doppler 70 series systems are c.w., three-beam (not switched) K-band radars. Adequate decoupling between transmitter and receiver is inherent in the design, so allowing the use of c.w. A local oscillator signal is used for mixing, so providing an intermediate frequency ± the Doppler shift. Further details of the system are included below.

Across-track error and track-angle error are usually available as outputs from a CDU for use by an autopilot. Obviously warning signals must also be provided to indicate the integrity of the steering signals to the user equipment.

Controls and Operation

We shall consider the Doppler 71 as an example, although obviously considerable variations exist.

P.B.D.I.
Indicator, controller and general purpose processor with programme capacity of 1500 16-bit words. Battery-protected memory.

Switches
1. DOP TEST: ground checking of sensor;
   ST BY: inputs inhibited, display flashes;
   LAND/SEA: allows correction for overwater calibration shift error to be switched in.
2. LMP TEST: check of display and lamps;
   HDG/VAR: display of heading input and insertion of magnetic variations;
   FIX: position displayed is fixed; Doppler incremental distances are stored; warning lamp flashes; slew switches operable;
   POS: aircraft latitude or longitude displayed;
   GS/DFT: ground speed and drift angle displayed;
   BRG DIST: bearing and distance to next waypoint displayed;
   WP: selected waypoint latitude or longitude.
3. WAYPOINT 1 to 10: allows for waypoint selection. Waypoints can be inserted or changed at any time.
4. LAT LONG: three-position latitude, longitude or both (alternately) displayed.
5. SLEW: two switches used for inserting variation, present position, waypoint co-ordinates and resetting the numeric displays as required.

Displays
1. Numeric: two groups of three seven-segment filaments show data selected by seven-position switch.
2. Sector display: indicates latitude north (N) or south (S), longitude east (E) or west (W).
3. Track error: analogue display showing track error, in degrees, to the selected waypoint.
4. Warning indicators: incorporated in analogue display to give warning of Doppler failure (or memory), computer failure or test mode selected.

Ground-Speed and Drift Meter
Display of ground speed up to 300 knots and drift
angle ± 30° (expanded scale).
Power failure and memory warning flags.
Manual setting of drift and ground speed provided for.

Hover Meter
Displays:
   along-heading velocity − range −10 to +20 knots;
   across-heading velocity − range ± 15 knots;
   vertical velocity − range ± 500 ft min^{-1}.

Characteristics

ARINC Characteristic 540, airborne Doppler radar,
was issued in 1958 and last printed in January 1960;
it is no longer maintained current. For this reason
details of a currently available system, the Decca
Doppler 71 are listed. Since this is primarily a
helicopter system a very brief data summary for the
Marconi AD 660 system aimed at the airliner market
has also been included.

Decca Doppler 71
Power: 100 mW
Frequency: 13·325 and 13·314 GHz.
Intermediate frequency: 10·7 MHz.
Beam width: 5° in depression plane, 11° in broadside
plane.
Depression angle: 67°.
Modulation: none, c.w.
Number of beams: three continuous.
Along-heading velocity range to computer: −50 to
+300 knots.
Across-heading velocity range to computer: ± 100
knots.
Supply: 115 V, 400 Hz, single-phase.
Altitude range: 0-20 000 ft over land or over water
when surface wind ⩾ 5 knots.
Accuracy of sensor − less than 0·3% or 0·25 knots
(whichever is the greater (overland)).
Acquisition time: within 20 s.
Indicated accuracy, ground speed and drift meter:
3·5 at 100 knots; 5 at 300 knots, drift ± 0·5°.
Indicated accuracy, hover meter: along and across
velocities ± 1 knot, vertical velocity ± 40 ft min^{-1}.

Marconi AD 660
Power: 200 mW.
Frequency: 13·325 GHz.
Modulation: f.m.c.w.
Number of beams: four, sequential.
Velocity range: 10-800 knots.

Drift angle range: ± 39·9°.
Altitude: 45 000 ft above ground level.
Supply: 28 V d.c., 2 A.

Testing

Modern Dopplers have a considerable amount of
built-in test equipment with which to carry out
checks. Synthetic signals may be generated by
switching antennas at a much higher rate than normal,
thus leading to the memory flag clearing and a given
reading possibly appearing on the ground-speed and
drift-angle indicator. This might be the effect of
pressing the test switch on the ground under memory
conditions. If airborne and in memory a similar
check could be carried out, but if in the signal
condition, i.e. Doppler shift present and s.n.r.
satisfactory, then a good and easy check is to operate
the slewing switches to offset ground-speed and
drift-angle readings; on release the readings should
return to their original positions. This check will
cause a small error in the computed position but this

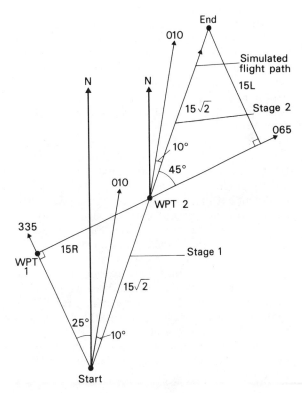

Fig. 10.23 Test conditions for simulated flight to check
computer (*see* text)

can be eliminated by slewing in the opposite direction by the same amount to produce a cancelling error.

To check the computer/display part of a Doppler navigator a course must be simulated by setting compass heading (d.g., directional gyro, selected), drift angle, ground speed and waypoint course and distance using appropriate slewing controls. Having set everything up the computer is switched on for a timed run, at the end of which the displayed readings should be as independently calculated. Usually a written procedure will give the necessary figures for such a check but in any case they are reasonably easy to work out. As an example, starting with the following:

Waypoint 1	track 335°	distance 15 nautical miles
Waypoint 2	track 065°	distance 15 nautical miles
Heading	010°	
Drift	10° starboard	
Ground speed	600 knots	

at the end of the simulated two-leg flight the across distance should be zero, the distance flown 42 nautical miles and the time taken 4 min 14·5 s, all to within the tolerance laid down for the system.

Ramp test sets have been produced for Doppler systems, usually purpose-built by the manufacturer of the radar and not general-purpose as are, for example, VOR, DME, ILS, etc. test sets. Sometimes one will find meters with associated switches which can be used to monitor various internal voltages and/or currents but this is more likely on older multi-unit equipment.

It is important for accuracy to ensure the antenna is aligned with the aircraft's longitudinal axis. The Doppler will interpret any slight misalignment as a drift-angle error. Initial alignment of all antennas is important but with a fixed antenna system once the hole is cut in the airframe, correctly aligned, the only cause for concern afterwards is that the antenna is fitted the correct way round. With moving-antenna systems an alignment procedure for the antenna mounting is carried out initially by using sighting rods on the mounting and the aircraft. Viewing the rods from a distance to ensure they are in line, and then tightening the securing bolts through the slotted holes in the mounting plate, will ensure that the antenna can be subsequently changed without a need for an alignment check — although one should be carried out on major inspections.

Appendix

Relationships Between Aircraft and Earth Co-Ordinates

As in Fig. A10.1 let i', j', k' be orthogonal unit vectors defining a right-handed co-ordinate system with the positive direction of the axis spanned by i' being forward along the aircraft's longitudinal axis and the positive direction of the axis spanned by j' being starboard along the aircraft's lateral axis.

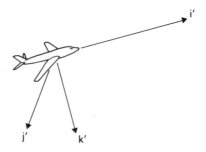

Fig. A10.1 Aircraft co-ordinates

As in Fig. A10.2 let i, j, k be orthogonal unit vectors defining a right-handed co-ordinate system with the positive direction of the axis spanned by i being forward along the aircraft's longitudinal axis projected on to a plane parallel to the ground and the positive direction of the axis spanned by j being starboard along the aircraft's lateral axis projected on to a plane parallel to the ground.

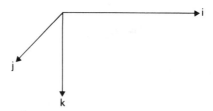

Fig. A10.2 Earth co-ordinates

Further let positive pitch be nose-up and positive roll be starboard wing-down, then from Figs. A10.3 and A10.4 we have:

$$i' = i \cos P - k \sin P$$
$$k' = i \sin P + k \cos P$$

$$j' = j \cos R + k \sin R$$
$$k' = -j \sin R + k \cos R$$

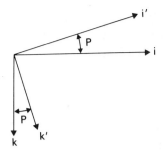

Fig. A10.3 Aircraft pitch

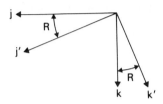

Fig. A10.4 Aircraft roll

Thus the matrix of transition from i, j, k to i', j', k' is given by:

$$\begin{bmatrix} \cos P & 0 & \sin P \\ 0 & 1 & 0 \\ -\sin P & 0 & \cos P \end{bmatrix} \times \begin{bmatrix} 1 & 0 & 0 \\ 0 & \cos R & -\sin R \\ 0 & \sin R & \cos R \end{bmatrix}$$

$$= \begin{bmatrix} \cos P & \sin P \sin R & \sin P \cos R \\ 0 & \cos R & -\sin R \\ -\sin P & \cos P \sin R & \cos P \cos R \end{bmatrix} = M$$

If the aircraft velocity vector V has co-ordinates V_H, V_A, V_V with respect to i, j, k and V_H', V_A', V_V' with respect to i', j', k' we have:

$$\begin{bmatrix} V_H \\ V_A \\ V_V \end{bmatrix} = M \times \begin{bmatrix} V_H' \\ V_A' \\ V_V' \end{bmatrix} \tag{A10.1}$$

i.e. $V_H = V_H' \cos P + V_A' \sin P \sin R + V_V' \sin P \cos R$
$V_A = \qquad\qquad V_A' \cos R \qquad - V_V' \sin R$
$V_V = -V_H' \sin P + V_A' \cos P \sin R + V_V' \cos P \cos R$

The Doppler Shifts for a Four-Beam Janus Configuration

The magnitude of the relative velocity vector V_R, in the direction of any beam is the inner product of the aircraft velocity vector V and the unit vector along the beam centroid, u. Thus:

$$V_R = V \cdot u$$
$$= (V_H' + V_A' + V_V') \cdot u$$

since V is the vector sum of V_H', V_A' and V_V'. Thus:

$$V_R = hV_H' + aV_A' + vV_V'$$

where h, a and v are the magnitudes of the projection of u on to each axis of the co-ordinate system

i.e. $u = hi + aj + vk$

From Figs A10.5, A10.6 and A10.7 we see that for:

beam 1 $h = -H$ $a = A$ $v = V$
beam 2 $h = H$ $a = A$ $v = V$
beam 3 $h = H$ $a = -A$ $v = V$
beam 4 $h = -H$ $a = -A$ $v = V$

where $H = \cos \theta \cos \alpha$; $A = \cos \theta \sin \alpha$; $V = \sin \theta$.

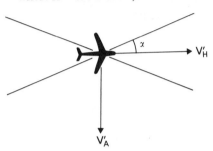

Fig. A10.5 Velocities in longitudinal/lateral plane

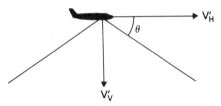

Fig. A10.6 Velocities in plane normal to longitudinal/lateral plane

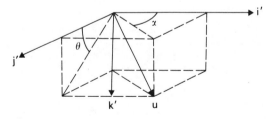

Fig. A10.7 Aircraft velocity vector

Now the Doppler shifts are given by $f_D = 2V_R f/c$, therefore:

$$\begin{aligned} f_1 &= 2f(-H V_H' + A V_A' + V V_V')/c \\ f_2 &= 2f(H V_H' + A V_A' + V V_V')/c \\ f_3 &= 2f(H V_H' - A V_A' + V V_V')/c \\ f_4 &= 2f(-H V_H' - A V_A' + V V_V')/c \end{aligned} \tag{A10.2}$$

The Aircraft Velocity in Earth Co-Ordinates Expressed in Terms of Doppler Shifts

From equations (A10.2) we have:

$$V_H' = \frac{c(f_2 - f_1)}{4fH} = \frac{c(f_3 - f_4)}{4fH}$$

$$V_A' = \frac{c(f_2 - f_3)}{4fA} = \frac{c(f_1 - f_4)}{4fA}$$

$$V_V' = \frac{c(f_1 + f_3)}{4fV} = \frac{c(f_2 + f_4)}{4fV}$$

(A10.3)

Substituting for V_H', V_A', V_V' from equations (A10.3) into equations (A10.1) we have:

$$\begin{bmatrix} V_H \\ V_A \\ V_V \end{bmatrix} = M \times \begin{bmatrix} K_H (f_2 - f_1) \\ K_A (f_2 - f_3) \\ K_V (f_1 + f_3) \end{bmatrix}$$

(A10.4)

where $K_H = \dfrac{C}{4f \cos \theta \cos \alpha}$

$K_A = \dfrac{C}{4f \cos \theta \sin \alpha}$

$K_V = \dfrac{C}{4f \sin \theta}$ are known constants.

M is obtained from pitch and roll signals and f_1, f_2, f_3 are the Doppler shifts measured on beams 1, 2 and 3. Note beam 4 is redundant but could be used for checking purposes.

11 Radio altimeter

Introduction

The meaning of the terms aircraft altitude or height is complicated by the various references used from which the height can be measured. A barometric altimeter senses the static pressure at aircraft level and gives a reading dependent on the difference between this pressure and the pressure at some reference level. For aircraft flying above about 3000 ft, the reference of paramount importance is that level corresponding to a pressure of 1013·25 mbar (29·92 in.Hg), the so-called mean sea level. The other barometric references used are local sea level and airfield level. The pilot is able to set the reference level pressure at 1013·25 mbar, QNH (local sea level – regional) or QFE (airfield level), the Q codes being used in communication with air traffic control (ATC).

Conversely the radio altimeter measures the height of the aircraft above the ground. If an aircraft is in level flight the barometric altimeter reading will be steady while the radio altimeter reading will be varying unless the aircraft is flying over sea or plain. It follows that radio altimeters are most useful when close to the ground, say below 2000 ft, and particularly so when landing providing the final approach is over a flat surface. As a consequence, radio altimeters designed for use in civil aircraft are low-level systems, typical maximum ranges available being 5000, 2500 or even 500 ft in the case of use in automatic landing systems. Military aircraft can utilize high-level radio altimeters.

Basic Principles

Radio height is measured using the basic idea of radio ranging, i.e. measuring the elapsed time between transmission of an e.m. wave and its reception after reflection from the ground. The height is given by half the product of the elapsed time and the speed of light: $h = 492\,t$ (t being the elapsed time in microseconds).

Energy is radiated at a frequency in the band 4200-4400 MHz. Modulation of the carrier is necessary in order to 'mark' the time of transmission, both f.m. and pulsed transmissions are used. The method of time measurement depends on the type of modulation used and the complexity of the airborne equipment which is acceptable. Three basic types of altimeter are marketed: pulse, conventional f.m.c.w. (frequency modulated continuous wave) and constant difference frequency f.m.c.w.

The basic principle of a pulsed system is simple, since the transmitted and received pulses clearly represent events between which the time can be measured. With f.m.c.w. there is no single event during one cycle of the modulating frequency; however specific times during one-half cycle can be identified by the instantaneous frequency being transmitted. Since the transmitter frequency is continuously changing, the received signal, which has been subject to delay due to the round-trip travel time, will be different in frequency to the transmitted signal at any instant in time. The difference frequency, f_h, can be shown to be proportional to the height as follows.

Assume a triangular modulating waveform of frequency f_m and amplitude such that the carrier, f_c, is modulated over a range Δf. This situation is illustrated in Fig. 11.1. The two-way travel time is $2H/c$ where H is the height and c the speed of light. The magnitude of the rate of change of transmitted frequency is $2\,.\,\Delta f\,.\,f_m\ (= 0{\cdot}5\,\Delta f/(1/0{\cdot}25\,f_m))$. The product of the elapsed time and the rate of change of frequency will give the difference in frequency between transmitted and received frequency thus:

$$
\begin{aligned}
f_h &= 2\,.\,\Delta f\,.\,f_m\,.\,T \\
&= 4\,.\,\Delta f\,.\,f_m\,.\,H/c
\end{aligned}
\tag{11.1}
$$

Thus the measurement of the beat frequency determines the height since $4\,.\,\Delta f\,.\,f_m/c$ is a known constant for any particular system.

The beat frequency is constant, for triangular modulation, except at the turn-around region twice per cycle. Since turn-around takes place in T μs we have that the average beat frequency for $2T$ μs is $f_h/2$ for the rest of the modulating cycle; the beat frequency is constant at f_h. If the average beat

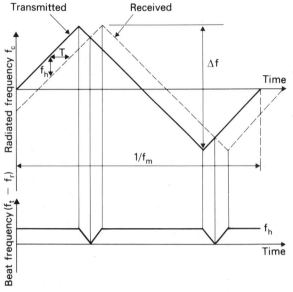

Fig. 11.1 A FMCW radio altimeter — frequency/time relationship

frequency over one modulating cycle is detected we will have a measured frequency f_h given by:

$$f_h = (((1/f_m) - 2T)f_h + Tf_h/2)f_m$$
$$= f_m(1 - 3Tf_m/2) \qquad (11.2)$$

With the aircraft at about 2000 ft and $f_m = 200$ Hz we have:

$$f_h = f_h(1 - 0.0012)$$

i.e. an error of about 2·4 ft at 2000 ft. On the ground there will still be an elapsed time, due to built-in delay, of about 0·12 μs corresponding to a residual altitude (see later) of 57 ft, say. When we use $T = 0.12$ μs and $f_m = 200$ Hz in equation (11.2) we find that the error on the ground due to the averaging of the non-constant beat frequency is about 0·002 ft which is insignificant.

In practice a perfect triangular modulating frequency is difficult to achieve, some rounding at the turn-around taking place. In fact with any reasonably shape-modulation waveform, it can be shown that the average beat frequency when used in equation (11.1) will yield a height reading which is correct within acceptable limits. Appendix 11.1 proves this for sinusoidal frequency modulation which is easier to obtain since the rate of change of carrier frequency is bounded in magnitude by unity.

If there is relative motion between the aircraft and the ground immediately below the received frequency will experience a Doppler shift, f_d (see Chapter 10).

This will result in a vertical displacement of the graph of the received signal in Fig. 11.1. The effect for a descending aircraft (positive shift) is shown in Fig. 11.2. As can be seen the beat frequency is $f_h - f_d$ and $f_h + f_d$ for equal periods. If we take the average over half a modulation period we get $(f_h + f_d + f_h - f_d)/2 = f_h$ as required. This assumes $f_h > f_d$ which will be the case with a radio altimeter.

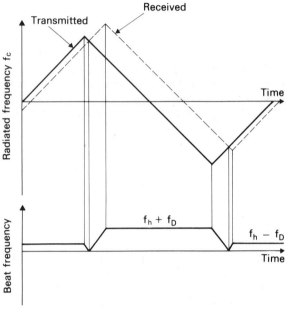

Fig. 11.2 The effect of Doppler shift on beat frequency

Using equation (11.1) we see that for a system with $\Delta f = 100$ MHz (4250-4350 MHz) and $f_m = 200$ Hz the beat frequency $f_h = (4 \times 100 \times 10^6 \times 200H)/(984 \times 10^6) \approx 80H$ so the range of f_h for a 0-2500 ft altimeter with a residual altitude of 57 ft would be 4·56-204·56 kHz. This wide bandwidth can be reduced by maintaining a constant difference frequency thus improving sensitivity. Since f_h depends on both Δf and f_m we can vary either in inverse proportion to the height so keeping f_h constant.

The necessary servo loop must monitor the difference frequency and control the modulator so as to change Δf or f_m accordingly. The control signal represents the height of the aircraft. Since the controlled variable is made inversely proportional to height it becomes difficult to employ the technique at lower heights, particularly when Δf is varied. This latter problem can be overcome by the compromise of operating conventionally at low altitudes and with constant f_h otherwise, or by modifying feedback in the loop such that f_h varies with any change in altitude but not over such a great range as it would with no feedback. The French manufacturer TRT produce altimeters with constant f_h at all heights, control being achieved by varying f_m; the tolerance ± 1 ft or 1 per cent is met.

Factors Affecting Performance

The accuracy of a radio altimeter depends fundamentally on the precision with which the time of transmission is marked. For precise timing a wide transmitted spectrum is required since this would lead to a steep leading edge in a pulsed system or, in the case of f.m.c.w., a large frequency deviation which effectively gives an expanded scale. Of course a finite spectrum is transmitted and in fact is limited to a total spread of between 4200 and 4400 MHz by international legislation (the band 1600-1660 MHz has also been allocated for use by radio altimeters but is no longer used).

In an f.m.c.w. system a counter may be used which measures the number of cycles or half-cycles in one period of the modulation. Since the counter is unable to measure fractions of a cycle, other than possibly a half, the count is a discrete number. The process results in a quantization error called step or fixed error. We may rewrite equation (11.1) as:

$$H = \frac{cf_m}{4\Delta f f_m} = \frac{cN}{4\Delta f} \qquad (11.3)$$

where $N = f_h/f_m$ is the number of beat frequency cycles (to nearest integer below) in the modulation cycle. Since N is an integer the height measured will be subject to a quantization error called step error equal to $c/4\Delta f$ which with Δf = 100 MHz is 2·46 ft.

In practice in any one modulation period the actual count will depend on the number of positive-going zero crossings of the beat frequency, this could be N or $N + 1$ depending on phasing. So if the phasing varies the count will jump between N and $N + 1$ and back so averaging out the step error providing the time constant of the indicating circuit is large compared with the time between count fluctuations. It can be shown that the count will change for a change in height of a quarter of a wavelength of the r.f. At the frequency used for radio altimeters a quarter of a wavelength is less than 1 in. and hence unless flying over very smooth surfaces the fluctuating radio height will cause averaging out of the error. Deliberately wobbling the

phase of the modulation frequency will also have the desired effect providing the wobbulation rate, say 10 Hz, can be filtered out.

If a frequency discriminator is used to measure frequency the step error is not present since measurement is continuous rather than discrete. With conventional f.m.c.w. altimeters, however, the range of frequencies to be measured is large and discriminator circuits sufficiently stable and linear are difficult to achieve. With a constant difference frequency f.m.c.w. altimeter a discriminator can easily be used to detect the small changes which occur in f_h.

The received signal strength varies with the height of the aircraft. From the radar range equation this variation is as the fourth power of the range; however with an altimeter the greater the range (height) the greater the area of the target (ground) is illuminated. For radio altimeters therefore, the variation is as the square of the range. The gain frequency characteristic of the difference frequency amplifier (f.m.c.w.) should be such that the higher frequencies are amplified more than the lower. Such a characteristic helps by reducing the dynamic range of the frequency-measuring circuit and also reduces low frequency noise.

Part of the two-way travel time is accounted for by the aircraft installation delay (AID). Since, ideally, the radio altimeter should read zero feet on touchdown, the residual altitude which accounts for the AID is made up of cable length, multiplied by a factor (typically 1·5) to allow for propagation speed, and the sum of the antenna heights. It is important that the system is calibrated so as to allow for AID. One method which has been used for an altimeter utilized for blind landing is to measure the difference frequency on touchdown on a number of flight trials of a particular type of aircraft. The frequency arrived at empirically can be injected into the difference frequency amplifier on the bench and the set can then be adjusted to give a zero feet output. A more common method is to calibrate by cutting the antenna feeders to an appropriate length; this will be described under the heading 'Installation'.

Transmitter-receiver leakage can be viewed as noise which limits the receiver sensitivity and also may cause an erroneous reading. Use of separate transmit and receive antennas will give space attenuation, a figure in the region of about 75 dB should be aimed for in an installation where the altimeter output is used in critical systems such as automatic landing and ground proximity warning (g.p.w.s.).

Signals occurring at near zero range are caused by reflections from landing gear and other appendages,

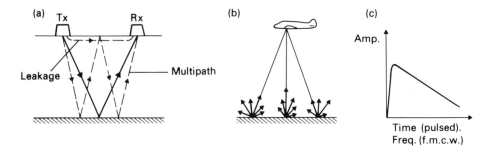

Fig. 11.3 Some factors affecting performance

as well as the leakage signal referred to above. In both constant-difference frequency and pulse altimeters a tracking loop is employed to follow the changes in altitude. Initially, the altitude will be unknown so a search mode is entered which, while seeking the correct altitude, will vary receiver gain. As previously discussed, at low altitudes the gain will be low, thus while searching in the frequency (f.m.c.w.) or time (pulsed) region of the unwanted signals the large gain reduction ensures they are weak. The ground return is relatively strong ensuring lock-on to the correct signal and hence indication of the actual radio altitude.

Multipath signals arise since the first-time-around echo will be reflected from the airframe back down to the ground and return as a second-time-around echo. While this multipath signal will be considerably weaker than the required signal the height-controlled gain will in part nullify this favourable situation. In tracking altimeters the initial or subsequent search can be in the direction of increasing altitude so locking on to the correct signal first, a similar approach to outbound search in DME.

Aircraft pitch and roll will mean that the beam centre is no longer vertical; however if the beam is fairly broad, at least part of the transmitted energy will take the shortest route to the ground. Provided receiver sensitivity is adequate there will be sufficient energy received from the nearest point for accurate measurement.

A consequence of broad beams is that in flying over rough terrain, reflections will be received from angles other than the vertical. Since the non-vertical paths have a longer two-way travel time the spectrum of the difference frequency will be spread (ground diffusion). The spectrum shape will be steep at the low frequency end corresponding to the correct altitude much the same as the pulse shape in a pulsed system will have a steep leading edge (see Fig. 11.3b and c). This spectrum widening is increased by aircraft roll and pitch. Leading edge tracking in

pulsed systems and lowest frequency tracking (spectrum filtering) in f.m.c.w. systems is used to retain accuracy.

The altimeter can be designed with a response time in the order of a few milliseconds; however one does not normally wish to follow the smallest variations of the ground below. The output is usually filtered with a time constant of say a few tenths of a second.

Block Diagram Operation

As already mentioned there are three main approaches to radio altimeters. Most altimeters are of the f.m.c.w. type, the majority of these being conventional for the sake of simplicity. Although tracking f.m.c.w. and pulsed systems are more complex they do have advantages over conventional f.m.c.w. as will be appreciated from the previous paragraphs. Simplified block diagrams for the three types will be considered.

Conventional f.m.c.w. Altimeters
The transmitter in a modern equipment comprises a solid-state oscillator frequency modulated at typically 100-150 Hz rate. While most of the power (0·5-1 W) is radiated from a broadly directional antenna a small portion is fed to the mixer to beat with the received signal.

The echo is mixed with the transmitter sample in a strip-line balanced mixer to produce the beat frequency. Use of a balanced mixer helps in reduction of transmitter noise in the receiver. The gain of the wide band beat frequency amplifier increases with frequency to compensate for the low signal level of the high frequencies (high altitude). Signal limiting removes unwanted amplitude variations and gives a suitable signal form for the counter.

A cycle-counting frequency-measuring circuit provides a d.c. signal to the indicator. Basically suitable switching circuits control the charging of a capacitor so that a fixed amount of charge is

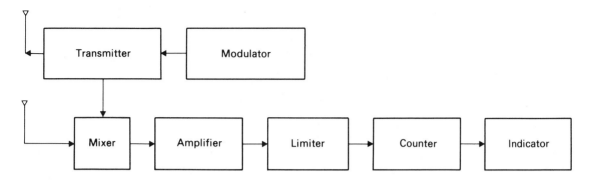

Fig. 11.4 Conventional FMCW altimeter block diagram

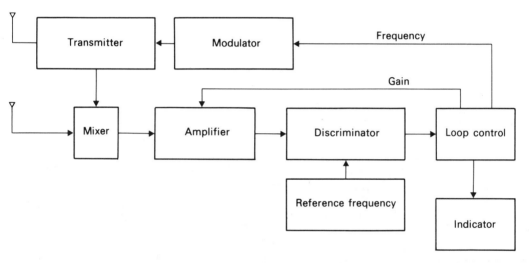

Fig. 11.5 Constant difference frequency FMCW altimeter block diagram

generated for each cycle (or half-cycle) of the unknown beat frequency. With the simplest type of indicator the total charge per second (current) is indicated on a milliammeter calibrated in feet.

Constant Difference Frequency f.m.c.w. Altimeters
This approach is similar to a conventional f.m.c.w. altimeter at the r.f. end. The beat frequency amplifier is a narrow band with gain controlled by the loop so that it increases with altitude. A tracking discriminator compares the beat frequency, f_b, with an internal reference, f_r; if the two are not the same, an error signal is fed to the loop control.

The outputs of the loop control circuit are used to set the modulator frequency, f_m (or amplitude if deviation, Δf, is controlled), to set the gain of the amplifier and to drive the indicator. The change in f_m (or Δf) is such as to make $f_b = f_r$. Obviously any change in height will lead to a change in f_b and

consequent loop action to bring f_b back to the required rate; in doing so the indicator feed will change. If f_b and f_r are far removed, search action is instigated whereby the modulator frequency (or Δf) is made to sweep through its range from low to high until lock on is achieved.

Pulsed Altimeters
A simplified block diagram of a typical pulsed altimeter is shown in Fig. 11.6. Such altimeters are manufactured by, among others, Honeywell; the figures mentioned in the description of operation which follow are for the Honeywell 7500BC series.

A p.r.f. generator operating at 8 kHz keys the transmitter which feeds the antenna with pulse of r.f. of 60 ns duration and frequency 4300 MHz. The radiated peak power is about 100 W. A time reference signal, t_0, is fed from the transmitter to initiate a precision ramp generator.

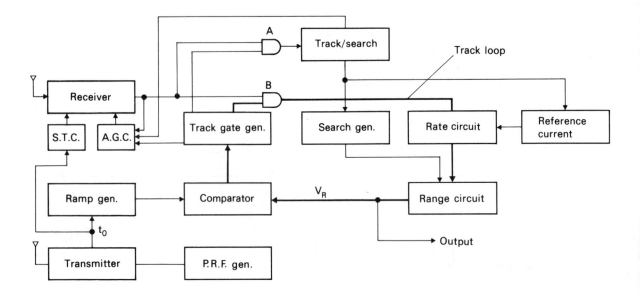

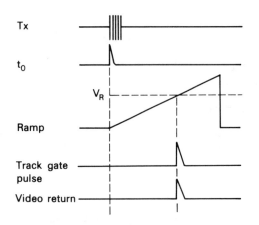

Fig. 11.6 Pulse altimeter block diagram

The ramp voltage is compared with the range voltage, V_R, which is proportional to the indicated height. When the ramp voltage reaches V_R a track gate pulse is generated and fed to gate B and an elongated gate pulse is fed to gate A. The detected video pulse is also fed to gates A and B. A further gate pulse is fed to the a.g.c. circuits.

Unless a reliable signal is detected within the elongated gate pulse the track/search circuit will signal the commencement of a search cycle and break the track loop by removing its reference current feed. During search the search generator drive to the range circuit ensures that V_R, starting from a voltage representing zero feet, runs out to a voltage representing 2500 ft. The search cycle repeats until a

reliable signal (five or six pulses) is received when the track loop becomes operational.

During track the overlap of the track gate pulse and video pulse determines the magnitude of a current which is compared with a reference (offset) current. Where the two currents are equal, the output of the rate circuit (integrator) is zero, otherwise a positive or negative voltage is fed to the range circuit. The range circuit (integrator) adjusts its output voltage, V_R, if its input is non-zero. Since V_R determines the timing of the track gate pulse any change in V_R will cause the previously mentioned overlap to alter until such time as the loop is nulled, i.e. overlap current = reference current. Any change in height will therefore result in a change in V_R to bring the loop back to the null condition.

Automatic gain control (a.g.c.) and sensitivity time control (s.t.c.) are fed to the receiver where they control the gain of the i.f. amps. During search the a.g.c. circuits monitor the noise output of the receiver and adjust its gain so as to keep noise output constant. The s.t.c. reduces the gain of the receiver for a short time, equivalent to say 50 ft after transmission, and then its control decreases linearly until a time equivalent to say 200 ft. This action prevents acquisition of unwanted signals, such as leakage, during the search mode.

During track the a.g.c. maintains the video signal in the a.g.c. gate at a constant level. This is important to ensure precise tracking of the received signal since any variation in amplitude would cause the area of overlap to track gate and video signals to change. At low heights on track the a.g.c. reduces the receiver gain, so helping to avoid the effects of leakage. When the height increases the leakage signal is, of course, gated out, giving time discrimination.

Monitoring and Self-Test

The integrity of the radio altimeter output is vital, particularly in automatic landing applications. Circuit redundancy and comparison is an effective way of dealing with the problem. For example two separate altitude-measuring circuits may accept a feed from the mixer and independently arrive at the aircraft's height. Should the two heights be different by more than an acceptable amount, a warning signal is sent to the indicator and any other systems to which the height information is fed. A disadvantage of using redundancy and comparison only is that no attempt is made to eliminate the cause of failure, so information is lost.

Self-calibration is an approach which is able to compensate for small errors. If a part of the transmitter output is passed through a precision delay line the resulting signal can be used to provide a 'check height'. For example in a conventional f.m.c.w. system the delayed transmitter sample may be mixed with an undelayed transmitter sample to give a beat frequency which may be compared with a suitable reference frequency. If the two frequencies are different the modulating signal is adjusted to bring them in line; for example, if the beat frequency is too low, equation (11.1) tells us that increasing Δf by increasing the modulating signal amplitude will, in turn, increase the beat frequency as required. Similar ideas may be applied to constant-difference frequency f.m.c.w. and pulsed altimeters where suitable parameters are adjusted as necessary.

A self-calibration loop such as described above may operate continuously using what is essentially redundant circuitry. However in equipment where the altitude is measured by means of a loop, such as a servoed slope (controlled f_m) f.m.c.w. system, we may have sequential self-calibration where the measuring loop is switched, perhaps three times per second, into self-calibrate mode.

Checking received signal quality is a feature of most altimeters. In a pulsed system the presence of detected received pulses in a gate pulse is feasible; in a constant-difference frequency altimeter the presence of a spectrum centred on the required beat is checked. With a conventional f.m.s.w. altimeter one cannot check a particular part of the time or frequency domain but signal plus noise to noise ratio may be monitored.

When the aircraft is flying above the maximum height reading of the radio altimeter it is likely that there will be a signal failure detected. Since this is due to attenuation because of excessive range, and not a failure or degradation of the altimeter, it is desirable that no warning of failure is given and that the pointer on the indicator is parked out of view. A cruise-monitoring circuit may be incorporated which, using a delayed and attenuated feed between transmitter and receiver, checks continuing satisfactory operation in the absence of a detectable received signal. Any warning to the autopilot must not be affected by cruise monitoring; it should be active whenever there is a loss of r.f. or when any other failure is detected. Contrary to the above, many radio altimeters react to a loss of signal by parking the pointer and displaying the flag.

The antenna and feeder, if not properly matched to the transmitter, will give rise to a reflection which may cause problems since it will be delayed with respect to the transmitted signal. A directional coupling circuit may be used to monitor the reflected signal and so give a warning of excessive v.s.w.r.

The monitoring and self-calibration circuits vary greatly in detail and in how comprehensive a check is carried out. All, however, on detecting a failure will provide a warning signal to operate a flag in the indicator and a similar, but usually separate, warning signal to other systems, dependent on radio altitude information. In particular if a tie-in with autopilot has been established, the warning signal will control an interlock circuit within the autopilot system which prevents erroneous information dictating the flight path. Some manufacturers provide latched indicator lights on the front panel of the transmitter-receiver which give an indication of the area of failure.

A self-test facility is usually provided whereby a delay line, ideally between antennas, is switched in, thus giving a predetermined reading on the indicator. A disadvantage of such a facility is that it introduces electromechanical devices such as co-axial cable relays which are, of course, something else to go wrong. It may be argued that checking that the reading on the ground before take-off is some specified figure near zero is adequate, but nevertheless, some form of in-flight test facility is usually required.

On pushing the self-test button, providing the equipment is operating correctly, the failure warning output should be active so causing the warning flag to appear on the indicator and, more important, preventing the autopilot utilizing radio altimeter information. As an extra safeguard, an interlock should be provided so as to prevent self-test once the autopilot or any other system has begun to make use of the radio altimeter height output.

Indicator

As mentioned previously, a milliammeter may be used to indicate height but an alternative is a servo-driven pointer. A decision height (DH) facility is also provided. The pilot sets the DH bug to the required height reading and in doing so determines the voltage V_d, fed to a comparator. The other comparator input is a d.c. analogue altitude signal which if less than V_d will cause the DH lamp to light, so warning the pilot that the aircraft is flying below the DH setting. A block diagram of an indicator is shown in Fig. 11.7, where isolation amplifiers have been omitted for simplicity.

used particularly laterally to avoid roll error in which case leading-edge tracking (pulsed) or spectrum-filtering (servoed slope f.m.c.w.) must perform adequately. The antennas must be mounted sufficiently far apart to avoid excessive leakage but not so far apart as to produce a large parallax error at touchdown, a spacing between 20 in. and 8 ft may be required.

If the spacing between antennas, mounted longitudinally, is 8 ft and the midpoint of the line joining the antennas is, say, 7 ft above the ground on touchdown, then half the shortest distance between the antennas via the ground will be $(4^2 + 7^2)^{0.5} \approx 8$ ft giving a parallax error of 1 ft on landing. This may be taken into account when calculating the residual

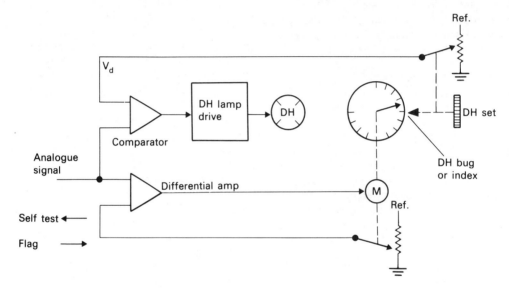

Fig. 11.7 Simplified servo-driven indicator

Installation

Figure 11.8 illustrates a single radio altimeter installation showing interface and selection links. Co-axial feeders pass r.f. energy to and from the separate transmit and receive antennas by way of switches. When self-test is activated the transmitted energy is fed to the delay unit where it is attenuated and delayed before being fed back to the receiver. For a particular installation feeder length and delay is known so the correct reading on self-test may be calculated and entered in the pilot check list and functional test procedure.

The antennas are broadly directional, flush-mounted horns often being employed giving a beam width between about 20° and 40°. Broader beams may be

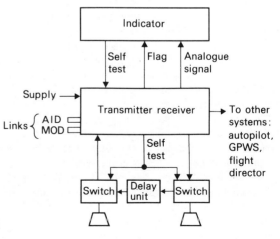

Fig. 11.8 Radio altimeter installation

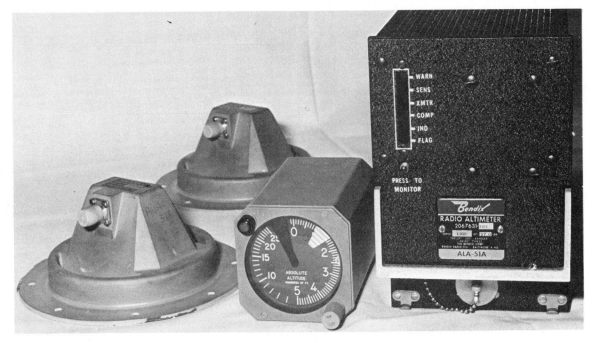

Fig. 11.9 ALA-51A (courtesy Bendix Avionics Division)

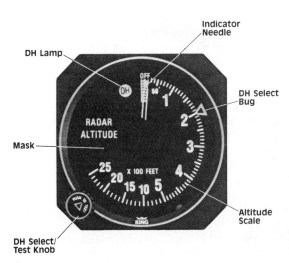

Fig. 11.10 KI 250 indicator for use with KRA 10 radio altimeter (courtesy King Radio Corp.)

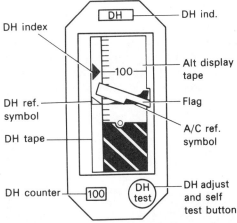

Fig. 11.11 Typical moving vertical scale indicator

altitude. Good performance in respect of leading edge tracking or spectrum filtering will make parallax error worse. A further consideration in antenna positioning is avoiding excessive reflections from protuberances such as the undercarriage; in this respect side lobe energy must be kept low (say 40 dB down).

The transmitter receiver must be mounted within reach of the antennas since the feeder length is critical. Since the transmitter is relatively low power, cooling is not a severe problem but forced-air cooling able to cope with up to 50 W of dissipated energy may be required. The power supply will be 115 V a.c. 400 Hz if the equipment is to ARINC specifications but 28 V d.c. equipments will be found.

Aircraft Installation Delay

Aircraft installation delay (AID) is the elapsed time

between transmit and receive when the aircraft is at touchdown, and is due to the delay in the feeders and the height of the antennas above the ground. In order that the indicator will read zero feet on landing the installation must be calibrated. Various methods have been used, by far the most common being that laid down in ARINC 552A; AID is defined by the formula:

$$AID = P + K(C_t + C_r) \tag{11.4}$$

where:

P is total minimum path length between transmit and receive antennas via the ground when the aircraft is in the touchdown position (minimum path length is specified to avoid parallax error);

K is the ratio of the speed of light to the speed of propagation of the co-axial cable (typically 1·5);

C_t is the transmitter feeder length;

C_r is the receiver feeder length.

(AID is not in fact aircraft installation delay since AID is an elapsed time whereas the right-hand side of (11.4) is in feet. A more accurate term would be residual altitude.)

Calibration is achieved by cutting the cables to a length which gives an AID of 20, 40 or 57 ft (figures of 40, 57 and 80 ft are quoted in draft proposals from ARINC in 1978). The transmitter-receiver is bench calibrated for the 57 ft AID standard. Grounding one of three pins on the t.r. plug by means of a jumper external to the unit selects the appropriate zero-bias adjustment to give the 20, 40 or 57 ft AID as required. The result of choosing this method is

interchangeability of transmitter-receivers between different installations.

In practice on a new installation, having determined suitable positions for the antennas, a minimum cable length for feasible t.r. location will be found. Equation (11.4) can now be used to decide the AID and to calculate the cable lengths. ARINC 552A and, usually, manufacturers' installation manuals provide a graph from which cable length can be read off. As an example consider $P = 10$ ft, minimum total cable length = 10 ft and $K = 1·5$. We have $P + K(C_t + C_r) = 25$ ft so the 20 ft AID cannot be used. If we choose 40 then total cable length is $(40 - 10)/1·5 = 20$ ft, whereas with 57 we have 31·3 ft. One should be careful, when using a graph, to ensure that it corresponds to the type of cable being used (RG − 9/U in ARINC 552A) and further check the axes which may be total cable length or each cable and total path or antenna height (each cable *vs.* antenna height in ARINC 552A).

Interface

Were it not for the use which is made of radio altitude information by other systems, it is doubtful whether many civil aircraft would carry radio altimeters. The outputs available are height, rate of change of height, trip signals and validity (flag or warning) signal. Some of these will be fed to the autoland/autopilot system, the g.p.w.s. and a flight director.

Most frequently used are a d.c. analogue of aircraft height wherever a system needs to continuously monitor radio height and, essential, a switched, fail-safe validity signal (invalid low). The rate signal, i.e. rate of change of height, may be derived in the system utilizing the height signal, but if provided will take the form of a phase-reversing a.c. analogue signal (ARINC 552A). The trips are switchable d.c. voltages, switching taking place when the aircraft transits through a pre-set height, the DH bug is sometimes called a pilot set trip. Again trip signals may be generated in those systems using the height analogue signal.

Autoland or blind-landing systems must have radio height information which will be used to progressively reduce the gain of the glideslope signal amplifier (not radio) in the pitch channel after the aircraft passes over the outer marker, and will also be used to generate trip signals within the autoflare computer. The following is a brief summary of events with radio heights:

140 ft (a) radio altimeter interlock switched in;

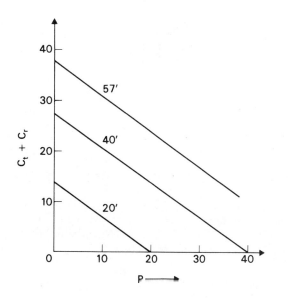

Fig. 11.12 An AID calibration chart ($k = 1·5$)

(b) changes in response to glidepath signals;
120 ft (a) preparatory functions;
 90 ft (a) check 140 ft operation;
 50 ft (a) glidepath signal disconnected;
       (b) throttle closure initiated;
       (c) pitch demand maintains correct descent
           rate;
 20 ft (a) rudder servo disconnected;
       (b) ailerons centred.

This sequence is applicable, for example, to a BAC 1-11 series 500 aircraft using an Elliott series 2200 auto touchdown system. The 140 and 90 ft trips are fed from the radio altimeter; the others are generated in the autoflare computer.

The g.p.w.s. needs radio height trips on all modes since the profile changes abruptly at different heights. Mode 2 operation is excessive terrain closure warning and so depends on the rate of change of radio height. The trip signals and the rate signal will normally be generated within the g.p.w.s. using valid height information from the radio altimeter.

Some multi-function flight director instruments have a rising runway symbol which moves up to meet an aircraft symbol as the aircraft descends to touchdown. Operation is typically over the last 200 ft. The vertical movement of the rising runway depends on the height analogue signal from the radio altimeter, while its lateral movement is controlled by the ILS localizer output. Failure of either radio altimeter or localizer causes the rising runway to be obscured by a 'RUNWAY' flag.

Multiple Installations

All-weather landings will only be safe if information fed to the autoland system is reliable. To achieve reliability of radio height a multiple installation is used. Whether dual or triple installations are used depends on the probability of an undetected degradation; consequently dual radio altimeters will only be used where monitoring, self-calibration and redundancy are deemed sufficiently comprehensive and reliable.

As soon as one fits more than one radio altimeter to an aircraft the possibility of interference exists. If the number 1 system were to receive a leakage signal from number 2 a false height reading may result. Also since the antennas are broadly directional and all facing downwards the echo from number 1 will be received by number 2 (and 3) and vice-versa.

Various safeguards are employed. Minimum coupling may be achieved by separating the pairs of antennas sufficiently (at least 8 ft, say) and possibly ensuring that the E fields of adjacent pairs are at right angles (*see* Fig. 11.13).

As a further precaution multiple-installation altimeters will employ different modulation frequencies. As an example of how this helps, consider Fig. 11.14 where we have two altimeters, one operating with a modulation frequency of 100 Hz,

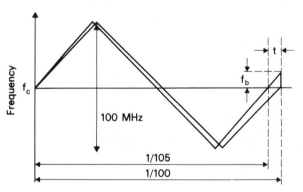

Fig. 11.14 Dual-installation modulation frequencies (100 and 105 Hz)

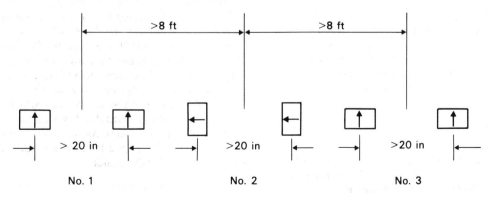

Fig. 11.13 Triple-installation aerial arrangements

the other 105 Hz (e.g. Collins ALT 50). Assume that at one instance in time 't_0' in one of the receivers we have two signals both at f_c (= 4300 MHz) and both increasing in frequency; one at 100 Hz rate, the other at 105 Hz rate. One-hundredth of a second later there will be a non-zero beat frequency f_b given by rate of change of frequency of the most rapidly changing signal multiplied by the time lag of the slowest. So:

$$f_b = (\Delta f \times 10^6 \times 100 \times 2) \times (t)$$
$$= (100 \times 10^6 \times 100 \times 2) \times (1/100 - 1/105)$$
$$\approx 9 \cdot 5 \text{ MHz.}$$

Thus after one cycle of f_m the interfering beat is well out of range of the difference frequency amplifier bandwidth. The beat will change at a 5 Hz rate, reaching a maximum of 100 MHz.

The different modulation frequencies are selected in a similar way to AID, i.e. by a jumper between appropriate pins, the jumper being part of the fixed installation. A similar technique for pulse altimeters could be to employ sufficiently different p.r.f.s to ensure that the 'height' change due to an interfering pulse would be at a rate fast enough to prevent lock-on by virtue of the altimeter time constant.

Characteristics

The following are selected and summarized from ARINC 552A.

Input/Output r.f. Coupling
50 Ω RG-9/U (or equivalent) co-axial cable.
Cable + antenna s.w.r. less than 1·1 : 1 over frequency range 4210-4390 MHz.

Altitude Range
From 2500 ft to a 'few feet' below touchdown.

Loop Gain
Sufficient to ensure proper operation up to 2500 ft assuming a total feeder cable length of 30 ft of RG-9/U, a ground reflection coefficient of 0·01 and with an additional 9 dB loop gain for contingencies (e.g. longer or different type of cable).

Outputs

Basic
(a) d.c. altitude analogue: $V = 0 \cdot 2h + 0 \cdot 4$ below 480 ft; $V = 10 + 10 \ln((h + 20)/500)$ above 480 ft (ln being log to the base e).
Accuracy: greater of ± 2 ft or 2 per cent up to 500 ft, 5 per cent thereafter. Time constant 0·1 s.

(b) Two trips: single make contacts switching supply from user equipment below pre-set height. Adjustable 0-2500 ft ± 6 per cent and 500-1500 ft ± 6 per cent.

Optional (additional to above)
(a) Synchro output representing height to be employed for display purposes. Same accuracy as (a) above.
(b) Altitude rate 400 Hz phase reversing, 200 mV 100 ft^{-1} min^{-1}.
Accuracy: greater than ± 20 f.p.m. or ± 10 per cent up to 50 ft; ± 30 f.p.m. or ± 10 per cent 50-500 ft.
(c) Additional trips: three at 0-200 ft ± 3 per cent ± 3 ft; two at 0-500 ft ± 3 per cent ± 3 ft; one at 1000-2500 ft ± 6 per cent.

Ramp Testing and Maintenance

It is important to stress that due to the extensive interface it is essential that the radio altimeter outputs are compatible with those systems which it feeds. If we also consider the program pins used to select modulation frequency and AID and, further, critical feeder lengths, it is clear that replacement of units or parts of the fixed installation must only be carried out when complete compatibility, both internal and external, has been established.

A functional test on the ramp is quite straightforward. The radio altimeter should read nearly zero feet when switched on. If the antennas are mounted forward of the main wheels the reading will be less than zero; if aft of the main wheels greater than zero. The flag should clear showing the r.f. path is not broken but not proving the loop gain is sufficient; attenuation should be introduced to check this but is unlikely to be called for.

When self-test is operated the correct reading should be obtained and the flag should appear. While keeping the self-test switch pressed the DH bug may be adjusted from a higher to a lower reading than the height pointer, the DH lamp being first lit and then extinguished as the bug passes the pointer.

Special-to-type test sets are available which allow variation of simulated altitude; this is useful for checking trip signals. On some altimeters operating the self-test causes the pointer to sweep again due to a variation in simulated altitude.

Appendix

Sinusoidal Frequency Modulation

If the carrier $V_c \sin 2\pi f_c t$ is frequency modulated by a sinusoidal waveform, $V_m \sin 2\pi f_m t$, then the output of the transmitter, v_t, and the received signal, v_r, are given by:

$$v_t = V_t \sin (2\pi f_c t + m \sin 2\pi f_m t) \qquad \text{(A11.1)}$$

$$v_r = V_r \sin (2\pi f_c (t - T) + m \sin 2\pi f_m (t - T))$$
$$\text{(A11.2)}$$

where T is the two-way travel time and m is the modulation index (constant in this application).

If received and transmitted signals are fed to a multiplicative mixer we have, after some manipulation, a difference frequency signal of:

$$v_h = k V_t V_r \sin (2m \sin(\pi f_m T) \times \\ \cos (2\pi f_m (t - T/2)) + 2\pi f_c T) \qquad \text{(A11.3)}$$

where k is a constant of proportionality. Since T is much smaller than $1/f_m$ we may write:

$$\sin \pi f_m T \approx f_m T$$

Also $m = \Delta f / 2 f_m$, where Δf is total range of frequency variation so:

$$v_h = k V_t V_r \sin (\pi \Delta f T \cos (2\pi f_m t - \pi f_m T) \\ + 2\pi f_c T) \qquad \text{(A11.4)}$$

The beat frequency may be found by differentiating the argument (angle) in (A11.4) with respect to time and dividing by 2π to give

$$\overline{f_h} = -((\pi \Delta f T)(2\pi f_m) \sin (2\pi f_m t - \pi f_m T))/2\pi \\ = \pi \Delta f T f_m \sin (2\pi f_m t - \pi f_m T + \pi) \quad \text{(A11.5)}$$

Note the minus sign resulting from the differentiation of the cosine term has been replaced by a phase shift of π radians. The average beat frequency over half a modulating cycle, $1/2 f_m$, is:

$$\overline{f_h} = 2 f_m \left(\int_0^{1/2 \text{fm}} f_h d_t \right) \\ = \pi \Delta f f_m T \cos \pi f_m T \qquad \text{(A11.6)}$$

Again since $T \ll 1/f_m$, $\cos \pi f_m T \approx 1$, so:

$$\overline{f_h} \approx 2 \Delta f f_m T \\ = 4 \Delta f f_m H / c \qquad \text{(A11.7)}$$

This is the same as equation (11.1) derived assuming a linear modulating waveform.

12 Area navigation

Development of Airspace Organization

Before radio aids were available, pilots navigated by visual contact with the ground and were responsible for their separation from other aircraft. With the advent of radio and improved instrumentation it became possible to fly in situations where the ground could no longer be seen and separation could not be guaranteed. From such beginnings the need for air- and ground-based navigation aids and controlled regions became apparent.

In the 1930s the airspace surrounding certain busy airports began to be designated controlled zones with restrictions, relating to weather and to qualifications, placed on those who wanted to enter the zone. With the growth of air traffic has come the growth of a worldwide controlled airspace system.

The 'shape' of this controlled airspace was influenced by the introduction of one of the earliest ground-based navigation aids, radio range. This equipment, introduced in the 1930s, gave four beams which suitably equipped aircraft could follow. Beam flying was continued and intensified with the adoption of VOR and so confirmed a system of controlled airways which radiate from ground stations. The airways link control areas where a number of airways converge over centres of high-density traffic. Neither the airways nor the control areas start at ground level, as do control zones which are centred on one or a group of airports.

The airways, control zones and control areas constitute controlled airspace within which instrument flight rules (IFR) are in force. Only instrument-rated pilots flying aircraft fitted with a minimum equipment complement can use controlled airspace for navigational purposes although, for non-conforming flights, a special visual flight rules (VFR) clearance can be obtained from air traffic control (ATC) to enter or cross. Within controlled airspace separation is the responsibility of ATC, whereas in uncontrolled airspace it is the responsibility of the pilot who, however, can be given a separation service if in an advisory service area or on an advisory route.

The above description of the structure of controlled airspace is lacking in detail but is sufficient to make clear the disadvantages. With heavy traffic we have many aircraft occupying a relatively small proportion of the airspace, in particular the scheduled air transport aircraft in the airways. To free aircraft from the airways one needs a navigation system which can be safely used over a large area, hence area navigation, and not irrevocably tied to fixed points, such as VORTAC beacons, on the ground. But one can go too far; the thought of aircraft converging on an airport from all directions is frightening. What is needed is new airways which can remove 'dog legs' and parallel existing ones, thus shortening routes and flight times.

The benefits of area navigation are not always easy or even possible to realize. For example in the United Kingdom the areas most used by air traffic of the scheduled transport type is largely covered with airways, control areas and zones already and an extension to area navigation which will benefit economically is difficult to achieve. However, in geographically small but busy regions such as Britain, area navigation equipment is an extremely useful boon to the large number of general aviation aircraft which potter around beneath the airways and in uncontrolled airspace generally. It was possible before, but with the correct equipment it is now much easier.

Generalized Area Navigation System

Area navigation equipment is not new although the acronym RNAV is fairly recent. In fact RNAV could have been implemented in the 1950s had the choice for an international standard been the Decca Navigator. Other equipments providing navigation facilities over a wide area and not tied to fixed points are Loran and Omega of the ground-based systems and Doppler and Inertial Navigation Systems of the self-contained variety. Unfortunately all of these systems are more expensive than VOR/DME which is in widespread use. The advent of airborne computers has now made possible sophisticated navigation systems including an RNAV system based on

VOR/DME. The trick is to 'shift' the position of the co-located beacons to a phantom beacon or waypoint location chosen by the pilot. The pilot uses his VOR/DME instrumentation in the same way as before, except that steering commands are related to a waypoint remote from the beacon.

The computer power, of course, allows much more than the generation of steering commands to phantom beacons, several navigation sensor and air data outputs may be mixed to provide a means of lateral and vertical navigation and a display of data which can take many forms. The all-purpose system is illustrated in Fig. 12.1.

heading and drift angle or
track angle and ground speed or
wind direction and speed or
cross-track distance and track error, etc.
Analogue presentation on HSI:
   heading and track
   course display and setting
   desired track
   lateral steering command.
Analogue presentation on attitude director:
   pitch and roll steering commands.
Analogue map presentation:
   route, beacon and waypoint data.

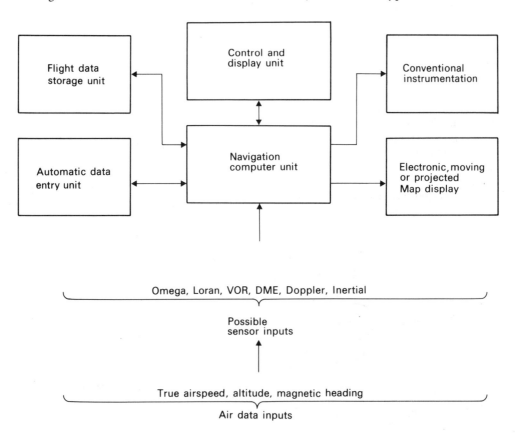

Fig. 12.1 General area navigation system

The computer, using stored data and inputs from a variety of sensors, calculates the aircraft position absolutely in terms of latitude and longitude and also relatively in terms of deviation from the desired flight path. A variety of display formats may be used as follows.

Digital readout on display and control unit:
   present position, latitude/longitude or

No attempt has been made here to give a definitive list of displayed data since there is considerable variation.

The data required for the computer to perform its function are of three types and can be input to the system in three different ways. For regularly flown routes 'hard' data such as location, elevation and frequency of VORTAC beacons and airports, standard departure and arrival routes (SIDS and STARS) etc. will be stored in a flight data storage unit (FDSU), typically on magnetic tape. Waypoint position, 'soft' data, may be entered or amended in flight by means of a keyboard and 'scratchpad' display on the control and display unit (CDU). Real-time data from navigation and air data sensors are continuously available for input from a variety of sources.

The data relating to waypoints are 'soft' in the sense that they can be amended but they may be stored as 'hard' data on a magnetic or punched card and input via an automatic data entry unit (ADEU). This facility is useful since an operator could have the waypoint data for all regularly flown routes recorded on cards, the correct one being chosen for a particular flight.

Since the information from the sensors is in analogue form analogue to digital conversation (A/D) is necessary before the computer can handle it; A/D circuits may be in the area navigation system itself or in the systems which feed it.

The form of area navigation systems is by no means finalized, and with the variety of inputs and outputs possible it seems unlikely that functional standardization will be achieved to the same extent as it has with other systems such as ILS, VOR, ADF, etc. One could write a book on those RNAV and VNAV (vertical navigation) equipments available now

(1979) but here space will only allow a brief discussion of VOR/DME-based RNAV, with examples, and ARINC Characteristic 583-1. Future developments depend on use of microcomputers and utilization of flexible c.r.t.-based display systems (*see* Chapter 13).

VOR/DME-Based RNAV Principle

The basic idea is simple; signals from existing VOR and DME co-located beacons are used to give range and bearing, not to the station but to a waypoint specified by its range and bearing from the station. To achieve this the RNAV triangle (Fig. 12.2) has to be continuously solved.

We have:

ρ_1: distance between beacon and aircraft;
θ_1: magnetic bearing from beacon to aircraft;
ρ_2: distance between beacon and waypoint;
θ_2: magnetic bearing from beacon to waypoint;
ρ_3: distance between aircraft and waypoint;
θ_3: magnetic bearing from aircraft to waypoint.

The quantities ρ_1 and θ_1 are known from normal VOR/DME operation, the quantities ρ_2 and θ_2 are entered by the pilot, hence two sides and an included

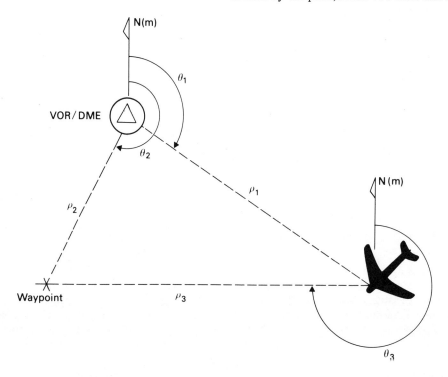

Fig. 12.2 RNAV. triangle

angle of the RNAV triangle are known, so ρ_3 and θ_3 can be found.

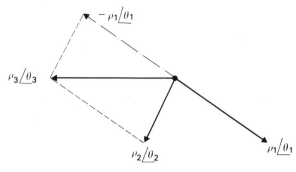

Fig. 12.3 Vector solution of RNAV. triangle

The solution of the triangle can be found by analogue methods as in one of the earliest RNAV computers for the general aviation market, the King KN74. The vectors $\rho_1\underline{/\theta_1}$ and $\rho_2\underline{/\theta_2}$ are represented by square waves whose amplitudes are proportional to ρ_1 and ρ_2 and whose phases represent to θ_1 and θ_2 respectively. From Fig. 12.3 we see that:

$$\rho_3\underline{/\theta_3} = \rho_2\underline{/\theta_2} - \rho_1\underline{/\theta_1} \tag{12.1}$$

where the minus sign indicates vector subtraction. Thus if we reverse the phase of the square wave representing $\rho_1\underline{/\theta_1}$ and add this to the square wave representing $\rho_2\underline{/\theta_2}$ we will have a waveform the fundamental of which represents ρ_3 and θ_3 in amplitude and phase respectively.

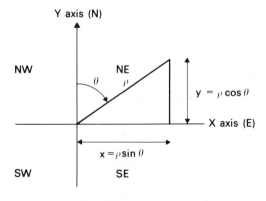

Fig. 12.4 Cartesian (X, Y) and polar (ρ, θ) co-ordinates

The solution may also be found by a digital computer. Expressions for ρ_3 and θ_3 can be found by converting to cartesian co-ordinates (*see* Fig. 12.4) then reverting to polar co-ordinates. Thus:

$$\rho_3 = ((x_2 - x_1)^2 + (y_2 - y_1)^2)^{0.5}$$
$$\theta_3 = \tan^{-1}((y_2 - y_1)/(x_2 - x_1)) \tag{12.2}$$

where $x_k = \rho_k \sin \theta_k$
$y_k = \rho_k \cos \theta_k$ $\quad k = 1, 2$

If $(y_2 - y_1)/(x_2 - x_1) > 0$, θ_3 is in either the north-east or south-west quadrant; if $(y_2 - y_1)/(x_2 - x_1) < 0$, θ_3 is in either the north-west or south-east quadrant, if $y_2 - y_1 = 0$, θ_3 is either 0 or 180°, while if $x_2 - x_1 = 0$, θ_3 is either 90 or 270°. The ambiguity can be resolved by observing that θ_3 will only change by a small amount for successive calculations. An example is given by Figure 12.5 where we have:

$\theta_1 = 90, \theta_2 = 180, \rho_1 = 40, \rho_2 = 30$; so:
$x_1 = 40 \sin 90 = 40, y_1 = 40 \cos 90 = 0$
$x_2 = 30 \sin 180 = 0, y_2 = 30 \cos 180 = -30$
$\rho_3 = ((-40)^2 + (-30)^2)^{0.5} = 50$
$\theta_3 = \tan^{-1}(-30/-40) = 36\cdot87$ or
$\quad\quad 180 + 36\cdot87 = 216\cdot87$.

If the previously calculated θ_3 was 216 then the new θ_3 is $216\cdot87$.

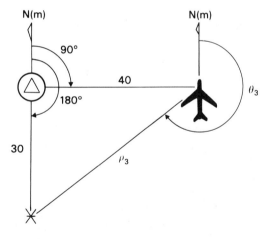

Fig. 12.5 RNAV. triangle example

The program for the solution of the RNAV triangle could be based on the above or some other formulation of the problem. Since the program is fixed it will be stored in read-only memory (ROM). The trigonometric function values may also be stored in ROM to speed up calculations. Note that complete sine and cosine tables need not be stored since $\sin \theta = \cos(\theta - 90)$, also

$\cos \theta = -\cos |180 - \theta|$ if $90 < \theta < 270$ and
$\cos \theta = \cos(360 - \theta)$ if $270 \leqslant \theta < 360$.

Thus, for example, a cosine table for angles 0 to 90 only is sufficient. A look-up table for the inverse tangent function is more problematical and can be avoided by a reformulation of the equations (12.2) to be solved, for example by using the cosine rule although here ambiguity is introduced in the solution for θ_3 which is slightly more complicated than that arising from (12.2).

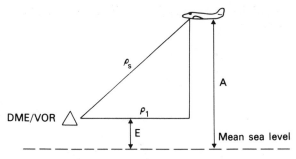

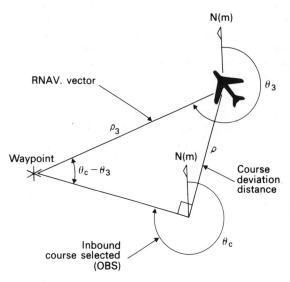

Fig. 12.6 Deviation triangle

Course deviation calculation involves the solution of another triangle shown in Fig. 12.6. It is normal with RNAV to give the deviation in terms of distance rather than angle, at least out as far as a specified range. Solution of the deviation triangle is possible since one side, ρ_3, and all angles are known. So using the sine rule:

$$\frac{\rho_3}{\sin 90} = \frac{\rho}{\sin (\theta_c - \theta_3)} \qquad (12.3)$$

$$\therefore \quad \rho = \rho_3 \sin (\theta_c - \theta_3)$$

If ρ is negative from (12.3) then the aircraft is to the left of the desired inbound course. For example in Fig. 12.6 if $\theta_3 = 270°$, $\theta_c = 306\cdot87°$ (to) and $\rho_3 = 50$ then $\rho = 50 \sin 36\cdot87 = 30$ nautical miles (a 3,4,5 triangle) with aircraft to right of course by 30 nautical miles, whereas if $\theta_3 = 306\cdot87°$ and $\theta_c = 270°$ then $\rho = 50 \sin (-36\cdot87) = -30$ nautical miles, i.e. aircraft to the left of course by 30 nautical miles.

In the above for accurate navigation the RNAV triangle should be in the horizontal plane, unfortunately distance to the DME beacon from the aircraft is given as slant range. To obtain ground

Fig. 12.7 Slant range triangle

distance (ρ_1) we need to solve the slant range triangle shown in Fig. 12.7. The beacon elevation must be fed into the equipment from a FDSU, ADEU or by means of a keyboard. Aircraft altitude is obtained from an encoding altimeter. Using the notation of Fig. 12.6 we have:

$$\rho_1 = ((\rho_s)^2 - (A - E)^2)^{0\cdot5}$$

Similar calculations are necessary if the system has VNAV capability, i.e. if steering commands in both pitch and roll are obeyed the aircraft will achieve a specified altitude at the active waypoint or at a specified distance from the current waypoint.

Bendix Nav. Computer Programmer NP-2041A

Introduction
The NP-2041A is a ten waypoint RNAV computer. The waypoint parameters may be entered from a keyboard on the front panel or from a portable magnetic-card reader. Bearing and distance to the active waypoint are found by solving first the slant range triangle then the RNAV triangle. In addition the unit can be used for frequency management for both v.h.f. communication and navigation.

The complete RNAV system comprises an NP-2041A, a CN-2011A comm./nav. unit, a DM-2030 DME, an IN-2014A electronic course deviation indicator and an encoding altimeter. Presentation of HSI and RMI is achieved through an IU-2016A interface unit. The above package can be complemented with an ADF and a transponder to make up a BX 2000 system. Other options are a weather radar interface and a magnetic-card reader (modified Texas SR52 or Hewlett-Packard HP-67 scientific calculator). Large business aircraft owners would be possible customers for a full or nearly full package, while small single-engined aircraft may be fitted with the basic VFR system; i.e. comm./nav. and an indicator.

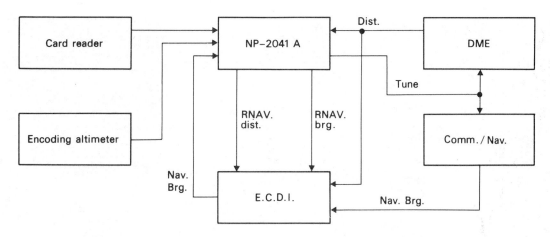

Fig. 12.8 Bendix NP-2041A-based RNAV. system

Although here we are concerned mainly with the RNAV computer, a brief description of the other units will be given. The CN-2011A (Fig. 2.2) is a panel-mounted unit containing two v.h.f. communications transmitter-receivers, two VOR/LOC receivers, an audio selection panel, glideslope receiver (optional), marker receiver (optional) and various system controls (a less comprehensive CN-2012A may be used with the NP-2041A). The IN-2014A indicator is discussed and illustrated in Chapters 4 and 5 (Figs 4.7 and 5.3). The IU-2016A remote-mounted interface unit converts VOR/LOC and glideslope outputs to levels that satisfy HSI and/or RMI requirements and performs other functions not of interest in this context. The DME, encoding altimeter, HSI and RMI require no comment here, having been dealt with elsewhere. The calculators are simply modified to attach a plug-in connector.

Display and Control
Figure 12.9 illustrates the front panel of the NP-2041A. There are seven separate digital displays each employing gas-discharge seven-segment indicators. The quantity displayed in each of the windows depends on the position of the Display Selector switch and, for some of the displays, the Mode Selector switch. With the Display Selector set to:

SBY: standby waypoint parameters shown in FREQ., BRG/KTS., DST/TTS, EL X100 and CRS windows.
ACT: active waypoint parameters shown as for SBY.
BRG/DST: displays bearing (BRG/KTS window) and distance (DST/TTS window) to active waypoint in RNAV or APR mode or to VOR/DME station in VOR/LOC mode.

KTS/TTS: displays ground speed (BRG/KTS window) and time to station in minutes (DST/TTS window) to waypoint in RNAV or APR mode or to VOR/DME station in VOR/LOC mode.
The SBY and ACT windows display the number (0-9) of the standby and active waypoint. The 'IN' legend is illuminated if course shown (CRS window) is inbound while 'OUT' legend (below 'IN' legend) is illuminated if course shown is outbound.

The Mode selector controls the mode of operation as follows:

OFF: self-explanatory.
VOR/LOC: conventional navigation, the waypoints are the stations.
RNAV: waypoints are remote from the associated stations. Left/Right course deviation is linear within 100 nautical miles, full-scale deflection (f.s.d.) being 5 nautical miles, from 100 nautical miles out deviation is angular.
APR: as RNAV but linear deviation up to 25 nautical miles, f.s.d. being 1·25 nautical miles.
'TEST': specified display for satisfactory operation.

Data is entered by means of the keyboard or by magnetic card reader. Of the 16 keys 11 are dual function e.g. FREQ./1, NAV.2/. (decimal point), etc. Data entry must always be in the correct sequence as follows:

1. press SBY WPT, FREQ., COM.1, COM.2, BRG, DST, EL, CRS, NAV.1, NAV.2, ADF or XPR (transponder) key as required to select appropriate address for data;
2. press number keys to enter data;
3. check data in appropriate window and if correct

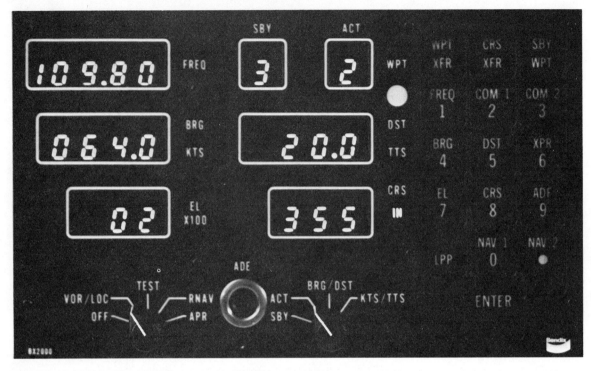

Fig. 12.9 NP-2041A (courtesy Bendix Avionics Division)

press 'ENTER' key.

An annunciator light indicates when a key is being pressed.

As an example the sequence for the entry of NAV.1 frequency is:

1. select KBD on COM./NAV. unit;
2. set mode selector to VOR/LOC;
3. press NAV.1 key, ensure dot in FREQ. window flashes;
4. press appropriate number keys, e.g. 109·80, ensure readout in FREQ. window (scratchpad) is correct;
5. press 'ENTER' key. Frequency will be transferred from FREQ. window to NAV.1 window in COM./NAV. unit within which the NAV.1 receiver will be tuned to that frequency.

A further example is given by the insertion of a waypoint parameter, say station elevation 200 ft for beacon associated with waypoint 3:

1. mode selector to any position other than 'OFF' or 'TEST';
2. display selector to SBY;
3. press SBY WPT key;
4. press number key 3, ensure 3 appears in SBY window;

5. press EL key, ensure dot in EL X100 window flashes;
6. press number keys 0 and 2 in that order, ensure 02 appears in EL X100 window (scratchpad);
7. press 'ENTER' key.

The other waypoint parameters i.e. FREQ., BRG, DST, CRS may be entered in a similar way. To enter outbound course we press the CRS XFR key having previously pressed CRS key and entered inbound course.

Two keys not previously mentioned are WPT XFR, which transfers SBY waypoint number to ACT, and LPP, which loads the present position of the aircraft into waypoint zero.

Block Diagram Operation

Microcomputer The heart of the NP-2041A is a microcomputer which comprises a central processor unit (CPU), system controller, ROM, RAM, system clock and input/output (I/O) ports. The CPU is an 8080A 8-bit microprocessor, the associated chips being drawn from the same 8000 series family e.g. 8224 clock generator 8228 system control and bus driver, 8255 programmable peripheral interface etc.

The microcomputer accepts data in a suitable form

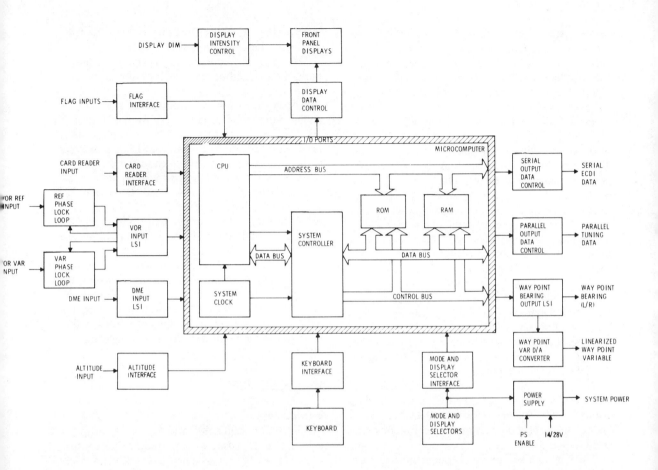

Fig. 12.10 NP-2041A block diagram (courtesy Bendix Avionics Division)

from the keyboard, selection switch, card reader, nav. receiver, DME receiver and altimeter. The input data is subjected to arithmetic and logical operations and then output in a suitable form to the ECDI, DME, comm./nav. and Interface units. The operations on data are performed by the CPU which obtains instructions and/or data from ROM, RAM or I/O ports. The list of instructions (program) is in ROM, the CPU storing the address of the current and next instruction in internal registers. An instruction may be to carry out an arithmetic operation as part of the solution of one of the triangles or to read data out of, or write data into, an I/O port.

The ROM provides a total non-volatile (permanent) memory of 96K bits (96 × 1024 = 98 304 bits). This storage space is used for the programs for the four basic service loops VOR/LOC, 'TEST', RNAV. and APR. The total non-volatile RAM is 2K bits providing storage for the parameters for 10 waypoints. The data in the non-volatile RAM in only retained as

long as a memory hold voltage (external) is maintained. In addition there is 2K bits of store in volatile RAM which provides a temporary storage for data from the CPU, distance to waypoint, bearing to waypoint, etc. Volatile memory is lost (dumped) when the equipment is switched off.

Inputs Waypoint parameters enter the microcomputer via the keyboard or card-reader interface. When a key is pressed the keyboard interface sets latches in an I/O port which remain set until serviced by the microprocessor during an appropriate service loop. A key can be pressed 60 ms after the previous one. The card-reader interface raises the signal level to that suitable for TTL operation and generates an Interrupt signal which causes the microprocessor to break the service loop in progress while it reads data into RAM.

Data from the VOR receiver is in the form of two constant amplitude square waves, reference (ref.) phase and variable (var.) phase. The phase difference between the ref. phase and var. phase signals representing the bearing to the VOR station. A voltage controlled oscillator (v.c.o.) is phase-locked to the ref. phase using an exclusive −OR type phase comparator. (If two square waves, of equal frequency and phase, switching between '0' and '1' are applied to an exclusive −OR gate the output will be zero since $0 \oplus 0 = 0$ and $1 \oplus 1 = 0$; if not in phase the mean level of the output will be non-zero). The ref. phase-locked signal is fed to the var. phase-lock loop where it is phase-compared with the var. phase, the difference controlling the repetition rate of pulses from a second v.c.o. The VOR LSI (large-scale integrated circuit) counts the pulses from the variable rate v.c.o. to obtain the bearing which is fed to the I/O ports as a four-digit b.c.d. number two digits at a time (since data bus is only 8 bits wide).

The DME distance data input is in the form of a pulse pair where the time interval between pulses represents the distance (12·36 μs per nautical mile). The DME LSI converts this time-interval into a four-digit b.c.d. number which, as in the case of the VOR LSI output, requires two readings to transfer the data through I/O ports.

An encoding altimeter feeds data via buffers (interface) to set latches in the I/O ports. The data changes in 500 ft increments since the C1, C2 and C4 lines from the encoding altimeter are not connected (*see* Chapter 8).

The flag signals of external equipment (e.g. nav. and DME) are monitored by the flag interface. If an invalid signal is detected the flag interface output is transferred through I/O ports to the computer.

Finally, the mode and display selector interface translate the information relating to the position of the appropriate switches into logic levels that are applied to the I/O ports.

Outputs Data to be displayed on the front panel is transferred through the I/O ports to the display data control. The data consists of b.c.d. address, b.c.d. data and decimal point. The display data control decodes the data and provides the necessary cathode and anode drives for the gas discharge displays.

The appropriate data will not be displayed but will be replaced by dashes if a flag signal is detected. For example the BRG/DST flag in RNAV mode will show for any of the following: nav. flag, DME search, DME test, DME not frequency paired with nav. 1, loss of nav. or DME input signals or ILS frequency selected. The RNAV flag signal generated by the computer must also be fed to appropriate external equipment.

The selected inbound or outbound course of the active waypoint and the computer distance to the waypoint are serially shifted out to the ECDI for display in the course and distance window.

Comm./nav. frequency management is achieved by parallel b.c.d. address and data outputs for tuning purposes.

The bearing to the waypoint is fed to the ECDI and also the interface unit in the form of the RNAV 30 Hz ref. phase and RNAV 30 Hz var. phase derived from the waypoint bearing output LSI and waypoint variable d/a converter. The feed to the waypoint bearing LSI from the I/O ports is in digital format. The ECDI processes the RNAV 30 Hz ref. and 30 Hz var. phases to produce left/right deviation signals to drive the 'bar'. The interface unit similarly provides left/right deviation signals for the HSI (and possibly autopilot).

The display intensity control sets the intensity level of the seven segment indicators and front panel annunciators in accordance with the setting of the 'DIM' control on the comm./nav. unit. A common 'DIM' control is used for all units of the BX 2000 system to ensure uniform intensity of lighting.

King KDE 566

Introduction
The KDE 566 is an automatic data input/output system (ADIOS) used with the KCU 565A control unit (Fig. 12.12) forming part of the KNR 665 digital RNAV system illustrated in Fig. 12.11. The complete system, which may have more units than those shown, will not be described since a system with similar capabilities has already been discussed.

We have not considered an ADEU in any detail so a brief description of the KDE 566 follows. In fact the unit is called an ADIOS rather than an ADEU since the magnetic cards may be recorded by the unit using data from the KCU 565A memory as well as providing the data entry or input function from pre-recorded cards.

The magnetic cards are about the size of a business card and can store the waypoint parameters (frequency, course inbound, course outbound, and waypoint distance and bearing from the beacon) for up to ten waypoints. A number of cards can be prepared for frequently travelled routes. The route (from-to) can be noted on each card and the top right corner clipped off to fix the data so that they cannot be changed.

Block Diagram Operation
The KDE 566 operation is best explained in terms of its modes of operation which are monitor, record,

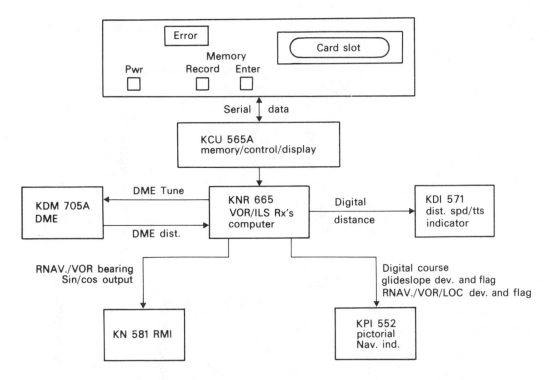

Fig. 12.11 King KNR 665 RNAV. system

Fig. 12.12 KCU 565A (courtesy King Radio Corp.)

enter and error. The mode control circuit monitors the record and enter buttons and the belt position detector to determine which mode should be active and so instruct the rest of the system.

MONITOR

Serial data is clocked in from the KCU 565A through the memory data gating and voltage translation circuit, the clock pulses coming from the master clock in the KCU 565A. Immediately prior to a data cycle

there is a synchronizing sequence of 6 bits set to 1 followed by 2 bits at 0. The data cycle consists of $10 \times 5 \times 16 = 800$ bits since there are 10 waypoints, 5 waypoint parameters and 16 bits for each parameter. A further 96 bits following waypoint 9 are designated 'test waypoint'. Thus we have a total of 904 bits from the KCU 565A which are stored in four shift register memories providing a more than adequate storage space of 1024 bits. In this mode the KDE 566 memory is a mirror image of the KCU 565A memory. Updating occurs every 11·3 ms.

RECORD

The record mode is activated whenever the record button is pushed. The mode will not be entered until the end of a memory-refreshing cycle as signified by the output of the memory synchronizer to the mode control circuit.

On inserting a card in the slot a microswitch is closed by the corner of the card unless previously clipped off. The record button switch is in series with the microswitch, thus when the button is pressed the memory is temporarily frozen, the motor drive system is activated and the card begins to travel out of the slot provided the card is whole and fully inserted. The motor drives a belt which has small holes in it at appropriate points allowing light from a

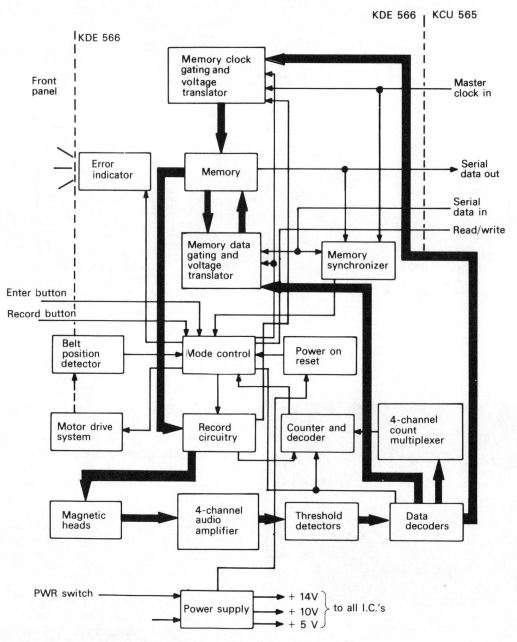

KDE 566 | KCU 565

KDE 566

Front panel

Memory clock gating and voltage translator

Master clock in

Error indicator

Memory

Serial data out

Serial data in

Read/write

Memory data gating and voltage translator

Memory synchronizer

Enter button

Record button

Belt position detector

Mode control

Power on reset

Motor drive system

Record circuitry

Counter and decoder

4-channel count multiplexer

Magnetic heads

4-channel audio amplifier

Threshold detectors

Data decoders

PWR switch

Power supply

+ 14V
+ 10V } to all I.C.'s
+ 5 V

Fig. 12.13 KDE 566 block diagram (courtesy King Radio Corp.)

lamp to shine through onto a photoresistor in the belt position detector input.

When the card has built up speed the mode control is notified by the position detector that all is ready for recording. The data is clocked out of the four shift registers to four magnetic heads which record the digital data at the appropriate points on the card by magnetizing the ferromagnetic oxide in one of two directions, depending on whether 0 or a 1 is to be recorded. A system counter is advanced one count each time the memory is clocked. Between writing 4 bits (at a time) the card advances and previously recorded data is erased. After 256 counts the data has all been recorded and the system returns to the monitor mode.

ENTER

A card, on which a set of data are recorded, is pushed fully home in the slot closing a microswitch so positioned that it will close even though the corner of the card is clipped. When the enter button switch, in series with the microswitch, is pressed, the motor drive system is started and the card travels outward. When the card reaches a position slightly before where data recording began the belt position detector notifies the mode control when then enables all enter circuitry.

The magnetic heads read data from the cards since the changing magnetic field, as the card passes over a magnetized part, will cause a current to flow in the coil wrapped around the head core. Because of the way in which the data were recorded this current occurs in pulses, positive or negative depending on whether 1 or 0 was recorded. Each of the four heads feeds an amplifier and thence the threshold detectors which provide digital data outputs. The digital data are fed to the data decoders which enter the data into the correct memory channel sequentially. The four-channel count multiplexer gathers the counts from all four channels producing one count output for the counter and decoder.

When the card has travelled past the end of the data tracks the belt position detector initiates the error check phase via the mode control. The counter and decoder output is examined to determine if $4 \times 256 = 1024$ bits have been counted. If the count is correct the mode control gates the master clock to memory, actuates the read/write line to the KCU 565A and enters the contents of memory into the KCU 565A memory. After data transfer is complete the KDE 566 returns to the monitor mode.

ERROR

If the count from the counter and decoder is not 1024 the mode control initiates a flashing red error light and returns to the monitor mode. No attempt is made to enter data into the KCU 565A.

Standardization

The first meetings of the AEEC area navigation sub-committee were held in 1969 to discuss an ATA statement previously prepared. Three possible systems for airline use were proposed: a simple Mark 1, a sophisticated Mark 2 and a Mark 3 which involved an expansion of INS. The ARINC characteristics for the Mark 1 and 2 systems were published in 1970; however, before publication of the Mark 3 characteristic it was decided that the Mark 1 system,

which by this stage was no longer 'simple', and the Mark 3 system should be combined, hence the publication in 1974 of the ARINC Characteristic 583-1 Mark 13 area navigation system. The remainder of this section will be used to briefly describe the Mark 13 system.

The Mark 13 is a three-dimensional system designed for use in all types of commercial transport aircraft. The basic information required for lateral and vertical navigation is derived from a mix of VOR/DME and INS data plus altitude from an air data computer or similar source. If INS data are not available VOR/DME fixing with air data/magnetic heading smoothing is used in which case loss of VOR/DME data leads to an air data based dead reckoning mode.

The parameters of at least twenty waypoints are provided for using manual or automatic entry. Two successive waypoints define a great circle leg with respect to which navigation and steering command or deviation signals are fed to conventional indicators to give lateral and vertical commands and in addition are produced for use by the AFCS. Both parallel track and vertical positioning at any point on the track are capabilities provided by the system; in the latter case visual and aural altitude alert signals are generated.

The Mark 13 system comprises two units, a navigation computer and a control and display unit, with the possible addition of a flight data storage unit. Processing of the inputs and generating the outputs should be performed by the NCU while the CDU provides the pilot/system interface including control of the INS when used as an RNAV source.

The system inputs are as follows:

VOR omni-bearing: analogue or digital;
DME slant range: pulse pair, variable spacing;
INS: present position latitude and longitude;
INS: true heading and velocity (N/S and E/W);
altitude: analogue or digital;
barometric correction: only if analogue altitude uncorrected;
TAS: synchro, a.c. analogue or digital for data smoothing and d/r;
magnetic heading: synchro;
VOR warning: discrete high or low level;
DME warning: discrete;
altitude warning: discrete;
TAS warning: discrete;
magnetic heading warning: discrete;
program control: pins wired to choose input options;
a.c. reference phase: 26 V 400 Hz;
go-around: discrete from AFCS;

altitude alert cancel: discrete;
Mach number: synchro or digital;
IAS: synchro;
ILS localizer/glideslope deviation: d.c. analogue;
localizer failure: discrete;
glideslope failure: discrete;
AFCS engaged: discrete;
autothrottle engaged: discrete;
digital clock input: ARINC 585.

The system outputs are as follows:

omni-bearing to waypoint: sin/cos from four-wire resolver;
relative bearing to waypoint: synchro;
crosstrack deviation: high- or low-level d.c. analogue;
vertical track deviation: as crosstrack;
lateral track angle error: synchro or digital (b.c.d.);
drift angle: synchro or digital (b.c.d.);
lateral track change alert: 28 V d.c.;
vertical track change alert: 28 V d.c.;
lateral steering (roll command): a.c. or d.c. analogue;

Fig. 12.14 TIC T-34A RNAV. test set (courtesy
Tel-Instrument Electronics Corp.)

vertical steering (pitch command): as lateral;
to/from: high- or low-level d.c.;
desired lateral track: synchro or digital (b.c.d.);
track angle error plus drift angle: synchro;
distance to waypoint: digital (b.c.d.) 0-399·9
    nautical miles;
present position (lat./long.): digital (b.c.d.);
ground speed: digital (b.c.d.) 0-2000 knots;
time to go: digital (b.c.d.) 0-399·9 min;
crosstrack distance: digital (b.c.d.), 0-399·9
    nautical miles;
lateral track angle: digital (b.c.d.);
desired altitude: digital (b.c.d.) 0-50 000 ft;
second system data: two-wire data bus;
RNAV system failure: high- or low-level discrete;
altitude alert failure: discrete;
digital bus warning: discrete;
autotune valid: discrete;
altitude alert: discrete aural and visual;
VOR frequency: 2/5 selection;
system status annunciation: 28 V d.c. once per
    second;
high deviation sensitivity: 28 V d.c. when selected;
VOR frequency alert: 28 V d.c. when discrepancy;
parallel offset track alert: 28 V d.c. when selected;
speed error: d.c. analogue;
speed error warning: discrete.

The preceding list of input and output signals is
rather lengthy but illustrates the computing power
available in modern equipment. Details of the signal
characteristics can be found in ARINC 583. The last
eight of the inputs and the last two of the outputs are
designated as being growth inputs and outputs. The
method of achieving the necessary outputs, given the
inputs, is left to the designer and will vary in both
hardware and software.

Testing RNAV

An RNAV system is simply a computer which acts on
data from external sensors. In order to check for
standard operation these sensors must give known
inputs to the RNAV system. For example we could
use appropriate VOR and DME test sets to give a
bearing and distance from beacon of 180° and 30
nautical miles respectively, then with a waypoint
position of 090° and 40 nautical miles from the
beacon the RNAV bearing to the waypoint should be
53·13° and the RNAV distance 50 nautical miles
since we have set up a 3 : 4 : 5 triangle. This simple
example can be extended to incorporate the other
inputs demanded by more sophisticated systems.
Flag operation must be thoroughly tested. A self-test
which checks the display and display drive and
perhaps other circuits is usually provided.

Tel Instrument Electronics produce an RNAV test
set, the T-34A, which is in fact a combined DME/VOR
ramp tester. The convenience of such an
arrangement is obvious. The DME section is virtually
the same as the TIC T-24A (Chapter 7) the VOR
section is similar to the TIC T-27B (Chapter 4) but
with additional features, i.e. 108·05 MHz r.f. and
bearings of 45°, 135°, 225°, 315°.

It should be remembered when trouble-shooting
that, if the system includes an ADEU or FDSU,
mechanical problems may occur affecting input of
data. Poor contact between reading head and
magnetic card or tape can cause a loss of data. If the
card or tape drive slows down but the reading
frequency remains the same then the rate of magnetic
flux is slower and hence the head output is lowered.
When recording a slow drive causes bits to be written
on top of each other (pulse crowding losses) while if
the drive speeds up the bit is recorded over a longer
length of track leading to incorrect head output if
replayed at normal speed.

13 Current and future developments

Introduction

Changes in aircraft radio systems occur more and more frequently due to the improving state of the art. The first airborne radio equipments used thermionic devices, cat's whisker detectors and large parallel plate tuning capacitors; power, weight and size were restrictions on the development of such equipments. In the 1950s transistorized equipment began to appear although not completely transistorized, the r.f. stages being reluctant to succumb to solid state. Even now the thermionic device is still with us in the shape of the magnetron and the c.r.t. but not, I think, for very long. Claims concerning an all solid-state weather radar were made about mid-1979, a commercially viable equipment appeared in 1980 (e.g. Collins WXR700). The c.r.t. will remain with us for many years but will, I'm sure, eventually be replaced by a matrix of electroluminescent elements.

Transistorized equipment is of course still marketed, but many of the transistors, diodes and resistors now appear on integrated circuits. The emergence of first small scale integration (SSI) then medium scale (MSI) and now large scale integration (LSI) of ever more components on one chip has revolutionized the design of air radio systems. In particular using LSI techniques to produce microprocessors opens up a whole new world.

The rate of development in the last decade or so means that many aircraft fly with a range of technologies represented in their electronic systems. It is not inconceivable that an aircraft could be in service with a valve weather radar, a transistorized ADF and an RNAV system employing a microprocessor, or some other combination which would make it a flying electronics museum. That this happens and will continue to do so is the company accountant's choice not the engineer's or the pilot's. The replacement of one system by another performing essentially the same function must be justified in terms of increased safety, increased pay load, increased reliability or an improvement in performance which allows flights to be made in conditions where previously the aircraft would have to be grounded.

The reluctance to replace an equipment which is performing adequately reduces the size of the market for the radio system manufacturer. Of course there is no problem with new aircraft which will have the latest proven equipment fitted. Paradoxically, the situation we have is that the aircraft fitted with equipment employing the latest state of the art are more likely to be in the general aviation category, since that market is very much bigger than that for commercial airliners.

Completely new systems do not appear very frequently, although when they do it is often because the improvement in the state of the art has made the impossible possible. An airborne Omega receiver was not a viable proposition until the computer power and memory capacity necessary could be economically made available in a box of reasonable size.

Systems such as VOR, DME, ILS, etc. require enormous capital investment and so once adopted on a large scale tend to last an extremely long time. During and immediately after World War II many airborne radio systems were developed but only a few survived; new systems developed since the 1950s have not been internationally agreed replacements for existing systems but provided competition for them. The microwave landing system (MLS) which will succeed ILS will be the first replacement system, as opposed to competing system, for decades.

It must be mentioned in the introduction to a chapter such as this that the changes we are seeing, have seen and will be seeing, are to a large extent due to vast expenditure on defence and space research. Having stated the obvious, I will now briefly give my thoughts, occasionally supported by facts, on what is to come.

The State of the Art

The microprocessor and other LSI circuits are used in the current generation of radio systems (1979). It seems clear that such circuits will be used more and more for succeeding generations not only for computing purposes, in the conventional sense, but also for control of virtually everything. Often, in equipments, a microprocessor will be under-utilized but nevertheless it will still be a cheaper approach than using the minimal amount of hard-wired logic and furthermore spare processing power is available for expansion. All one needs to do is add the necessary software. I doubt if special-purpose LSI circuits will appear in great variety since the volume of production required for a reasonable unit cost is very large. Having said that, we already see special LSI chips for VOR and DME signal processing.

The complete all-purpose airborne computer is not with us yet and may never be. By 'completely all-purpose', I mean a computer system which monitors all sensors, drives all displays, performs all control functions and is the only equipment with which the pilot can communicate directly. Such a computer could be built today but there are problems such as reliability, duplication or triplication being necessary, the need for performing several tasks at the same time and the huge I/O interface. Certainly in the near future, and indeed now, airborne computers will work in specific function areas such as navigation, flight control, flight management, etc. although some of these functions may be combined and performed by one computer.

Interwiring is beginning to change radically in aircraft installations due to our ability to handle large quantities of fast time multiplexed digital data. The prospect of a main serial digital data highway with spurs out to sensors, for incoming data, and control and/or display units, for both incoming and outgoing data, is a very real one. Again we have the problem of reliability but the saving in interwiring will be significant. This is happening now in certain functional areas such as frequency control and passenger entertainment systems, and will be extended. In this context mention should be made of the use of optical fibres which can handle data at a very much faster rate than conventional cables (15×10^6 bits per second; cf. 2400 bits per second, say). In addition to the increased capability the cheapness of the raw materials and the immunity to interference are advantages which make it virtually certain that we shall see fibre optics used in the future and would see them now were it not for the difficulties encountered in connecting them together.

The increase in the use of digital signals and the ability to process them has a most noticeable impact in the aircraft in that controllers, displays and facilities are all changed, meanwhile progress in the

r.f. field continues with perhaps less obvious results. A logical outcome of the development of low-noise, reliable, small, solid-state r.f. amplifiers and sources must be to mount t.r.s adjacent to antenna downleads so that r.f. cables and waveguides longer than a couple of inches are a thing of the past. Reliability is the key in this latter development since such t.r.s would be relatively inaccessible.

The Flight Deck

The flight deck will be radically different in future with flexible electronic displays replacing conventional instrumentation and a keyboard with alphanumeric and dedicated keys replacing a mass of rotary and toggle switches. The trend has already started, examples being discussed in Chapters 9 and 12. This is not to suggest that conventional display/control will disappear completely; electromechanical instrumentation will be needed as back-up for the electronic displays and toggle switches will always be used for certain functions. As examples of the way things are going, work by Boeing and British Aerospace will be discussed.

Boeing 767

There are a number of features of the 767 flight deck worthy of mention, such as spaciousness, visibility and comfort; our main concern here, however, is the display and control of radio systems. Rockwell-Collins are to provide their multi-colour EFIS-700 electronic flight instrument system which includes two shadow mask c.r.t. indicators: an electronic attitude detector indicator (EADI) and an electronic horizontal situation indicator (EHSI). Computation and alphanumeric display will be provided by the Sperry flight management computer system (FMCS). There will be an EADI, EHSI and FMCS for each pilot, while an additional centrally placed electronic display will be used as part of the caution and warning system.

The EADI presentation is similar to a conventional attitude-director indicator, one of which is fitted as a back-up. Blue and black fields represent sky and earth respectively with a white line, separating the two fields, as the artificial horizon. There are scales for roll (upper), glideslope (left), speed deviation (right) and pitch (vertical centreline). In addition there is a rising runway symbol and a radio altitude digital readout. The information displayed from radio aids is glideslope deviation against a scale, localizer deviation by lateral movement of a symbolic runway and radio altitude by vertical movement of

Fig. 13.1 Boeing 767 flight deck mock-up (courtesy Boeing Commercial Aeroplane Co.)

the symbolic runway and by digital readout. Decision height selected and operating modes are also displayed. The facility exists, with an EADI, for blanking of scales not in use.

The flexibility of a computer-driven c.r.t. display is fully utilized in the EHSI by providing for operation in three modes: map display, full compass display or VOR/ILS mode with a full or partial compass rose. Weather radar data can also be displayed making a dedicated weather radar display an optional extra. When presenting data in map form the display is orientated track up; a vertical track line with range marks joins a symbolic aircraft at bottom centre to a boxed digital readout of the track at top centre. Heading and preset course are given by distinctive

pointers on a partial scale near the top of the display. Ground speed (from INS), a three-segment trend vector (projected path), wind direction and speed, planned flight between named waypoints, vertical deviation, range scale, operating mode and weather radar data are all shown. A variety of colours are used to avoid confusion in the interpretation of the large amount of data in a 4·7 × 5·7 in. display. A conventional RMI provides back-up.

The FMCS will mix stored data and data from several radio and non-radio sensors to provide position fixing, optimized flightpath and speed guidance, drive for the EADI and EHSI and also hardware and software monitoring to assist in trouble-shooting. A four-million-bit disk memory system will be employed to provide storage of data such as location of airports and VOR stations, selected company routes, standard departure and arrival routes (SIDS and STARS) and aircraft/engine parameters. Communication with the system is provided by a 14-line c.r.t. display with 24 characters per line, for display of navigation and performance data, and also a full alphanumeric keyboard plus dedicated keys.

British Aerospace Advanced Flight Deck

Work by the British Aircraft Corporation and Hawker Siddeley Aviation on the evolution of flight decks into a form which would include integrated electronic displays began back in the early 1970s. The results were sufficiently encouraging to commence, jointly, an advanced flight deck program in January 1975. Electronic displays and controls have been studied with regard to engineering feasibility and human factors.

The program has come up with an exciting view of the flight deck of the future. The main display consists of seven 9 in. c.r.t.s split into two discrete sub-systems. Three displays (S1, S2 and S3) centrally located on the instrument panel present aircraft systems and engine information while four displays (F1, F2, F3 and F4) split two each side of the panel, present flight information. In addition, two further c.r.t.s (D1 and D2) are provided, one each side of the main instrument panel, for documentation, e.g. checklist, performance data, etc.

The flight information displays are an EADI and an EHSI. Presentation of information is in a conventional format, the EADI being similar to an ADI but with information in both analogue and digital form surrounding the ADI earth/ground circle. The EHSI can present a conventional HSI type display with full compass rose and lateral deviation bar or a map-like display complete with route and weather radar data. Like the EADI the EHSI has flight information either side of the main display but in this case in digital form only. A facility to switch the display from one c.r.t. to the other will help should a malfunction occur. In addition there are conventional back-up instruments.

Alternative Instrumentation

The Boeing and British Aerospace developments discussed above do not depart from the conventional display format for the main part of the EADI and the EHSI display. Obviously in using electronic displays showing computer-generated symbols a wide range of possibilities for display formats exist; however, any departure from convention would require pilot retraining and would have to be justified in terms of easier and safer interpretation. Work has been done by NASA using a Boeing 737 in which the EADI display format is such as to give the pilot the next best thing to the VFR view when landing (*Flight*, 11 September 1976).

As conventional electromechanical instruments give way to c.r.t.s so c.r.t.s will one day give way to solid-state devices. Litton Systems of Toronto have recently announced (1979) a 3 X 4 in. display made up of nearly 50 000 LEDs. The matrix is computer-driven to provide the required display. The advantages over the c.r.t. are reduced size and longer life (m.t.b.f.).

A display technique particularly suitable for ILS approaches is that of a head-up display. Such displays are commonplace on modern military aircraft. When landing using panel-mounted instruments the pilot must look up to establish visual contact. If such contact is not possible looking down again to return to instruments could create problems of fast assimilation of the data on instruments. With a head-up display the approach guidance symbols are projected by some arrangement of optical devices so that they can be viewed through the windscreen. Civil airliners will be fitted with such displays (e.g. Airbus A300) although it should be noted that with two pilots one could be eyes-up and one eyes-down during approach to avoid an abortive attempt to acquire visual contact.

Multi-System Packages

With the advent of micro-electronics and the consequent small unit size, it is possible to bring various systems together in one package. In the days of valves we had one system — many boxes, whereas now it is possible to think in terms of one box — many systems. In fact we have already discussed examples of multi-system packages in Chapter 12. As a further, and yet-to-be-implemented, example, consider a Doppler radar antenna. There is no reason why the electronics for the Doppler radar, an inertial sensor, a radio-navigation sensor, such as Loran or Omega or VOR/DME, and a navigation computer should not all be mounted on top of the fixed Doppler antenna forming a single package. Control, display and radio sensor antennas would all need to be remote in such an installation.

Data Link

A two-way digitally encoded automatic information

Fig. 13.2 Experimental advanced flight deck (courtesy British Aerospace)

link has been the subject of periodic discussion by various working groups for over 30 years. If and when the system will be implemented and what r.f. channels will be used if any are still unknown. ARINC project paper 586 provides detailed information on a possible system with an entertaining appendix on the history of automatic communications for aircraft by the then Chairman of the AEEC, W.T. Carnes.

In fact an ATC automatic data link does exist in the form of the secondary radar surveillance radar system (Chapter 8) which will probably be extended some time in the future (*see* ADSEL/DABS below). Here we are only concerned with a two-way automatic data link utilizing v.h.f., h.f. or Satcom for universal use.

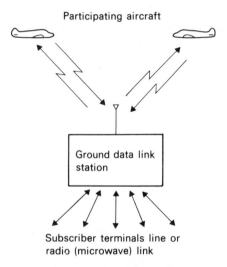

Participating aircraft

Ground data link station

Subscriber terminals line or radio (microwave) link

Fig. 13.3 Data link system

The data link is essentially ground-controlled. Aircraft participating in the system are 'polled' by the ground station which transmits a sequence of digital signals split into messages each of which contains a particular address (aircraft registration number) and suitable text. The airborne equipment responds if it recognizes its address in the polling sequence which is repeated at a rate determined by the ground station. Messages will be either to/from ATC or to/from the airline company and may relate to clearances, altitude changes, position reports, flight-plan change, weather data, etc. The text of the messages will be routed to/from terminals on the ground via a point-to-point communications network interconnecting the ground station and the terminals.

ADSEL/DABS

The problems of fruit and garbling were discussed in Chapter 8; such problems increase with traffic density. Address selective SSR (ADSEL) and discrete address beacon system (DABS) have been developed in the UK and USA respectively in an effort to postpone the date by which the ICAO SSR system would become saturated. In addition a new system will provide for a transfer of more information than is possible with current SSR, enable more accurate and reliable tracking by ATC and so help in the development of automated approach control systems (CAAS – computer assisted approach sequencing) and further, form an indispensable part of a proposed beacon-based collision avoidance system (BCAS).

A memorandum of understanding was signed by the FAA (for the USA) and the CAA (for the UK) early in 1975 to allow for future development of selectively addressed SSR systems on a co-operative basis. We are still some way off an ICAO standard system, but whenever it comes it will be compatible with SSR so that existing airborne equipment may continue to be used.

ARINC Characteristic 718 (November 1978 – draft) lays down a specification for a transponder which forms part of the standard SSR system (ATCRBS – ATC radar beacon system) and DABS. In that characteristic P1, P2 and P3 pulse parameters, frequencies and SLS provisions are as for standard SSR but the ability to respond to modes A and C interrogations only is required rather than A, B, C and D.

Two types of interrogation will be possible with the new system, an ATCRBS/DABS all-call or a DABS only. The all-call interrogation will consist of three pulses P1, P3 and P4 together with a SLS control pulse P2. The P1, P2 and P3 pulse parameters are as for the ICAO SSR while P4 is a $0.8\ \mu s$ pulse the leading edge of which is $1.5\ \mu s$ after the leading edge of P3. An ICAO transponder will ignore P4 while a DABS transponder will recognize the interrogation as all-call and respond with the all-call reply.

A DABS interrogation consists of P1 and P2 preamble pulses and a data block. The data block is a single r.f. pulse either 15·5 or 29·5 μs long employing differential phase shift keyed (d.p.s.k.) modulation. With this type of modulation a 180° phase change of the carrier at a data bit phase reversal position represents a '1' while no phase change represents a '0'. The first phase reversal occurs 0·5 μs after the leading edge of the data block, this is the sync. phase reversal. Subsequent phase reversal positions occur at time $0.25\ N\mu s\ (N \geqslant 2)$ after the sync. phase reversal. The maximum value of N is 57 or 113 giving 56 or 112 data bits transmitted at a $4\ M$ bit/s rate. The trailing edge of the data block has 0·5 μs of r.f. added to ensure the demodulation of the last bit in the data block is completed without interference.

An optional P5 may be radiated as an SLS control pulse in the same way that P2 is radiated from an ICAO interrogator. P5 will be transmitted 0·4 μs

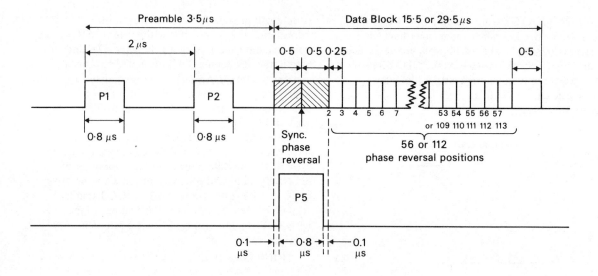

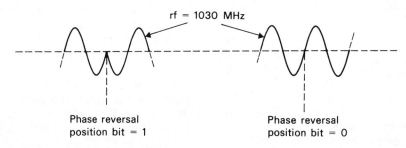

Fig. 13.4 ADSEL/DABS interrogation format

before the sync. phase reversal. For an aircraft fitted with a DABS transponder the received P5 amplitude will exceed the amplitude of the data block hence the transponder will not decode the d.p.s.k. modulated signal. An ICAO transponder equipped aircraft will not reply to a DABS interrogation since the P2 pulse will trigger the SLS suppression circuit.

A DABS transponder will generate ICAO replies (12 information pulses) in response to ICAO interrogations and DABS replies in response to all-call and DABS interrogations; DABS transponders also generate squitter at random intervals to allow acquisition without interrogation (similar to DME auto-standby, Chapter 7).

A DABS reply is only similar to an interrogation in so far as it contains a preamble followed by a data block of 56 or 112 bits. The preamble consists of four 0·5 μs pulses with the spacing between the first pulse and the second, third and fourth pulses being 1·0, 3·5 and 4·5 μs respectively, measured from leading edge to leading edge. The data block begins 8 μs after the leading edge of the first preamble pulse and uses pulse position modulation (p.p.m.) at a data rate of 1 M bit/s. In the 1 μs interval allotted to each data bit a 0·5 μs pulse is transmitted in the first half if the data bit is a '1' and in the second half if a '0'. The data block is thus 56 or 112 μs long. The r.f. is 1090 MHz as for the ICAO SSR.

There are four types of interrogation from an ADSEL/DABS interrogator all of which have the same preamble. The all-call data block contains a sequence of 28 ones in a 56-bit block, the all-call reply contains the aircraft address, details of data interchange equipment on board and parity bits for error-checking purposes. A surveillance interrogation of 56 bits contains address and parity bits and also a repeat of the height information received on the ground. An aircraft recognizing the address in a surveillance interrogation will reply with a 56-bit data block containing the altitude or identity. The remaining interchanges of data are in 112-bit blocks both ways, a comm.-A interrogation giving rise to a

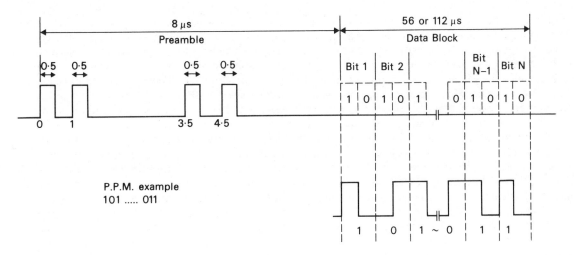

Fig. 13.5 ADSEL/DABS reply format

comm.-B reply and a comm.-C interrogation giving rise to a comm.-D reply. The A-B interchange involves altitude or identity as well as other data, and can be used for tracking purposes while the C-D interchange contains an extended-length message segment of 80 bits in both directions. One thing not yet decided is the method by which data will be transferred into and out of the transponder from various sensors and to various displays via a suitable processor. Two methods are proposed for the interface, firstly using ARINC 429 digital information transfer system (DITS) format, secondly a synchronous 1 M bit/sec interface which would allow data requested in an uplink to be contained in the next downlink.

The system has only been briefly described; the reader is referred to ARINC 718 for further details.

Satcom. and Satnav.

There are many satellites in orbit around the earth being used for relaying telephone and television signals, weather sensing, observation and military navigation and communication. (For a comprehensive review *see Flight*, 28 October 1978.) Unfortunately none so far are used by civil aircraft and it is not known (by the author) when such use will occur. However, brief comments can be made on the principles involved.

A possible v.h.f. Satcom. system is described in ARINC Characteristic 566. The satellite is simply a repeater for voice and data communications between air and ground. If the satellite is at synchronous altitude (22 000 nautical miles) the service area would be 41 per cent of the earth's surface. A double-channel simplex system employing frequency modulation would be used with uplink and downlink frequencies separated by between 4 and 10 MHz. Aircraft Satcom. antennas would be broadly directional, possibly with switchable lobes.

The accuracy of any Satnav. system will depend on the knowledge of satellite position and so a number of tracking stations are required on the ground. Since the airborne equipment must have the data relating to the satellite position a link must be established between the tracking station and the aircraft, most probably via the satellite. Knowing the position of the satellite the airborne equipment must establish the aircraft's position relative to the satellite in order to obtain a fix.

The various methods by which a fix can be obtained involve some combination of measurement of angular elevation of a satellite, range of a satellite and rate of change of range of a satellite (Doppler shift). Direction of arrival of a signal at the satellite may be found using interferometer methods whereby the satellite antennas are mounted on long booms (say 50 ft) and the phase difference in signals arriving at the antennas is measured. Range measurement may be obtained in a similar way to that employed in DME. In a range-rate system the Doppler shift of a signal from the satellite is recorded over a period of say 10 min, then the aircraft position can be computed from the time of zero Doppler shift and the slope of the frequency/time graph at zero shift.

The range-rate method can provide an accurate fix about once every $1\frac{1}{2}$ h, using a satellite in a 500-mile circular orbit, obviously for aircraft a large number of satellites must be used to reduce the time-interval between fixes. The aircraft velocity and altitude must be accurately known during the time taken to obtain a fix as the satellite makes a pass over the line of closest approach to the aircraft. The US Navy use such a system for surface ship navigation.

Angle-only, range-only or angle-range methods may be used. In these systems, by using a two-way link between the aircraft and a ground station via the satellite, the computation of aircraft position can be carried out on the ground, the data being sent to both aircraft and ATC. A range-only system which should come on line in the 1980s is the Global Navigation System (NAVSTAR.) using 24 satellites; however use may be restricted to military aircraft and ground personnel.

The frequencies involved for Satnav. are likely to be v.h.f. or around 1·6 GHz. It will obviously be advantageous if a group of satellites could be used for both communication and navigation.

Microwave Landing System (MLS)

The long, controversial and heated argument about which system will be adopted as the successor to ILS ended in 1978 with the choice of a time-referenced scanning beam (TRSB) system. The requirement was for a landing system that would allow for a variety of curved or straight-line approaches within a large volume of airspace and that would not suffer to the same extent as ILS from multipath effects.

The main contenders by the time the final decision was made were the USA with TRSB and the UK with a commutated Doppler. Demonstrations and

simulations showed that both systems would do the job and the choice must have been difficult. One factor which helped swing the vote must have been a reduction in cost of the TRSB system brought about by the development of cost-minimized phased-array techniques (COMPACT) by Hazeltine. A conventional electronic beam scanning array consists of many radiating elements each of which is fed by an electronic phase shifter. Changing the phase of the r.f. energy radiated by each element causes the far field beam to scan. With COMPACT there is nearly a 4 : 1 reduction in the number of phase shifters each of which feeds all radiating elements through a patented passive network. The result is accurate beam scanning with low side lobes at a reduced cost.

The principles of TRSB are quite simple. Consider a radio beam scanned rapidly to and fro; an appropriately tuned receiver on an aircraft within range of the beam source would receive two pulses in one complete scan, as the beam swept past twice. The pulse spacing is related to the angle made between the centroid of the scanned sector and the line joining aircraft to beam source. Note that the system as described is ambiguous since the computed angle could be either side of the centroid of the scanned sector. Ambiguity may be removed by knowing which is the 'to' and which is the 'fro' scan, or by knowing the scan cycle start time, i.e. the commencement of the 'to' half cycle. For accuracy precision timing circuits must be used.

For lateral and vertical guidance azimuth scanning and elevation scanning beams are required. Preamble instructions must be used to identify the beams which

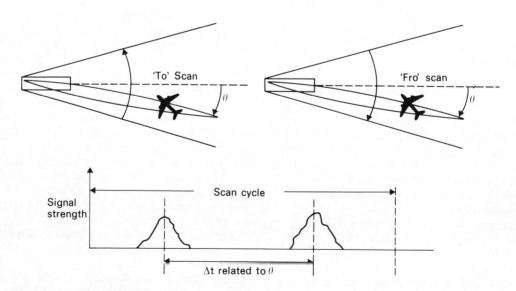

Fig. 13.6 Principles of TRSB

are synchronized so that one time difference for each beam is measured in a 150 ms frame. Back beam and flare measurements are also possible on a full system which will be used in conjunction with a high-accuracy DME. Reflected beam reception can be eliminated by time gating (echo suppression). The r.f. employed will be in the Ku band.

The battle for ICAO recognition is not the whole story of MLS, systems having been developed for special applications; MADGE (microwave aircraft digital guidance equipment) is an MLS-based on-ground derived interferometry, developed by the British company MEL (*see below*); SCAMLS (small community airport MLS) is a Hazeltine product using their COMPACT antennas for the TRSB system.

Microwave Aircraft Digital Guidance Equipment (MADGE)

Introduction

MADGE is a microwave secondary radar system which provides guidance to a landing site for any suitably equipped aircraft within a range of about 15 miles. As well as providing flexibility in the approach path, as one would expect in any successor to ILS, a two-way data link is established which results in deviation and range information being available not only in the air but also at the landing site.

The MEL Equipment Company Limited (A Philips Company) have won sufficient military orders to assure the future of MADGE. The first extensive civilian use will be in the North Sea oil fields where, one platform is already equipped.

Basic Principles

The system provides both range and angular data. The range is derived in the same way as with DME, i.e. measurement takes place in the airborne equipment after an air-to-ground interrogation and a subsequent ground-to-air reply. The air-derived range may be contained in the interrogations, subsequent to the recognition of valid replies, in order to make this information available on the ground.

Azimuth and elevation angles are ground-derived, using interferometry or, in the case of elevation, radio altitude and range. If the latter is the case both range and radio altitude data must be transmitted from air to ground in order that the elevation triangle may be solved for elevation angle. The angular data is contained in the reply to the airborne equipment's interrogation.

Modes of Operation

There are three modes of operation, namely AB, C1 and C2. The particular mode used depends on the aircraft fit and the type of ground station.

Mode AB Angular and range information is available using a standard land-based MADGE station. The direction from which the aircraft is interrogating is measured by the ground station interferometers, the subsequent reply containing horizontal and vertical deviation from an approach or overshoot path determined by the siting of the ground antenna arrays. The azimuth deviation with respect to the approach path centre line is displayed on a purpose-built precision range and azimuth meter (PRAM), while on a standard cross-pointer deviation indicator azimuth and elevation guidance is given to an approach path selected by the pilot. The overshoot path is selected by the pilot in azimuth only, elevation deviation is with respect to the ground-defined overshoot path.

Range data, derived by measuring the elapsed time between interrogation and reply, is displayed on a PRAM. With an appropriate link in the wiring of the airborne installation or on receipt of a command in the ground station reply the range data is sent to the ground interlaced with subsequent interrogations. The two types of air-to-ground transmission are referred to as A channel − interrogation; B channel − range data.

Mode C Two alternatives for Mode C are available, both providing guidance to a point offset horizontally from the landing site, by at least 200 metres. Such guidance is suitable for helicopters operating to offshore platforms. In addition to azimuth and elevation and range data one of two arrows on the PRAM indicates to the pilot on which side of his aircraft the landing site is situated.

Unlike Mode AB the pilot-selected angular offset of the approach path is not available with Mode C. The particular approach path used is ground-defined, hence Mode C is known as the ground controlled mode (GCM). The platform installation is rotated to the correct compass bearing within one of four sectors chosen by the pilot, the choice being relayed by r/t.

The two Mode C alternatives are Mode C1 and C2 which differ in the way elevation guidance is derived. With Mode C1 radio altitude and range are transmitted to the landing site, where the elevation angle can be computed since the sine of the angle is equal to the ratio of the radio altitude to the (slant) range. With Mode C2 elevation information is derived as in Mode AB.

Mode C1 allows greater flexibility of approach. The aircraft can be guided down a glideslope to a point remote from the landing site (say 0·5 nautical miles away) from where the final approach is completed in level flight. The parameters of the approach path are under the control of the ground station for both Mode C1 and C2.

Interferometry

A basic interferometer consists of two antennas feeding receivers, the outputs of which are compared in phase. If the radiated wave arrives from a direction other than normal to the plane of the two-antenna array then the energy arriving at one antenna will have travelled further than that arriving at the other by a distance d. The phase difference between the antenna signals will depend on d which, in turn, depends on the direction of arrival.

A two-antenna interferometer is of little use since an ambiguous measure of the direction of arrival is obtained. For example consider the antennas spaced ℓ cm apart and a wavelength of the radiated wave equal to λ cm. If $d = 0, \lambda, 2\lambda$, etc. the measured phase difference will be zero corresponding to directions of arrival θ, measured with respect to the

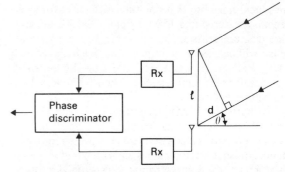

Fig. 13.7 Two antenna interferometer

normal, given by $\sin \theta = 0, \lambda/\ell, 2\lambda/\ell$, etc. Thus with $\ell = 100$ cm, say, and $\lambda = 6$ cm, then for zero phase difference θ could be 0, 3·44, 6·89, etc. degrees.

To resolve the ambiguity several antennas must be used in a linear array. Phase difference measurements can be made between any two antenna signals to give collectively an unambiguous direction of arrival. With the spacing of the antennas chosen to be in the ratio 2 : 4 : 8 : 16 : 32 the derived angle word can be coded directly in binary.

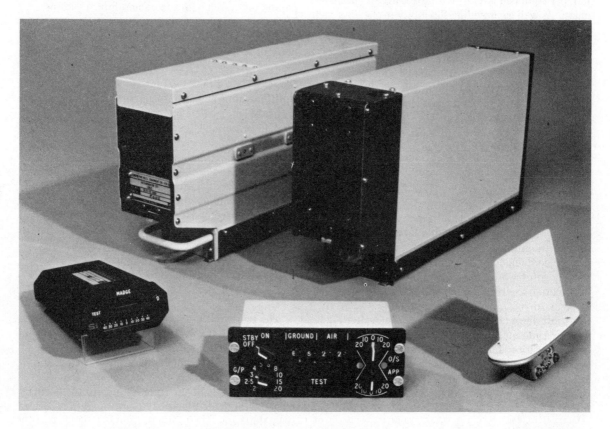

Fig. 13.8 MADGE hardware (courtesy MEL Equipment Co. Ltd)

Controls and Instrumentation

A Mode AB controller has the following controls:

1. 'OFF/STANDBY/ON'. When in standby the input to the modulator is inhibited with a 3-min warm-up delay for the transmitter is initiated.
2. GROUND/AIR control. Four thumbwheel switches which select the ground and air address and the frequency of operation.
3. Angle offsets. Three rotary switches which allow the pilot to select one of a variety of elevation and azimuth angles for approach. For overshoot azimuth offset only is provided.
4. 'TEST'. A push switch which activates the built-in test equipment (b.i.t.e.).

In addition, if the controller is dual mode i.e. Mode AB and C an 'ANGLE OFFSETS'/'SECTOR GCM' five-position switch is provided to allow the pilot to select which of the four approach sectors he desires for Mode C (GCM) operation or, if using a Mode AB station, the angle offset controls may be enabled by selecting 'ANGLE OFFSET'.

The PRAM and crossed-pointer deviation indicator have been mentioned previously. In addition three optional indicators may be fitted:

1. Overshoot warning. Only active during Mode AB operation. There are two active states of this magnetic indicator, in one of which indication of the serviceability of the ground overshoot interferometer is given; the other giving overshoot warning. 'Off' is displayed when the indicator is not active.
2. Low-fly warning. Similar to (1) above except that the active states show either that the elevation failure warning flag is pulled in (elevation safe) or that the aircraft is low.
3. Excess azimuth deviation. Only used in Mode C. A lamp which flashes when the aircraft is more than 60 metres from the approach path and within 1 nautical mile of the landing site.

Block Diagram Operation

The installation comprises an interrogator set (logic unit), an interrogator set (transmitter-receiver), a controller, an antenna selector, two antennas and up to five different indicators, possibly duplicated, as described previously. All electronic circuitry is contained within the logic unit and transmitter-receiver (t/r) with the exception of that contained in the PRAM.

The length and message content of the interrogation word, which is assembled in the logic unit, depends on the mode of operation. For A channel (Mode AB) a 25-bit word requesting guidance information is transmitted at a jittering mean rate of 50 Hz. B channel, containing range and other data in a 60-bit word, can be interlaced with A channel interrogations at a factory set rate of 2·5, 5, 10 or 50 Hz. C modes use only one interrogation word 60 bits long at a jittering mean rate of 100 Hz. Both C1 and C2 interrogations contain guidance interrogation data and range, but in addition mode C1 transmits radio altitude information. Appropriate air and ground address codes, as selected on the controller, form part of the guidance interrogation.

The interrogation word pulse train, suitably processed in a line receiver and pulse modulator, controls the grid voltage of a travelling-wave-tube which amplifies the r.f. from a solid-state source phase-locked to 56 times a reference oscillator crystal. A 4-bit parallel code, determined by the frequency selection at the controller, selects which of four crystals is to be used as a reference. The pulse code amplitude modulated frequency of between 5·1825 and 5·2005 GHz is fed via a low-pass filter and circulator in the microwave assembly to one of two antennas selected by a switch which is controlled by the logic unit.

Received signals are amplified and detected in a double-superhet receiver, then passed to the logic unit. Incoming noise pulses are combated by reducing the receiver sensitivity as the rate of received pulses increases. Interference from multipath echoes is avoided by setting a threshold level in accordance with the amplitude of the first pulse of the incoming word. The weaker multipath echoes will be unlikely to exceed this threshold which returns to zero at the end of each received word.

The reply is clocked into a shift register and then checked for validity and parity. Validity is determined by comparing air and ground address codes received with those selected. A range clock, which was started when the interrogation took place, is stopped on completion of a successful validity and parity check.

The system functions in either search or track. Until the rate of validated replies is acceptable the logic unit causes the t/r output to switch between forward and rear antennas at a 0·5 Hz rate. Having acquired a reliable range value, a tracking gate is generated so that only those replies within 1 μs before, and 2 μs after, the expected time of arrival are accepted. With replies regularly falling within the tracking gate the range of change of range is

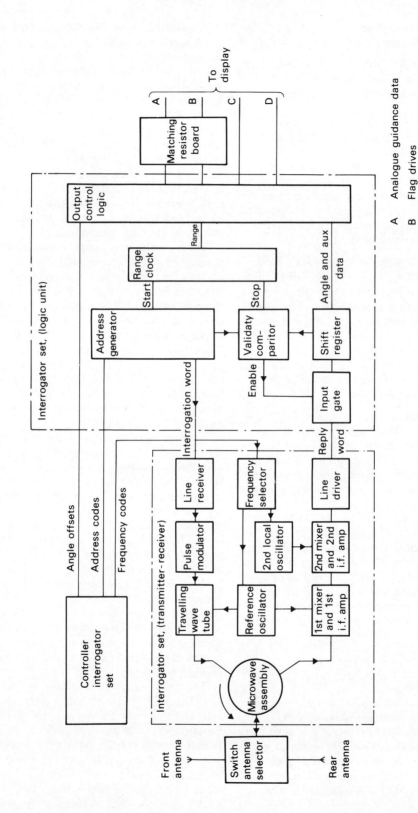

Fig. 13.9 MADGE simplified block diagram (courtesy MEL Equipment Co. Ltd)

A   Analogue guidance data
B   Flag drives
C   Digital navigation data
D   Warning signals

computed. If the rate exceeds 30 knots antenna-switching ceases, the forward antenna being selected for decreasing range, the rear antenna for increasing range. Each antenna has a polar diagram which is $180°$ wide in the horizontal plane and $40°$ wide in the vertical plane.

With validity and parity confirmed range and angle data is fed to the output control logic circuits. Digital range and azimuth information is fed to the PRAM, the azimuth information being unaffected by the selection of angle offsets. Azimuth and elevation information is compared with the selected angle offsets, the resulting digital differences are then converted into analogue guidance outputs which are fed via matching resistors in the interface junction box to the cross-pointer deviation indicator. The d/a converter gain is progressively reduced as the range decreases from 1 nautical mile. This reduction in gain is known as beam-softening and results in meter deflection being proportional to lateral rather than angular displacement from the approach path.

Warning signals are generated within the logic unit. Flag drives are fed to the cross-pointer instrument being 28 V for valid information, 0 V during a fault condition. A low-fly warning is provided in Mode AB, or an excess elevation deviation signal in Mode C. Azimuth warnings are the excess azimuth deviation in Mode C and the overshoot signal in Mode AB. The PRAM display is enabled by the azimuth flag signal.

For Mode C1 a radio altimeter interface unit is required to digitize the analogue height signal from the radio altimeter. As a check the digitized height is converted back into analogue form, then compared with the height input. A fault signal is fed to the logic unit if a discrepancy greater than ± 25 ft is detected. The fault signal is also generated if the radio altimeter's flag output shows a fault condition. With a fault detected the elevation flag shows and the height information present bit in the interrogation word is negated.

Selected System Parameters

Transmitter peak power: 150 W nominal.
Transmitter frequency channels: 5182·5, 5188·5, 5194·5, 5200·5 MHz.
Receiver frequency channels: 5004·5, 5010·5, 5016·5, 5022·5, 5028·5, 5034·5 MHz.
Interrogation word rate: 50 Hz mean (A channel); 100 Hz mean (C channel).
Word jitter: ± 2 ms (A channel); ± 1 ms (B channel).
Message bit rate: 1·01125 MHz nominal.
Interrogation word length: 25 bits (A channel); 60 bits (C channel).
Reply word length: 60 bits (all channels).

Message format: non-return-to-zero (n.r.z.).
Height data, down link: 11 bits (binary).
Range data, down link: 16 bits (b.c.d.).
Elevation data, up link: 9 bits.
Azimuth and flag data, up link: 15 bits.
Analogue azimuth guidance: selectable $\pm 2·5$ to $\pm 10°$ full scale.
Analogue elevation guidance: selectable $\pm 0·5$ to $\pm 5°$ full scale.
Azimuth coarse output: $\pm 45°$ full scale.
Elevation coarse output: $\pm 25°$ (A channel); -5 to $+20°$ full scale (C1 channel).
Range output: 25 nautical miles at 10 V; 30 nautical miles at 12 V.
Velocity output: ± 200 knots full scale.
Digital outputs: 1·01125 MHz, bi-phase n.r.z.
Angles and flags: 28-bit word at reply rate.
Range data: 18-bit word at interrogation rate.
Digital resolution: azimuth $0·235°$; elevation $0·144°$; range 9·26 metres.

Collision Avoidance

Up until 1979 collision avoidance has been the responsibility of ATC for aircraft flying under IFR while pilots are responsible for their own safety under VFR. This situation is likely to continue for some time in the future even though a workable collision avoidance system (CAS) has been developed.

A self-contained system would protect the equipped aircraft regardless of whether other aircraft were similarly equipped or an ATC service was available. Such a system could be built measuring range, range-rate of change, and direction of all aircraft within a certain volume of space around the protected aircraft. Received data could be used to compute projected paths so that the risk of collision could be evaluated and, if necessary, a warning given or automatic manoeuvre initiated. The cost of such a system providing the accuracy required is prohibitive, at least for the time being.

As an alternative, we may have a co-operative system and this is an area in which work has been done. Two possibilities exist:

1. an interrogator/transponder secondary radar system which could measure range and range-rate in much the same way as DME does but with obvious problems in crowded airspace where the system is most needed;
2. a time multiplexed system in which all aircraft transmit in turn without interrogation.

The calculation of the range at nearest approach

(miss distance) is complicated and requires present relative positions, including altitude, and the speed and track of each aircraft involved. One approach is to use the component of relative velocity perpendicular to the line joining the aircraft as shown in Fig. 13.10 where V_A, V_B, V_R are the velocity vectors of aircraft A, aircraft B and B relative to A respectively, while X is the measure of the risk of collision. Another, simpler method is to use the range divided by the range-rate, measure of the risk being known as tau (τ). In both methods a minimum value of the risk measure is set, below which evasive action is taken. With the latter method, however, when the closing velocity is small τ is not a good measure of risk and a minimum range criterion should be included in the system.

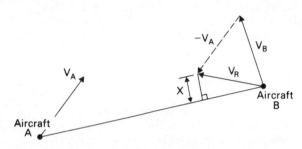

Fig. 13.10 Collision threat geometry

As an example of a system we will briefly consider the Bendix CAS which was workable as long ago as 1969. The system involves an airborne clock, computer and transmitter-receiver while on the ground synchronization and clock accuracy of the system is assured by means of an atomic clock. During a 3 s interval known as an epoch, each participating aircraft transmits during one of 2000 time-slots each of 1·5 ms duration; while one is transmitting the rest listen. Transmission of altitude and other data (e.g. heading) is made.

The ground station keeps all aircraft synchronized in time; and frequency of transmission and hence range may be measured from propagation time and range rate from Doppler shift. Thus τ may be calculated once during each epoch for all reporting aircraft. Commands to the pilot based on the computer's evaluation of the risk are: aircraft above, prepare to dive, dive, aircraft below, prepare to climb, climb and fly level. The commands are given by back-lighted legends on one indicator.

Any CAS which may eventually be adopted will not necessarily be like the Bendix system, but certainly some of the factors and techniques discussed above will be relevant.

The Current Generation of ARINC Characteristics

In 1979 a number of new ARINC Characteristics (700 series) were adopted by the AEEC. The systems covered include radio altimeter, DME, ILS, VOR, ADF, Selcal., p.a. amp., v.h.f. comms, weather radar and ATC transponder. These characteristics detail the airline standards for radio equipment in the 1980s. There are obviously many minor differences between new and old characteristics and some major ones such as the incorporation of DABS into the ATC transponder. However, the most significant change is the switch to serial digital signals for both system outputs and control. The details of the digital information transfer system (DITS) are given in ARINC Specification 429-2 published 1 March 1979. Additional information is given in project papers 453 and 720, the very high speed (VHS) bus and digital frequency/function selection (DFS) respectively, although these papers had not been adopted by May 1979.

The DITS describes the standards for the transfer of digital data between all avionics systems, not just radio. Data flow is one way only, via twisted and shielded pairs of wires at a rate of 100K bits per second (Kbs) or 12 to 14·5 Kbs (1000 Kbs for VHS bus). The system is based on 32-bit words. The encoding logic for each bit is based on a voltage transition, a 'Hi' state at the beginning of a bit interval returning to a 'Null' state before the end of that interval represents a logic '1' similarly a 'Lo' to 'Null' represents a logic '0'. The transmitter voltage levels are +10 ± 1 V, 0 ± 0·5 V and −10 ± 1 V for the 'Hi', 'Null' and 'Lo' states respectively.

Information is coded in one of several ways: binary coded decimal (b.c.d.), two's complement fractional binary (b.n.r.) or the International Standards organisation (ISO) alphabet No. 5. Code for graphics data has not yet been defined. Discrete data such as on/off switching is simply a 1-bit 'code'. Words are synchronized by a gap of at least 4 bits between words, a gap is recognized by the fact that there is no voltage transition. Error checking is carried out by one parity bit per word, the required parity is odd, i.e. the total number of '1s' in a word is odd.

The basic organization of each word is label, source/destination identifier (SDI), data field, sign/status matrix and finally, bit 32, parity. The first 8 bits of each word are assigned to a label which identifies the information contained in the data field, e.g. v.h.f. comm. frequency, DME distance, selected course, etc. Bits 9 and 10 are used for the SDI where a word needs to be directed to a specific system of a multi-system installation or the source system of a multi-system installation needs to be identified. The SDI is not available for alphanumeric words (ISO alphabet No. 5) or where the bits are used as part of the data field when the resolution required demands it. Bits 30 and 31 are used for the sign/status matrix which represents +, North, right, to, test, no computed data, etc. If several words are used to transmit a message too long for one word then the sign/status matrix is used to indicate final word, intermediate word, control word or initial word.

The above ideas are best illustrated by examples:

1. ADF, typical word
   0 0 0 1 1 0 1 0 0 0 0 0 0 1 1 0 1 0 0 0 0
   1 1 0 0 0 0 0 1 0 0 0
   The label '0 0 0 1 1 0 1 0' is followed by SDI '0 0' the all-call code. Data field bits 11, 12 and 13 are b.f.o. — on/off (0 for off), ADF/antenna mode (0 for ADF) and spare respectively. Data field bits 14-29 are the frequency select bits with bits 27-29 the 1000 kHz selection, bits 23-26 the 100 kHz, bits 15-18 the 1 kHz and bit 14 the 0·5 kHz selection. The example shown reading from bit 14, is
   1   1 0 1 0   0 0 0 1   1 0 0 0   0 0 1
   0·5 + 5   +   10   +   800   + 1000
   = 1815·5 kHz.
   Sign/status is not applicable here but in any case 00 can be read as positive. The final bit is set to 0 to make total one count odd.

2. ATC transponder, typical word
   0 0 1 1 1 0 1 1 0 0 0 0 1 0 0 0 0 0 0 0 1
   0 1 0 1 0 1 0 0 0 0 1
   The data field bits 11-17 in ascending order are altitude reporting on/off (0 for on), inertial reference system/flight management computer, i.e. IRS/FMC inputs which are reserved for future use (0 for IRS), ident. on/off (1 for on), altitude data source select (0 for No. 1), IFR/VFR which is reserved for future use (0 for IFR) and X-pulse on/off (0 for off). Data field bits 18 to 29 represent pilot-selected code for Mode A replies with bits 18-20 the D code group select, 21-23 the C, 24-26 the B and 27-29 the A code group select. The example shown reading back from bit 29 is
   0 0 1   0 1 0   1 0 1   0 0 0
     1   2   5   0   = code

3. DME distance (b.c.d.)
   1 0 0 0 0 0 0 1 0 0 0 1 1 0 0 0 0 1 1 1 1
   0 1 0 1 0 0 1 0 0 0 0
   The data field is used exclusively for the DME

distance with the most significant bit (m.s.b.) of the most significant character (m.s.c.) being bit 29. The example shown reading back from bit 29 is
0 1 0   0 1 0 1   0 1 1 1   1 0 0 0   0 1 1 0
  2   5   7   8   6
nautical miles

DITS words representing parameters are generated in units such as VOR receivers, DME interrogators, etc. and will terminate in navigation computers, display drivers or indicators. The rate of transmission of such words varies, for example the minimum rate for DME distance is 6 times per second while radio height is 20 times per second; DITS radio control words such as examples (1) and (2) above are transmitted 9 times per second.

Concluding Remarks

This book has considered current radio systems with examples of a range of technologies. The final chapter has attempted to show directions in which radio systems may progress. We will certainly see MLS and most probably ADSEL/DABS. Flight decks will make full use of flexible electronic displays but a minimal complement of conventional instruments and controls will remain indefinitely.

Modulating signals will probably remain analogue in propagating systems, since to go digital would require a shift up the frequency scale to accommodate the wider bandwidths required. Even though the basis of the systems will be analogue signals, they will 'go digital' as early as possible in the circuitry. Computing power will increase beyond that which we can employ; this has happened already, the power is there, all we need to do is think of the applications, after which there will be yet more computing power.

Perhaps the biggest question mark is over the future of VOR/DME as the standard ICAO navigational aid. Possible replacements are v.l.f./Omega, Satnav. in one form or another, or even Loran C; the advantages of these being that they are long range.

A possible scenario is an aircraft fitted with a variety of dead reckoning and position fixing nav. aids in a minimum number of boxes backed up by accurate ground tracking, immensely powerful ground computers and a comprehensive data link. With a multiple CAS and MLS of the required accuracy the aircraft of the future could go from ramp to ramp without the intervention of the pilot and in almost perfect safety. This could be developed now, but would be cost prohibitive; and anyway who wants a robot flying the 'plane?

Recommended reading

As the reader is probably aware there is a dearth of books on avionics; those that exist and concern themselves with aircraft radio are perhaps a little dated. In contrast the number of books available on electronics, computers and radio is staggering.

I have chosen to list most books available on avionics which I think are worthy of the reader's attention. For sources of background material on basic theory of electronics and radio the reader is perhaps best advised to visit a suitable library or bookshop and pick out those which seem to suit him or her best. Since this is a formidable task, I have listed some books which I think may be useful. A brief note is given as a guide to content and level of each.

1. M. Kayton and W.R. Fried (Editors), *Avionics Navigation Systems*. John Wiley and Sons (1969).
   Authoritative book which is still of considerable interest. Covers radio and non-radio aids. Postgraduate engineer level.
2. G.E. Beck (Editor), *Navigation Systems*. Van Nostrand Reinhold (1971).
   Similar to Kayton and Fried, also considers marine navigation systems. Equally worthy but not, perhaps, as comprehensive since it has almost 300 fewer pages.
3. B. Kendal, *Manual of Avionics*. Granada (1979).
   Biased towards air traffic control aspects of aircraft operations. Complementary to this book.
4. E.H.J. Pallett, *Aircraft Electrical Systems*. Pitman (2nd edition, 1979).
5. E.H.J. Pallett, *Aircraft Instruments*. Pitman (2nd edition, 1981).
6. E.H.J. Pallett, *Automatic Flight Control*. Granada (1979).
   All of Pallett's books are well written with good illustrations. Very useful to avionics engineers. May be considered as companion volumes to this book.
7. N.H. Birch and A.E. Bramson, *Flight Briefing for Pilots*, Volume 3, *Radio Aids to Air Navigation*. Pitman (4th edition, 1979).

A very good book but the emphasis is on operational use so the theory given is brief. Complementary to this book.

8. S.E.T. Taylor and H.A. Parmer, *Ground Studies for Pilots*, Volume 1, *Radio Aids*. Granada (3rd edition, 1979).
   Covers the needs of prospective commercial pilots in so far as the use of radio aids is concerned.
9. J.L. McKinley and R.D. Brent, *Electricity and Electronics for Aerospace Vehicles*. McGraw-Hill (2nd edition, 1971).
   Covers fundamental theory and briefly describes avionics systems. Basic.
10. D.C. Green, *Transmission Systems*, II. Pitman (1978).
11. D.C. Green, *Radio Systems*, II. Pitman (1978).
12. D.C. Green, *Radio Systems*, III. Pitman (1979).
13. D.C. Green, *Electronics*, II. Pitman (1978).
14. D.C. Green, *Electronics*, III. Pitman (1978).
    All of Green's books are well written and illustrated. Technician level.
15. J.E. Fisher and H.B. Gatland, *Electronics from Theory into Practice*. Pergamon (2nd edition, 1976).
    Mainly concerned with design of circuits. Undergraduate and practising engineers.
16. G.A. Streitmatter and V. Fiore, *Microprocessors Theory and Applications*. Reston (1979).
    One of the best of a recent number of books on microprocessors.
17. A.J. Baden Fuller, *Microwaves*. Pergamon (2nd edition, 1979).
    Undergraduate level. Useful descriptions of components and devices.
18. *Telecommunications Systems Units*, 1-6. Course Chairman: G. Smol. The Open University Press (1976).
19. *Electromagnetics and Electronics*. Course Chairman: J. J. Sparkes. The Open University Press (1972).
    Both 15 and 16 are highly recommended as course material.

I am sure I have omitted many books which are equal in merit to those listed. The editions referred to (1st unless otherwise indicated) are those with which I am familiar; the reader is advised to check that these are the latest editions.

I have not mentioned any mathematics textbooks, but for those who wish to study aircraft radio systems in depth, considerable mathematic maturity is needed. Many books have titles which are variations on the theme 'Mathematics for Technicians' most of which will be useful. The Open University is again a useful source for those requiring applied mathematics at undergraduate level.

A huge source of material on avionics comes from organizations which are not publishing houses. The reader is advised to consult the publications lists of national aviation authorities, such as the CAA and FAA, and also ARINC and ICAO. Aircraft and equipment manufacturers produce comprehensive manuals of varying standards which will be consulted by the reader, as a matter of course, in the execution of his duties in the aircraft industry.

Glossary

a.c. – Alternating current: current flow which changes direction periodically.

Acquisition – The recognition of a signal.

ACU – Antenna Coupling Unit.

A/D – Analogue to Digital conversion.

Address – A group of bits which identify a particular location in memory or some other data source or destination.

ADF – Automatic Direction Finder: a system capable of automatically giving the bearing to a fixed radio transmitter.

ADI – Attitude Director Indicator: an instrument which demands attitude changes which, if executed, cause the aircraft to fly a path determined by radio or other sensors.

ADSEL – Address Selective SSR: British development of SSR, compatible with DABS.

a.f.c. – Automatic frequency control: automatic tuning of a radio receiver.

AFCS – Automatic Flight Control System.

a.g.c. – Automatic gain control of a radio receiver.

AID – Aircraft Installation Delay: the time elapsed between transmission and reception in a Radio Altimeter installation when the aircraft is in the touchdown position.

Air Data Computer – A unit which senses, evaluates and outputs quantities associated with altitude, airspeed, vertical speed and Mach number.

Air speed – The speed of an aircraft relative to the air mass through which it is flying.

AIS – Audio Integrating System: the electronic interface between crew members and audio sources and destinations.

Algorithm – A sequence of steps which always leads of a conclusion.

Alphanumerics – Displayed characters which may be letters or numerals or both.

Altimeter – Pneumatic: a pressure measuring device calibrated in feet; also barometric, pressure and servo altimeter. Radio: a system which measures the height of an aircraft above the earth's surface.

Altitude hole – Loss of signal in an f.m.c.w. radar due to round trip travel time being equal to the modulation period: of importance in Doppler navigation systems.

Altitude trip – A discrete signal from a radio altimeter which changes state as the aircraft passes through a pre-determined altitude.

a.m. – Amplitude modulation: meaningful variation of the amplitude of an r.f. carrier.

Analog, analogue – A quantity or signal which varies continuously and represents some other continuously varying quantity; hence an analog circuit which processes such signals, an analog computer which performs arithmetic operations on such signals.

AND gate – A logic circuit which gives an output of 1 if, and only if, all its inputs are 1.

Angle of cut – The angle between two hyperbolic or circular l.o.p. at their point of intersection.

Antenna, aerial – A device specifically designed to convert r.f. current flow to electro-magnetic radiation, or vice versa.

a.o.c. – Automatic overload control: a circuit which prevents an excessive rate of triggering of a transponder.

APU – Auxiliary Power Unit: a motor-generator fitted to an aircraft for the purpose of providing ground power and starting the main engines.

A/R – Altitude Reporting: automatic coded transmission of altitude from aircraft to ATC in an SSR system.

Array – A group of regularly arranged devices, for example, antennas or memory cells.

ASP – Audio Selection Panel.

Associated identity – The identification of co-located VOR and DME beacons by synchronized transmissions of the same Morse code characters from each beacon.

Astable – Having no stable state.

ATC – Air Traffic Control.

ATE – Automatic Test Equipment.

ATU – Antenna Tuning Unit.

A-type display – A c.r.t. display in which the timebase deflection is horizontal and the signal deflection is vertical.

Automatic standby – *see* Signal controlled search.

Backlash – Play in driven mechanical linkage such as scanner drives.

Balun – Balanced to unbalanced transformer: used, for example, in connecting a co-axial feeder (unbalanced) to a centre fed half wave dipole antenna (balanced).

Barometric setting – The reference pressure level of a barometric altimeter as set by the pilot.

Base – The integral value of the number of symbols in a counting system. The central region of a bipolar transistor.

Baseline – The line joining two ground stations in a hyperbolic navigation system.

b.c.d. – Binary coded decimal: a positional code in which each decimal digit is binary coded as a 4-bit word.

Beam softening – Progressive reduction in gain of demand signal channel in landing systems.

Bearing – The angle, measured in a clockwise direction, between a reference line through the aircraft and a line joining the aircraft and the object to which bearing is being measured. The reference line may point to magnetic or true North or be in line with the aircraft's longitudinal axis for magnetic, true or relative bearing respectively.

Beat frequency – The difference frequency resulting when two sinusoids are mixed in a non linear device.

b.f.c. – Beat frequency oscillator: an oscillator, the output of which is mixed with an incoming c.w. signal in order to produce an audible beat frequency.

Bi-directional – Refers to an interface port or bus line which can transfer data in either direction.

Binary number system – A counting system using 2 as its base and employing the symbols 0 and 1.

Binary signal – A signal which can take on one of two states, one representing the bit 0, the other the bit 1.

Bipolar transistor – A solid state device utilizing two types of current carriers: holes and electrons; capable of amplifying or switching functions when used in suitable circuits.

Bistable – Having two stable states.

Bit – A single binary digit, i.e. the symbol 0 or 1.

BITE – Built In Test Equipment.

Blade antenna – A rigid quarter wave antenna, the blade shape of which gives operation over a wide band of frequencies; electrical components may be housed within the blade for the purpose of improving the performance.

BNR – Signal representing a binary number.

Bonding – Electrical: interconnecting metal parts with conductors in order to eliminate potential differences. Mechanical: joining parts to one another by methods other than those involving bolts, screws and rivets.

Boolean algebra – The algebra of two state, or binary, variables.

Buffer – A circuit used for isolating or matching purposes.

Bug – A fault, usually in software. A mark, fixed or set, on a meter face.

Bus – One or more conductors used as an information path. A conductor used to carry a particular power supply to various user equipments.

Byte – A specific number of bits (usually 8) treated as a group: 8-bit word.

c – Standard notation for the speed of propagation of e.m. waves in free space: $c = 3 \times 10^8$ metres per sec = 186 000 miles per sec = 162 000 n.m. per sec.

CADC – Central Air Data Computer.

Capsule – An evacuated airtight container used to detect changes in pressure.

Capture – The sensing of a radio beam such as occurs in ILS.

CAS – Collision Avoidance System.

CDI – Course Deviation Indicator: an instrument which presents steering signals to the pilot which, if obeyed, cause the aircraft to follow a particular flight path.

CDU – Control Display Unit.

Cell – A circuit or device used for storing one character or word, the location being given by a particular address. A single chemical source of electro motive force (e.m.f.).

Chip – A collection of interconnected electronic components formed on a single silicon wafer.

Choke flange – A type of waveguide joint which, by use of a short-circuited half-wave stub, gives a good electrical connection across the joint.

CIWS – Central Instrument Warning System.

Clarifier – Tuning control for the inserted carrier oscillator needed for s.s.b. reception.

Clear – To place one or more storage locations in a particular state, usually 0.

Clock – The basic synchronizing circuit in a system; the waveform from such a circuit.

Clutter – Unwanted radar returns.

Co-axial cable – A pair of concentric conductors separated by an insulating material and used for line transmission of r.f. currents up to about 4 GHz.

Code – A system of symbols and rules used for representing information such as numbers, letters and control signals.

Colocation – VHF navigation and DME beacons sharing the same geographical site; such beacons will operate on paired frequencies and use associated identity.

Commutator – A mechanical or electronic rotating contact device.

Compass rose – A circular scale marked in degrees and used for indicating aircraft heading.

Computer – A machine or system which performs arithmetic and logical functions; may be analogue or digital, electronic or mechanical.

Contour – Blanking of the strongest signals in a weather radar.

Control bus – A bus used to carry a variety of control signals.

CPU – Central Processing Unit: a device capable of executing instructions obtained from memory or other sources; a term often used for a microprocessor.

Cross modulation – Modulation of a desired signal by an unwanted signal.

Crosstrack deviation – The perpendicular distance between aircraft position and the desired track.

c.r.t. – Cathode ray tube: an evacuated thermionic device which has an electron gun at one end and a fluorescent screen at the other; the electron beam from the gun writes a pattern on the screen which is a function of analogue signals applied to the device.

Crystal – A frequency sensitive device used to determine and maintain the frequency of oscillators or establish narrow pass or stop bands within close limits. A point contact diode which may find use as a mixer or rectifier in microwave systems.

CVOR – Conventional VOR (beacon).

CVR – Cockpit Voice Recorder.

c.w. –Continuous wave: continuous transmission of unmodulated r.f. during the time the transmitter is keyed.

Cycle – One of a recurring series of events.

D/A – Digital to Analogue conversion.

DABS – Discrete Address Beacon System: American development of SSR; compatible with ADSEL.

Data – That on which a computer or processor operates; singular: datum.

Data bus – Usually either 8 or 16 bi-directional lines capable of carrying information to and from the CPU, memory or interface devices.

Data save memory – A memory device which does not lose the data stored in it when power is switched off. May require a battery.

dB – Decibel: unit of relative power or voltage measured on a logarithmic scale with multiplying factors of 10 and 20 respectively.

dBm – Unit of power: decibels relative to 1 mW.

d.c. – Direct current: current flow in one direction only.

d.d.m. – Difference in depth of modulation: refers to the 90 Hz and 150 Hz modulating frequencies used in ILS.

Dead reckoning – Calculation of position using vehicle speed or acceleration, time in motion, direction and the known co-ordinates of the initial position. The absolute error in a dead reckoning system increases, without bound, with distance flown.

Decca navigator – A c.w. hyperbolic navigation system.

Decimal number system – A counting system using 10 as its base and employing the symbols 0, 1, 2, 3, 4, 5, 6, 7, 8, 9.

Decometer – A phase meter used in the Decca navigation system; three are employed: purple, red and green.

Detector – An electronic circuit which de-modulates amplitude or pulse-modulated waveforms.

D/F – Direction Finding.

DH – Decision Height: the height at which the runway should be in view when on an approach.

Differentiator – A device which gives an output proportional to the rate of change of input.

Digital – A system or device using discrete signals to represent particular values of a varying or fixed quantity numerically; a signal in such a system.

Diode – A semiconductor or thermionic device which prevents flow of current in one direction.

Dipole, half wave – An antenna consisting of two co-linear lengths of conductor each one quarter wavelength long at the desired frequency of operation. The two poles may form a 'V' shape if a more omni-directional polar diagram than a figure of eight is required.

Direct access – Capability of reading data from a particular address in memory without having to access through preceding storage area.

Disc – Storage device giving large capacity and almost direct access.

Discrete signal – A signal characterized by being either 'on' or 'off'.

Discriminator – A circuit which converts frequency or phase differences into amplitude variations.

DITS – Digital Information Transfer System: ARINC 429.

DME – Distance Measuring Equipment: a secondary radar system capable of measuring the slant range of a fixed transponder.

Doppler effect — The change in frequency noted when a wave source is moving relative to an observer.

Doppler navigation system — A dead reckoning system consisting of a Doppler radar and a computer which, with heading information from a compass, calculates the position of the aircraft.

Doppler radar — A primary radar system which utilizes the Doppler effect to measure two or more of ground speed, drift angle, longitudinal velocity, lateral velocity, vertical velocity.

Doppler shift — The difference between transmit and receive frequencies in a system subject to the Doppler effect.

Doppler spectrum — A band of Doppler shift frequencies produced by a Doppler radar with a finite beam width.

DPSK — Differential Phase Shift Keying: a form of digital modulation in which a phase reversal indicates the binary digit '1'.

Drift angle — The angle between heading and track.

d.s.b. — Double side band: transmission of both side bands of an a.m. wave, the carrier being suppressed.

Duplexer — A device which permits sharing of one circuit or transmission channel by two signals in particular use of one antenna for reception and transmission.

DVOR — Doppler VOR (beacon).

d.v.s.t. — Direct view storage tube: a type of c.r.t. with a high intensity display.

Dynamic RAM — A type of RAM in which data stored will fade unless periodically refreshed.

EADI — Electronic ADI: similarly ECDI and EHSI.

EAROM — Electrically Alterable ROM: *see* EPROM.

Earth — *see* Ground.

ECL — Emitter Coupled Logic: logic circuits employing bipolar transistors giving very fast operation, reasonable fan-in and very good fan-out.

e.h.t. — Extra high tension: a source of e.m.f., usually measured in kilovolts, used as a supply for c.r.t.'s and high power transmitters.

Elapsed time — The time between transmission and reception in a radar system.

Electroluminescent — A property of devices which convert electrical energy to light.

e.m. waves — Electromagnetic waves which include radio and light waves.

e.m.f. — Electromotive force.

Enable — A signal which allows a circuit to give an output; alternatively a gate (signal).

Encoding altimeter — A pneumatic altimeter with a parallel coded output of 9 to 11 bits representing the aircraft's height above mean sea level to the nearest 100 ft.

EPROM — Erasable Programmable ROM: a ROM which, using suitable equipment, can be erased and re-programmed.

Fan-in — The number of inputs that can be handled, usually by a logic circuit.

Fan marker — A position fixing aid for en route airways navigation: also Z marker.

Fan-out — The number of circuits which can be driven from an output terminal, usually of a logic circuit.

Fast erect — The application of a larger voltage than required for normal running to a gyro in order to reduce the time taken to achieve operating speed.

f.e.t. — Field effect transistor: a solid state device utilizing one type of current carrier (c.f. bipolar transistor).

Fetch — The part of a digital computer cycle during which the location of the next instruction is determined, that instruction is taken from memory and entered into a register.

Filter — A circuit which selects wanted or rejects unwanted signals, usually on the basis of frequency.

Firmwave — Instructions stored in ROM and hence not easily amended.

Flag — A signal which has two discrete states, one of which (low) usually indicates failure.

Flag bit — The software equivalent of a flip flop which may be used as an indicator, for example, to indicate the beginning or end of a piece of data.

Flare — The final phase of a landing during which the rate of descent is reduced with height.

Flash over — Discharge through air between conductors across which a large potential exists.

Flight level — With a pneumatic altimeter reference set at 1013.25 mbar or 29.92 in.Hg the indicated height, to the nearest hundred feet, is the flight level; the reply from an ATC Transponder to mode C interrogations.

Flight log — A device which records an aircraft's flight path in the horizontal plane, for example, a roller map.

Flip flop — A circuit having two stable states, often referred to as a bi-stable. The circuit remains in one state until triggered, two triggers being required to revert to the original state. A mono-stable may be referred to as a flip flop.

Flowchart — A diagrammatic representation of a sequence of operations which are often algorithmic.

f.m. — Frequency modulation: meaningful variation of the frequency of a carrier.

Fruit — Unwanted SSR replies.

Frequency pairing — The permanent association of frequencies in different systems such as VOR/DME and Localizer/Glideslope.

Freeze − Not allowing updating of a weather radar picture.

f.s.d. − Full scale deflection.

Garbling − Received signals overlapping in time.

Gate − A circuit, the output of which depends on certain input conditions being met; for example AND, OR, NAND, NOR gates. A switching waveform. The region of an f.e.t. which controls the output current.

Gimbal − A frame in which a gyro is mounted so as to allow freedom of movement about an axis perpendicular to the gyro spin axis.

Glidepath/glideslope − The vertical plane approach path to a landing site. That part of ILS which provides vertical guidance.

GPWS − Ground Proximity Warning System.

Gray code − A one bit change code.

Grey region − A condition of uncertainty.

Ground − A point of zero potential; also earth.

Ground plane − A surface which completely reflects e.m. waves and which, at the frequency of interest, behaves as if it extends to infinity in all directions.

Ground speed − The speed of an aircraft projected on to the earth's surface.

Ground wave − A radio wave which follows the earth's surface.

Gunn diode − A solid state device utilizing the bunching of current carriers and finding application as an oscillator in microwave systems.

Gyroscope, gyro − A spinning mass free to rotate about one or both of two axes perpendicular to one another and the axis of spin. In the absence of external forces the spin axis direction is fixed in space.

Handshake − Electrical verification that a data transfer has taken place.

Hard data − Data which remains in memory with power removed.

Hardware − The sum total of components of a system which have a physical existence.

Hard μV − Hard micro volts: the voltage across an open circuit load.

Head up display − Equipment which allows information to be visually presented to the pilot while looking through the windscreen.

Heading − The tail to nose direction of the aircraft longitudinal axis measured in degrees clockwise from either magnetic or true North.

Height ring − The ground return from a vertical sidelobe in a Weather Radar gives a bright height ring on the p.p.i. centred on the origin.

Hexadecimal number system − A counted system using 16 as its base and employing the symbols 0, 1, 2, 3, 4, 5, 6, 7, 8, 9, A, B, C, D, E, F.

High level language − A vocabulary, together with grammatical rules, in which each statement corresponds to several machine code instructions so making the task of programming less tedious; examples are BASIC, FORTRAN, ATLAS, PASCAL, etc.

Hot mic. − A microphone which is permanently live irrespective of crew operated switch positions; live output is fed to the CVR.

HSI − Horizontal Situation Indicator: an instrument displaying information from the compass and v.h.f. navigation aids, the latter being in the form of deviation signals which, in the case of VOR, relate to a course selected on the same instrument.

Hyperbolic navigation − A means of navigation using a co-ordinate system of hyperbolic lines defined by ground based radio transmitters.

i.c. − Integrated circuit: a device containing electronic circuits inseparably fabricated as an integral part of the device itself; often referred to as a chip.

i.f. − Intermediate frequency: the fixed frequency at which most of the amplification and selection takes place in a superhetrodyne receiver.

IFF − Identification Friend or Foe: military version of SSR.

IFR − Instrument Flight Rules: apply when VFR are excluded by virtue of flying in controlled airspace or lack of visibility.

ILS − Instrument Landing System: the current standard ICAO approach aid.

Impatt diode − Impact avalanche transit time diode: a silicon p-n junction reverse biased to its avalanche threshold; can be arranged to act as a negative resistance in microwave circuits, hence its use in oscillators.

Impedance − The total opposition to the flow of current; in general impedance varies with frequency.

in.Hg − Inches of mercury: a unit of pressure measurement; the height of a column of mercury supported by the pressure being measured; 29.92 in.Hg = 1013.25 mbar = 1 standard atmosphere, i.e. the pressure at mean sea level.

Inhibit − A signal which prevents a particular circuit from performing its function.

INS − Inertial Navigation System: a non radio navigation aid which computes the aircraft's position by dead reckoning using the measured acceleration of an airborne gyro stabilized platform.

Instruction — Coded information which causes a computer to perform an operation usually on data available at an address which forms part of the instruction.

Instruction set — The sum total of instructions which can be executed by a particular computer.

Integrator — A device, the output of which is proportional to the sum of past inputs.

Intensity Modulation — Variation of the velocity of the electron beam in a c.r.t. so as to cause a corresponding variation in intensity of the brightness of the display.

Interface — The point at which two parts of a system or two systems meet.

Interferometer — An antenna array, together with phase discriminators, capable of measuring the direction of arrival of an e.m. wave.

Interlace — Time multiplexing of modes of interrogation in a secondary radar system; in particular modes A and C may be interlaced in SSR.

Interrogator — The independent part of a secondary radar system.

Interrupt — The suspension of the execution of a current routine while a computer carries out an alternative routine; the signal which triggers such an action.

I/O — Input-Output.

IRS — Inertial Reference System: the heart of INS.

Isodop — The line joining those points on the earth's surface from which reflected e.m. waves, originating from an airborne transmitter, suffer the same Doppler shift.

Jitter — Random variation of frequency; employed in DME and MADGE in order that wanted replies may be recognized.

Key — To turn on a radio transmitter.

Keyboard — A device which allows an operator to input information into a computer; the keys or switches may represent alphanumeric characters or dedicated functions.

Klystron — A thermionic device employing velocity modulation of an electron beam and capable of oscillating or amplifying continuously at microwave frequencies.

Knot — The unit of speed used in air and marine navigation; 1 knot = 1 nautical m.p.h.

Lagging edge — The edge of a pulse which occurs last in time, i.e. the right-hand edge if the pulse is viewed on an oscilloscope or drawn against a time scale increasing to the right.

Lane — A region bounded by lines of equal phase in the Decca or Omega navigation systems.

Latch — A circuit that may be locked into one of two particular stable conditions.

Leading edge — The edge of a pulse which occurs first in time; cf. lagging edge.

Leakage — Unwanted coupling between transmit and receive antennas.

LED — Light Emitting Diode: a semiconductor diode which emits light when forward biased.

Limiter — A circuit which limits the voltage excursion of a waveform.

Linear array — A one-dimensional array of antennas arranged to produce a beam which is narrow in one plane, for example, a slotted waveguide.

l.o. — Local oscillator: the circuit used to provide an output which is mixed with an incoming r.f. in order to produce the i.f. in a superhetrodyne receiver.

Load — A device which draws current; to connect such a device.

Localizer — That part of ILS giving azimuth guidance.

Logic circuit — A circuit which processes binary signals in accordance with the rules of Boolean algebra; extensively used in digital systems.

Look-up table — A circuit, the output of which is the function value corresponding to the input which represents the argument; usually a ROM which, for example, might store the sine (function values) or a large number of different angles (arguments).

Loop antenna — An antenna consisting of a coil of wire, usually wound on a ferrite core, which, ideally, reacts only to the changing magnetic field in an e.m. wave; an ADF or an Omega loop antenna has two mutually perpendicular coils.

l.o.p. — Line of position.

Loran — Long range aid to navigation: a pulsed hyperbolic position fixing system; Loran A — obsolete, Loran C — current, Loran D — short range version of Loran C (Loran B — never operational).

LSA diode — Limited Space — charge Accumulation diode: similar to Gunn diode.

l.s.b. — Least significant bit in a binary word. Lower sideband: the sideband of an a.m. transmission which is of lower frequency than the carrier.

LSI — Large Scale Integration: a large number of circuits (usually 1000 or more) on a single i.c.; similarly SSI (small), MSI (medium) and VLSI (very large).

Lubber line — A reference line against which a moving scale is measured.

Machine language — The basic instructions, in binary code, executed by a computer; may be written down in hexadecimal or octal code.

MADGE — Microwave Aircraft Digital Guidance Equipment: a secondary radar system with civil application as an approach aid to offshore platforms.

Magnetron — A thermionic device employing velocity modulation of an electron beam in a magnetic field and capable of oscillating at microwave frequencies with very high power output for short periods.

Magslip — A four wire synchro resolver commonly used to resolve a timebase waveform into sine and cosine components with respect to the azimuth angular position of a radar scanner.

Main bang — The transmission from a pulsed radar.

Main lobe — The predominant cigar-shaped part of a directional antenna polar diagram.

Marker beacon — A radio aid transmitting a vertical directional beam so allowing a pilot to fix his position on an approach path or airway.

mbar — Millibar: a unit of pressure measurement; 1013.25 mbar = 1 standard atmosphere i.e. the pressure at mean sea level.

Memory — A device which stores information for future use.

Microcomputer — A complete digital computing system the hardware of which comprises a microprocessor and other LSI circuits such as memory and input/output ports; a single chip with circuits capable of providing control, arithmetic/logic operations, memory and input/output.

Microphone, mic. — A transducer which converts sound waves to electrical signals.

Microprocessor — A chip which provides the control and arithmetic/logic operations required by a digital computer; a chip capable of processing information in digital form in accordance with a coded and stored set of instructions in order to control the operation of other circuitry or equipment.

Microstrip — Transmission lines and passive components formed by depositing metal strips of suitable shapes and dimensions on one side of a dielectric substrate, the other side of which is completely coated with metal acting as a ground plane.

Microwaves — A vague term used to describe radio frequencies above 1000 MHz.

MLS — Microwave Landing System: replacement for ILS.

m.o. — Master oscillator: the circuit which provides the frequency reference in a radio transmitter.

Modulation — Variation of one or more characteristics of a carrier wave in order to impress information on it.

Monostable — A device or circuit with one stable condition to which it will return, after a specified delay, when disturbed.

Morse code — Combinations of dots and dashes assigned to letters of the alphabet and to numerals.

MOSFET — Metal-Oxide-Semiconductor FET: an f.e.t. where the gate connection is insulated from the drain to source channel by an oxide of silicon.

m.p.e.l. — Maximum permissible exposure level: in relation to microwave radiation.

MP mode — Multipulse mode: a transmission sequence which allows lane ambiguities to be resolved in a Decca Navigation System.

m.s.b. — Most significant bit in a binary word.

m.s.l. — Mean sea level.

MTL — Minimum Triggering Level: the signal amplitude required to initiate an action; of significance in secondary radar systems.

Multiplexing — Transmitting more than one signal over a single link; signals may be separated in time or frequency.

Multivibrator — A circuit which can be in one of two states, neither, one or both of which may be stable, hence astable, monostable and bistable multivibrators.

NAND gate — A logic circuit which gives an output of 0 if, and only if, all its inputs are 1.

NDB — Non-Directional Beacon: a radio transmitter at a known geographical site for use by ADF.

Negative logic — Representation of the bit 1 by a low voltage and the bit 0 by a high voltage.

n.m. — Nautical mile: the length of a minute of arc of longitude on the equator; approximately 6076 ft or 1852 m.

Noise figure — The s.n.r. at the input of a receiver divided by the s.n.r. at the output; a measure of receiver 'noisiness'.

Non-return to zero — A binary signal which makes a transition only when the bit 1 needs to be represented.

Non-volatile memory — A memory that holds data after power has been disconnected.

NOR gate — A logic circuit which gives an output of 1 if, and only if, all its inputs are 0.

Null — A no error signal condition in servo systems.

OBI — Omni-Bearing Indicator.

OBS — Omni-Bearing Selector: the control with which the pilot selects the desired VOR radial.

Octal number system — A counting system using 8 as its base and employing the symbols 0, 1, 2, 3, 4, 5, 6, 7.

Omega — A c.w. hyperbolic navigation system giving worldwide cover.

Omnidirectional antenna — An antenna which radiates in or receives from all directions equally; impossible to achieve in three dimensions.

Omni-station — A VOR ground transmitter.

One bit change code — A binary code in which only one bit in the word changes with each count, for example, Gray code.

One shot — A monostable multivibrator.

On-line — Refers to equipment in direct interactive communication with a computer. Refers to the installation and commissioning of a system or the state of a system when operational.

ONS — Omega Navigation System.

Open centre — A p.p.i. display in which the radial timebase line has its origin on an arc of non zero radius, the arc representing zero n.m. range.

OR gate — A logic circuit which gives an output of 0 if, and only if, all its inputs are 0.

Origin — A point with zero co-ordinates; the illuminated spot on the screen of a c.r.t. at the start of the timebase.

Orthogonal — At right angles (in two or three dimensional spaces).

PA — Passenger Address system. Power amplifier.

Page — A number of words treated as a group; within memory typically 4096 consecutive bytes; for display purposes a portion of memory which can conveniently be displayed on a VDU.

Paired frequencies — *see* Frequency pairing.

Parallax error — The reading error resulting from viewing an instrument or display from other than head on.

Parallel operation — Used by a digital system in which one line or circuit deals with only one bit in a word.

Parity — A bit or bits added to a group of bits such as to make the sum of all bits odd or even, hence odd or even parity which can be checked for error detection or correction.

p.e.p. — Peak envelope power: a measure of power in s.s.b. systems; since carrier power cannot be quoted the r.f. power dissipated at the peak of the modulating waveform is given in specifications.

Performance index — A global measure of the quality of a Weather Radar system; related to maximum range.

Peripherals — Units or devices that operate in conjunction with a computer but are not part of it; more generally, units or systems connected to a system under consideration but not part of the system.

Phantom beacon — A waypoint, in an RNAV system based on VOR/DME, at which no actual radio beacon exists, its position being defined in terms of bearing and distance from the nearest in-range beacon.

Photosensitive — A device which changes its electrical characteristics when exposed to light; for example photocell, photodiode, phototransistor.

PIN diode — P-type/Insulator/N-type diode: may be used as a high power switch at high frequencies.

Pitot pressure — The dynamic air pressure on an aircraft caused by its movement relative to the air mass surrounding it; dependent on both air speed and static pressure.

Planar array — A two-dimensional array of antennas arranged to produce a beam which is narrow in two planes, for example a flat plate slotted array as used in Weather Radar systems.

p.l.l. — Phase lock loop: a circuit which, by using a phase discriminator to generate an error signal, controls an oscillator so as to make its output equal in phase and hence frequency to an input or demand signal.

Polar diagram — A plot of points of equal field strength which gives a diagrammatic representation of the directional properties of an antenna.

Polarization — The plane of the e-field in an e.m. wave.

Polling — Interrogation of circuits, units or systems to determine their state of readiness to receive or transmit information; scanning interrupt lines to determine which, if any, require servicing by a computer.

Port — A circuit providing electrical access (in or out) to a system, usually a computer system.

Position feedback — A signal representing the position of the output of a position control servo system which may be compared with an input or demand signal so as to produce an error signal.

Position fixing — Finding the position of a vehicle in relation to a ground feature such as a radio beacon.

Positive logic — Representation of the bit 1 by a high voltage and the bit 0 by a low voltage.

Potentiometer — A three terminal variable resistor; the resistance between the wiper terminal and either of the end terminals varies with adjustment; the resistance between the end terminals is fixed.

p.p.i. — Plan position indicator: a radar display which shows the relative position of targets in a plane; targets on the same bearing will be superimposed on the display if they have the same slant range.

p.p.m. — Pulse position modulation: transmission of information by varying the position (in time) of pulses within a group.

p.r.f. – Pulse repetition frequency: the number of pulses per second; may be used to quantify pulse groups per second.

Primary radar – A radar (radio detecting and ranging) system which detects the reflections of its own transmissions from an uncooperative target.

Program pins – A group of connector pins some of which may be grounded to select particular modes of operation of a system from several options available.

Programmable – The capability of accepting data which alters the electrical state of internal circuitry so as to be able to perform one of several possible tasks.

Programme counter – A CPU register which holds the address of the next instruction to be fetched from memory; automatically incremented after a fetch cycle.

Programme, program – A set of instructions, arranged in an ordered sequence, which determine the operations carried out by a computer.

PROM – Programmable ROM: programmed after manufacture according to the user's specifications; generally not reprogrammable.

p.r.p. – Pulse repetition period: the reciprocal of p.r.f.

p.t.t. – Press to transmit or press to talk.

Pulse compression – A technique used in radar systems which allows a relatively wide pulse to be transmitted and a narrow pulse to be processed in the video circuits.

Q-code – A code used in R/T operations to identify the nature of commonly used messages, for example: QFE – atmospheric pressure at airfield level; QTE – true bearing from ground station; QNH – atmospheric pressure at local sea level.

QE – Quadrantal Error: the error introduced in ADF due to re-radiation from the airframe.

Q-factor – A measure of the selectivity of a tuned circuit.

Quadrature – At right angles: a $90°$ phase difference between signals.

Quarter-wave antenna – One of the conductors of a half wave dipole mounted on a ground plane which serves to 'reflect' the quarter-wave conductor so as to produce, effectively, a dipole.

Radar mile – The time taken for an e.m. wave to travel 1 n.m. and back, approximately 12.36 μs.

Radial – One of a set of straight half lines terminating at a fixed point; a line of radio bearing from a VOR station.

Radio, radar altimeter – *see* Altimeter.

Radome – A detachable aircraft nose cone made of dielectric material; more generally any dielectric panel or antenna cover.

RAM – Random Access Memory: a memory which affords immediate access to any location whereby information may be written in or read out.

Raster – The pattern traced by the electron beam in a c.r.t.

RBI – Relative Bearing Indicator: displays the relative bearing of an NDB.

Read – To sense information contained in some device such as memory or an input port.

Real time – Computation relating to a process during the time that the process occurs; the results of such computation may be used to control the related process.

Refreshing – The process of restoring the charge of capacitors which store the contents of dynamic RAM: at intervals of, for example, slightly less than 1 μs cells are automatically read, the results then being written into the same cells.

Register – A memory device with minimal access time used for the temporary storage of binary coded information; usually a collection of flip flops, one for each bit which can be stored.

Resolver – A device which can give signals representing the sine and cosine of an angle.

r.f. – Radio frequency.

Rho-Rho-Rho – A position fixing system which relies on measurement of distance to fixed points; rho-rho systems give ambiguous fixes.

Rho-theta – A position fixing system which relies on measurement of distance and bearing of a fixed point.

Rising runway – A runway symbol on a flight director driven laterally by localizer signals and vertically by radio altimeter signals.

RMI – Radio Magnetic Indicator: an aircraft instrument which indicates relative and magnetic bearings derived from VOR and ADF.

RNAV – Area navigation: navigation which does not necessarily confine the aircraft to a fixed airways system.

ROM – Read Only Memory: contains permanently stored information written in during manufacture; random access is available to all stored information.

Routine – A list of correctly sequenced computer instructions; the terms routine and program are often interchangeable but the former is usually applied to a commonly used set of instructions which may be called by other programs.

R/T – Radio telephony: speech communication by modulated radio waves.

Scan conversion — In position: the conversion of co-ordinates from rho-theta (angle and distance) to X-Y (orthogonal grid). In time: the conversion between rate of receipt of data and (usually faster) rate of display.

Scanning — The process of causing a directional beam of e.m. radiation to sweep through a sector of space. The process of polling interrupt lines or devices.

Scott-T transformer — Used in synchro systems for three-wire to four-wire conversion or vice versa.

Scratchpad — Memory, often on the CPU chip, in which data needed for subsequent operations may be temporarily stored. Display on which data may be checked before being entered into the main memory.

Search — The process leading to acquisition.

Second trace echo — An echo or return of a radar transmission which gives a false range reading since it arrives at the receiver after a transmission subsequent to the one giving rise to the echo.

Secondary radar — A radar system which requires a cooperative target; a radio link is established by an interrogator, the return or reply being supplied by a transponder on receipt of the interrogation.

Selcal — Selective calling: automatic alerting system using a v.h.f. or h.f. ground to air link to a particular aircraft or group of aircraft.

Sequential access — Reading data from a particular address in memory having gone through preceding storage area in order to find that address; for example, storage on magnetic tape.

Serial operation — Used by a digital system in which one line or circuit deals with all the bits in a word sequentially.

Servo loop — A system in which a signal representing the output is fed back for comparison with an input reference, the amplified difference, or error signal, being used to control the output.

Seven-segment indicator — Seven small bar-shaped light sources arranged in a figure of eight pattern, such that activating particular combinations of the seven sources causes a character to be displayed.

Shadow mask c.r.t. — A type of c.r.t. commonly used for colour displays.

Shift register — A register which is accessed serially both in and out; variations can give parallel to serial or serial to parallel conversion.

Sidebands — Those bands of frequencies, either side of the carrier frequency, produced by modulation.

Sidelobe — Those parts of a directional antenna polar diagram either side of the main lobe.

Signal controlled search — Allowing DME to commence searching and hence transmitting only when squitter is received; known also as automatic standby.

Skin effect — The tendency of a.c. at h.f. and above to avoid the centre of a conductor so reducing the useful cross sectional area and hence increasing resistance to current flow.

Skywave — A radio wave refracted back to earth by the ionosphere.

Skywave contamination — Reception of a skywave and ground or space wave simultaneously; an example of multipath propagation.

Slant range — The actual range of a target in a plane which is not necessarily horizontal.

SLS — Side Lobe Suppression: a technique used in SSR to prevent interrogation by sidelobes.

s.m.o. — Stabilized Master Oscillator.

s.n.r. — Signal to noise power ratio.

Soft data — Data which is lost when power is removed.

Software — Programs, languages and procedures of a computer system: no part of software has a physical existence other than as written down on paper or stored in code as represented by the state of a signal or device.

Spacewave — A radio wave which travels in a straight line being neither refracted nor reflected.

Spectrum — The sum total of frequency components of a signal.

SPI — Special Position Indicator: an additional pulse of r.f. which may be radiated by an SSR transponder for identification purposes.

Squitter — Random transmission of pairs of pulses of r.f. from a DME beacon as required for the operation of signal controlled search.

s.s.b. — Single sideband: the transmission of one sideband of an amplitude modulated wave.

SSR — Secondary Surveillance Radar: a secondary radar system employing an airborne transponder which transmits information relating to identity and/or altitude; range and bearing is available by measuring elapsed time and using a directional interrogation.

Stable — A mechanical or electrical state which is automatically restored after a disturbance.

Static memory — Memory which stores information in such a way that it does not need refreshing.

Static pressure — The air pressure due to still air; decreases with height.

s.t.c. — Sensitivity time control: variation of receiver gain with time so as to make the output amplitude independent of the range of the received signal source.

Subroutine — A small program or routine which may be called by a larger program or routine to perform a specific operation.

Super flag — A high level warning signal providing sufficient current at 28 V d.c. to energize a relay so indicating valid or no-warning status.

Superhetrodyne receiver, superhet — A radio receiver in which the received signal is mixed (hetrodyned) with a tuneable locally generated signal in order to produce a constant i.f.

Swept gain — An alternative term to s.t.c.

s.w.r. — Standing wave ratio: *see* v.s.w.r.

Synchro devices — A type of transducer which converts angular position to an electrical signal or vice versa; all synchros are transformers with both rotatable and stationary coils. Three wire devices establish a unique relationship between the rotor angle and the voltage distribution in the three coil stator; four wire devices establish voltages which depend on the sine and cosine of the rotor angle and are thus termed synchro resolvers. Designations are STRX or TR: synchro torque receiver; STTX or TX: synchro torque transmitter; DTTX or TDX or CDX: differential synchro torque transmitter; CT: control transformer; RS: synchro resolver.

Synchronization — Changes related in frequency, time or position.

TACAN — Tactical Air Navigation: a military system which gives rho-theta navigation; the ranging part has the same characteristics as DME.

Tape, magnetic — Storage device using sequential access.

Telephone, tel. — A transducer which converts electrical signals to sound waves.

Time base — A waveform which changes linearly with time; the term is normally applied to the waveform which causes regular deflection of the electron beam in a c.r.t. so as to trace a line representing a time axis, the line also being referred to as a timebase.

Time constant — A measure of the degree of resistance to change: if a system is subject to an external influence which causes it to change from one state to another and it were to execute that change at a rate equal to the initial rate it would complete the change in a time equal to the time constant.

To/From — Refers to selected VOR radials or omni-bearings; if the pilot complies with VOR derived steering commands he will be flying towards the beacon if a 'to' flag is in view and away from the beacon if a 'from' flag is in view.

Topple — The effect of allowing the angular velocity of a VRG to fall below that at which it exhibits the properties of a gyro.

Track — The actual direction of movement of an aircraft projected onto the earth and measured in degrees clockwise from magnetic North.

Track angle error — The angular difference between track and desired track.

Transducer — A device which converts input energy of one kind into output energy of another kind which bears a known relation to the input.

Transponder — The triggered part of a secondary radar system.

t.r.f. — Tuned radio frequency: a basic radio receiver in which selection and amplification of the modulated signal is carried out in the r.f. stages, there being no i.f.

Trigger — A signal, usually a pulse, which initiates a circuit action.

Tri-state buffer — A buffer which can assume one of three states: 0 or 1 when required to feed a load, high impedance otherwise; the high impedance state exists in the absence of an enable signal.

TRSB — Time Referenced Scanning Beam: adopted by the ICAO as the technique to be employed by MLS.

TTL — Transistor-Transistor Logic: logic circuits employing bipolar transistors fabricated on i.c.s. giving fast operation and good fan-in and out.

Tunnel diode — A type of semiconductor device which can be made to exhibit a negative resistance characteristic under certain conditions.

TVOR — Terminal VOR: a low power VOR station situated at an airfield.

Two from five code — A code commonly used for frequency selection; any two from five wires may be grounded giving ten possible combinations, one for each of the digits 0—9.

USART — Universal Synchronous/Asynchronous Receiver/Transmitter: a device which interfaces two digital circuits the timing of which may or may not be related; similarly UART and USRT.

u.s.b. — Upper side band: the sideband of an a.m. transmission which is of higher frequency than the carrier.

UVEROM — Ultra-violet Eraseable ROM: an EPROM.

Varacter diode — A voltage controlled variable capacitance; the capacitance varies with reverse bias.

v.c.o. — Voltage controlled oscillator.

Velocity feedback — A signal which is proportional to the rate of change of position of the output of a servo system; in position control systems such feedback is used to limit hunting, i.e. an excessive number of overshoots.

VFR — Visual Flight Rules: apply in uncontrolled airspace when visibility allows; limitations on pilot qualifications and equipment fitted are minimal under VFR.

Video signal — The post detector signal in a radar receiver.

Volatile memory — A memory that loses stored data when power is disconnected.

VOR — VHF Omni-Range: a system giving the bearing to a fixed ground radio beacon.

VORTAC — VOR and TACAN beacons on the same geographical site, i.e. co-located, are termed collectively a VORTAC beacon.

VRG — Vertical Reference Gyro: a gyro to which gravity controlled forces are applied by an erection system such as to maintain the spin axis in the vertical plane; used to give signals proportional to pitch and roll.

v.s.w.r. — Voltage standing wave ratio: the ratio of the maximum to minimum voltage of the standing wave set up on a mismatched line;
$$\text{v.s.w.r.} = (1 + (P_r/P_f)^{0.5})/(1 - P_r/P_f)^{0.5}) \geqslant 1$$
equality indicating a perfect match, P_r and P_f being the reverse (or reflected) power and forward (or incident) power respectively.

Waveguide — A hollow, round or rectangular, metal tube which is used to transmit e.m. energy at microwave frequencies.

Wavelength — The distance between points of identical phase angle; wavelength $\lambda = c/f$.

Waypoint — A significant point on a route.

Wheatstone bridge — An electrical measuring circuit consisting of four impedance arms connected in a closed chain; with an excitation supply connected to two opposite terminals in the chain the current drawn from the other two terminals is determined by the ratio of the impedances.

Whip antenna — A quarter-wave antenna made from a thin metal rod.

Word — A group of bits treated as an entity; it may represent an instruction, address or quantity.

Write — To record information in some device such as a memory or output port.

X-Y display — A p.p.i. display on which target position is determined in terms of horizontal (X) and vertical (Y) displacement from a datum point; it may be referred to as t.v. display.

Zenner diode — A diode operated with reverse bias so that breakdown occurs, the breakdown voltage remaining constant for a wide range of reverse currents.

Zone — A region bounded by hyperbolic lines separated by a distance equal to half a wavelength of the fundamental frequency of a Decca chain.

Exercises

The following exercises are given to test the reader's knowledge and understanding of the content of this volume; this aim will be best achieved if the questions are not read until one is ready to attempt them. Having worked through each chapter the exercises associated with that chapter should be attempted. Six test papers are given which should be attempted only after the whole book has been read. It is recommended that one hour be devoted to each test paper; the answers are not given but are to be found within the relevant chapters. Ideally the test papers should be marked independently, however, the reader should be able to give an assessment, albeit subjective, of his attempt at the written answer-type papers. An accurate assessment can be achieved from test paper 6 by giving one mark for each correctly attempted question, deducting half a mark for each incorrectly attempted question, leaving the score unchanged for each question not attempted, then multiplying the result by 10/6 to give a percentage.

Some of the questions can be used to generate others, for example, those concerned with drawing block diagrams, ramp tests, listing controls, etc. could apply to any of the systems described herein. Even with an extended set of questions, as suggested, it is unlikely that the syllabus for any course will be completely covered. For example, prospective aircraft radio maintenance engineers will be required to satisfy examining bodies and/or employers in the following areas:

basic electrical and electronic principles
legislation
ramp, hangar and workshop practices
reading wiring and schematic diagrams
fault finding skills, etc.

In addition they must show evidence of having had sufficient experience to assume the responsibilities of an engineer.

Chapter 1

1. Comment on the significance of bandwidth in an information link.

2. Draw a block diagram of an f.m. transmitter.
3. Draw a block diagram of a superhet receiver.
4. Describe *four* different ways in which binary digits may be represented in electronic circuits.
5. Describe *two* codes commonly used for airborne radio frequency selection.
6. Compare analogue and digital representation of data.
7. Discuss briefly the following: I.C.A.O., ARINC, ATA 100, national aviation authorities.

Chapter 2

1. Describe typical antenna tuning arrangements in a general aviation 20 channel h.f. comms system.
2. List and state the function of typical audio systems on a large passenger aircraft.
3. Describe what happens when a crew member transmits on v.h.f. comms.
4. Draw the block diagram of a CVR showing clearly the sources of the inputs.
5. Discuss typical v.h.f. comms antennas.
6. Tel. to mic. feedback in an AIS leads to a howl; how would you isolate the fault?

Chapter 3

1. List the sources of errors affecting ADF operation.
2. Describe quadrantal error and explain how it may be corrected.
3. Describe how an ADF ground loop swing is carried out.
4. Draw a situation diagram and a dual pointer RMI presentation for an aircraft on a heading of 200°(M) with an NDB due north of the aircraft and another at 300° relative to which numbers 1 and 2 ADFs are tuned respectively.
5. Explain the basic principles of ADF.
6. Draw an ADF block installation diagram.

Chapter 4

1. Describe the differences between the radiated signals from Doppler and conventional VOR stations and explain why airborne equipment operation is not affected.
2. Explain the terms automatic and manual VOR.
3. Draw a situation diagram for an aircraft on a heading of 090°(M) with a selected radial of 280° and with a fly right demand and from flag showing on the flight director.
4. Draw a dual VOR block installation diagram.
5. Describe how information derived from a VOR receiver is presented to the crew.
6. Discuss typical VOR antennas.

Chapter 5

1. Explain why a marker sensitivity switch is required.
2. Describe the need for and a typical implementation of loading compensation for an ILS installation.
3. Draw a block diagram of a glideslope receiver.
4. Describe the outputs from ILS to the aircraft's instrumentation and to other systems.
5. Describe ILS and marker channelling arrangements stating how selection is made.
6. Describe, in general terms, how you would carry out a ramp test of an ILS.

Chapter 6

1. Explain how, in distance related phase measuring navigation systems, errors due to changes in clock offset can be minimized.
2. List the factors affecting propagation of Omega signals stating for each, how, if at all, compensation is made.
3. Describe briefly the general procedure for skin mapping prior to deciding the position of an Omega antenna.
4. Describe how Decca chains are designated.
5. Explain how lane ambiguities in Decca may be resolved by using the MP mode.
6. Describe the characteristics of the radiated signals from a Loran C chain.

Chapter 7

1. Describe the *four* possible modes of operation of a DME interrogator (assume switched on and any warm up time expired).
2. Explain how echo protection can be achieved in DME.
3. Why might a DME interrogator receive less than 100% replies?
4. Describe the arrangements for co-located beacons.
5. Describe, in general terms, how you would carry out a ramp test of DME.
6. Draw a simplified DME block schematic diagram.

Chapter 8

1. Explain the need for and the implementation of SLS in SSR.
2. Explain the terms fruit and garbling as applied to SSR.
3. What is successive detection and why is it necessary in an ATC transponder?
4. Draw a block schematic diagram and explain the action of a decoder in an ATC transponder.
5. Describe how barometric altitude may be encoded into a form suitable for selecting the reply to a mode C interrogation.
6. Draw a typical ATC transponder controller, stating the purpose of each control.

Chapter 9

1. Compare platform and line of sight stabilization.
2. Describe, briefly, video signal processing in a digital weather radar.
3. Describe how a p.p.i. display can be used to present information relating to weather ahead of the aircraft.
4. How does a weather radar flat plate antenna achieve a narrow directional beam?
5. Describe the safety precautions to be observed when operating weather radar, stating the possible consequences of not doing so.
6. Describe how you would check a waveguide run for condition.
7. Discuss contour, STC and AGC in a weather radar.
8. Describe how range and bearing resolution may be improved in a weather radar stating the disadvantages of taking such measures to give improvement.
9. Explain the basic principles of operation of a Ryan Stormscope.

Chapter 10

1. Describe the Doppler effect as utilized in an airborne Doppler radar.
2. Explain how a moving antenna Doppler radar measures drift angle.
3. Discuss factors leading to a choice of f.m.c.w. for Doppler radars.
4. Explain the need for a land/sea switch.
5. Draw a simplified block diagram of a Doppler navigation system.
6. Describe, in general terms, how you would carry out a ramp test of a Doppler navigator.

Chapter 11

1. Distinguish between barometric and radio altitude commenting on the usefulness of both.
2. Explain the basic principles of an f.m.c.w. altimeter.
3. Why does Doppler shift have a negligible effect on a radio altimeter?
4. List the sources of error in radio altimeter systems.
5. Explain the main advantages of using constant difference frequency altimeters over conventional f.m.c.w. altimeters.
6. Draw a block schematic diagram of a pulsed radio altimeter.
7. Which systems require signals from a radio altimeter? What are the signals involved?

Chapter 12

1. Draw the block diagram of a general area navigation system.
2. Explain the basic principles of RNAV based on VOR/DME beacons.
3. Draw and label typical RNAV, deviation and slant range triangles.
4. Describe the functions performed by a typical digital navigation computer being part of a VOR/DME based RNAV system.
5. Explain the action of a typical data entry/record unit.
6. Describe, in general terms, how you would carry out a ramp test of a VOR/DME based RNAV system.

Chapter 13

1. Describe in general terms, the instrumentation of

the airliner of the 1980s and beyond, paying particular attention to the presentation of information from radio sensors.
2. Explain the basic principles of how an automatic data link using h.f. and/or v.h.f. comms could be set up.
3. Compare ADSEL/DABS with current SSR.
4. Explain one way in which satellites could be used for navigation purposes.
5. Describe, briefly, a TRSB MLS.
6. Explain how a collision risk measure may be arrived at.
7. Compare DITS with current methods of information transfer.
8. Explain the principles of interferometry.

Test Paper 1

1. Compare, briefly, the different types of antenna which may be found on aircraft.
2. Draw a simplified block diagram of a computer and state briefly the function of each block.
3. Draw and explain a simple anti-crosstalk network.
4. With the aid of a block diagram explain the action of an h.f. ATU.
5. Describe how information from an ADF is presented to the pilot.
6. Explain how displayed noise is reduced in a digital weather radar.

Test Paper 2

1. Describe two ways of modulating a c.w. carrier.
2. Discuss navigation using radio aids under the headings, dead reckoning, rho-theta, rho-rho-rho, theta-theta and hyperbolic.
3. Draw a simplified block diagram and explain the action of a frequency synthesizer paying particular attention to selection.
4. Draw a block diagram of a VOR receiver.
5. Define the terms jitter and squitter.
6. Describe, in general terms, how you would carry out a ramp test of a line of sight scanner stabilization system.

Test Paper 3

1. Describe the modes of propagation used with airborne radio equipment.

2. Define the terms hardware and software.

3. Describe, with the aid of a sketch, a typical h.f. wire antenna installation paying particular attention to safety features.

4. Sketch a typical error curve for ADF stating QE, loop and field alignment errors for your curve.

5. Draw and explain a simplified ATC transponder block diagram.

6. Draw a typical weather radar control panel stating purpose of each control.

Test Paper 4

1. Describe how a capacitive type antenna operates; list systems which might use such an antenna.

2. Explain how an interrupt signal might be used to achieve a data transfer from a radio sensor to a navigation computer.

3. Describe briefly the basic principles of ILS.

4. List the facilities provided by a typical general aviation AIS.

5. Draw a simple interlock arrangement for a dual h.f. installation.

6. Describe how the possibility of interference is minimized in a multiple radio altimeter installation.

Test Paper 5

1. Describe, briefly, the fetch-decode-increment-execute cycle of a computer.

2. List sources of interference to aircraft radio systems and state methods used to minimize the effects of such sources.

3. Discuss the term squelch.

4. Explain the principles of lane ambiguity resolution in ONS.

5. Describe, in general terms, how you would carry out a ramp test of a VOR.

6. At a point in a 180 n.m. leg of a flight the following situation exists:

heading	090°(M)
drift	10° port
distance to go	80 n.m.
desired track	085°(M)

Draw the situation diagram and calculate the across distance reading if the wind and heading have remained unchanged for the leg so far. (Assume 0.017 radians/degree and that $\sin \theta = \theta$ if $\theta \leqslant 0.2$ radians).

Test Paper 6

1. An e.m. wave of frequency 30 MHz will have a wavelength of (a) 10m, (b) 10cm, (c) 10 ft.

2. A loop antenna is used for (a) VOR and ADF, (b) ADF and Omega, (c) Omega and VOR.

3. Above 30 MHz propagation is by (a) space wave, (b) sky wave, (c) ground wave.

4. Fading at l.f. and m.f. may be due to (a) poor receiver sensitivity, (b) atmospheric attenuation, (c) simultaneous reception of sky and ground wave.

5. A carrier of amplitude 5 V is amplitude modulated by a signal of amplitude 3 V, the percentage modulation is (a) 15%, (b) 16.7%, (c) 60%.

6. A constant amplitude modulating frequency of 500 kHz causes a carrier to vary between 8798.5 MHz and 8801.5 MHz, the modulation index is (a) 1/3, (b) 3, (c) 6.

7. Which of the following is not equivalent to 23_{10}? (a) 10111_2, (b) 27_8, (c) 15_{16}.

8. The b.c.d. equivalent of $3C_{16}$ is (a) 0110 0000, (b) 111100, (c) 0011 1100.

9. Which of the following, where the l.s.b. is an odd parity bit, represents 68_{10}? (a) 10001001, (b) 11000100, (c) 10001000.

10. An address bus usually consists of (a) 16 bi-directional lines, (b) 16 uni-directional lines, (c) both bi- and uni-directional lines.

11. Rho-theta navigation is the basis of (a) VOR/DME, (b) Omega, (c) ADF.

12. To avoid earth loops in audio systems cable screens should be (a) earthed at both ends, (b) not earthed at either end, (c) earthed at one end only.

13. An aircraft v.h.f. communications transceiver will provide (a) 720 channels at 50 kHz spacing, (b) 360 channels at 25 kHz spacing, (c) 720 channels at 25 kHz spacing.

14. An aircraft at flight level 100 will be able to communicate with a v.h.f. ground station at 100 ft above m.s.l. at an approximate maximum range of (a) 123 n.m., (b) 12.3 n.m., (c) 135 n.m.

15. The minimum 1000 Hz, 30% modulated signal level to achieve an output s.n.r. of 6 dB from an airline standard v.h.f. receiver is (a) 1 μV, (b) 3 μW, (c) 0.18 x 10^{-12} W.

16. A typical a.f. response of a v.h.f. transceiver is (a) 500 to 2000 Hz, (b) 300 to 2500 Hz, (c) 300 to 4000 Hz.

17. Typical radiated power from an airline standard v.h.f. comms transmitter would be (a) 10 W, (b) 30 W, (c) 50 W.

18. In an airline standard h.f. installation the ATU would reduce the v.s.w.r. of the antenna and ATU

combined to better than (a) 1.1:1, (b) 1.3:1,
(c) 1.5:1.

19. An ARINC standard h.f. comms system has a typical power output of (a) 400 W p.e.p., (b) 700 W p.e.p., (c) 1000 W p.e.p.

20. A Selcal transmission is coded by (a) the number of r.f. bursts, (b) the pulse spacing, (c) the modulating tones used.

21. An anti-crosstalk network (a) reduces radiated interference, (b) reduces conducted interference, (c) prevents transmission on both h.f. systems simultaneously.

22. Airline standard ADFs will, after QE correction, have an error bound of (a) $3°$, (b) $5°$, (c) $8°$.

23. The average of the absolute values of the peaks of an ADF error curve give (a) field alignment error, (b) loop alignment error, (c) QE correction.

24. If the variable phase leads the reference phase by $30°$ the magnetic bearing to the VOR station will be (a) $30°$, (b) $210°$, (c) $150°$.

25. With a selected omni-bearing of $090°$ and the variable phase lagging the reference phase by $280°$ the flight director will show (a) fly right; from, (b) fly right; to, (c) fly left; to.

26. The frequency range of a VOR receiver is (a) 108 to 117.95 MHz, (b) 108 to 111.95 MHz, (c) 118 to 135.95 MHz.

27. The VOR audio identification tone is at (a) 1350 Hz, (b) 1000 Hz, (c) 1020 Hz.

28. Which of the following is a localizer frequency? (a) 110.20 MHz, (b) 109.15 MHz, (c) 112.10 MHz.

29. In which of the following bands does glideslope operate? (a) h.f., (b) v.h.f., (c) u.h.f.

30. If the 90 Hz tone predominates in a localizer receiver the deviation indicator will show (a) on course, (b) fly left, (c) fly right.

31. The v.s.w.r. of a localizer antenna should be no more than (a) 5:1, (b) 3:1, (c) 1.5:1.

32. An ONS, using software correction for predictable errors, will give aircraft position to an accuracy (r.m.s.) of (a) 1–2 nm, (b) 0–1 nm, (c) 2–5 nm.

33. Omega gives worldwide navigation facilities using (a) five stations transmitting on 10.2, 11.33 and 13.6 kHz, (b) eight stations transmitting on 10.2, 11.33 and 13.6 kHz, (c) strategically placed stations transmitting frequency multiplexed signals.

34. A Decca chain usually consists of (a) a master and three slaves, (b) a master-slave pair, (c) independent stations.

35. The usable night range of Decca is about (a) 120 nm, (b) 240 nm, (c) 360 nm

36. Loran C radiates (a) pulsed r.f. at 100 kHz, (b) pulsed r.f. at 14 kHz, (c) c.w. at 100 kHz.

37. TACAN beacons transmit in the range (a) 962 to 1213 MHz, (b) 1030 to 1090 MHz, (c) 978 to 1213 MHz.

38. DME gives (a) range, (b) slant range, (c) ground speed.

39. If a DME is in track subsequent loss of signal will cause the equipment to (a) search, (b) automatically standby, (c) go into memory.

40. Mode A and C pulse spacing are, respectively (a) 8 and 21 μs, (b) 12 and 36 μs, (c) 8 and 17 μs.

41. Selection of 5237 on an ATC transponder will give the following pulses, in order of transmission (a) F1 A1 A4 B2 C1 C2 D1 D2 D4 F2, (b) F1 C1 A1 C2 A4 D1 B2 D2 D4 F2, (c) F1 C1 C2 A1 A4 B2 D1 D2 D4 F2.

42. The output of an encoding altimeter for an altitude of 7362 ft would give the code (a) A1 A2 A4 B1 B2 C2 C4 D2, (b) A1 A2 A4 B4, (c) A2 A4 C1 C2.

43. The -3dB bandwidth of an ATC transponder receiver is (a) 6 MHz, (b) 3 MHz, (c) 12 MHz.

44. An ATC transponder should not reply if (a) $P1 \geqslant P2 + 9$ dBs, (b) $P1 \geqslant P2 + 4.5$ dBs, (c) $P1 \leqslant P2$.

45. An X-band weather radar will operate at (a) 9375 MHz, (b) 5400 MHz, (c) 8800 MHz.

46. Second trace echoes are avoided by (a) choosing a p.r.f. greater than some minimum, (b) choosing a p.r.p. greater than some minimum, (c) increasing either or both of the receiver sensitivity and transmitter power.

47. The pilot reports pronounced ground returns to one side of the display, the most likely cause is (a) system permanently in the mapping mode, (b) scanner tilt faulty, (c) gyro toppled.

48. Broken radial lines are observed on the weather radar indicator, the most likely cause is (a) a.f.c. circuit sweeping, (b) dirt in the magslip, (c) interference from another radar.

49. A weather radar with a p.r.f. of 200 and a duty cycle of 10×10^{-3} would have a bandwidth of approximately (a) 1 MHz, (b) 500 kHz, (c) 3 MHz.

50. A typical memory size for a digital weather radar employing an X-Y display is (a) 4 kbit, (b) 8 kbit, (c) 32 kbit.

51. If P and R are the VRG pitch and roll signals respectively and θ is the azimuth angle then the demand signal for a line of sight stabilization system is (a) $P\sin\theta + R\cos\theta$, (b) $P\cos\theta + R\sin\theta$, (c) $P\cos\theta \times R\sin\theta$.

52. An X-band Doppler radar shows a ground speed of 400 knots, a reasonable estimate of the Doppler shift would be (a) 5 kHz, (b) 500 Hz, (c) 12 kHz.

53. An f.m.c.w. Doppler radar operating at a frequency of 8800 MHz, modulated at 500 kHz with a depression angle of 60° will have altitude holes at multiples of approximately (a) 500 ft, (b) 2000 ft, (c) 8000 ft.

54. Wobbulation in a Doppler radar is used to overcome the effects of (a) reflections from the dielectric panel, (b) overwater calibration shift errors, (c) altitude holes.

55. A radio altimeter would not be connected to (a) MADGE, (b) a flight director, (c) an ATC transponder.

56. The DH lamp comes on when the aircraft is (a) over the outer marker, (b) below a pilot set barometric altitude, (c) below a pilot set radio altitude.

57. It is found that the most suitable positions for a radio altimeter transmitter-receiver and antennas leads to a minimum total feeder length of 9 ft and an antenna-ground-antenna path length of 8 ft; what would be a suitable AID setting? (a) 20 ft, (b) 40 ft, (c) 57 ft.

58. A phantom beacon is (a) a co-located VOR/DME beacon with no identity transmission, (b) a TACAN beacon, (c) related to a VOR/DME beacon by pilot set distance and bearing.

59. An aircraft is 20 n.m. and 045°(M) from a VOR/DME beacon; the range of the current waypoint, which is due east of the beacon, is shown as 20 nm; approximately how far is the waypoint from the beacon? (a) 20 nm, (b) 30 nm, (c) 40 nm.

60. MADGE mode C1 derives elevation information by using (a) radio altitude and slant range, (b) interferometry, (c) a directional beam narrow in elevation.

Index